Three Faces of Being

THE CENTURY PSYCHOLOGY SERIES

Kenneth E. Clark, Gardner Lindzey &
Kenneth MacCorquodale

EDITORS

Three Faces of Being

Toward an Existential Clinical Psychology

Ernest Keen
Bucknell University

New York

APPLETON-CENTURY-CROFTS
Educational Division
MEREDITH CORPORATION

Library of Congress Card Number: 78-128900

PRINTED IN THE UNITED STATES OF AMERICA

390-49770-3

ACKNOWLEDGMENTS

Ludwig Binswanger, "The Case of Ellen West," reprinted from *Existence*, edited
by Rollo May, Ernest Angel, and Henri Ellenberger, published by Basic
Books, Inc., Publishers, New York, 1958. Reprinted by permission of the
publishers.

Carl Frankenstein, *Psychopathy*, published by Grune & Stratton, New York,
1959. Reprinted by permission of the publishers.

Sigmund Freud, *The Standard Edition of the Complete Psychological Works of
Sigmund Freud*, revised and edited by James Strachey. Reprinted by per-
mission of Sigmund Freud Copyrights Limited, The Institute of Psycho-
Analysis, and The Hogarth Press. *The Collected Papers of Sigmund
Freud*, edited by Ernest Jones, M.D., Basic Books, Inc., Publishers, New
York, 1959. Reprinted by permission of the publishers.

Hermann Hesse, *Demian*, pp. 5-6, 75-77, 81. Copyright 1925 by S. Fischer Verlag.
Copyright © 1965 by Harper & Row, Publishers, Incorporated, New York.
London, Peter Owen and Vision Press. By permission of the publishers.

Lara Jefferson, *These Are My Sisters*, as written by Lara Jefferson and published by Vickers, 1947. Reprinted by permission of the publishers.

Ernest Keen and Robert Laird, "The Two Worlds of the Prison Inmate," from
the *Pennsylvania Psychiatric Quarterly*, 1968. Reprinted by permission.

R. D. Laing, *The Politics of Experience*, first published by Penguin Books, Ltd.,
Harmondsworth, Middlesex, England. Copyright © 1967 by R. D. Laing.
Reprinted by permission.

Jean-Paul Sartre, "Une idée fondamentale de la phénoménologie de Husserl:
L'intentionnalité" from *Situations I*, published by Gallimard, © Editions
Gallimard 1947. Translated and printed by permission of the publishers.

H. F. Searles, *Collected Papers on Schizophrenia and Related Subjects*, 1965,
reprinted by permission of the author, The Hogarth Press Ltd., and International Universities Press.

Marguerite Sechehaye, *Autobiography of a Schizophrenic Girl*, translated by
Grace Rubin-Rabson, published by Grune & Stratton, New York, 1951.
Reprinted by permission of the publishers.

V. E. von Gebsattel, "The World of the Compulsive," reprinted from *Existence*,
edited by Rollo May, Ernest Angel, and Henri F. Ellenberger, Basic Books,
Inc., Publishers, New York, 1958. Reprinted by permission of the publishers.

To MMK *and* IWRK

Preface

This book is intended for students, graduate and undergraduate, and for professionals, who seek to understand how existential psychology may be relevant to clinical problems. Part I argues that psychology is and should be involved in an evolution toward an existential orientation. The demands upon psychologists for new ways of thinking, talking, and seeing, for new foci of our attention, and for new approaches to our subject matter, are substantial. The existential-phenomenological approach answers these demands but itself makes new demands on psychologists, for better theory, new metaphors, and different attitudes.

Part II looks to existential philosophy for several new concepts. This section is not an account of existential philosophy, but it selects a few ideas and shows their psychological relevance. The first two parts of the book, therefore, establish an existential point of view (not *the* existential point of view) from which to observe clinical phenomena of neurosis, psychosis, psychopathy, and psychotherapy. The chapters in the first two parts each close with a short glossary of "technical terms" as a kind of summary and a way to keep one's bearings in the difficult task of threading one's way through a pioneer area of psychology. Each of Parts I, II, III, and IV closes with a short summary as well.

Parts III and IV confront directly the relationship between an existential orientation to psychology and concrete problems of the psychological clinic. The most difficult problems, from the author's point of view, are: (1) How are we to understand persons who are "mentally ill"? (2) How is that understanding related to how we diagnose and treat them? (3) How are our understanding, diagnosis, and treatment related to our intellectual assumptions and our existential commitments?

In Part V, we address ourselves finally to the even more difficult issues of how everything so far is related to social values, to a systematic methodology, and to the existential situation of being a psychologist in the twentieth century.

The book is somewhere between being an account for strangers of existential psychology and a statement of innovations within the community of existential psychologists. It also stands between the tasks of detached description of others' thought and personal advocacy of my own. It is both impersonal and personal, observing and participating, in the evolution of psychology toward a more adequate, more mature, more self-conscious, and more relevant science of man.

I am indebted to my students and my colleagues, but most especially to my predecessors. Should this book provoke further interest in existential psychology, I would suggest the work of Bugental (*The Search for Authenticity*, 1965), Van Kaam (*Existential Foundations of Psychology*, 1966), Van den Berg (*The Phenomenological Approach to Psychiatry*, 1955), and of course the pioneering collection edited by May, Angel, and Ellenberger (*Existence*, 1958).

E.J.K.

Contents

Preface

PART I   PSYCHOLOGY IN TRANSITION

Chapter 1   Introduction   3

    1. Existential and traditional psychology
    2. Psychology and consciousness

Chapter 2   The Self   13

    1. The self as subject and object
    2. The self-as-subject
    3. Self-objectification

Chapter 3   Being as an Object of Psychological Inquiry   24

    1. Aspects of being
    2. Movement
    3. Movement in the interview
    4. Meaning
    5. The perversion of being

Chapter 4   The Development of Being   39

    1. Stages of development
    2. The psychology of lying
    3. Identification

SUMMARY OF PART I   58

PART II   EXISTENTIAL THOUGHT IN PSYCHOLOGY

Chapter 5   Anxiety and Choice   63

    1. Anxiety and choice
    2. Anxiety and self-as-subject

    3. Existential and neurotic anxiety

    4. Anxiety and choice in psychotherapy

Chapter 6   Intentionality and the Self-World Relationship   81

    1. Intentionality and personal history

    2. Intentionality and transference

    3. Intending the traumatic past

Chapter 7   The World as a Psychological Category   92

    1. Space

    2. Time

    3. The two worlds of the prison inmate

    4. The body: conversion hysteria

SUMMARY OF PART II   109

PART III   THERAPY AND NEUROSIS

Chapter 8   The Case of Paula Kress   115

    1. The life-history

    2. Analysis of the life-history

Chapter 9   Being an Obsessive   152

    1. The rat man

    2. The world of the obsessive

    3. The obsessive structuring of time

    4. An existential obsession

Chapter 10 Therapy and the Dynamics of Being   166

    1. Interaction among the three levels of being

    2. To let the other be

    3. Healthy being

Chapter 11 The Structure of Psychotherapy   186

    1. Gross structure

    2. Intermediate structure

    3. Fine structure

SUMMARY OF PART III   205

PART IV   PSYCHOSIS AND PSYCHOPATHY

Chapter 12   The Psychotic Struggle   211
    1. The existential platform
    2. Panic
    3. The psychotic struggle

Chapter 13   The Psychotic Resolution   232
    1. Notes on Dr. Schreber
    2. Megalomania
    3. Symbols and psychotic expression
    4. The politics of psychosis

Chapter 14   The Case of Ellen West   248
    By Ludwig Binswanger

Chapter 15   Binswanger's Analysis of Ellen West   287
    1. The world of Ellen West
    2. The death
    3. Time

Chapter 16   Being a Psychopath   306
    1. The world of the psychopath
    2. The psychopathic self
    3. Confronting the psychopath

SUMMARY OF PART IV   318

PART V   TOWARD AN EXISTENTIAL CLINICAL PSYCHOLOGY

Chapter 17   Psychotherapy and Values   325
    1. The politics of psychotherapy
    2. Being a bureaucrat
    3. Therapy and the bureaucrat

Chapter 18   Methodological Puzzles   335
    1. Measurement in psychology is not objective

2. The point of view of the actor

3. Husserl and method

Chapter 19   Conclusion   347

Epilogue   357

Index   359

Three Faces of Being

PSYCHOLOGY IN TRANSITION   I

Introduction 1

1. Existential and Traditional Psychology

In the last decade, existential psychology has appeared in America—a continent whose psychology has been dominated by two main traditions, behaviorism and psychoanalysis. Let us begin by looking at the relationship of existential psychology to these two predominant points of view.

The underlying philosophy of behaviorism states that psychology is the study of behavior. Only behavior is externally observable, and thereby measurable, and hence subject to the operations of science (as understood by behaviorists). There is an obvious validity to this line of thought that will not be labored here, but it is also clear that behaviorist principles and findings, perhaps *because* they are so close to quantifiable dimensions, are not very useful for understanding such phenomena as "mental illness." For example, the *habit,* as a mathematical relationship between a measured stimulus and a measured response, is an extremely small unit of analysis. It does not help us very much to understand something like psychosis, which is a phenomenon organized on a much higher level—something like the total relationship of the individual to the world.

Psychoanalysis, from its very beginning, was more willing to compromise measurability for the benefit of provocative, if unprovable, insights into human nature: for example, the concept of the Unconscious. The prime focus of psychoanalytic theory today is upon character structure. One's character is conceived as the accrued style of handling certain inevitable conflicts, such as between the sexual drive and the inhibitions society puts on sexual expression. Character structure is a larger unit of analysis than habit, and is (not by accident) uniquely suited to the understanding of neurosis. However, psychoanalysis has much in common with behaviorism. The *ego,* for example, is a concept that is embedded in a theory of man that is highly mechanical in style, biological in rationale, and if not strictly measurable, hopes some day to be so.*

Unlike behaviorism, the primary emphasis of existential psychology is not on behavior, and unlike psychoanalysis, not on biological instincts and their vicissitudes in the development of character structure. Existential psychology, like existential philosophy, takes *experience* as its starting point. In this respect, it is indebted to phenomenology. The behaviorist unit, habit, becomes important for the existential psychologist primarily in terms of how it is *experienced* by the person behaving. The psychoanalytic unit, the character structure, becomes important primarily in terms of how it is experienced by the person involved in the conflict.

In no sense does this make the insights of behaviorism and psychoanalysis irrelevant to the understanding of people. Principles of conditioning are essential to understanding the affective overtones of an action observed or performed. Understanding character structure is helpful in judging what a particular behavior means to the individual. But the existential approach to human psychology does not seek the conditioned habits or characterological peculiarities as *explanations* of the troubled person's troubles. They are only guides to understanding his experience of himself and the world. The abnormality, the problem that is attacked, is in the person's *experience* rather than in his behavior or his character structure. This approach is perhaps the psychological ramification of the philosophical view which places consciousness in the center of the definition of man, rather than on the periphery as an epiphenomenon.

Perhaps psychosis is not a matter of habits that violate cultural norms. What is most important may be the psychotic's expe-

---

* Federn's (1929) experiential definition of the ego is an exception to the natural-scientific thrust of psychoanalytic thought.

rience of the cultural norms, and of himself in relation to them. Nor is psychosis an ego structure that lacks certain fundamental characteristics that should allow for a sublime interaction between impulses on the one hand and society and reality on the other. What may be more important is the psychotic's style of experiencing his instincts (which may be to deny them) and of experiencing reality (which may be to deny it). Experience is thus the starting point and the ending point of existential psychology.

It may seem a little surprising that this starting point is new, and one must understand the historical development of psychology to account for the heretofore rejection of the "subjective." But in fact it is relatively new for American psychology, and in the face of psychology's modest success in treating "mental illness," it is worthwhile to follow this new approach wherever it will lead.

It is possible that beginning with experience may yield a new delineation of abnormal syndromes, a new understanding of their origin, and we hope, new techniques for their treatment. We shall look into these matters. So far, existential psychology has been rather self-consciously trying to justify itself philosophically, and the progress toward a new understanding of persons in psychological distress has been slow. This is not to say the philosophical enterprise is unworthy and best left to philosophers alone. Such a position has too long led psychologists to philosophically naive conclusions. It is clear, however, that the writing of an existential psychology is a long way off.

2. Psychology and Consciousness

If we take seriously the idea that consciousness is not just an epiphenomenon but rather must stand in the center of our definition of man, then we are involved in a radical redefinition of man and of what psychologists are seeking to understand. It is a revolution of sorts, but hopefully it has more thoughtfulness and less impetuosity than that term often connotes. The redefinition of man in this way is bound to have far-reaching consequences for psychology, however, and so let us examine a few of these consequences.

1. The whole notion of an "intervening variable" between stimulus and response must be reconceptualized. Between input and

output stands experience, but experience is more than a connecting link. It becomes central and informs the input as well as the output. According to the traditional model, the causal sequence runs:

STIMULUS INPUT $\longrightarrow$ EXPERIENCE $\longrightarrow$
BEHAVIORAL OUTPUT

Taking experience more seriously would lead to a schematization something like this:

STIMULUS $\longleftarrow$ EXPERIENCE $\longrightarrow$ BEHAVIOR

A given stimulus is not really "given" apart from the experience of it and the meaning imposed upon it by the person. Similarly, the meaning of responses cannot be assumed to be self-evident without the context of the person's experience of it.

2. To have a psychology with conscious experience in the center therefore implies a radical shift in our metaphors, in the very categories in terms of which we think. If I see a tree and reconstruct this event as light, bouncing off the tree in certain wavelengths, hitting my retina, causing a series of electrical-chemical impulses to traverse my optic nerve to my occipital lobe, in turn causing various circuits in association areas to fire, then I am not taking consciousness seriously. I am taking seriously a theoretical reconstruction along the lines of particular metaphors. This theory explains what may go along with consciousness in physical terms, but this is not a theory about conscious experience. The electrical-chemical events may be construed as correlates, causes, or prerequisites *of* consciousness, but they are not the same as consciousness. My conscious experience of a tree must be described in terms of the content of my conscious experience, not in terms of a model of physical events. The tree has a certain appearance and a certain meaning to me. The experience of it may follow patterns of figure-ground or nuances of feeling, or a thousand other subtleties. These terms, terribly underdeveloped in psychology, seek to take consciousness per se seriously, and psychology should too. The fact that the physical events transpire as described is not remarkable except in the metaphysical sense that it is remarkable that there is something instead of nothing. But the facts that I know about trees, that I can reconstruct a theory of physical correlates, and that I can reflect on both of these, and upon my reflection—these facts are

remarkable for psychology. And these are facts of conscious experience; they are entirely different in nature from the facts of physical events.

Therefore, the crucial problem for a psychology that can handle consciousness is to find a language that is not a language of *things*. Even such a sophisticated scholar as Arieti, who has made a very serious attempt to use the data of experience to formulate a total theory of the individual mind, gets trapped in his metaphors when he says, for example, "Whatever seems to go on between the individual and the object is something that is experienced *in* the organism [Arieti, 1967, p. 30, italics are Arieti's]." To say this is to give the experience a spatial location, which is to impose upon it a metaphor of things that have their reality *in* space, as objects are in space. Experience is not an object and cannot be described in metaphors that are derivative of the object world. Laing has put it this way:

> Bertrand Russell once remarked that the stars are in one's brain.
>
> The stars as I perceive them are no more or less in my brain than the stars as I imagine them. I do not imagine them to be in my head any more than I see them in my head.
>
> The relation of experience to behavior is not inside my head. My experience of this room is out there in the room (1967, pp. 6–7).

Hence the "something" that goes on between an individual and an object, such as an object relationship in the psychoanalytic sense, or simply an individual experiencing an object, is neither *in* the organism, nor *in* the object, nor *in* some space between them. It is not any *where;* this coordinate of object-language is not appropriate for experience. Freud's language, which uses the metaphor of electricity, in which objects become "charged" relative to a subject, is a metaphor of a "field" that is defined by relationships between things and not by things in their spatial dimensions. Freud is therefore closer to an accurate description of the relationship of an experiencing subject to an object than Arieti's metaphors permit. But by far the best metaphors for describing this situation and these events are those of phenomenology. Objects are said to "shine forth" for a subject, and subjects are said to "illuminate" objects.

We will have occasion to show how such metaphors are more than just nice poetry; they are necessary for a psychology that takes consciousness seriously and helpful for a clinical approach that takes patients seriously.

3. There is the problem of unconscious behavior, behavior which clicks off automatically without any apparent correlate in experience. Provoking another person to anger or blinking an eye may be equally "unconscious," but these two cases obviously have to be seen differently. The former, an unconscious provocation, is purposive in the sense of the individual's purposes in his relations with others; * the latter, an unconscious eyeblink, is purposive in the sense of the organism's adaptation to the environment in a self-protective way. The provocation involves meanings that can be understood only by understanding the individual's total experience of himself in the world; the eyeblink can be understood *impersonally* as a response any organism will emit under certain circumstances. It is also worth noting that the eyeblink can be conditioned to a neutral stimulus. This stands as an intermediate case; conditioning can be seen as a process in which the meaning of stimuli are changed, although on a very primitive level. Somewhat more complex is the eyeblink response to dirty words, which takes on communicative value and becomes subject to yet another network of meaning.

Be that as it may, we will focus in this book on behavior that is at the personal and complex end of the continuum. An unconscious provocation will have to be understood by any clinical psychology. Does the fact that it is unconscious indicate that it does not mean anything to the individual? Certainly not; Freud convinced us of the meaningfulness of accidents long ago. But the meaning of the act to the actor may well be obscured by other ways of interpreting oneself and the world, and the goal of an existential psychology is to elucidate that meaning and the ways it is obscured.

4. The focus on experience is a rejuvenation of an old ideal in psychology, to investigate the "psyche" immediately. The earlier attempt was burdened by an atomistic psychology and a mind-body

---

* We are excluding here "inadvertent" provocation; indeed it is well to be suspicious whether provocation is ever totally inadvertent in the sense of accidental.

dualism. Existentialism and phenomenology make substantial gains over these assumptions, although we may find that the newer assumptions will lead into as blind an alley as the structuralist psychology of Wundt and Titchener. Perhaps we have learned something from this failure.

Such a rejuvenation does, however, recall a number of old problems. Consciousness as an "object of study" is notoriously difficult. It is only because of our conviction that consciousness is a definitive part of man that we try at all. Although we have an intersubjectivity, there is something private about consciousness. There is also something highly individual about it. And if these were not problematic enough for the methodologist, there exist in the scientific tradition precious few metaphors in terms of which to think and formulate. Conscious experience is active and dynamic, slippery and elusive, practically impossible to talk about in terms of our usual way of construing scientific subject matter.

For psychology, then, the focus on man as primarily experiential implies a radical shift in the very form of our thought. Even as I write I must make a conscious effort to avoid the thought habits that have traditionally made psychologists incapable of dealing with experience as subject matter. Almost certainly that effort has been only partly successful so far.

5. One occasionally hears the view that insight is not enough for therapy, that a change in the subjective experience of the individual is not therapy if it does not change his behavior.* We need not disagree, but such a view assumes that behavior occurs independently of experience. Some behavior does occur independently of our consciousness, but it should not escape our notice that in many cases as soon as there is consciousness of our behavior, we have the option of performing the behavior or not performing it. It is indeed no accident that most scientific research on humans must conceal the purpose of the research from the consciousness of the subjects in order to avoid the multiple random factors that are introduced as soon as the subject is most vividly human. Our scientific psychology is a psychology of unconscious organisms. It is a psychology of man as an object. Man is, indeed, part object; my flesh

---

* cf. London (1964) for a thorough discussion of this issue.

burns, I cannot fly, I am not a disembodied spirit, and these limitations are important "givens" in the existential situation. But putting consciousness into the center of our definition of man yields a study of man as subject, as experiencing.

With respect to clinical problems, it was clear early in Freud's career that "insight" is not enough for cure. Insight at that point was to be informed about the causes of one's symptoms according to psychoanalytic theory. Such insight is an insight into oneself as an object. It is a consciousness of self that does not really take consciousness seriously. The whole notion of "insight" therefore must take on a new meaning for us as soon as we take consciousness seriously.

6. The traditional comfort that scientific psychology has enjoyed by being "value-free" is rapidly coming to an end. How can we define psychological health and how, once we define it, does one get it or give it to another? Psychology is obliged to attack both questions. The definition of psychological health is a profoundly moral issue, just as the attempt to change people, to cure their illness or give them health, is a profoundly moral (as opposed to value-free, scientific) enterprise. The question of *how* to instill, produce, or facilitate health, once we define it, is a scientific question, just as the attempt to discover what cures an illness is a scientific enterprise.

It violates the tradition of value-free science to wed scientific and moral considerations, but a few far-sighted psychologists have taken a tentative step. This tentative step has met with a tremendous response among certain segments of our population and of our profession, as seen in the popularity of such terms as "self-actualization," and "self-realization." These concepts can be found in Goldstein (1945), Horney (1950), Rogers (1961), and finally explored systematically by Maslow (1954). It is only a tentative step because it is not explicitly moral and it maintains the scientific motif of empirical investigation. The specifications of self-actualization are seen as a "finding," a discovery of *what is the case.* The logic seems to say, "Once we discover what the nature of man is, then we can use this nature as a criterion for value decisions." "Good" acts are acts that aid man to "actualize" the "self" that he essentially is; "bad" acts are those that violate this inherent nature of man. In a word, this approach, which we have characterized as tentative, is clearly essentialistic. Man has an essence; the moral problem is solved by discovering the essence and conforming to it. Value issues are solved by a cognition and a recognition of truth as it is given.

The existential tradition is quite different. One can and must recognize essences and confront that which is given with honesty and rigor, of course. But man is more than an essence. If we take man's consciousness seriously, his growth is more than the unfolding of an innate plan and his moral dilemma cannot be resolved by a cognition. A process different from discovery comes into play if we pay attention to the phenomena of consciousness, namely, the process of decision. These two processes, cognition and decision, are not really separable, just as essentialism and existentialism are not really separable (cf. Tillich, 1961). One cannot decide in a cognitive vacuum, but also one cannot cognize in a moral vacuum. Each implies the other: cognition—decision, essence—existence, object—subject, fact—value, actuality—possibility, finitude—freedom, limits—transcendence, determinism—self-determination. It is when we view man as conscious that the second term in each of these pairs becomes a psychological problem.

The relationship between cognition and decision is a complex one. It is one thing to be in favor of racial equality, peace on earth, love and happiness for mankind. It is quite another thing to be able to think about human problems in such a way that allows us to achieve these noble ends. Is it possible that the metaphors in terms of which we think are arbitrary? Yes. Is it possible that the choice of such metaphors happens largely unconsciously? Yes. That the choice of metaphors makes a difference in what we can see and understand? Yes. That if we can see and understand things more clearly we will be able better to achieve our goals? Yes. Finally, is it possible that the terms of our psychology are not really appropriate for the achievement of our noble ends and that we really must choose our metaphors consciously, with one eye on the ends that we want? Yes, it is possible, and, I submit, true.

We therefore have, in any moral problem (such as clinical treatment), also an intellectual problem. And the creation of a new intellectual theory, which this book attempts to facilitate, is also a moral enterprise.

References

Arieti, S. *The Intrapsychic Self.* New York: Basic Books, 1967.

Federn, P. Das Ich als Subjekt und Objekt in Narcissmus. *Internationale Zeitschrift Psychoanalyze,* 1929, XV.

Goldstein, K. *Human Nature in the Light of Psychopathology.* Cambridge, Mass.: Harvard University Press, 1945.

Horney, K. *Neurosis and Human Growth.* New York: Norton, 1950.

Laing, R. D. *The Politics of Experience.* New York: Pantheon, 1967.

London, P. *The Modes and Morals of Psychotherapy.* New York: Holt, Rinehart and Winston, 1964.

Maslow, A. *Motivation and Personality.* New York: Harper, 1954.

Rogers, C. *On Becoming a Person.* Cambridge, Mass.: Houghton Mifflin, 1961.

Tillich, P. Existentialism in psychotherapy. *Review of Existential Psychology and Psychiatry,* 1961, I, 8–16.

The self 2

1. The Self as Subject and Object

Consider the experience of oneself. The "self" has been a concept in psychology for a long time, but it has frequently been confused with the ego. "The ego" does not refer to an experience but rather to a set of functions, as seen from the point of view of an "outside" observer constructing a formulation about a patient. The self, as understood here, is a concept referring to the assumptions about, judgments of, and feelings toward oneself as a person—a part of his subjective, experiential life. This concept has been part of psychology since Rogers (1942), who contributed the related concept of the "ideal self." Horney (1950) contributed the related but different concept of the "idealized self." Before that time one could find passing references to such subjective experiences, but never in the center of psychology. William James (1890) wrote extensively on the self as it appears in experience, but psychology has been unable to extend or even to use his insights, largely because experiential psychology was atomistic (Titchener's structuralism) and not phenomenological. Adler's notion of "fictional finalism" suggests a phenomenological viewpoint, when he says: "Experience, traumata, sexual development mechanisms cannot yield an explanation, but the perspective in which these are regarded, the individual way of seeing them, which subordinates all life to the final goal, can do so (1956, p. 92)." But Adler's phenomenology was not a well developed one. He was sensitive to the importance of self, of future, and of the inferiority-superiority dimension, but not to "world," temporality, and aspects of being that come from phenomenology. His use of bodily awareness, early in his career, also suggests phenomenology; but his formulations about the structure of experience were limited to organ inferiority and other medically conceived metaphors.

Gestalt psychology (cf. Köhler, 1947) is largely phenomenological, but it has primarily concentrated on the psychology of perception rather than on the psychology of the self. Perls, et al. (1951) is a notable exception. The experience of self is not only central to the existential approach but in addition, insights into the nature of this experience from existential philosophy have rather direct relevance for psychology.

Passing over the metaphysical problem of the self for a moment, let us draw a distinction between two entirely different ways of experiencing oneself. My self seems to be, first of all, that which I am, with certain traits and characteristics, talents and limitations.* These attributes constitute my *essence*: I am X and not Y; "Xness" is a part of my *essence* and "Yness" is not. My self thus has *essential* characteristics that cumulatively define *what* I am. This sort of experience of myself is thus the object of my attention. Let us call this the experience of oneself *as-object*.

The experience of *what* I am is at times dwarfed by the experience *that* I am. This is a second, entirely different sort of self-experience which we shall call the experience of *self-as-subject*. Rather than viewing myself as an object of my self-conscious scrutiny, I am now living the part of the viewer, the subject of the act, "I-see-me." The "I" experience does not contain attributes, characteristics and traits, as the "me" experience does. Rather than being experienced as a fixed entity, the "I" is experienced as a dynamic, open-ended activity without the stability of the me-as-object, i.e., without an essence. The "I" is pure existence, noteworthy because it *is,* not because it is *such and such.*

At this point description becomes difficult because our lan-

* cf. Wylie (1960) for a summary of data collected before 1960 in relation to this experience of self.

guage is geared to describing objects and their essences and is very poorly equipped to describe existential experience. Nevertheless, the experience is real enough and must be described. The "I" is an activity and not a continuous thing that remains static over time. It is an activity, and as such, the permanence of things does not apply. Sartre (1956, Part I, Ch. 2), it is interesting to note, calls this "I" experience the genuine one, in contrast to the "me" experience which is fraudulent—bad faith, self-deception. His point is a metaphysical one, that in fact "I" am exactly "nothing," and the attempt to give myself the permanence of a thing is an attempt to escape the responsibilities of being free to become whatever I want to become. It is bad faith to steal "because I am a thief," as if it were a matter of one's essence and not a choice.

Both of these ways of experiencing oneself are possible points of psychopathology. We are familiar with the celebrated "inferiority complex" which, in these terms, would be a poor balance of derogatory to complimentary self attributes of the me-as-object experience. Or the delusion that one is Jesus Christ reflects faulty judgment of the identity (and essence) of "me." But what is the experience of a totally withdrawn schizophrenic? What must one's perception of the self-world relationship be in order to promote such a blanket and massive style of life? From reports of psychotics in remission (cf. Kaplan, 1964), from careful observation and trial and error in the attempt to understand psychosis, and from existential-phenomenological theory, there is reason to suspect that the "I" experience is the focus of disorganization in psychosis. Or perhaps it is better to say that the "I" experience is an important focus of organization of experience for all of us, and psychotic withdrawal is the outward manifestation of the disordering, or even disappearance, of this focus. Somehow the experience of agency, of living out into that open-ended future within my grasp and under my control, is a key ingredient in sanity, and its loss a key ingredient in madness.

Of course, behaviorist and psychoanalytic theory have contributed many valuable suggestions about schizophrenia; but the experience of the loss of self-as-subject has been relatively neglected. We suppose that it must have developed in some kind of systematic fashion, but what are the early stages of structuring the experience of the world and self in this way? Why do certain objective conditions that we know antedate schizophrenia yield this sort of self-world relationship?

The point is that schizophrenia may not be merely a problem of essences—that the psychotic individual has such and such attributes, or sees himself as having such and such attributes. Schizophrenia may be an existential problem: a disturbance of the experience *that* I am, in addition to, perhaps prior to, a reckoning of *what* I am. It is this highly subtle, but often massive experience of self-as-subject that characterizes the existential component of life and the concern of the existential psychologist.

Existentialism and essentialism are two traditions in philosophy as well as, now, in psychology (cf. Tillich, 1961). Essentialism, which is the philosophic underpinning of behaviorism and psychoanalysis, attempts to stand apart from the object of study and ascertain its essential attributes. This yields natural science and is one orientation for psychology. As pointed out above, it is also one way we all experience ourselves. Existentialism, on the other hand, attempts to study the immediate experience of existence and everything that follows from it. This includes the experiences of one's body (again, as-subject as well as as-object), the experience of time, of space (including geometric "rational" space, but also hodological space; affective as well as linear distance, etc.). Each of these experiences is a focus of experiential organization and is subject to disorganization, such as in psychopathology.

Existential psychology has a difficult task, running counter to deeply ingrained intellectual habits and traditions, and yet it may be a key to man's groping hope to come to terms with himself.

2. *The Self-as-Subject*

We have noted the difficulty that is inherent in talking about this experience, for our language is most suited to a description of essential rather than existential issues, but let us consider what is involved in the experience of self-as-subject.

Philosophers, notably Husserl and Kant, have explored these experiences and felt that they were important enough to formalize into a metaphysically conceived "transcendental ego." We shall still retain our psychological orientation and sidestep specific metaphysical conclusions in order to see, if we can, the role of the experience of self-as-subject within the experiential field as it is experienced. We must resort, for this task, to various metaphors, some of which may be more successful than others.

First, I find myself-as-subject to be a kind of "ground" against which I experience the "figure" of the world, to use a metaphor from the Gestalt theory of perception. It is clear that I can experience a figure only as it has some kind of contrast to a surrounding ground, against which it stands in contrast. The world, as I experience it, is clearly "not-me" and gains some stability of definition by being "not-me." At the same time, however, it is clear that something in the world makes sense only as it has some relationship to a self-as-subject who perceives it and whose existence supplies the necessary ground for that perception to be there at all.

This suggests another metaphor: the self-as-subject is a context in which the world becomes meaningful. It is clear that a single word apart from a context is ambiguous, and a sentence out of context is not as meaningful as it is when it is surrounded by a number of other meaningful sentences. Myself-as-subject is a context in terms of which the world takes on meaning, and without that context it is meaningless.

It is interesting to note that Sartre, especially in his novel, *Nausea* (1959), describes experiences of objects losing their meaning, and that in his philosophy he formulates the self to be exactly nothing, empty, contentless and transparent. When we experience the "nothingness" of ourselves, is it not an inevitable concomitant to experience the world as meaningless? What is more, this experience is built into the structure of man and reality, according to existential philosophy. Laing has put the matter this way:

> . . . in saying "the sky is blue," we say "the sky" "is." The sky exists and it is blue. "Is" serves to unite everything and at the same time "is" is not any of the things that it unites.
>
> None of the things that are united by "is" can themselves qualify "is." "Is" is not this, or the next, or anything. Yet "is" is the condition of the possibility of all things. "Is" is that no-thing whereby all things are.
>
> "Is" as no-thing, is that whereby all things are. And the condition of the possibility of anything being at all is that it is in relation to that which is not (1967, pp. 22–23).

By and large, the context of my being-in-the-world has to
do with my desires, feelings, fears, all of which I refer to a central
"place"—myself—and without which one could hardly imagine anything having any meaning. But the context is also one of physical
space and time. I see objects from a point of view; I experience
life from a point of view that I recognize as limited; and yet, in
that limitation, there is a kind of boundary to which I can refer
for stability and definition of experience. Certainly, I never forget,
in one sense, that I am existing in time and space, and should I
experience something that challenges these coordinates, things I
perceive become unreal and strange. Some people lose this perspective when they examine the stars, for the experience of a perspective
of cosmic time and space undermines the stability of ordinary meanings and familiarity.

It is also important to me, as I experience the world, that
I am able to understand that this experiencing is taking place in
continuity with what I experienced yesterday, last year, and twenty
years ago. Without this point of reference, how could I feel that
what passes through my awareness has any organization or sensibility at all? These first metaphors point to the experience of self-
as-subject as a kind of *point of orientation* in terms of which to
organize and give meaning to my experience.

A second aspect of the experience of self-as-subject involves
the feeling of agency, or power, in relation to the world around me.
It is helpful, in organizing my perception, to be able to reach out
("at will") and move an object from one place to another. The fact
that I can do this when I want to makes the "I" into something
more than a mere point of reference. The experience of self-as-
subject is an experience of having some control over what I experience. It is important to me that what I desire in the world is not
merely a separate and unrelated experience from that of the world
itself. I can translate these desires into changes in the world and
then observe, with some satisfaction, the effect of this translation.
Anyone who has observed an infant closely may agree that the repetitive grasping and letting go, of shaking and watching move, of
babbling and listening are early realizations of this experience that
are not only pleasurable but also are essential for the normal psychological growth of the child. Piaget's concepts of circular reactions
and especially of "intentionality" in the first year of life speak to

this point (cf. Flavell, 1963, Ch. 3). These two aspects of the experience of self-as-subject, as an *orienting point of reference,* and *as active agent,* are crucial experiences that have been neglected in psychology, because they are difficult to talk about and because they are so commonplace as to escape notice.

Laing has stated the matter in the following way:

> I wish to define a person in a twofold way: in terms of experience, as a center of orientation of the objective universe; and in terms of behavior, as the origin of actions. Personal experience transforms a given field into a field of intention and action: only through action can our experience be transformed (1967, p. 8).

A third aspect, which may also be built into the experience of self-as-subject, has to do with myself as a party in a relationship. When I am interacting with a person, I suppose that that person is responding to more than my body or words. He is responding to my immediate desires and feelings, even though, upon reflection, I may conclude that he cannot know these except as they are mediated by my externalized words and deeds. But most of the time I am not reflective in this way, and it is always something of a shock to realize that we are misunderstood. Perhaps more shocking, upon reflection, is that fact that we are so often *not* misundertsood. When someone talks to me, he is not just talking to a body or a machine; I understand him to be talking to a consciousness, and I respond as if we both understood that we are in some kind of meeting of the minds. People do more when they talk than try to manipulate and influence me through adding additional causal input to my system. They try to make me understand; they try to effect a change in my subjective organization of the world, and I understand this desire perfectly. I, too, assume I am a subject, a consciousness, and something other than a complex machine.

3. Self-Objectification

If the experience of oneself-as-subject is to be characterized as "existential," then the experience of oneself-as-object should be

characterized as "essential." These terms call attention to the form
as well as the content of the experience. That is, the experience of
oneself-as-subject has an entirely different format than the experience of the self-as-object. The subject experience of self does not
objectify, attributes are not given to the self in this experience
(as we assign attributes to objects), and the self is the "looker" and
not the "looked at." The experience of oneself-as-object, on the
other hand, does objectify, attributes are assigned, and the self is
the object of attention. It follows that the experience of self-as-
subject is immediate, that is, is not mediated by symbolic formulations of any kind. The self-as-subject is not "known," for knowing
always implies a conceptual scheme in terms of which to know. The
self-as-subject can only be "lived." The self-as-object, on the other
hand, is an experience that is mediated by symbols, is cast in terms
of some symbolic form, and therefore is "known" rather than
"lived."

Our experience with objects is to separate them from ourselves, to scrutinize them dispassionately and judge them impartially.
Self-objectification is the experience of doing that to oneself. A
total inability for self-objectification would be an inability to reflect
upon oneself, and such an individual would hardly be human.
Self-objectification is not only inevitable and given in the shape of
human experience, it can also be quite valuable and healthy. However, there are certain kinds of self-objectification that strike us as
pathological. The conditions under which this is the case can be
specified as whenever self-objectification has become so pervasive
in the experiential life of the individual that he can no longer
experience himself as a subject. This is a danger, but such a loss
implies a second danger: without a firm feeling for the subject
pole of experience,* one loses one's immediate relationship to the
world. It is one thing to love, in which one has an implicit recognition *that* he is; it is something quite different to reflect on *what
kind of lover one is* to the degree of losing the beloved from view,
losing contact with that which formed the very basis of the love
experience.

The first of these dangers is what May (1961) has referred

---

* Kostenbaum (1962) has called this experience "the sense of subjectivity."

to as the "loss of sense of self." In Jaspers' terms, it is an inability to transcend *Dasein* (empirical existence) into *Existenz* (nonobjectifiable mode of being) (cf. Tymieniecka, 1962, p. 79). Laing (1962) presents a thorough discussion of this danger under the rubric, "ontological insecurity," and makes the remarkable Sartrean point that, for the ontologically insecure person, self-objectification, in the unpleasant extreme of losing one's sense of subjectivity, results automatically from seeing the "other" as a person, a subject who can objectify him.

The second of these dangers, the corollary that one also loses contact with the world, is what Frankl (1955, 1956) terms "existential vacuum" and what is described by Riesman, who points out that today's psychiatric patients'

> limbs work and their sexual organs work, but somehow life does not live up to its billing for them. . . . They need, usually without knowing it, a new vision and not merely a new way of talking about themselves . . . (1960, p. 4).

In general this condition may be described as a lack of commitment, and with the rise of cultural relativism, suspicion has been thrown on all commitments. The ideologies that people have believed for centuries, that have meaningfully related the individual to his immediate and ultimate surroundings, have become suspect in the light of our awareness of the effect of economic, social, and cultural influences upon our personal ideals. This broad cultural trend will continue.

If commitment is valuable, and we will later argue in a complicated way that it is, then it follows that self-objectification can work against our values. But it is also clear that commitments made without the reflective appraisals of self-objectification are particularly vulnerable, and make the individual particularly vulnerable, to the pressures of our peculiarly modern kind of self-awareness. Self-objectification is like a vaccination: a sense of oneself-as-subject that has survived it is in a position to survive the objectification of ourselves that inevitably comes at the hands of others and of our increasingly bureaucratic and impersonal society.

Technical Terms

Self: The self as experienced by the individual himself; a part of our internal, subjective experience.

Self-as-object: The way of experiencing oneself from a point of view that is detached, objective, and uninvolved. Such experience of oneself is like the experience of a thing in that it attributes characteristics to the object, which defines the object's essence or nature. The experience of *what* I am. Essentialistic experience of self.

Self-as-subject: The way of experiencing oneself as viewer (rather than viewed). Such experience of oneself is not like the experience of a thing but is more like an activity or process. The experience *that* I am. Existential experience of self.

Essentialism: The philosophic tradition of defining essences of things, their nature and qualities as objects.

Existentialism: The philosophic tradition of exploring or exhorting the experience of self-as-subject.

self-as-point-of-orientation
self-as-active-agent
self-as-party-in-a-relationship
} ingredients of the experience of self-as-subject, without which we experience meaninglessness, depersonalization, anxiety.

References

Adler, A. The principle of internal causation. In H. L. Ansbacher & R. R. Ansbacher (Eds.) *The Individual Psychology of Alfred Adler.* New York: Basic Books, 1956.

Flavell, J. *The Developmental Psychology of Jean Piaget.* Princeton: Van Nostrand, 1963.

Frankl, V. *The Doctor and the Soul.* New York: Knopf, 1955.

Frankl, V. *Theorie und Therapie der Neurosen.* Vienna: Urban and Schwarzenberg, 1956.

Horney, K. *Neurosis and Human Growth.* New York: Norton, 1950.

James, W. *Principles of Psychology.* New York: Henry Holt, 1890.

Kaplan, B. (Ed.) *The Inner World of Mental Illness.* New York: Harper & Row, 1964.

Koestenbaum, P. The sense of subjectivity. *Review of Existential Psychology and Psychiatry,* 1962, II, 47–64.

Köhler, W. *Gestalt Psychology.* New York: Liveright, 1947.

Laing, R. D. Ontological insecurity. In A. R. Ruitenbeek (Ed.) *Psychoanalysis and Existential Philosophy.* New York: Dutton, 1962.

Laing, R. D. *The Politics of Experience.* New York: Pantheon, 1967.

May, R. Existential psychotherapy: An evaluation. *Journal of Religion and Mental Health,* 1961, I, 31–40.

Perls, F., Hefferline, R. F. & Goodman, P. *Gestalt Therapy.* New York: Dell, 1951.

Riesman, D. The search for a challenge. *New University Thought,* 1960, Spring.

Rogers, C. *Counseling and Psychotherapy.* Cambridge, Mass.: Riverside Press, 1942.

Sartre, J.-P. *Being and Nothingness.* New York: Philosophical Library, 1956.

Sartre, J.-P. *Nausea.* Norfolk, Conn.: New Direction Books, 1959.

Tillich, P. Existentialism and psychotherapy. *Review of Existential Psychology and Psychiatry,* 1961, I, 8–16.

Tymieniecka, A. T. *Phenomenology and Science in Contemporary European Thought.* New York: Noonday, 1962.

Wylie, R. *The Self Concept.* Lincoln, Neb.: University of Nebraska Press, 1960.

Being as an object of psychological study   3

In the last chapter, we defined two kinds of self-experience. We shall return to these experiences presently, as aspects of "being." Let us now establish the metaphor of "being" as clearly as we can. Existential psychology must develop new categories and metaphors. Through the study of "being," it is hoped that there may be some new insight into problems that traditionally have been poorly understood. Hence, being is the object of our study.

There is a certain ambiguity about the notion of "object." The meaning of the term, "object," here is simply where we direct our attention. Being is not a *thing*. Indeed, being is exactly that part of our subject matter that is not a thing nor thing-like, not objective (in the usual sense) and not alien to our subjectivity. Therefore, being is a somewhat different focus of psychological attention from traditional ones (although there are predecessors). Let us try to describe the nature of this category as an object of study.

Being has been defined by Bugental (1965) as "self-aware existence." "Self-aware," here, indicates the crucial role that consciousness plays in being. We have to be especially careful not to objectify consciousness, however, because Titchenerian structuralism formulated consciousness in thing-like fashion and failed to enlighten us (cf. Boring, 1957). It is an antecedent of the study of being that is easy to confuse with phenomenology. Titchener objectified consciousness both in applying an atomistic formula and in trying to "make it hold still" for introspective examination. Naturally, such a program could only lead to failure, for as soon as one makes consciousness into an object (in this sense), one has lost consciousness. Consciousness clearly is *not* an object, a thing, or even a state of a thing. It is perhaps best described as an activity and hence its theoretical name would better be a verb than a noun. It is an unfortunate historical accident that the term "conscious" is taken to be an attribute of a thing, such as its color or its size. Similarly, the noun, "consciousness," is an awkward abstraction from what was originally seen as an attribute, such as greenness.

Consciousness is, however, crucial for being. That which is not conscious has no being. Being is the activity of being self-aware, or conscious of one's self and it is therefore an activity that we all engage in. Perhaps in our search for theoretical terms, the concentration upon verbs and verb forms should have taken us to the English "aming" or "I-aming." Although these terms are awkward, they do not lead us into the temptation to solidify the activity of being into a thing. Aming is clearly something we all do; in fact, it is the most central thing that we all do and we are "beings" only insofar as we do it, or we could say that we all *are* only insofar as we do it.

To explicate the conditions, the modes, and the exigencies of aming is the existential-psychological goal. Clearly this is a quest for a totalistic psychology of the person, for whatever goes on in one's life accrues its most important meaning only within the processes of his aming, or his being. A conditioned habit may not affect his being very much and hence is not very important; an experience of being loved or hurt that does affect his being is very important. There may be habits that are central to one's being, but being is not just a conglomeration of habits. All habits fit into a larger (the largest) *Gestalt* of how the person is aming (what the person is), and hence being is the ultimate context in which habits or experiences of them make sense. Apart from the context of being, habits make only limited sense. They are meaningful to the psychologist, perhaps, in terms of his psychological theory, but his psychological theory, insofar as it encompasses less than the activity of being, will not illuminate the relevance of a habit for a human life.

For example, I have a habit of smoking a pipe. This behavior is made up of various muscle movements that are repetitive and woven into standard larger patterns which developed according to some regular process of development of motor habits. But pipe smoking is also (and more importantly) a part of the way I present myself to myself and to the world, and within this context it takes on larger and more significant meaning, such as the dynamics of role-playing or of the self-concept. This frame of reference is closer to the totalistic one of my being, but role theory or self-concept theory are still partial theories. The most complete and important meaning of this activity is clear only in the context of my central activity of aming.

The study of being per se leads one away from the specific activities of one's life into a larger realm of the meanings of activities. For one's being is an activity of juggling meanings, as we will try to show. It is precisely this juggling of meanings that constitutes the most important addition that existential psychology has to offer traditional psychology. "Meaning" here, however, is the meaning of being, which has to be distinguished (for historical reasons) from meaning as understood by associationistic psychology. Let us for now simply reject explicitly the notion of meaning as the sum of associations that a stimulus may evoke within an organism. Not only are we not particularly interested in stimuli per se, but also we want to recognize explicitly the fact that meanings are organized according to the contexts in which they are embedded. One's activity of being is the ultimate context into which we cast everything, the frame of reference within which a stimulus or a response, a feeling or an image, becomes meaningful.

1. Aspects of Being

We therefore want to study being. Analysis of an object of study into its component parts is a frequently used scientific procedure. While we must recognize the danger of destroying the larger *Gestalt,* it will be our procedure in this book. Furthermore, *three* seems to be a popular number for analysis (perhaps second only to two and four): id, ego, and superego; conation, cognition, affection; Father, Son, and Holy Ghost. The trilogy we have in mind is similar to the three modes of bodily experience as described by Sartre (1956, Part III, Ch. 2). The activity of being is really three simultaneous activities, or perhaps we could say it is an activity that proceeds on three levels. There is a "natural" separation of the three and yet an intricate interaction among them; they vary independently some of the time and at other times they move together. Like the Christian Trinity, they are "three in one," or three aspects of one phenomenon.

A. Being-in-the-world

We *are*, first, in the sense that we are desire, fear, thought, etc., *of* something that is implicitly seen as outside ourselves. This way of being entails an experience of oneself-as-subject: *I* desire a steak; *I* fear a germ; *I* think of an idea. Our term for this level of being, "being-in-the-world," means approximately the same thing in all existential literature, although it is not usually counterposed to two other aspects of being.

B. Being-for-myself *

We *are*, second, in the sense that we represent *what* we are to ourselves. This aspect of our being entails the experience of oneself-as-object. We reflect upon our desires, fears, and thoughts, name them, judge them, reason about them and have feelings about them. Furthermore, I am a "me" to myself, with certain attributes and characteristics. With dispassionate detachment, I can, upon reflection, do everything to myself that I can do to the world. The content of this process is a second activity of being.

C. Being-for-others

We *are*, third, in the sense of presenting ourselves to others, anticipating what others are thinking or feeling about us, and guiding our externally observed behavior so as to have a certain kind of effect on others, to make a certain kind of impression. This is yet a third activity of one's being (one's aming), and while it goes on simultaneously with the other two, it is distinguishable.

* This term is not to be confused with the Sartrean category, "being-for-itself," which is approximately equivalent to consciousness.

The ontological significance and basis of this tripartite division can be seen only by going back again to the notion of being and
what one is doing when he is aming. Aming (being) is experiencing
oneself as a "going concern," as a person-in-process. This process
of aming is central to my life and "it wouldn't be the same" without it. But just what do I experience when I experience myself
aming? To use an intellectualized metaphor, we may say that there
are three kinds of "data" that feed into this experience: (*a*) the
data of the world that is implicitly referred to "my" point of view,
(*b*) the data of myself as I objectify myself for my own scrutiny and
(*c*) data as fed back to me through my interpretation of others'
interpretation of me. These three classes of data are all that we
have in being; this is an exhaustive, and also a mutually exclusive,
list.*

No matter how separable one aspect of being is from the
others, according to the kinds of "data" that go into the process,
the interpretation of the data of any one source always depends on
a supraordinate context of my being in general. What I think others
think of me (my being-for-others) is important to me only in terms
of how it fits the context of what I think of them (my being-in-the-
world) and what I think of myself (my being-for-myself).

Let me anticipate what will come later. The sort of "neurotic"
who is likely to be called "depressed" because of a self-degredation
that is designed to evoke love and pity from others is caught without this supraordinate context of his being in which to interpret
social feedback. His only context of meaning is the question "Am I
loved?" and he is (he ams) exclusively "for-others." Somehow the
"security" or "self-esteem" that protects most of us most of the time
from this sort of behavior is missing. But *what* exactly is missing?
It is the meaningfulness and relevance of the other two activities of
being for his being in general. It is a cruel twist of fate that condemns such a person, whose being is totally "for-others," that he
will drive people away and thus be disappointed in his vain attempt to fill up his emptiness. The person who is not so dependent
upon being loved will in fact be more lovable and loved more by
others. The rich get richer and the poor get poorer. This fact indi-

* That the list is exhaustive and mutually exclusive is problematic. A
more modest claim would be that it is a convenient list. Which is the better
claim entails an ontological argument that goes beyond the scope of this book

cates the fundamental nature of the tripartite division. No one or two of the three is enough. Healthy being is a three-level operation; less than a three-level operation violates the ontological structure of being and leads to psychological (existential) illness.

Let us look at a segment of Sinclair's experience in Hesse's novel, *Demian* (1965), where Sinclair is going through a difficult stage of reshuffling his experience of himself. First he tells us what he looks like "from the outside," which refers here to the point of view of his teachers and parents. Later in the same paragraph he tells us that from the point of view of different "others," namely, his classmates, he is a "hell of a fellow." Both of these are being-for-others, and as so often happens, the relevant others don't agree among themselves about their expectations, and this leaves being-for-others in a kind of internal conflict. Later Sinclair tells us what he feels more immediately as he watches children, which is an expression of his being-in-the-world and conflicts with both versions of his being-for-others. His being-for-himself, in this passage and throughout this part of his life, is particularly confused and shifting, without a stable orientation and without what one would call "a sense of identity."

> Meanwhile, viewed from the outside, I was going rapidly down-hill. My first drunken frenzy was soon followed by others. There was much going to bars and carousing in our school. I was one of the youngest to take part, yet soon enough I was not merely a fledgling whom one grudgingly took along, I had become the ringleader and star, a notorious and daring bar crawler. Once again I belonged entirely to the world of darkness and to the devil, and in this world I had the reputation of being one hell of a fellow.
>
> Nonetheless, I felt wretched. I lived in an orgy of self-destruction and, while my friends regarded me as a leader and as a damned sharp and funny fellow, deep down inside me my soul grieved. I can still remember tears springing to my eyes when I saw children playing in the street on Sunday morning as I emerged from a bar, children with freshly combed hair and dressed in their Sunday best. Those friends who sat with me in the lowest dives among beer puddles and dirty tables I amused with remarks of unprecedented cynicism, often even shocked them; yet in my inmost heart I was in awe of everything I be-

littled and lay weeping before my soul, my past, my mother, before God. . . .

The more I realized that I was to remain perpetually
lonely and different within my new group of friends the less I
was able to break away. I really don't know any longer whether
boozing and swaggering actually ever gave me any pleasure.
Moreover, I never became so used to drinking that I did not
always feel embarrassing after-effects (1965, pp. 62–63).

2. Movement

Let us introduce another term, namely, "movement." Some movement of being has long-term ramifications for one's being in the
future, while other movement does not. We will want to focus our
attention on the relatively important movements. If I light my
pipe with this match rather than that, it is a movement of little
consequence, but if I have a religious conversion, it is a shift with
far-reaching implications.

One can make a movement on one level of being without
changing very much on the other two levels. I may discover that
people see me as aggressive, and so I can change my behavior to
fit what I want them to think of me without changing very much
of how I spontaneously *am* (feel, think, etc.) in-the-world or how I
represent myself to myself. Or I can discover that I have been
telling myself a lie about a particular feeling and can change my
judgment or reckoning of myself without changing very much of
my being-in-the-world or of my being-for-others. However, it becomes clear in these examples that no one activity of being is totally
independent of the others, for a movement in one realm cannot
fail to have some implications for my being in general. The kinds
of implications, of course, the degree and direction, the qualitative
relationships among them, are the most important questions that
this analysis raises, and some examples follow to show how these
relationships are crucial in understanding being.

3. Movement in the Interview

Suppose that a patient on a particular day is angry at me, but I see
it only in little cues, little nuances of his behavior or in distant im-

plications of what he says. It is clear that he cannot integrate his anger at me into how he conceives of himself, nor into how he would like to appear to me. So he tells me that while he is not really getting anywhere in therapy (implication: I am a bad therapist), he also thinks that I am really a very good therapist. Note that there is a certain out-of-jointness among the three levels of his being. For some reason his being-in-the-world made a movement toward anger at me, which necessitated his being-for-himself to make a concerted effort to avoid a movement (maintain the status quo, don't get well, thus justifying the imperfectly perceived movement on the first level, namely, anger at me). This in turn necessitated a movement in his being-for-me toward an appreciative and respectful patient.

We will not, at this point, address ourselves to the motivational question as it is traditionally asked and answered. One might well see this as "defensive behavior." Defenses are mobilized for the purpose of reducing anxiety or achieving security, or whatever one's motivational theory states. Let us delay an explanation of the particular direction of his behavior until we understand more about what being wants. That is, the hypotheses that it was to reduce anxiety or to ensure security are embedded in a frame of reference that is less than total, less than encompassing the juggling of meanings by being in general (i.e., aming), which will probably turn out to be highly individual anyway. Being in person X and being in person Y must have some things in common, and indeed, we want to describe them. Our understanding of this particular defensive behavior, however, will necessarily not be complete until we understand this individual's own being.

Now suppose that I say to the patient that he is really quite angry at me today. He may answer: "You are absolutely right, doctor, I am angry at you. Isn't that crummy of me, after all that you are trying to do for me . . . I'm no damn good," etc. This is a definite movement, on the level of his being-in-the-world, from anger to anger + submission. On the level of his being-for-himself, the movement is justification to self-blame and self-derogation. And on the level of his being-for-others, there is *no movement at all*. He is still presenting himself to me as a "good patient" with admiration and respect and the rest of it.

There are now several alternatives open to me. I may want to interpret his lack of movement in his being-for-others, in this case his being-for-me. Or, I may want to question the meaning of his movement in his being-for-himself, for example, that it is a way not to experience his anger as he originally experienced it, but to shift its direction from me to him, *in how he presents himself to himself*. Or I may want to question the sincerity of his movement on level one by asking why he isn't angry any more. Which, if any, of these strategies I may choose will depend now on the interaction among the three levels of my being. Am I angry at him? We may hope there will be less out-of-jointness among the three activities of my being than among the activities of his being.

Although the example is fairly minute, we have arrived at a point at which we can reap some benefits from the analysis. I want to propose now some general principles of being which will be elaborated in the next chapters: (*a*) Mental health is the relative lack of what we have called "out-of-jointness." Perhaps the various kinds of psychopathology can be described in terms of the kinds of out-of-jointness among various aspects of being. (*b*) The task of psychotherapy is to unify or integrate being, to bring to light the context of a person's being as a new source of meaning of his own behavior and feelings. (*c*) This is achieved by facilitating certain kinds of movements in the patient's own being. (*d*) The necessary therapeutic movements in a patient's being will be dependent upon the pathogenic movements he has made in the past, and insofar as we understand the movements of various kinds of psychopathology we will understand the kinds of therapeutic movements that are necessary for its treatment.

It is noteworthy that Sinclair, the hero of Hesse's *Demian,* whose being was severely out of joint, was able to achieve a temporary integration on the basis of a relationship with a girl to whom he never talked. His being-for-this-particular-other pervades all levels of his being and integrates them on the basis of a fantasy relationship. The following passage describes this movement, which, incidentally, exemplifies the function of an "ego ideal" (from psychoanalytic theory), which in turn is always a matter of being-for-others.

Although I never addressed a single word to Beatrice, she exerted a profound influence on me at that time. She raised her image before me, she gave me access to a holy shrine, she transformed me into a worshiper in a temple. From one day to the next I stayed clear of all bars and nocturnal exploits. I could be alone with myself again and enjoyed reading and going for long walks.

My sudden conversion drew a good deal of mockery in its wake. But now I had something I loved and venerated, I had an ideal again, life was rich with intimations of mystery and a feeling of dawn that made me immune to all taunts. I had come home again to myself, even if only as the slave and servant of a cherished image (Hesse, 1965, pp. 66–67).

4. Meaning

We have postponed the issue of meaning long enough. We must understand meaning, that is, meaning in the sense of being. We began with the task of discussing being as an object of psychological study. Being was defined as "aming" and aming was analyzed into three concurrent activities. But what goes on when an individual is aming? A central aspect of it is a primordial process of interpreting the world and one's place in it. The meaning one imposes on oneself and the world always occurs within a frame of reference, a context that supplies the ground without which we cannot see the figure. If a patient says to me, for example, that he hates me and everything that I stand for, this "stimulus" has no predictable effect apart from the interpretation I give his statement, and this interpretation will in turn depend on my being at the time. I may be undergoing a personal crisis, in which my being-for-myself is in an unusual state of flux, or I may be having feelings toward him (my being-in-the-world) that could influence my interpretation of his remarks, or I could be involved in some kind of impression-making game in which I am put very much on my guard in order to prevent exposing what I implicitly recognize as my real feeling toward him or toward myself. The crucial point here is that I will manipulate the meaning of what he says according to the meanings I have at my disposal at the time, and these possibilities will be limited by the movements within my own being.

Similarly, the things that I say to him will be subject to the same interpretations. If I don't realize this, I may provoke movements in his being that are quite antitherapeutic. For example, when I told the patient in the example above that he was angry at me, his "good patient" enterprise was the one that did not move. The other two activities of being changed to fit the agenda of his being-for-others. His being-for-others was the context that proved relevant to his perception of my comment and he created the meaning of my remark as a threat to my view of him as a good patient. He could as well have denied the remark explicitly by saying, "I certainly am not! I'm not the sort who gets angry." This reaction would have maintained his being-for-himself and thus revealed to me that he created the meaning of my comment as a threat to how he perceived himself. But he did not maintain this enterprise; in fact, he agreed that his first judgment of himself (as victimized by his problems) was wrong and moved to self-criticism. Apparently his being-for-himself is in a state of flux. Or he may have said, "Of course I am angry at you! What do you expect when every time you turn around your behavior is being interpreted?" This would have been maintenance of his being-in-the-world, namely his anger; and it would have indicated that this aspect of his being was the context from which he created the meaning of my remark.

It is not clear from what we have said about this patient which of the possible movements I could have provoked would have been most therapeutic. The point here is that the central activity of being is the creation of meaning, the interpretation of the significance of events. This process goes on according to the quality of one's being at the time; giving meaning to experience is a central part of being. The three activities of being, therefore, may be seen as three meaning contexts that may be used in interpreting the events in one's life.

5. The Perversion of Being

Certain roles in society or certain kinds of activities seem to exemplify the dominance of one aspect of being over the others so that one's being is pervaded by the exigencies of that aspect. For example, a movie star makes a profession out of being-for-others, often at the tragic expense of being-in-the-world (cf. Sartre, 1954), even while he is playing at being-in-the-world or being-for-himself.

Sartre cogently argues that our being-for-others often leads us into various poses and role-playing that robs our being of the immediacy of being-in-the-world and of the reflectiveness of being-for-oneself. This kind of "playing at being" is often a core of a neurosis. Even Freud, in the notion of the superego, suggests that behavior is controlled "as if" father were in fact watching. Freud and other theorists, however, have failed to note the degree to which such a perversion of being by such a lopsidedness is the central dynamic of the pathology. The notion of secondary gain, for example, which is meant to refer to the sympathy and other interpersonal benefits that come from having symptoms, is contrasted to the primary gain of surreptitiously indulging oneself in unacceptable impulse gratification or translating a central conflict into symptomatic behavior. But secondary gain is often not secondary at all, especially in the subtle cases of interpersonal distortion such as described by Sullivan (cf. Mullahay, 1949).

Overemphasis on being-for-oneself is also a frequent source of what we think of as neurotic behavior. The maintenance of an "idealized self," for example, as described by Horney (1950) in order to boost self-esteem or justify behavior, is a pervasion of being by the exigencies of being-for-oneself. Suppose that a man sees himself as an extremely masculine person and is faced with an emotional scene. He may not, even in private, admit to himself that the scene touched his emotions or approached his iron-hard nerves, for to surrender this idealized self (being-for-himself) would cost too much in terms of the self-definition that he feels secure with. In these cases, as in the "depressed" person described some pages back, it is easy to see how pervasion of being by one or another of the three aspects of being can lead to what is ordinarily called neurotic behavior. It may be possible for an individual to live in only one aspect for a whole lifetime without ever coming to terms with the experiences sacrificed in so doing.

Neurotic behavior, however, is never simple, and the classification of the pathology of being must be more complex than the three category division of being. As an attempt to get more leverage from the tripartite division, let us propose the notion that there are primordial experiences connected with each of the three activities of being. In fact, let us develop two sets of such experiences, "healthy" and "unhealthy." It is important to realize that

all six experiential terms are a part of all lives, but that the quality
of one's being may be pervaded by one or more of these "primordial
experiences":

	being-in-the-world	being-for-oneself	being-for-others
healthy	care	self-esteem	identity
unhealthy	frustration	guilt	shame

Instead of the old diagnostic categories based on an uneasy combination of manifest symptoms and inferred psychodynamics, looking at psychopathology through the fashions of being may yield
new insights into the nature of psychopathology. It may be that
descriptions of psychopathology, when not related to an individual's
process of aming, are descriptions in terms that cover only part of
the person. Furthermore, the part of the person covered is likely
to be foreign to his view of his problem. The formulations of his
problem as given by a patient are always more than just rationaliza-
tion. They tell the way that his aming is currently going on and
constitute the core of the problem for him. This is not to deny
that there may be affects of which he is "unconscious" and which
are not part of his formulation. But if a patient formulates his
problem with the omission of one of the primordial experiences,
he is formulating the problem around it, about it, on the fringe of
it, focusing negatively, as it were, upon it.

     If the three aspects of being that have been singled out here
do have ontological significance, that is, are built fundamentally
into the very structure of human aming, and if we have named the
experiences correctly, then we can ask ourselves the question about
any patient, "What are his frustrations?" "About what does he feel
guilty?" etc., just as psychoanalytic theory directs our attention to
sexual and aggressive instincts and their ramifications in character
structure.

     Let us close this chapter by returning to the general principles
of being outlined above. We said first that psychopathology is the
existence of a certain out-of-jointness among the three aspects of
being. Let us take the enterprise of diagnosis seriously, even though
its usefulness has had a checkered history. The classification of psychopathology should be primarily descriptive, but it is important to

describe the right thing. Describing the movements of one's being is the right thing. Describing symptoms or behavior patterns is the wrong thing, because they will always be seen within some context that is smaller than (such as psychodynamics) or different from (such as the cultural definition of "right" behavior) the most central activity that we all engage in, namely, being. This descriptive work is exactly what must be done, and the formulation of primordial experiences is only a crude beginning.

We said, second, that psychotherapy has the task of integrating what had previously been out-of-joint. This formulation of the goal is similar to the psychoanalytic goal of eliminating dissociation, but it is a broader concept. For the meanings that emerge at the various levels of one's being can be integrated only if there are certain movements in an individual's being. One must shift his aming from a for-others orientation, say, but this can only follow a meaningful experience of his aming on the other two levels. To facilitate this is the therapeutic task; and as the descriptive categories mentioned above become more and more elaborate, the therapeutic program for any individual patient will be more and more clear.

Technical Terms

Being: The activity of being self-aware: the total process of being who we are, which supplies the context in terms of which all life events are meaningful.

Aming: Being.

Being-in-the-world: That aspect of my being that focuses on an object in the world and results in the experience of myself-as-subject.

Being-for-myself: That aspect of my being that focuses reflectively on myself-as-object.

Being-for-others: That aspect of my being that focuses on myself as seen by others.

Movement: Some change in my posture or process of being on one, two, or all three (above) levels.

Primordial experiences: An attempted catalogue of experiences that are universal, related to the ontological structure of being, and can become the basis for personality description.

References

Boring, E. G. *The History of Experimental Psychology*. New York: Appleton-Century-Crofts, 1957.

Bugental, J. F. T. *The Search for Authenticity*. New York: Holt, Rinehart
and Winston, 1965.

Hesse, H. *Demian*. New York: Harper & Row, 1965.

Horney, K. *Neurosis and Human Growth*. New York: Norton, 1950.

Mullahay, P. *A Study of Interpersonal Relations*. New York: Hermitage
House, 1949.

Sartre, J.-P. *Being and Nothingness*. New York: Philosophical Library,
1956.

Sartre, J.-P. *Kean on Disorder and Genius*. London: Hamish Hamilton,
1954.

The development
of being 4

We have argued and will continue to assume that some things in life are "given" and essential and some things are open-ended, with many possibilities, no one of which is "given" in the sense that the essence of rubber is to stretch. Events, historical and present, are given; their significance is not. One's body and physiology is given; its meaning for one's life is not. Conditioning contingencies of our individual histories are given, but their role in our future is not. Those things that are not given are open to choice, insofar as we have an awareness of options. One's ability to see options may be great or small, depending on one's past; but as long as one is alive and conscious, the limits of this ability are subject to change. The goal of psychotherapy is, among other things, to broaden this ability, and this goal can be achieved only through an increase in our openness to our experience of ourselves and the world.

Our openness to our experience, or our lack of it, is a crucial outcome of development. One's ability to see options is dependent on an ability to face the "givens" of human existence. The inability to face these givens may well grow out of childhood conditions that we know about. But the nuances and styles of this inability are highly idiosyncratic and the attempt in this chapter is to state some of the factors that are involved. We will try to integrate this major theme with some ideas about the development of the three aspects of being introduced in Chapter 3.

This chapter is speculative and based on theoretical as well as observational sources. But the developmental perspective is a helpful one, so long as we avoid the oversimple determinism that says, "trauma *A* caused symptom *B*." The complexities come, of course, not simply from the complexity of the causal matrix. They come also from the challenging realities of human consciousness— its spontaneity and freedom.

1. Stages of Development

Let us begin with an outline of four stages of development. Like all such schemes these stages are not meant to be a rigid schedule; they obviously blend into one another, and in any given child there will be multiple partial progressions and regressions that complicate the picture. However, the sequence of events described here is an educated guess about the way one's experience of self and world evolves through childhood. We will talk about four stages: fusion, separation, satellization, and similarity.

A. Fusion

The label for this earliest kind of experience signifies the lack of differentiation between subject and object, between "in here" and "out there," between me and not-me, hypothesized by numerous theorists from James, through Freud, to Piaget. Consciousness and the world are one; when the child's experience is filled with pain, the whole world is pain. There is no body image or object concept. We find that we have little to say about this experience, which is indeed fortunate since we have no way of talking about such experiences anyway.*

B. Separation

Sometime during the first year, we suppose that experience becomes differentiated along the lines of "me" and "not-me." The development of a body-image defines the limits of "me" and the acquaint-

---

* The speculations of Harry Stack Sullivan (1953) about the intricacies of this experience are perhaps the most suggestive. Also see Jacobson (1964).

ance with the stability ("conservation," Piaget calls it) of objects becomes apparent. This differentiation is not without its drama. The child must come to recognize the intransigence of reality and its independence of his own wishes. Most important along these lines is probably the discovery that his mother is an independent person. This recognition is one of the first opportunities the child has to confront the limitations of life (the very first such opportunity is probably the experience of bodily pain). A limited kind of choice exists for the child at this stage, but it is a frequent one and no doubt in many ways a crucial one. He can either recognize the truth of this painful "given" or he can deny it. It is probably the case that fantasies frequently occur well into the second year in which this existential fact is avoided.

Separation anxiety is a frequent experience, and the anxiety may be tolerable only because one's feeling of agency begins to develop. A year-old child is an indefatigable explorer and experimenter with objects in his world. The repetitious production of sights and noises, under his own control, is for most children adequate compensation for the lack of power to produce mother's warmth by merely wishing for it. Indeed in the second year, the child's adamant affirmation of his own independence seems overdone. It is as if he were saying, "I like it this way, I want it this way, I insist on having it this way." Learning to traverse space at his own command, to deposit fecal material in the appropriate (or inappropriate) place under his own control, to move furniture and manipulate parents, all of these experiences place him in a position of power and agency that he plays to the hilt.

During this time, we suppose that the "me" versus "not-me" dichotomy is profound. The child experiences himself as a center of the universe; everything is his object and he is the universal subject. It is probable that he sees himself as the only consciousness in the world and he becomes, in his own eyes, the center of gravity for all events.

C. Satellization

Sometime during the preschool years, and this may occur very early in certain respects or circumstances, the child's experience of subjectness and objectness reverse themselves. Perhaps this is a subterranean feeling all along, but it becomes quite apparent by around age four. The center of gravity has shifted; the universal subject is now located outside himself in the persons of god-like parents. Around these gods he can only revolve as a satellite. He can appease them, establish covenants with them (and hope to become "chosen"), but finally he has no choice but to worship them. For they are all-powerful and he is weak. He becomes a frail reed blowing in the winds of their power; he becomes their object.

Oneself, now, which has been the triumphant center of subjectivity, becomes an object. The former object, the parent, becomes the subject that objectifies him. If there had been a profound being-in-the-world in the previous stage, we have a profound being-for-others in this stage. Again there is a grim reality to face, namely, his new-found powerlessness, and again there are options, many more options now. He can accept the fact with a kind of infinite resignation, or he can fight the fact by reasserting his power over parents, or he can subjugate himself completely to their superior will, or he can, in fantasy, become the god-parent himself and preserve his dignity through vicarious power. Most children no doubt do all of these things in varying degrees. The particular choice he makes in a concrete situation may come to be an investment, so that he feels he needs to perpetuate the chosen posture in the eyes of his parents.

But the situation is not all bleak. For most children there are tremendous gains in satellization. Unless his parents are consistently cruel or indifferent, there will be glorious moments of safety and security in the protective gaze of his god-like parents. The gods are probably not without kindness and compassion. They give orders but they also give love and food and encouragement. The admiration becomes a gratifying apprenticeship and like all apprentices, the child begins to rediscover his competence and capabilities.

D. Similarity

Certainly by about seven years old the child has begun to discover a new way of experiencing himself and his parents. If separateness put the center of subjectivity solely within himself and satellization put it solely within his parents, he eventually discovers that there are multiple centers of subjectivity. It is a great revelation to discover in the early grade school years that one's parents have parents. Grandparents become more than subsidiary gods; they become gods of the gods. And if the gods have gods, then these god-parents become somewhat less remarkable. The cognition of generations may well come before the realization that the covenant was really a contract between two parties of equal status. It is with this plateau of self-esteem that the child escapes the disturbing issues of family jealousies and frustrations and embarks upon the expanding discoveries of the world in the grade school years. Sometimes this occurs so late that it is immediately interrupted by adolescence. Other times it occurs early enough for one to get involved in many layers of intrigue and power with one's peers. Peers are there in any case, and the experience of oneself in relation to peers is never independent of the experience of oneself in relation to one's family.

The grade school years are thus immensely complex mixtures of satellization and similarity, with parents, siblings, peers, and teachers all playing various roles. The options open to the child during this time are much too numerous to mention, but he probably experiences those options most acutely in relation to rules. He has parental rules, peer rules, teacher rules, and no doubt by this time a few self-rules. They conflict hopelessly in a rich conglomeration of situations, each of which demands a choice and each choice demanding a justification. Furthermore, his attempt to impose rules on others opens a myriad of options, both of ends and of means. Standards of decision making become solidified, some stemming from a perseveration of satellization, some from the rigorous reward system of the peer group, some from convictions of his own inner worth or lack of it.

2. The Psychology of Lying

In each of the stages we have outlined, we are able to point to some of the options that the child faces. In any given concrete situation, the child does not face the options as stated by us in abstract terms, but he faces a choice among concrete alternatives about how to perceive and interpret events and how to respond to them.

Among the alternatives in any given situation, some are

better than others. "Better than" here does not refer to "more rewarding" in the sense of behaviorism, or "more adaptive" in the sense of functional theories such as psychoanalysis. By "better" here we want to say "more honest." We want to focus our attention on the attitude of openness to experience, for such openness is crucial in the ability to see options. The breadth and depth of openness involves an attitude of long standing in any adult. The moral connotations of the term "honesty" should not divert us, in an overzealous desire to make psychology a value-free science, from a recognition of what is important in development. It does not follow, of course, that every "dishonesty" deserves moral condemnation. If the metaphor is helpful, let us use it.

A. Lying-for-others

Sometime during the stage of satellization, the child discovers that he can misrepresent himself to the gods with some success. The recognition of this fact must have profound implications for how he experiences himself and others. Let us see if we can understand some of these implications. First, one's being-for-others takes on a new flavor. Lying is always a choice. The ability to deceive is a remarkable increment in power, and no doubt serves to enhance the feeling of agency with complex strategies and far-reaching effectiveness. Second, the choice to lie occurs first in the face of the gods. The actual personalities of the child's parents, then, are crucial in determining what this choice will eventually mean to the child. Tolerant and forgiving parents obviously have a higher likelihood of evoking the truth than stringent and punitive ones. Furthermore, the feeling of investment in the lie, the need to support it with further lies, is effected by the same considerations.

Third, every lie eventually comes to be accompanied by the fear of discovery. The experience of being caught in a lie is one of shame. Any given lie, depending on how important it is, will be accompanied by a degree of impending shame. If we move from the particular case of a single lie to the more general case of a complex network of lies, built up over years of small but cumulative deceptions, we have a particularly painful kind of being-for-others. Very often the specific content of the lies is forgotten, perhaps misperceived according to the contingencies of lying-for-oneself, and all that remains is the vague and diffuse feeling that "if people really knew" what I am, they would withdraw love and respect.

Children probably always feel somewhat fraudulent in relation to parents and peers. The question is the extent to which this experience preempts one's total being. In any given adult there are probably multiple layers of shame, some very important and some very unimportant. A significant feature of the shame of most adults is its relationship to their guilt. It is one thing to deceive others and know one might be exposed. It is something else to have this experience complicated by the feeling that in so lying one is violating a personally felt standard of behavior, and regardless of the other's objectification and judgment of you, there remains the objectification and judgment of oneself.

B. Lying-for-oneself

The experience of satellization is a significant one, for it consolidates the experience of oneself-as-object. The relationship between the experience of oneself as one's own object and oneself as the object of another is a complex one. It is probably safe to assume that the ability to see oneself as an object is tied up with the evolution of the ability to "take the role of the other," as described by Mead (1934). Cooley's (1902) concept of the "looking-glass self" refers to this earliest kind of self-objectification and necessarily assumes the presence of others from whose point of view one may look at himself. Buber (1958), Jaspers (1964, pp. 349–355), Marcel (1927, pp. 63–145), and Sartre (1956), have all made the same point. Sullivan (1947) terms self-objectification "reflected appraisals" and Spitz (1959) notes the use of the child's "No" in "objectivating the self."

Be that as it may, the acquisition of a self-concept, a series of attributes one feels one has (like a car "has" speed, mileage, and maneuverability), is a crucial developmental event. When the child lies to his parents, he implicitly knows that his and his parents' views are different, and he therefore has the experience of himself-as-object. If a child is accused of stealing cookies and denies it when in fact he stole them, his denial is a presentation of himself to his parents as a "good boy" when he secretly knows that he is a "bad boy."

The standard of judgment by which "good" and "bad" are reckoned comes first from the parents and only later from within himself. The experience of performing an act and being punished for it yields a conflict between the original criteria of the decision to act and the criteria of judgments of acts enforced by parents. This conflict is most easily resolved by "internalizing" the parental criteria and building them into the criteria for future decision-making. The experience of performing an act *that one already knows* is judged *by his parents* as bad is halfway to the experience of performing an act *that one decides for oneself is bad.* This final experience is the experience of guilt. The experience of guilt generalizes to the *desire* to perform some forbidden act, and so is not an uncommon experience of childhood.

There comes a time in the life and lying of the child when he comes to believe his own lies. This is a highly subtle and yet very important phenomenon. When the child presents himself to his parents as "good" and knows he is "bad," that is not a lie-for-oneself. But when a child invests so much in the being-good-for-his-parents that it becomes an overwhelming concern, then his honesty in confronting himself is likely to suffer. Extremely punitive parents, therefore, undermine the child's honesty with himself. The experience of guilt can be so threatening that one effectively loses contact with what one really feels or desires. In the place of this honest reckoning of oneself emerges an "idealized self," as Horney (1950) has called it, which may come to dominate one's entire being.

It is not clear how, exactly, it is possible to lie to oneself. If I claim I am all-loving and never hostile, I must hide my hostile feelings from myself. In order to do that, I must selectively perceive my own feelings, and the selection process must be systematic and regular. On some level, in some way, I "know" what not to perceive. Can I know what not to know about myself?

Freud's theory of repression accounts for this phenomenon in terms of a hypothetical interaction of forces within the personality. Sartre's attack of this theory is the obvious one that one must know what not to know about oneself. His alternative is in terms of "bad faith," or as it has sometimes been translated, "self-deception." This point of view assumes that one would not have to deceive oneself, that one *could* face the truth, in other words, that it is a choice. Let us adopt this solution; self-deception is a choice.

What are the implications of such a choice on future choices? We can see a snowballing effect with respect to lying-for-oneself. Having established a self-concept that is idealized and unrealistic, the child is faced with the subsequent choice either to try to maintain the deception through future good works or at least good intentions, or to face the guilt. Having not faced the guilt once almost certainly makes the possibility even more frightening a second time. Lie begets lie, being-for-oneself becomes lying-for-oneself.

For any particular situation, the effect of this process may not be particularly important, unless of course the guilt is very great because of very punitive parents or because of a very bad act. But if we again move from the particular case of a single lie to the more general case of a complex network of lies built up over years of small but cumulative deceptions, we have a particularly painful kind of being-for-oneself. The guilt is always there, vigilance must be very great, and more and more elaborate distortions of one's being result. From this point, the emergence of obsessive symptoms, for example, is indeed a short step.

There are two issues about which lying-for-oneself is particularly likely, from childhood through adolescence to adulthood and old age. This is the temptation to misconstrue what is given and what is not, to fail to see accurately the *necessities* and the *possibilities,* to separate those things that are essential and not subject to choice from those issues that are existential and subject to choice. Let us consider the example of two children in relation to their school work. Child *A* feels that if he were only "good" enough, that is, if he simply tried hard enough and chose to do so, he could learn all the multiplication tables by next week. Such an unrealistic assessment of his possibilities does not take into account certain necessities or givens, such as the limitations of information processing. This child is stuck with a situation in which guilt is built in from the start. It is easy to imagine how learning the tables means "being good" to him, and how he feels the necessity to be "good" because of the investment in an idealized concept he has of himself, which in turn has emerged from a series of lies he has told himself over the course of years.

Child *B* is convinced, say, that he cannot learn to read. The situation is construed by him as one in which it is *given* that he will not be able to learn to read. One can imagine here too the kinds of lies that have led to this kind of self-deception. Suppose that the child discovered that by appearing helpless to his parents he could get their attention, and that he wanted their attention so much that he was willing to lie to get it and was willing to accept it in the form of paternalistic and degrading acts of "helpfulness" on the part of his parents. In the perpetration of this lie, the child comes to believe that in fact he is incapable of tying his own shoes, of cutting his own food, etc. The generalization to the school situation is not at all unlikely if this particular lying-for-oneself comes to dominate his being. Furthermore, while these examples are of the very practical school situation, it is easy to imagine that love-hate, or male-female could be the issues at stake instead of success-failure. In addition, it is easy to see how the achievement situation of the school would inevitably be effected by other, more earthy and familiar issues, when the child's being-for-himself is permeated by lies-for-himself.

C. Lying-in-the-world

This is obviously the most difficult kind of lying to detect in one-self and in adulthood we are aided in our detection by honest and rigorous being-for-oneself. Suppose that a sibling is born to a three-year-old child, and suppose that he feels acutely the inevitable jealousy as he perceives the new "second-fiddle" quality of his own status. Anger at the intruder is a common and nearly inescapable reaction. He finds, however, that his expression of anger at the newborn only further subverts his stock with his parents, and so he learns to hide his feelings from them. Here we have a version of lying-for-others. He also finds that there is something especially "bad" about being angry and feels like he's bad for having such feelings. With a little time, he is able to convince himself that he is not the sort of lad who has such bad feelings. Here we see a version of lying-for-oneself.

Lying-in-the-world is yet a third dimension of this maneuver. It is one thing to misrepresent *oneself* to others or to oneself, to misconstrue oneself-as-an-object. It is quite different to misrepresent *the world* to oneself and misconstrue oneself-as-subject. The new-born sibling becomes, in an extreme reaction formation, a desirable and attractive object and the child's relationship to this object, on a spontaneous and immediate level, becomes one of love and devotion. Such a lie invades the very core of experience and profoundly interferes with one's ability to confront the world honestly.

This is not to say, of course, that every child who makes peace with his younger siblings is caught in a damning lie that forever undermines his own integrity; but there is an important difference between the child who works out an acceptance on the basis of facing the facts and learning to live with them and the child whose devotion to the baby is arrived at in the short, easy way—by misconstruing his real feelings in their subject-like reality as well as objects of his own reflection.

Another example: suppose a child must confront the reality of a loss of a parent. We can see this example as a mild, temporary loss, as when mother goes to the store, or as a severe, permanent loss as in death or divorce. The harshness and persistence of the loss dictates the importance of the choice of how to perceive this "given." A posture of honesty with respect to this given is difficult and indeed we hardly expect uncompromising courage from children under all circumstances. If the goal of life is to avoid anxiety, then any kind of distortion of reality that protects us from such a truth is a "good" one. The avoidance of anxiety, however, at the cost of one's openness to experience is a "bad" choice. The normal process of mourning, as described so well by Freud, is a process of progressively facing the many ramifications of a loss, over a period of time, at a rate that makes the trauma bearable.

Lying-in-the-world, in both of these examples, is no doubt accompanied by various kinds of lying-for-others and lying-for-oneself. But the latter do not necessarily imply lying-in-the-world. All such lies are costly in terms of one's openness to experience, and insofar as the issues are profound ones in the life of the child and the network of lies is a complex and integrated style of being, one's being becomes a lie. This whole series of bad choices involves one in a psychological morass in at least two ways. First, there are bound to be internal contradictions that are confusing at the least and produce symptoms in the extreme case. This is the "out-of-jointness" we talked about in Chapter 3. Second, the more profoundly one's being is pervaded by a lie, the less open one becomes to any experience that reveals the contradictions, causes the confusion, and the more limited one is in facing the challenges of the given exigencies of life.

One of the most important exigencies that is given to the human being and constitutes part of the intransigent reality with which he must deal is one's biological organism. The human being is not just consciousness; he is not a disembodied spirit. Freud's theory of man, resting as it does on a theory of instinct, gives full recognition to this aspect of the existential situation. Binswanger (1963) and other existentialists have noted this revolutionary challenge of Freudian thought, but they have generally objected to Freud's hypostasis of the insight into a total theory of man.

Be that as it may, our immediate relationship to the world is not under total conscious control. Impulses toward objects in the world, positive and negative, love and hate, are part of the given, at least in their physiological aspects. The range of events from glandular response to investment of an emotion with meaning is a unitary phenomenon, and yet it is clearly part "given" and part "chosen." Sartre goes the furthest in seeing the phenomenon as chosen (cf. Fell, 1965); Freud goes the furthest in seeing it as given.

Lying-in-the-world is a way of not facing this aspect of the given. For the child to experience himself-as-subject in a way that does not permit expression of what is given in being-a-subject is to begin on the road of alienation of his experience from its very foundation. The question is not whether the child should feel free to act out his spontaneous feelings. Murderous impulses in action are not "good." The question is whether these impulses and feelings are experienced as-subject, whether this fact of life, which impinges upon one's being-in-the-world, is integrated into one's being or lost in the morass of interferences that come from various sorts of lies.

The resulting loss of openness to experience yields a loss of contact with this aspect of reality which in turn yields a loss of the ability to bring it under the control of conscious choice, that is, to see options in what to do with feelings. Frustration is inevitable under these circumstances, for one does not know what one wants or where one is going. As in the cases of shame and guilt, frustration may remain as a conscious experience, without the particular lies that underlie it being at all apparent. One is therefore left with vague feelings of unhappiness with all sorts of lies-for-oneself and lies-for-others covering up that aspect of the given that is not being faced.

Before we leave our "psychology of lying," it is well to reflect on what is involved in the use of that metaphor in describing the being of the child. The term seems to imply that there is a hard-core reality that "honest" people face and neurotic people do not. This is indeed too simple. By focusing on existential "givens," we are setting a kind of absolute standard, but it is unwise, I think, to insist that there is only one truth or one "right" way to interpret a given situation. There are multiple perspectives to everything, and it is well to remember this when we as psychologists argue among ourselves about the nature of man and when we seek to help the patient come to terms with life. And certainly we must avoid condemning children and patients because they "lie."

There are profound philosophical problems lurking in the background here. Are we to settle for the old distinction between "primary" and "secondary" qualities of an object, the former being objectively given and the latter being subjectively determined? Our discussion about man's relation to his physiology and impulses seems to imply such a view. Actually existentialism offers a serious alternative to this kind of metaphysics, and we must be willing to stretch our concepts a little to see the point. And the point is, concisely stated, that experience is always both objective and subjective and never exclusively either. The theory of intentionality and the phenomenological meaning of the term "world" begin to show how this is so. But most important of all, we need to see that in choosing a metaphor for describing childhood, neurosis, or whatever, we are being simultaneously objective and subjective, and this is always and inescapably the case. This issue comes up again in the chapter on methodology at the end of the book.

3. Identification

Being develops over time. By the time one is an adult, the activities of his being are a complex conglomeration of styles, operating on three levels at once, partly perpetuating old lies, partly replacing them with truth and gaining momentum in coming to terms with the given, partly giving up old truths in the production of new lies as life weaves its way through the myriad of circumstances and events. It is hardly any wonder that psychology has had difficulty collecting scientific data that successfully generalizes about the core of human existence.

Identification is one of the concepts that names a process originally conceived by Freud. It has since become a label for a problem area of empirical and theoretical work in psychology. In our thinking too, we must see the phenomena that are usually included under this label as highly significant for the development of being. We must, of course, redefine the concept in terms of the progress we have made in reducing the complexity of being to a less complex map of the terrain.

Let us begin with a typical pattern of a satellized child. He feels very weak and insignificant in comparison to his father, who is, let us assume, a stern disciplinarian. His father often tinkers with the car, wielding screwdriver and socket wrenches with great skill. The child, while his father is away at work, sneaks into the garage and "repairs his car" just as he saw his father do. Sockets are snapped into place with authority. The screwdriver is deftly whipped from pocket to task and back again. During this game, the child does not feel quite so small, quite so insignificant. In fact, the fantasy is that he *is* his father, and therefore that he possesses all the skills, authority, and interests of his father. When he is discovered playing with daddy's tools, he is soundly punished, for sockets were lost and ratchets broken. Later the child is seen punishing an imaginary playmate for having broken his paint brush and spilled his paint, and this scolding uses the same language and technique that were used on him.

Observers of human nature have long seen this as important behavior. Imitation was seen by some of the nineteenth century as the key to all social behavior.* Freud focused our fascinated attention on it with his ingenious theory of identification, and since that time we have tried to understand just what happens in identification and how it fits into the development of personality. Perhaps phenomenological psychology is particularly well suited to describe the import of this phenomenon, for it may be that what is taking place is taking place primarily within the child's experience of himself and the world.

* Gabriel Tarde was such a theorist. cf. Timasheff (1955).

Let us define identification as a process of self-definition in terms of a model, probably a parent but often an historical or mythical hero. This definition puts the phenomenon squarely in the realm of being-for-oneself. However, we must at this point be particularly attentive to the interaction of one's being-for-himself with being-in-the-world and being-for-others. When the child is faced with some decision in relation, say, to his peers, he may consciously ask himself, "How would father feel about this?" This may mean, "What would father say if I do such and such?" in which case we see being-for-others (namely his father), or it may mean, "What would father do in this situation?" in which case the question is about father's being-in-the-world. Somewhat later, after identification is more advanced, the child may merely get himself into the well-practiced "father attitude" and respond to the situation as his father would. Here identification has influenced directly the child's being-in-the-world. All children almost certainly do all of these, in various proportions, using various models in various situations.

Let us focus our attention on the question of punishment and its relationship to identification, for research findings seem to indicate that warm and loving parents evoke more identification than cold and cruel ones, or at least the kind of identification that can be readily measured.* According to psychoanalytic theory, however, it would be somewhat easier to explain heightened identification in the case of parents whose punishments are severe. A phenomenological and existential approach opens up new possibilities for understanding the mysteries of the relationship between identification and punishment.

The crucial difference between mild punishment, or we might call it a supportive curbing of undesirable behavior, and harsh and severe punishment, which can be either physical violence or psychological manipulation through the threat of the withdrawal of love, might be found within the experiential field of the child. The mild version, we will argue, opens up options and the severe version closes them off.

Any time a parent reprimands a child for having done something, he sends the message to the child, "You did not have to do

* For a complete account of research in this topic, cf. Hoffman & Hoffman (1964).

that. If you think of doing it again, I want you also to think of the fact that it will be followed by punishment." Such a message places the child in the position of making the choice next time in light of superior information about the consequences of his acts and increases the meaning of the choice to do it or not to do it. Punishment therefore enhances the child's experience of himself-as-subject in the sense that it gives him more control over his interaction with the world than he had before. It also enhances his experience of himself as the object of others by making the child feel the power of the other. And it enhances his experience of himself as his own object in that it introduces certain behavioral criteria for self-judgment that perhaps had not been present before.

The facilitation of the experience of oneself-as-subject is of immediate interest. Increasing the options the child sees with respect to his own behavior, making them more meaningful and continuing their availability, all serve to break down satellization and lessen the importance of the experience of oneself as the object of the god-parent. Punishment, if it is not so severe as to make a particular option unthinkable, therefore forces the child to make behavioral decisions that have wider meaning than whether simply to do it or not to do it.

Part of that wider meaning has to do with what the child wants to become for himself and for others. Both of these activities have histories, of course, and a network of meanings of these two kinds will have already been built up. But the preservation of options gives him relatively more control over his being-for-himself and his being-for-others. One's being-for-oneself, the most crucial dimension of which is probably an evaluative one ("I am a good boy/bad boy"), is thus grounded in the experience of having made decisions and is not subject to undue being-for-others.

Suppose, however, that the punishment is very severe, that the child really would have to risk the unriskable, such as the good will of the gods. This makes certain options literally unthinkable, or in other words, takes them out of the realm of what is possible. They are no longer live options. The child's field of choice is thereby narrowed and his experience of himself becomes lost amid a certain kind of satellization, namely, the feeling that one must be constantly on one's guard against offending the gods. One's being-for-others comes to be relatively more important under these circumstances, just when one's experience of himself-as-subject who can choose among alternatives is being undermined.

Let us now consider the quality of guilt under the two circumstances. One kind of guilt is to know one has chosen badly, that one did not live up to standards that have become internalized when one could have chosen differently. This is a guilt for what one has *done*. It is an entirely different kind of guilt that comes not from what one has done, by having chosen badly, but rather from what one *is*, as an object rather than as a subject. Satellization that is perpetrated by severe punishment may not be a passing stage of childhood but may come to be a permanent part of oneself-as-object. This is understandable whenever one loses contact with oneself-as-subject and ceases to be-in-the-world, an activity that becomes swamped by being-for-oneself and particularly by being-for-others.

We can understand this better by asking further about the processes of internalization of parental standards in the two cases. In the case of supportive curbing of undesirable behavior, the standards for behavior emerge from having chosen, from a number of alternatives, and a corresponding willingness to take responsibility for that choice. In the case of severe punishment, the standards are internalized not into a spontaneous and personally felt preference among alternatives in-the-world, but rather from a preemptory being-for-others which becomes a haunting being-for-oneself. The second, more pathological, case is even more understandable in light of the lying-for-oneself that becomes a part of one's psychology. In spite of the lie, there is the nagging awareness, vaguely experienced, that one's standards are not one's own. The "idealized self" is an attempt to deny this awareness, but it leads, as we have seen, to failure, and one becomes enslaved to a morality that has no support from one's being-in-the-world. That such standards may well be rather unreliable as psychological controls of impulses becomes quite understandable. One is caught in a "struggle with the introject," a struggle to appease and rebel, alternately or simultaneously, gods that one no longer understands or feels comfortable with.

We have spoken as if the severity of punishment were the single factor that makes this important difference. This is of course an oversimplification, especially when we recall what the experience of satellization is really like. Parents can act quite neutrally at certain times, and if the child's being-for-others is right for it, the parental action will be construed as a damning condemnation. Furthermore, good-bad is not the only dimension that becomes involved: weak-strong, success-failure, male-female all are subject to the complex workings of being, with subtle interaction among the three levels that changes from instant to instant. Over the course of the first five years, it is indeed altogether possible that the child's ability to see options, to experience the crucial task of making decisions, and to develop being-for-himself and being-for-others that are not out of joint, becomes lost amid the confusions of life.

Technical Terms

Fusion: That earliest experience in infancy before the self is differentiated from the world.

Separateness: The experience immediately following fusion, which is characterized by both the joys of independent power (as reflected in two-year-old initiative) and the anxiety of separation from the primordial experience of fusion with the parent.

Satellization: The experience of oneself as the object of god-like parents, in which one's joys of independence are submerged in the recognition of one's relative powerlessness, but in which the anxiety of separation is submerged in the feeling of safety under the protection of the gods.

Similarity: The experience of oneself in relation to parents in which the opposition of separateness and the subjugation of satellization is replaced by a recognition that both parent and child are subject to equality before the authority of reality.

Lying-for-others: Lying in the usual sense of knowing that one's presentation of oneself to the other is deceptive.

Lying-for-oneself: The extension of the deception from being-for-others to being-for-oneself; the development of an idealized self; self-deception.

Lying-in-the-world: The extension of the deception from content about oneself to content about the world as it is immediately experienced in one's being-in-the-world.

Guilt for what one does: Guilt that grows out of having chosen wrongly; created by punishment that leaves options open; healthy guilt.

Guilt for what one is: Guilt that grows out of being unacceptable to the gods of satellization; created by severe punishment during satellization; tends to be neurotic guilt.

References

Binswanger, L. Freud's conception of man in the light of anthropology. In J. Needleman (Ed.) *Being-in-the-World.* New York: Basic Books, 1963.

Buber, M. *I and Thou.* New York: Scribners, 1958.

Cooley, C. *Human Nature and the Social Order.* New York: Schreibners, 1902.

Fell, J. P. *Emotion in the Thought of Sartre.* New York: Columbia University Press, 1965.

Hoffman, M. L. & Hoffman, L. W. *Child Development Research I.* New York: Russell Sage Foundation, 1964.

Horney, K. *Neurosis and Human Growth.* New York: Norton, 1950.

Jacobson, E. *The Self and the Object World.* New York: International Universities Press, 1964.

Jaspers, K. *General Psychopathology.* Chicago: University of Chicago Press, 1964.

Marcel, G. *Journal Metaphysique.* Paris: Gallimard, 1927.

Mead, G. H. *Mind, Self, and Society.* Chicago: University of Chicago Press, 1934.

Sartre, J.-P. *Being and Nothingness.* New York: Philosophical Library, 1956.

Spitz, R. *No and Yes: On the Genesis of Human Communication.* New York: International Universities Press, 1957.

Sullivan, H. S. *Conceptions of Modern Psychiatry.* Washington, D.C.: William Allison White Institute, 1947.

Sullivan, H. S. *The Interpersonal Theory of Psychiatry.* New York: Norton, 1953.

Timasheff, N. S. *Sociological Theory.* New York: Random House, 1955.

SUMMARY OF
PART I

In the last four chapters, we have spoken about psychology in transition. The transitions are actually many and constant, but we are focusing here on the move toward an existential orientation. In summary of what has been said so far, let us state the main elements of that transition.

First, existential psychology seeks to take consciousness seriously. Our inability to deal with conscious experience as a part of psychological subject matter is an embarrassment at the least and in the worst case a scientific myopia. Consciousness is important and can no longer be ignored if we are to have an adequate science of man. Second, taking consciousness seriously forces us into a direct confrontation with *subjective experience* as subject matter and as data. An examination of the experience of self leads to a fundamental difference between experiencing oneself-as-subject and oneself-as-object. These different experiences correspond to the philosophical traditions of existentialism and essentialism respectively. This correspondence is no accident; these two great traditions of Western thought appeal to different kinds of experiential data. Third, a phenomenological examination of *experience* leads us to seek new metaphors in terms of which to talk and to think. The most obvious need is to arrive at some way to formulate our observations that avoids the essentialistic and object-geared language of natural science. The metaphor of "being" was described as fulfilling the qualifications for a way to deal with phenomenological data. It was pointed out that being is the most important context in which to interpret any psychological event, for it is the overarching activity of human life.

Fourth, we have said in Chapter 3 that man's being has "three faces," that his activity of being the person he is can usefully be divided into three "levels" of being: (*a*) Being-in-the-world, in which he experiences the world directly and as meaningful in terms of his own desires. His experience of himself in this aspect of being is "as-subject," over against the world of objects in which he is involved. (*b*) Being-for-oneself, in which one's object of attention is not the world, and one's style of attention is not prereflective and immediate, but rather the object is oneself and the style is reflective. Out of this experience of oneself "as object" comes the notion of "self-concept" and the casting of oneself into substantive terms so that there is some kind of solid "me" or definition which one can use to make decisions about what to do, how to act, etc. (*c*) Being-for-others, in which oneself is experienced through the eyes of others, and one becomes the object of "the other." Hence we gear our behavior to the expectations of others all the time, and indeed, if we did not do so, our relationships would be so full of surprises and inconsistencies that we would hardly get along with one another at all.

Fifth, these three activities may fit together into an integrated way of being or they may be more or less out of joint with one another. This out-of-jointness constitutes the core anomaly of psychopathology.

Sixth, it was assumed that life is made up of necessities and possibilities, of contingencies that are "given" and into which we are "thrown" without our consent, and of an open-ended future that is decided by the individual as he goes along. The experience of "deciding," which is alleged to be illusory according to the natural-scientific doctrine of determinism, has a developmental history in the individual that goes through discernible stages described in Chapter 4. Seventh, it was found that "lying" is a metaphor in terms of which it is possible to see the development of the out-of-jointness we call psychopathology. Three types of lies were described that parallel the three faces of being, and each introduces into being certain kinds of experiences that appear in the psychological clinic. These were called "primordial experiences" insofar as they constitute the core around which human experience is organized.

These chapters therefore describe the direction of a transition in psychology from a mere natural science to a more complete existential orientation that takes consciousness seriously. This transition is a moment of growth for psychology into a new relevance and a new adequacy as a science of man.

In Part II, we will move from traditional topics in psychology, such as clinical examples, interview phenomena, development, identification and the self, into experiential phenomena and concepts that come from existential philosophy. These experiences too should be a part of a psychology that seeks to take consciousness seriously, and they are intricately related to the findings so far. We shall focus on existential anxiety, its relationship to choice and to the experience of self-as-subject, on "intentionality" as a concept that ties together several threads of existential and psychological thought, and on "the world" as a psychological category.

EXISTENTIAL THOUGHT IN PSYCHOLOGY II

Anxiety
and choice   5

In the next three chapters, we will seek to understand experiences and concepts that are not part of traditional psychology but come instead from existential and phenomenological philosophy. There are important ways in which the issues already discussed demand these new concepts, for the various experiences of being are described by key concepts that emerge from existential literature. In this chapter, we will focus on the experiences of anxiety and of choice.

Let us for now dodge the issue of "free will *versus* determinism," by emphasizing that in terms of concrete experience, where existential psychology must operate, both are meaningful concepts. We sometimes feel determined and sometimes feel free. This is true of all of us, regardless of how well formulated or elaborate our ideological convictions may be. All too often the argument of this issue becomes a rational duel that reflects only indirectly how the participants are being and ignores the experiential fact that both theoretical views have relevance to certain aspects of immediate, experiential data.

1. Anxiety and Choice

The conditions of our decision-making have changed radically in the last century. Religious and other institutional values that used to help us to make decisions have broken down. A century ago, only an intellectual elite understood Nietzsche's announcement that God is dead; now God is popularly dead. The old faith that organized our lives is relevant only to the small minority of remaining devout, and this change has made the whole matter of making decisions much more of a problem for modern man.

We are freer from externally imposed restraints, such as institutional values, but we are also faced with a kind of ambiguity that has not been mankind's usual condition. The necessity for making decisions and the lack of a doctrine according to which to make them creates a particular paradox for human beings. In concrete experience, this paradox yields anxiety. How will I know that the values I hold will not prove to be mere products of my social class? Of my sibling position? Of my historical situation? How do I know that my decisions have any more validity than the accidental circumstances of my life history?

There are perhaps two ways in which people make choices. First, one can follow what appears to be rather clear evidence about what is right, such as recognizing matters of fact or following some value or principle that seems beyond question. Second, one can affirm a value in the face of no objective (external) evidence or in the face of some ambiguity about the ultimate validity of a value. The first is more like a cognition than a choice, for one really feels coerced into a particular path, and one is merely processing information about where to turn. If I choose not to take heroin, for example, it is probably because I have a clear cognition of the likely results of such action. Or if I believe in the absolute validity of the Christian ethic, I am similarly bound "from the outside" to follow it. Even if I choose to reject a career as a poet, it may well be because I know that objectively speaking, I haven't the talent, and this condition is imposed from the outside in the sense that I haven't any control over the genes that determined my brain cells.*

The second kind of choice, on the other hand, forces one to confront an absence of external guides and to create an internal one, one that has no justification beyond oneself. If I take seriously

---

* Note that this last example, the decision not to become a poet because I haven't the talent to do so, comes dangerously close to placing responsibility for my choice elsewhere, in my genes and in my essence, and would be labelled "bad faith" by Sartre.

the possibility that being a heroin addict is just as good a way of life as any other, or that the Christian ethic is culturally relative, or that whether I become a poet is more a matter of whether I want to discipline myself, then to make a decision about these issues is to affirm where I stand on the basis of my own criteria. Such choice makes me alone responsible for the content of my behavior and makes my values into *my* creations instead of something imposed from the outside.

Sartre (1947) tells the story of the youth who came to him with the following dilemma. If he were to join the resistance, he would have to leave his aging mother and she would surely die. If, on the other hand, he were to stay with his mother, he would forego the obligation to resist the Nazis and he would support their presence by not resisting. Which should he choose? The appeal to Sartre for help in sorting out the contingencies of this decision was an attempt to make the problem go away. The fact is, Sartre tells us, that the boy had already decided, but that he was not willing to face the consequences of that choice. What he really wanted was to find some way to make his abdicated responsibility less burdensome. Had Sartre decided for him, that would have solved the problem of responsibility for the youth, a problem that is exacerbated in the absence of an absolute ethic to which we can appeal in such situations. But had Sartre said anything at all about the matter, he would have interfered in the most crucial of existential processes: making a choice and then taking responsibility for that choice.

The only way out of such a dilemma is not to "discover" which obligation is the greater, but to make it so by deciding it is so. One does not "discover" moral standards; one makes them. And in the process of making them, we become authentic.

It is therefore in the making of choices of the second kind, where there are no established criteria to follow, that we have the most salient experience of ourselves-as-subject. To choose this or that course, to opt for one value or another under conditions of cognitive ambiguity, is to have control over oneself, to be an agent and to establish oneself as valid. Such a birth of self-as-subject, however, takes place amid the anxiety of not knowing whether one is "choosing the right thing." Indeed we never know what is right, and indeed we feel anxious in not knowing, and indeed to establish what is right we must survive anxiety. The ambiguity of the human situation is not amenable to any cognitive tricks; it is a hard game that must be played honestly if one is to experience the self-as-subject. Authentic being, resting on self-as-subject, is born of anxiety.

Tillich (1952) has specified three sources of existential anxiety and Bugental (1965) has adapted them directly to the psychological situation, adding a fourth contingency of human existence that inevitably makes us anxious. The first existential "given" is the fact of human finitude. There is nothing more certain than death—not even taxes—and no conscious person can forget this inevitability indefinitely. This leads, as does all existential anxiety, either to a confrontation of the anxiety of our finitude or to an avoidance of it through typical maneuvers of denial and distortion. Very few American psychologists have considered death to be of abiding importance, for it seems to be a mildly aversive topic that has relevance only at the death of a loved one or in direct anticipation of death in terminal illness. One can argue from this fact either that death is not a very important phenomenon or that psychologists have participated in the denial and evasion. We opt for the latter interpretation. A serious contemplation of one's own death is very difficult to sustain, more difficult than to contemplate seriously other biological events, such as birth, sex, and maturation.

Perhaps one of the reasons why death has always seemed irrelevant to American psychologists is that it is, for each of us, always in the future. Future events, according, to the natural scientific model, never have any relevance for the present, for American psychologists have rejected teleological and eschatological thinking decades ago. A phenomenology of life, however, cannot reject the relevance of the future, and yet death, unlike any other future event, is scrupulously avoided in our ordinary experience. The fact is simply that a serious contemplation of our own death makes us anxious.

There are indeed many supporting distractions from the culture to aid us in avoiding the anxiety. When one is able to break through the temptations of denial and avoidance and to tolerate the anxiety that inevitably comes, life changes its character. The shape of that change is not the same for everyone. Some of us find that life becomes more urgent, others that it becomes more precious, and yet others that it becomes meaningless. The change, in any case, is profound, even if only temporary. This poignantly suggests the relevance of death to life.

Death is the logical extreme of human finitude. We are also powerless in a number of other respects: against accidents and fate, against chance factors that control us without our assent. Together, these elements of the human situation have been the key data that feed into the formulation of life as "tragic" in the classical sense.

The second contingency that inevitably produces anxiety is that of the potential, indeed the necessity, to act. Here the demands of life to make choices, combined with the modern uncertainty of how to do so, of which we have spoken above, produces the continual threat of being profoundly guilty. We must take responsibility for decisions made in relative ignorance of their ramifications. We hurt people regularly without meaning to do so; indeed the most vicious of human cruelty is performed in the name of some kind of goodness. We are constantly subject to such self-deception, and experience has taught each of us how prone we have been toward it in the past.

Perhaps the most abstract, but no less vivid, contingency of human existence that produces anxiety is the threat of meaninglessness. We have a kind of orientation to life, ordinarily, that allows us to see what we do as meaningful. For one man, life's activities give him pleasure, for another, they produce beauty, for another they further the causes of goodness and virtue. But these orientations are open to question. When they are questioned, the issue becomes not how to act or how to live, but whether life *means* anything. Of course there are any number of glib dismissals of the issue; life simply means nothing. But such an *experience,* as opposed to a mere intellectual conclusion, is the occasion of the shaking of the very foundations of our lives. Even the orientation through which we see this or some intellectual problem is at stake. We may *say* that life is meaningless because we can find no meaning intellectually, but to *live* life under the threat of meaninglessness is accompanied by anxiety. Even the saying of the intellectual conclusion must take place within some orientation that gives the act meaning. To experience meaninglessness is another matter indeed.

Bugental's fourth contingency, which he considers separately from the other three and which Tillich considers within the other three, is the isolation of the individual. Regardless of how intimate I may become with another person, I can never be he or he I; we are inevitably separated from one another by the gulf of our own individuality. That hiatus cannot be overcome. To be embedded in some kind of community, such as a family, a fraternity, or a profession, relieves us of the acute pain of loneliness. But the relief is never permanent. Other people are intransigently themselves and I am intransigently myself. We "share" experiences and yet we never totally understand the other nor are understood by him. To ask for such a total communion is, of course, logically absurd, and we have all learned to live with the logical conclusion of our ultimate loneliness. But we have not learned to experience that loneliness without anxiety. We may frantically seek each other out, or we may agree to pretend that we are one with another, or we may find the frustration of others so aversive that we give up trying. But we never overcome this contingency.

The four contingencies specify further the origins of existential anxiety. They are not, of course, independent of one another. For any one of us, one or another of them may have more salience. But they are all there, quite inescapably, for they are given and can be avoided only at the expense of the constriction of our consciousness. Together, these contingencies have been called "nonbeing," and nonbeing is the perpetual context of being. These givens are matters of *necessity;* and hence they are a negation of being-as-a-subject, which is by definition conscious, open-ended, and is the realm of *possibility.*

Being survives to the extent that it takes nonbeing into itself; it perishes to the extent that it attempts to affirm itself by avoiding nonbeing. Being can affirm itself only through affirming nonbeing. More concretely, the self-as-subject can *be* only through confronting and surviving anxiety. To avoid anxiety is to avoid nonbeing in its various forms. To avoid choice and its anxiety, for example, is to fail to be-a-subject. The flight into the experience of self-as-object is like paying blackmail. It serves to keep anxiety at bay temporarily, but it solves nothing in the long run and eventually impoverishes the victim. I may solve the problem of how to make decisions by appealing more and more to an objectification of myself, but such a maneuver eventually enslaves me to an idealized self and limits my ability to be-in-the-world-as-a-subject. The progressive impoverishment of one's sense of himself-as-subject in the extreme case leads, we shall argue below, to a more devastating invasion of anxiety.

2. *Anxiety and Self-as-Subject*

In Chapter 2, an attempt was made to describe the experiences of self-as-subject. We concluded that at least three crucial things are involved: (*a*) The self as a point of orientation or a context of meanings that makes the experience of the world meaningful, (*b*) The self as an active agent, which can translate desire into behavior that has a real effect on the external world, and (*c*) The self as a pole of consciousness in a field of two or more centers of consciousness, which gives interpersonal experience a profoundly different flavor from interaction with a thing.

Above we have argued that to decide is to survive anxiety and to establish a valid being based on the experience of self-as-subject. Let us now turn the matter around. Might we define anxiety also as the loss or absence of the experience of self-as-subject?

Let us now ask what happens when (if) we lose the experience of self-as-subject. First, without the self as a point of orientation, it is clear that things will not mean the same thing. One can, indeed, ask if experience would mean anything at all. Put another way, one can ask whether the organization of experience that is gained by referring it to a central clearing house of meanings is necessary. We can only say, at this point, that one's being-in-the-world would be extraordinary without it. Perhaps the "loss of reality" experience is not a breakdown in perception (in the sense of organs functioning) as much as it is a breakdown of meaning and of the organization of experience.

Second, the experience of self as agent seems to be an integral part of one's relationship to the world. To imagine experience without this feeling of agency is to imagine experience that is wholly passive, alienated, and encapsulated from the world of objects and people. We can only say that such a profound helplessness is difficult to imagine. Perhaps the common nightmare of being chased and being unable to run is the closest thing in most of our experience to the panic and futility of this loss.

Our third characteristic, that has to do with the kinds of assumptions we make, indeed must make, in order to relate to other people, also appears quite necessary when we consider its absence. To operate on the assumption that other people are not really people, not really conscious, has been a suggested feature of the psychopath's experience (Frankenstein, 1959), for his behavior betrays no identification with others at all. More to the point, perhaps, are the common complaints of psychotics that other people do not understand them and are not really "with them" in the ordinary sense. Their esoteric language augments this effect, of course. That fact is not apparent to them, but their alienation from others and absolute loneliness is quite apparent and frightening.

Experience without a self-as-subject would certainly, therefore, be different. Indeed it would be terrifying. We might say that our base of operations has been pulled out from under us, or that we have lost our "security." May has suggested that "An individual experiences various fears on the basis of a security pattern he has developed; but in anxiety it is this security pattern itself which is threatened (1950, p. 191)." Laing (1960) has emphasized the relationship of anxiety to depersonalization and the loss of ontological security. The term "security" in both contexts has to do with the organization of the experience of life into a pattern that is meaningful and familiar, that has stability and relevance, and in which the "I" has some control and power. The loss of this experience, or the threat to it, involves potential disorganization, instability, and helplessness. It is a matter of losing the "I," of depersonalization, and of meaninglessness. When we feel anxious, we feel this threat. A patient who becomes anxious in therapy is threatened by the loss of the organization that he has been able to achieve, and such anxiety is not easy to endure even if that organization has proved in various ways to be inadequate.

Let us again now consider the breakdown of institutional values and the resulting paradoxes of making decisions. Whatever else is true of the modern condition, man is aware of more aspects of himself than he has ever been before. The social sciences have made our position within various causal chains more salient and given us more solid reason to experience ourselves as caused phenomena. Laing points out:

Under the heading of "defense mechanisms," psychoanalysis describes a number of ways in which a person becomes alienated from himself. For example, repression, denial, splitting, projection, introjection. These "mechanisms" are often described in psychoanalytic terms as themselves "unconscious," that is, the person himself appears to be unaware that he is doing this to himself. Even when a person develops sufficient insight to see that "splitting," for example, is going on, he usually experiences this splitting as indeed a mechanism, an impersonal process, so to speak, which has taken over and which he can observe but cannot control or stop.

There is thus some phenomenological validity in referring to such "defenses" by the term "mechanism." But we must not stop there. They have this mechanical quality because the person as he experiences himself is dissociated from them. He appears to himself and to others to suffer from them. They seem to be processes he undergoes, and as such he experiences himself as a patient, with a particular psychopathology (1967, p. 17).

This dissociation undermines the experience of self-as-subject in all three respects. I can no longer rely on myself as a point of orientation if I must see myself as a mere element within a larger system of causal relationships. I can no longer feel like the master of my own fate when I become aware of the input to my very experiential propensities from family, social class, and personal history. And I can no longer involve myself in a relationship with others as readily as I could before I was aware of all these mechanical determinants of my own and the other's behavior.

Hence, the paradoxes of not knowing where to look to validate one's choices, and of not knowing all the long-term effects of my choices, even while choice is necessary to get on with life—these paradoxes are given further intensity by the additional undermining of my experience of myself-as-subject by my increased awareness of myself as an object of causal forces. The reciprocal is also true: the undermining of my experience of myself as-subject makes the paradoxes more poignant. The anxiety that results from the paradoxes thus augments the anxiety of the loss of self-as-subject and vice-versa. In both cases, a restoration of the self-as-subject is an antidote, but an increasingly difficult one to achieve within the snowballing of anxiety.

Anxiety, as we have been talking about it, deserves the

characterization, "existential," in two senses: first, it stems from exigencies of the human situation and is not merely a failure of an organism to perform its assigned task; and second, it involves the loss of the existential experience of oneself, that is, the experience of oneself-as-subject.

3. Existential and Neurotic Anxiety

Existential anxiety, as we have discussed it above, is commonly differentiated from neurotic anxiety (Bugental, 1965; May, 1967). Traditional psychology has seen anxiety as neurotic, and, in fact, has seen anxiety as a central factor in the production of clinical symptoms. Freud, in his earlier work (1959), conceived anxiety as an overflow of excess libidinal energy that did not find normal discharge in sexual gratification. Later Freud (1936) tended to see anxiety as an experience rather than as a physiological phenomenon; but its systematic status was that of a danger signal that motivates the organism (according to the pleasure principle) to avoid some dangerous situations, such as the pressure of impulses from the id. Behaviorism, on the other hand, has seen anxiety largely as a conditioned response that interferes with more adaptive habits and should be extinguished (cf. Eysenck & Rachman, 1965). Here, too, the experiential and the inevitable qualities of anxiety have been badly neglected. A phenomenological and existential psychology can fill the gap in our understanding of anxiety as a part of human experience.

The paradoxes of the existential situation have always been there for man. He has never been able to predict all the consequences of his decisions, and he has always run the risk of being foolish in the eyes of history. But the modern age is more acutely aware of these limitations and hence more subject to the anxiety of the paradoxes. Existentialism, as a philosophy, is a direct response to this historical situation. Sartre tells us that we must accept our "facticity" and our limitations (cf. Greene, 1963), and Tillich (1952) tells us we must have "courage" to make decisions in spite of the paradoxes and limitations. The modern condition of man is both a threat and a possibility. The threat is that the anxiety may overwhelm us and the possibility is that if we survive the threat, our experience of self-as-subject can be richer and more autonomous than ever before.

Existential anxiety, seen in this light, is not pathological. It is a normal experience that inescapably accompanies the paradox of the human condition. Furthermore, such an experience is not limited to philosophers and intellectuals, although they are of course the ones who have agonized about it in print. The lack of clear guidelines for making decisions and the pain of knowing one must decide—this is a universal human experience.

Existential anxiety leads to pathological symptoms, however, (to neurotic anxiety) when we undergo certain experiential contortions in response to it rather than confront it head on and make decisions in spite of it. In general these experiential contortions involve an increasing "out-of-jointness" due to the pervasion of being by being-for-myself and being-for-others and a loss of contact with my being-in-the-world. This experiential conceptualization of the role of anxiety in the production of symptoms is markedly different from seeing it as a conditioned response or as a characterological anomaly among the functions of personality.

We have argued above that the "healthy," "authentic," or "good" way to live is to affirm oneself according to the immediate experience of one's self-as-subject, to be aware of one's immediate relation to the world, which is one that demands choices from us, and to make those choices, to be a subject, in spite of the anxiety. To ignore the necessity for choice and the anxiety and to try to guide one's behavior according to attempts to maintain the experience of self-as-object (put another way, to be unwilling to change one's being-for-himself), leads to neurosis. And to let my being-for-others usurp the guiding role at the cost of my being-in-the-world also creates experiential anomalies that lead to behavior that is seen clinically as symptomatic.

Suppose, for example, that a man denies his desire to be loved because he has an image of himself as quite independent of others and in need of no one's love, or because he wants very much to appear that way to others for whom he is performing. Such a person may hasten into an action that obeys these agendas and that may well conflict with his most basic and real desires. Having invested some action, energy, and some of his reputation and self-esteem in the particular action he took, he has lied-for-others in such a way that he feels obligated to support the lies with additional actions for the benefit of maintaining a consistent self in the eyes of others. Eventually he lies to himself: "I don't want to be loved." Continuation of this course leads finally to the lie-in-the-world: love from others is experienced immediately as a matter of indifference. His original and quite natural involvement in loving and being loved becomes totally submerged. His experience of himself-as-subject is lost in the maintenance of himself-as-an-object of others and of his own reflective appraisals. The result is the neurotic effects of shame, guilt, and frustration.

The escape into being-for-myself and being-for-others is motivated by an attempt to escape the anxiety of decision. In our example there are two layers of ambiguity: First, how does he know that a particular course will yield love instead of hate; and second, how does he know that he deserves being loved, even if he knew how to provoke it? No doubt the desire to be loved is nearly universal; but for some, it cannot be a simple matter of making oneself lovable. The uncertainties of childhood—and the accompanying anxieties—may have been very great for some of us. Perhaps we received contradictory demands from our parents so that we could not escape their punishment (cf. Bateson, et al., 1956). Or perhaps we found it expedient to define ourselves very rigidly as a way to conform to extreme parental standards, or we discovered that it was very dangerous to follow—or even be aware of—our own immediate feelings in relation to the world we grew up in.

One can imagine how the experiences of being-for-myself and being-for-others can grow in childhood into various lies that poison adulthood. Part III below will specify this line of thought. For now we need only to note that under the right conditions, any immediate experience of being-in-the-world may be totally lost amid the lies. We thus become "alienated from ourselves" as Fromm (1955) has put it, and become slaves to the expectations of others or to contrived and exaggerated conceptions of ourselves. R. D. Laing (1960) has described how this separation within ourselves progresses into a schizoid split in experience, and eventually to schizophrenia. His clinical descriptions are vivid exaggerations of what we can all experience on a small scale in ourselves; we all find it necessary to take flight into a self-concept or into a social role when the ambiguities of life raise our anxiety to a higher level than we are able to tolerate.

4. Anxiety and Choice in Psychotherapy

Psychotherapy, conceived existentially, is a process in which one must eventually learn to tolerate anxiety and to choose. People enter psychotherapy for all kinds of reasons. The standard diagnostic categories of psychopathology are an attempt to classify these reasons. These categories will no doubt be useful for years to come, even though they are based on a mixture of experiential, behavioral, and psychodynamic considerations.

It is helpful clinically to take off our diagnostic glasses occasionally and ask some experiential questions. One such question is: "How does the individual experience his world?" This will be discussed in Chapter 6. Let us ask here whether instead of experiencing "care," an individual is stuck with "frustrations"; instead of experiencing "self-esteem," he is stuck with "guilt"; and instead of experiencing "identity," he is stuck with "shame."

Care, self-esteem, and identity, as experiencies, all imply choices. Frustration, guilt, and shame, as experiences, all imply that we are victimized by forces outside our own control. When a person cares for someone or something, in the sense we mean it here, he has the option of withdrawing that concern. Frustration, on the other hand, is intransigent. Self-esteem is, by definition, earned by one's choices; one cannot, however, choose to feel guilty or not guilty. And by identity, I mean what Erikson means, "the accrued confidence that one's ability to maintain inner sameness and continuity (one's ego in the psychological sense) is matched by the sameness and continuity of one's meaning for others (Erikson, 1959, p. 89)."

What happens in psychopathology in general is that the self-as-subject, as an experience, is lost. The process of pursuing life according to being-an-object for myself and/or for others yields a frustration of the original immediate experience of the world. The individual then attempts to fill that gap by trying to live his lies, by trying to live up to a self-image or to the expectations of others.

The flight into being an *object* for oneself or for others is doomed to failure, for there is no substitute for the original experience of being-in-the-world. The self-as-subject must be expressed in (rather than submerged by) the other experiences of being in order for there to be healthy being. Hence, the flight into being-for-oneself is a flight from the experience of being-in-the-world and its anxiety, but this flight leads inevitably to guilt because being-for-myself is never completely satisfactory. Or a flight into being-for-others, for similar reasons, yields shame. In Part III we shall see how this works in different ways for different kinds of psychopathology.

The goal of psychotherapy is to replace frustration, guilt, and shame with care, self-esteem, and identity; or, in other words, to change one's experience from being determined to being free to choose; or put yet another way, to restore the experience of self-as-subject and thus to help the person overcome his out-of-jointness.

Lest this description sound too simple, let us immediately direct our attention to the difficulties of the task. The greatest difficulty is anxiety. The process of escape from anxiety, as it originally occurred, was a temporary solution and a long-term failure. In the first place, original anxieties of childhood must eventually be confronted, for they lie behind the lies. To face the truth is not easy to do. Second, anxiety is not something that one can dismiss as having happened in childhood and is now over. It is built directly into the human situation and must now be faced in its adult forms as well as its childhood forms. And third, even though the temporary solutions are long-term failures, there is a powerful substitute gratification in the "safety" of them, because they are familiar and habitual and have protected the person from anxiety for so long. Bugental (1965) has happily equated these difficulties with the psychoanalytic concept of "resistance," which makes a helpful connection between these therapeutic goals and the valuable and extensive literature of psychoanalysis as therapy.

Bugental has also described the therapeutic task as to help the patient experience himself-as-subject, which is equivalent to experiencing oneself as free to choose. We have shown that this freedom is necessarily accompanied by anxiety and that the solution comes not in eliminating anxiety but in facing it—and deciding in spite of it. Such a reorientation to life is monumental, and the achievement of this "authentic" orientation comes only by weathering "existential crises."

"Existential crisis" is Bugental's term for those situations that come up in the course of one's life—and always in therapy—when the individual has come face to face with a crucial decision. The alternatives in the existential crisis are: (*a*) maintenance of the protective escape into an experience of oneself that insulates one from the anxiety of freedom and choice—those modes of self-experience that preclude the existential anxiety inherent in the human situation, or (*b*) a leap into an unknown and perhaps terrifying abyss of freedom, in which one not only must garner the courage to face the heretofore denied pain of his own life but also must be willing to face the present and the future without those symptomatic distortions that provide excuses for not exercising one's freedom.

This description applies well to certain crucial points in psychotherapy. Bugental offers an example of a patient who failed to meet the challenge of a situation in which his life pattern and the therapeutic intervention were coming to a head. The failure was due, in part if not entirely, to the fact that both patient and therapist failed to appreciate the totalistic nature of the issues involved. It was, in short, an opportunity to reorganize his entire being.

The therapist's interpretation was clever, and even correct within a traditional psychological frame of reference, but it was existentially trivial. And it was the existential issue, not the psychodynamic one, that was at stake. Without the benefit of a full realization of the ultimate nature of this situation, by either patient or therapist, it was no wonder that the patient did not find the courage. In other words, there simply are situations in which the issue is one's total being. The psychodynamic formulation, no matter how skillfully presented, makes the situation appear trivial when it is profound, makes the person feel like a passive recipient of forces beyond his control, when in fact that feeling is his greatest resistance, and thus fails to mobilize the patient's experience of his subjectness and freedom. In this particular instance (and one cannot help wondering how many instances occur regularly without our understanding of them) the less-than-ultimate interpretation supplied the patient with a set of terms and a way of seeing that reduced the poignancy and intensity of the choice and failed to mobilize the strength and courage that was needed for real change. Both the ultimate escape motive and the ultimate potential to decide not to escape were overlooked.

Laing offers the following formulation of the difficulty encountered in personal change during psychotherapy:

> In the idiom of games theory, people have a repertoire of games based on particular sets of learned interactions. Others may play games that mesh sufficiently to allow a variety of more or less stereotyped dramas to be enacted. The games have rules, some public, some secret. Some people play games that break the rules of games that others play. Some play undeclared games, so rendering their moves ambiguous or downright unintelligible, except to the expert in such secret and unusual games. Such people, prospective neurotics or psychotics, may have to undergo the ceremonial of a psychiatric consultation, leading to diagnosis, prognosis, prescription. Treatment would consist in pointing out to them the unsatisfactory nature of the games they play and perhaps teaching new games. A person reacts by despair more to loss of the *game* than to sheer "object-loss," that is, to the loss of his partner or partners as real persons. The maintenance of the game rather than the identity of players is all-important (1967, p. 30).

The experiential movements within psychotherapy must therefore be very complex. For one person to help another person to make the movements necessary to reconcile the "out-of-jointness" among the levels of his being is, indeed, a herculean task. Certainly, no general map can yet be laid out and one suspects that any such map would have to be too general to be of much value in any individual case.

Technical Terms

Choice: A decision among alternatives, particularly in the absence of criteria outside oneself to which to appeal and with awareness that we cannot predict all the ramifications of our decision. Such experiences are more frequent in the modern age when institutional values have lost their validity.

Existential anxiety: That anxiety that is built into the exigencies of the human situation, and which derives from the paradoxes of choice. Also defined as the meaninglessness, depersonalization, and helplessness that comes from a loss of the existential experience of self, that is, the self-as-subject.

Neurotic anxiety: That anxiety that is derived from frustration, guilt, and shame, which in turn result from an escape into being-for-myself or for-others and in an inability to face existential anxiety.

Frustration: The remnant of the experience of self-as subject when choices are not made.

Guilt: The failure to live up to an "idealized image" of oneself, an enterprise that was attempted as a compensation for the lack of the experience of choice.

Shame: The failure to live up to the expectations of others, an enterprise that was attempted as a compensation for the lack of the experience of choice.

Security: That which is threatened in anxiety. It may involve any single aspect of being predominantly, in which case it is a false and particularly vulnerable security, or all three in a consistent "identity."

References

Bateson, G., Jackson, D. D., Haley, J., & Weakland, J. Toward a theory of schizophrenia. *Behavioral Science,* 1956, I, Whole No. 251.

Bugental, J. F. T. *The Search for Authenticity.* New York: Holt, 1965.

Erikson, E. Identity and the life cycle. *Psychological Issues,* 1951, I, Whole No. 1.

Eysenck, H. J. & Rachman, S. *The Causes and Cures of Neurosis.* San Diego, Calif.: Knapp, 1965.

Frankenstein, C. *Psychopathy.* New York: Grune & Stratton, 1959.

Freud, S. *The Problem of Anxiety.* New York: Norton, 1936.

Freud, S. Instincts and their vicissitudes. In *The Collected Papers of Sigmund Freud,* Vol. IV. New York: Basic Books, 1959.

Fromm, E. *The Sane Society.* New York: Rinehart, 1955.

Greene, N. N. *Jean-Paul Sartre: The Existentialist Ethic.* Ann Arbor, Mich.: University of Michigan Press, 1963.

Laing, R. D. *The Divided Self.* Chicago: Quadrangle Books, 1960.

Laing, R. D. *The Politics of Experience.* New York: Pantheon, 1967.

May, R. *The Meaning of Anxiety.* New York: Ronald Press, 1950.

May, R. *Psychology and the Human Dilemma.* Princeton, N.J.: Van Nostrand, 1967.

Sartre, J.-P. *Existentialism.* New York: Philosophical Library, 1947.

Tillich, P. *The Courage to Be.* New Haven, Conn.: Yale University Press, 1952.

Intentionality and the self-world relationship   6

The making of choices organizes our experience of self and world, gives it meaning, helps us to feel we are in control of life, and is necessary in order to conduct our lives. Anxiety is inherent in making choices and yet is dispelled by making them, by the affirmation of ourselves-as-subject. This is true, we suppose, in the beginnings of experience in childhood. The process of development is a continual race between the ability to make choices and the escape of choices by developing more and more reliance upon the experiences of self-as-object for myself and for others. Neurosis is, experientially, a loss of the experience of self-as-subject, an accompanying exacerbation of anxiety, and a resulting dependence on being-for-myself and being-for-others. In this chapter, we want to explore further the notion of making choices and we will conclude that we choose not only our actions but our perceptions, not only our responses but also our stimuli.

As originally conceived by Brentano (1960), intentionality is inherent in psychic acts and is an important aspect of consciousness. Husserl (1958) generalized this concept to all conscious experience. Heidegger (1962) further generalized the concept to all of Being.*

"Intentional" is an adjective that describes experience *as*

* For a secondary source that unravels some of the relevant ideas in these two complex works by two difficult philosophers, I recommend Wild (1959).

experienced, rather than the hypothesized mechanisms that under-lie experience. For example, if one were to speak of a smile in inten-tional terms, one would address himself to the intentions of the person smiling—what he means by it—rather than to the change of the facial configuration due to muscle contractions, etc. The latter orientation is analogous to the way traditional, natural-scientific psychology would approach the matter. That is, the focus would be on the objective behavior rather than the subjective intentions of the smiler.

In a traditional psychological analysis, the *meaning* of the smile would emerge from the frame of reference of the observer, not from the person smiling. That is, a smile is a response to X stimulus, or the outcome of a tension-reducing mechanism, or whatever the frame of reference of the observer dictates. From the intentional point of view, it is the smiling person, not the observer, who is the "center of meanings." The smile's meaning comes from the context of the experience of the smiler, not from the theory of the observer. When a person smiles, he *means* something by it.

Understanding the experience of the person in the person's own terms is a program for psychology that phenomenologists are not the first to propose. Within American psychology, such sugges-tions have been made by Rogers (1947), Lewin (1935), Snygg and Combs (1949), Lecky (1945), McCurdy (1961), and others. The par-ticular formulation that occurs within existential psychology has the additional and most important thesis that there are gigantic barriers that stand in the way of organizing one's experience in a healthy way, and these barriers have particularly to do with anxiety, understood existentially. The traditional scientific approach in American psychology has been supplemented by these additions of the subjective point of view. Existential psychology, however, has at least one of the elements that traditional psychologists wanted, namely, a theory of motivation, and that theory is that in his escape of existential anxiety, the individual flees into neurotic patterns.

A person's whole life is intentional. People mean things in their behavior. They have a kind of orientation, or posture, with respect to the world, and this "intentionality" is basic to their lives. By intending life in this total way, a person casts a certain slant on the world. His perception of the world is heavily influenced by this orientation, and we may say that the "world" to person A is really a different "world" from that of person *B*. In Chapter 7, on "The World," this implication of intentionality will be followed through more completely. To understand person *A,* we must understand his world.

Subjectively, we experience our intentionality as our "taking a stand" in life. Existentialists, concentrating on the phenomenological data, therefore expand this "taking a stand" into the crucial part of a person's being. In fact, we "take a stand" in regard to everything that comes up, and thus terms like "will" and "decision" become central to existential psychology. Often this taking a stand is automatic or habitual, and its "willfulness" is not really given in the immediate phenomenological data. To argue that our "life orientation" is really a decision, under our personal control, is to interpret the data of experience in quite a different way from traditional psychology, where causality is emphasized. A deterministic frame of reference is one way to organize the data; the intentional point of view is another. Existential psychologists opt for the latter, but the situation becomes complex when we attempt to reconcile the two points of view into a coherent conception of man.

We dismissed the "free-will *versus* determinism" issue in the last chapter too quickly, for the entire language of choice and courage seems to contradict the empirically observable facts that certain kinds of childhood experiences predict certain adult behaviors as if there were a causal relationship behind this apparent experience of choice. Is it also a choice to be neurotic?

If persons really intend their lives, does this mean that we should "blame" an alcoholic for his behavior? If there is an empirically verifiable relationship between the conditions of one's childhood and his later life (and there is), how can this apparent causal connection be reconciled with the notion of intentionality? What of the contradiction between the notion of determinism and the common clinical observation that an individual is able to cope with his life-problems only when he is "willing" to take responsibility for his actions, to feel they are under his control? Can we say that a person is the author of the conditions of his own life, without saying that everything is his own fault and that he somehow "deserves it"? These are weighty issues.

It violates an implicit moral tradition to attribute an active role to the person for what he is and at the same time to have compassion for his plight and to make the commitment to try to help him do something about it. And yet that is exactly the paradox that the clinical psychologist must live with. To assume the individual is a purely passive recipient of forces playing upon him is not to do him a favor clinically. The goal of clinical psychology is to help the person appreciate and participate in the authorship of his self-world relationship, not to reinforce passivity by making it more comfortable; the goal is to promote responsibility, not to condone escape from it.*

1. Intentionality and Personal History

The term "intentionality" provides a very useful focus for clinical investigation. What does the person "intend"? This is another way of asking, "What aspects of the world does he attend to, and what meaning does he impose upon them?" Objective reality is singularly ambiguous; our interpretation of it is the source of its meaning. A tree is really a beautiful product of nature only insofar as we hold that intention and make that interpretation. A tree is beautiful, in other words, if we mean it to be. This perceptual aspect of intentionality involves the same kind of choice as what a smiler means by his smile. Both are acts, i.e., are active, motivated—in a word, intentional.

     In the course of growing up, the child selects certain parts of reality and ignores others, and the parts he does select are given meaning by him in accordance with his intentions. In this sense, each person "creates" his world. He chooses what aspects of reality to attend to and what to ignore, and he decides the major dimensions of meaning that will characterize his self-world relationship. The self-world relationship of an infant is (almost literally) potentially anything and actually nothing. Of course, what becomes *possible* and *impossible* is dependent on what happens to him, but by virtue of the nature of personality development, "what happens to him" becomes "what he can intend" of the world, which later

---

     * The author realizes that this is one of those inevitable value judgments that invade clinical work. Instead of arguing the moral issue here, the reader is referred to Rieff (1966) for a thoughtful treatment of this and related issues.

affects what happens to him in an increasingly complex circular reaction between himself and the world. "The world" for him becomes as unique as he is himself. In this respect, one's personal history is the history of his intentions.

Are men all greedy animals? They are only insofar as this is the intention of the beholder. They are, say, for women for whom this is the only possibility. In such a case, the person will "create" men in the same repetitive, stereotyped way, and will probably interact with them in the same neurotic way. The *possibilities* in this case are extremely limited; the world is narrowly defined, the person is severely blocked in her ability to create varied and realistic interpretations of social reality. Alternative interpretations of the reality, "men," are somehow not available, due to a lack of varied experience with men or, more likely, due to a perversion of being through the exaggerated importance of being-for-oneself or being-for-others. Such a perversion will also produce an out-of-jointness and a constriction of intentions. Constriction yields repetitive interaction and an inability for adaptive variability in perception and behavior.

A child discovers a rattle. His first intention probably emerges as a consistency in visual pattern and later as the motoric possibility: shake it. Eventually the visual and motor intentions are more thoroughly integrated until the rattle becomes, as Piaget says, an object. The child recognizes the object by virtue of having unified the two intentions, one visual and one motoric, into a single intention to which he will later apply the name "rattle." Auditory intentions enrich the experience. The intention, or as Piaget calls it, the "schema," is there before the name is, and the child applies it to various objects in the world, such as spoons. Eventually the child learns to intend a spoon as we do—as an implement of eating —and to discriminate the appropriate objects for appropriate intentions. In terms of relationships with people, which are central to personality development, the child builds up expectations and other conceptual intentions on the basis of experience, in combination with the emotional intentions he can allow himself. If he intends people as friendly, he will in fact evoke friendliness from them. If intends them as threatening, they constitute a threat for him. However, it is also true that expecting, say, aggression from others evokes in fact aggression. This latter phenomenon, the renowned "self-fulfilling prophesy," is an objective way in which the person "creates" his own world, in addition to the subjective creation in imparting meaning to the world.

This general pattern of intending objects, of imposing meaning (both cognitive and emotional) upon them, can be generalized to the totality of what the person does with the world. What a person does with the world, the meanings he imposes, follows some basic theme or pattern that is characteristic of him. His personality, then, can be seen as the organization of his intentions of the world, the pattern of possibilities of what the world can be for him. The pattern is not simply built up atomistically, one intention beside another, but probably involves a systematic or hierarchical organization of intentions. Some intentions will be the basis of more refined elaborations and supply a common thread that constitutes his more general style of creating the world.

In addition, his construing of the world also implicitly (sometimes explicitly) defines himself. It is quite inescapable that he will develop a self-definition and come to see himself as someone with such and such qualities; he will become something for-himself, he will be-for-himself. It is also inevitable that he will develop some conception of how he appears to others and will come to be-for-others as well. All of these are related to how he defines the world, of course. The three faces of being are interlocked and interdependent. There emerges an entire self-world relationship from the intentional reckoning of the world's possibilities and the implications of these possibilities for himself. Just as a person creates the world, so does he create himself and his relationship to the world.

By the time an individual arrives to the clinical situation as a patient, therefore, he has gone through an elaborate process of laying out the coordinates of this relationship. Listening to a patient in therapy is thus listening to his account of how this creation is going on now. The patient begins to speak and in the process of speaking he tells us how he is-in-the-world (what the world means to him), how he is-to-himself and how he is-for-others. How he is-for-others is particularly revealed in terms of what he tells us he looks like to us. How he is-in-the-world is particularly revealed in how he construes us. The relationship between patient and therapist is therefore the crucial source of data for both patient and therapist in their endeavor to understand what is happening in the life of the patient.

2. *Intentionality and Transference*

One of Freud's great contributions to clinical psychology was the discovery of transference. In the process of classical psychoanalysis, the feelings of the patient for the therapist came to be more and more colored by the infantile attitudes the child had for his parents. Eventually the whole neurosis, then viewed as largely an infantile matter, was concentrated in the analytic relationship. Thus developed the "transference neurosis" which became the theater of psychoanalytic therapy. Psychoanalysis was epitomized by analysis of the transference neurosis. The presence of the transference neurosis became the criterion of whether psychoanalysis was really going on.

Psychotherapy does not always involve a transference neurosis, but it does always involve transference—that is, the "transfer" of feelings from an earlier relationship into the therapeutic relationship. In fact, all relationships with people are, in the psychoanalytic view, various degrees and combinations of transference, all beginning with the original family. Whether we agree with Freud or not that an adult love relationship is really infantile in its more profound feelings, we have to agree that people, especially people we see in some kind of therapeutic situation, will treat us after the fashion of older, more basic relationships.

Let us restate this fact now in terms of intentionality. The individual will define the therapist as a person according to the intentions that are available to him in his creation of the interpersonal world. Indeed the content of his feelings toward the therapist may be infantile, if in fact he has not graduated from this very primitive intentional structure within himself. But whatever the content of the feelings toward the therapist, it is important to see that it is his imposition of meanings upon the ambiguous reality of the therapist. The patient creates the therapist in setting the mood and content of the relationship. And in so doing he creates himself as one pole of what comes to be an extremely complex and dynamic dialogue.

This definition of the therapist and of himself, and of the relationship, will be characteristic of his own pattern of creating the world. Insofar as he is having some difficulty in the interpersonal world, and he almost certainly is, he is relating to (or creating) some other person or persons in a constricted, nonadaptive way. The intentions that are available to him in creating relationships with others do not permit him to get along. Some people immediately define the counseling situation as a competitive situation. This signals a limited repertoire of intentions with which to define the interpersonal world, and it indicates the most highly lubricated channel of relating to others. Others immediately withdraw from the therapist. Where in his interpersonal world is this intention proving to be an inadequate way of relating? Whence the emphasis on this intention? Still others, and this is probably the most dangerous kind of transference, will immediately define the situation as one in which they "surrender" to the therapist.

Such a surrender frequently goes beyond the natural understanding by patients that they must cooperate; it is an abdication of self-as-subject and indulgence in being-for-the-therapist. One thus becomes an object for the therapist and adopts a passive position *vis à vis* the therapist. It is dangerous because it constitutes a defense against the most crucial benefit one can potentially get from therapy, namely, an awareness of oneself-as-subject and an understanding of one's own authorship of the direction of his life. The person is saying, in effect, "I am powerless; I have been victimized, and now I am submitting myself to your 'treatment' to solve my problems." The most unfortunate aspect of this situation is that so many therapists succumb to such seduction. It is tempting to play God, to assume all responsibility for the process of therapy, and ultimately, for the person's life. This not only assures an unnecessarily long therapy wherein the person cannot overcome his dependence on the therapist, but also it deprives the person himself of the very thing to be gained from therapy, namely, an ability to graduate from his stereotyped and repetitive, yet self-defeating style of creating relationships.

3. Intending the Traumatic Past

No one grows up without sustaining some more or less severe traumas. Certain growing pains are universal, such as separation from parents, disappointment in fulfilling the grandiose fantasies of childhood, etc. These are childhood paradoxes that are analogous to the existential paradoxes appreciated later in adulthood. Just as the adult wishes for answers to problems about which he can only choose, so does the child wish for unrealistic gratification and security, and so must he choose.

What is not universal, however, is facing such childhood traumas with unequivocal honesty, admitting our failures and tolerating the longings of separation. In general, the earlier the trauma, the less capable we are of dealing with it, of facing our own feelings about it and accepting the cruelty of life. In general, the earlier the trauma the more our infantile, undifferentiated and magical intentions will be mobilized in reckoning the significance of the event.

Suppose that a three-year-old child is faced with the unhappy fact that his mother hates him. As adults, when we realize that someone hates us, we first recognize the fact and second feel bad about it. The three-year-old can do neither. To recognize the fact shakes the very foundations of his security and so he must avoid intending his mother in a flexible, open-minded and reality-oriented way. The older intentions of idyllic peace will prevail and this will limit his ability to intend mother, mother-figures, and even women in general, in any but the most stereotyped and (probably) non-adaptive way. This denial is a lie-in-the-world.

The second step, to recognize his own feelings in the situation, is also not a real option to the child, for these are feelings of agony and anxiety. Thus, he learns to intend his own reaction to things in an unrealistic way, or, we might say, the ability to face the things that go on within himself is severely restricted. His being-for-himself becomes a lie-for-himself. Even more important, he will need to preserve this being-for-himself to avoid anxiety. We can see here a childhood version of adult neurosis as described in Chapter 3. The child may well vacillate between the magical thought that he will remain in the arms of his mother forever on the one hand, and absolute indifference to her as an important person in his life on the other. The very importance of his mother's feelings makes his ability to perceive reality, to intend reality with variable and open-ended intentions, all the more threatening.

It is at this point that the issue of free will *versus* determinism with which we began this chapter becomes resolved. We do not hold the patient morally responsible for the inability to face reality (we do not "blame" him in any punitive sense) and yet we face the fact that his creation of the self-world relationship is the source of the trouble. Even if the conditions of one's childhood choices were totally determinative, the construction of a self-world relationship is creative and intentional nonetheless. If such a trauma as being hated by one's mother is at the root of one's self-world relationship, if it is the guiding principle of his definition of the world, the patient must come to terms with it before any effective change can occur in his life.

"Coming to terms" with one's traumatic past is not just a matter of remembering it. Uncovering "repressed" memories may be an essential step in reorganizing one's world, but it is even more important to mobilize the person's ability to face the trauma in all of its affective splendor. He must be willing to undergo certain movements and to relinquish the defensive posture that allows him—indeed forces him—to create an unreal world and an unreal self. He must be willing to forego his lies and to reorganize his experience of himself and of the world.

Technical Terms

Intentionality: An inherent feature of immediate experience, its directedness toward a focus of attention (sometimes called "object"), and since immediate experience is central to being, it is inherent in being. The tripartite analysis of being in Chapter 3 and the dichotomy of self-experience in Chapter 2, divide up kinds of intentional acts. Intentionality as a feature of experience emphasizes that the meaning of experience is imposed by our intentions (it means what we mean it to mean); as a feature of being, it emphasizes that our being is as we mean (or intend) it to be.

Transference: Originally Freud's term for the concentration of cathexes, particularly pathogenic ones, in the therapeutic relationship, i.e., transferring feelings from parents to the analyst. Here transference is reconceptualized in terms of intentionality.

References

Brentano, F. The distinction between mental and physical phenomena. In R. M. Chisholm (Ed.) *Realism and the Background of Phenomenology.* Glencoe, Ill.: Free Press, 1960.

Heidegger, M. *Being and Time.* New York: Harper, 1962.

Husserl, E. *Ideas.* London: Allen and Unwin, 1958.

Lecky, P. *Self-Consistency: A Theory of Personality.* New York: Island Press, 1945.

Lewin, K. *A Dynamic Theory of Personality.* New York: McGraw-Hill, 1935.

McCurdy, H. G. *The Personal World,* New York: Harcourt, Brace and World, 1961.

Rieff, P. *The Triumph of the Therapeutic: Uses of Faith after Freud.* New York: Harper, 1966.

Rogers, C. Some observations on the organization of personality. *American Psychologist,* 1947, *2,* 358–368.

Snygg, D. & Combs, A. *Individual Behavior.* New York: Harper, 1949.

Wild, J. *The Challenge of Existentialism.* Bloomington, Ind.: Indiana University Press, 1959.

The world as a psychological category 7

When I am building a table, my world becomes narrowed down to the space in which I am working and the objects in that space exhaust the content of my experience. If I have reflected about my wood-working ability and maintain a degree of pride about it, I may have a different sort of experience. I will imagine how I overcame the disadvantage of never having been taught carpentry, and this may absorb me to the extent that I make a mistake with materials. Or I may indeed imagine how I would look to a neighbor who drops in, how romantically handy I appear, covered with sawdust. This is another kind of experience that may invade my original involvement in the task of building a table. These three kinds of experiences are now familiar as being-in-the-world, being-for-myself, and being-for-others.

There is something fundamental about the first. It is the arena in which my life is prereflectively acted out in relation to the environment. We assume that the reflective experiences of being-for-myself and being-for-others are not present in the animal kingdom apart from man, and if subhumans have experience at all, it is very much like this prereflective involvement. There is a kind of immediacy about prereflective experience. The shape of the world in that experience may guide my behavior without my being self-consciously aware of it. The "shape" of that world is a function, we have said, of my intentionality, and the world of one person is not the same world as that of another person.

The prereflective world is the "world" I am "in" during my "being-in-the-world." It has been divided into *Umwelt, Mitwelt,* and *Eigenwelt* by existential psychologists (See Chapter 15; cf. also May, 1958) and this distinction bears resemblances to the tripartite division of being. There is also some interest in the concept among nonphenomenologists, as seen in Arieti's (1967) concept of "phantasmic world."

In this chapter we will look briefly at space and time and then turn to some actual clinical examples that show some of the complexities of being-in-the-world. We will see that "the world" can become quite unreal under certain circumstances, can be split into real and unreal, or can be built up in layers. Phenomenological literature is full of such metaphoric descriptions, some of which enhance particularly our understanding of psychopathology.

When we listen to a patient, then, we listen for how he construes the world. The term "construing" will rightly remind some readers of the work of George Kelly (1955) who is clearly dealing with phenomenological data, but not within the tradition of phenomenological psychology.

"The world" and "self" each supply a meaning-context for the other. That is, when I view myself (as in being-for-myself) it is always within the context of the world as I see it. My "self" becomes a figure against the ground of world, to use again the *Gestalt* metaphor. And when I view the world (as in being-in-the-world), it is always within the context of myself as I see it. The "world" becomes a figure against the ground of my self. The "viewing" here is of course intentional, and the meanings that I impose on the world come also from other contexts as well, most notably from long-term assumptions I make about the world.

Hermann Hesse, in his novel, *Demian,* describes very well a unique world as seen by his ten-year-old hero:

> The realms of day and night, two different worlds coming from two opposite poles, mingled during this time. My parents' house made up one realm, yet its boundaries were even narrower, actually embracing only my parents themselves. This realm was familiar to me in almost every way—mother and

father, love and strictness, model behavior, and school. It was a realm of brilliance, clarity, and cleanliness, gentle conversations, washed hands, clean clothes, and good manners. This was the world in which morning hymns were sung and Christmas celebrated. Straight lines and paths led into the future: there were duty and guilt, bad conscience and confession, forgiveness and good resolutions, love, reverence, wisdom and the words of the Bible. If one wanted an unsullied and orderly life, one made sure one was in league with this world.

The other realm, however, overlapping half our house, was completely different; it smelled different, spoke a different language, promised and demanded different things. This second world contained servant girls and workmen, ghost stories, rumors of scandle. It was dominated by a loud mixture of horrendous, intriguing, frightful, mysterious things, including slaughterhouses and prisons, drunkards and screeching fishwives, calving cows, horses sinking to their death, tales of robberies, murders, and suicides. All these wild and cruel, attractive and hideous things surrounded us, could be found in the next alley, the next house. Policemen and tramps, drunkards who beat their wives, droves of young girls pouring out of factories at night, old women who put the hex on you so that you fell ill, thieves hiding in the forest, arsonists nabbed by country police—everywhere this second vigorous world erupted and gave off its scent, everywhere, that is, except in our parents' rooms. And that was good. It was wonderful that peace and orderliness, quiet and a good conscience, forgiveness and love, ruled in this one realm, and it was wonderful that the rest existed, too, the multitude of harsh noises, of sullenness and violence, from which one could still escape with a leap into one's mother's lap (Hesse, 1965, pp. 5–6).

The specific characteristics of the two realms as seen through these ten-year-old eyes are not precisely the same as the division of my particular world, but the division itself may be universal. Good–bad, me–not-me, safe–unsafe, familiar–foreign: these may be fundamental categories of human experience upon which much behavior is built.

Put another way, there is a kind of experience of one's self and one's world that is not quite conscious (i.e., the focus of attention) and not quite unconscious (i.e., an instinctual drive that is unacceptable) that constitutes the ground upon which the figure of our consciously purposive life is enacted. Lewin (1935) called this "level" of experience the *field*. It is the structure of space, with its paths and vectors, in which we move. It includes the linear space of the rooms and streets we live in, the temporal space of the minutes, days, and years we live in, and the affective space of feelings and moods we live in.

Pathology gives us unique insight into the structure of this world. Let us look for a moment at space, time, and body as experienced pathologically.

1. Space

Suppose a brain-damaged patient lives in a spatially very restricted world and then undergoes psychotherapy. While there is no change in the patient's neurological disorder, there may be, through therapy, a marked change in his world (Mendel, 1961). The point here can also serve as a general model for the proper relationship between neurophysiology and psychology: brain damage may be a stress that the organism must suffer, but a person may react in a number of ways, most commonly by "shrinking" the world. The world can be expanded again without neurological intervention. This indicates that the physiological organism does not exhaust a person's being. Being is more than the physiological organism. Man cannot be reduced to his physiological processes. The shrinking of the world (or whatever else may happen to it, say, in psychosis) is a different kind of disorder from the physical disorder, detected by physical means and formulated in physical terms. The details of the psychophysical relationship in the context of being remains a frontier for psychology.

We must be able to distinguish a number of spatial coordinates that structure our experience. There are, first of all, any number of physical "spaces," such as that between my eyes and the paper, that of the interior of my house, my neighborhood, my city, country, the world, and finally outer space. In physical terms, these are all related in the same coordinate of measured distance, but experientially these scales are not necessarily of the same order at all. I am likely to think of the distance between states in terms of driving time, for example, which is hardly the same space as that between my chair and the window. Second, there is an interpersonal space that is often a powerful factor in our experience and behavior. Some people are "close" to me, others are "distant," regardless of course of the physical measurements. Third, I may "distance" myself from an issue, a novel, or an idea, by withdrawing my involvement and examining it from a detached perspective. Objectification of persons creates this kind of "distance."

In addition to these "spaces," there are any number of specialized spaces—semantic, mathematical, aesthetic, or the "space" occupied by a concept when we say that it is "coterminous" with another concept. These specialized spaces are invented for particular purposes and we are quite conscious of how they organize our experience. The other "spaces," of physical, interpersonal, and emotional distance, are just as crucial in the organization of our experience and our being, but we are not usually explicitly aware of them. They provide a structure within which we *are*. Along with temporality and corporality, they constitute our "world," or perhaps we should say that *we* constitute our world according to these structural coordinates. Indeed it could not be any other way. We cannot say that we know another person unless we are able to see his map, to understand the various "spaces" in which he *is* and how they are layered or ordered in his experience.

When we as psychologists approach the study of man, we too invent a space. The space of "the world" in this chapter is quite different from the space of neurophysiology, and one must be able to live in the space of this chapter in order to understand, for example, the meaning of the Mendel (1961) paper mentioned above.

2. *Time*

Time is also an important aspect of experience, and a person's world definitely has a tempo, a rhythm, which provides another locus of psychopathology. Minkowski's (1958) description of schizophrenic depression demonstrates a blocking of the future in this kind of psychopathology.

The point here is that time is experienced not only as a straight line upon which each instant is a point, nor simply as a moment situated within an hour, day, and year. The present moment is never just the present moment, if we examine our experience carefully. Embedded in the experience of the present moment are (at least implicit) memories of our past and anticipations of our future. These *contextual* aspects of every experience serve to order experience into a coherent and manageable whole. I understand something that happens to me because I see it in the context of what has happened before and what I expect to happen in the future. There is a thread of continuity given to all my experience that makes it yield to my comprehension. I am the same person today that I was yesterday. "Well, it's not the end of the world," we may say in the face of a trauma. How can we say that? Because we do not experience the present in isolation from the past and future. And if we could not say that, if we could not assure ourselves of the continuity of our identity, if we did not have the ability to escape ("transcend," some existentialists would say) the exigencies of the present moment into a temporal perspective that makes the present moment make sense, then even the most trivial experience would be meaningless and our inability to "place" it may indeed make it quite threatening. It is this sort of disorder that makes certain drug experiences, some nightmares, and some psychotic experiences so terrifying.

We wish to call attention to the *historical* nature of our subject matter, a person. In so doing we seek to make psychology a historical science. To do so we must state that the subject matter of our science is conscious. It is by experiencing, by being a subjectivity, that a subject matter becomes historical. "Historical" implies "experiential," for it is human experience that is historical, that exists in a present that cannot be pulled out of its temporal context. I do not exist (I do not am) simply in the present. My aming is seen and executed by me as, and therefore by definition simply is, embedded in a temporal flux that has a past and a future.

My past is part of my present. So is my future. I do my aming in a present that remembers the past and hence I design my aming as related to the past, by rebelling against it, or trying to be continuous with it, or trying to grow from it. I am never without it. I also do my aming in a present that anticipates the future and hence I design my aming in relation to it, by planning for it, fearing it, or trying to change it. But I am never without it. The past and the future are therefore immanent in the present. The present is full of them. There is no present, for a conscious being, without time. To take *what* I am, just now, without its context of my past and my future as experienced by me now, is to take only a part, and for psychology a very small part, of the total phenomenon of what, how, and who I am.

As we shall discover in Binswanger's analysis of the case of Ellen West (Chapter 15), the way one temporalizes life is central to understanding his being. Temporalization is inevitable and universal; it supplies us with an order, or more accurately, we order our being temporally. Authentic or "healthy" being is pointed into the future. But "future" in experience cannot be merely fantasy that avoids integration with the past. The present moment is experienced as coming out of the past and moving into the future. Binswanger has put it this way:

> The existential sense of temporality in general forbids us to conceive of "future" only as the empty possibilities of the pre-established, the wished-for, and the hoped-for, as it also forbids us to see in the past only that which was present and is now over. Rather we must understand by the past in the existential sense the has-been, which decides that we not only have been but actually *are* from the viewpoint of "has-been" (Binswanger, 1958, pp. 302–303).

To the extent that the present takes account of its past, then:

> . . . the future by no means hangs in the air, and the possibilities of the future are not "empty" but are definite possibilities. To this extent existence is determined not only by the future, that is, by the comprehending of the being-able-to-be, but always also by its pastness; existence [read "aming"] has always been "thrown" into its being; it is already in its being, or is in a word already tuned to a certain key. All futurity of the existence of being is therefore "has-been" and all having-been is of the future (1958, p. 303).

The future is of particular interest to clinical psychologists. A healthy being-into-the-future, Binswanger tells us, must be rooted in and grow out of the past that is given even as the particular meaning of that past must derive from expectations of the future. Three common pathological futures will be called by us, "deteriorative," "fantastic," and "status-striving."

A. The deteriorative future

When one's experience of himself is pervaded by objectification, for-himself and for-others, the objective qualities of one's being exhaust what one is. The most obvious "thing" we are is bodily. If I take my bodily being as the central theme of my being, what does the future hold? If what I am bodily exhausts all that I am, the future is inevitably deteriorative, especially in our culture which is so heavily committed to the physical charms of youth. Yet another "thing" we are is our possessions. When a beautiful house and car, or bank account, permeates my being, the deteriorative effects of time constitute a definite threat. My only hope is to be able to acquire new things to replace the old. The common denominator between these ways of being is a perverse objectification of one's being. Objects, things, are static. Time can only mean deterioration, for things do not grow, do not develop and are not "going anywhere" except into oblivion. The future does not hold possibilities; it is burdened with necessities.

B. The fantastic future

Just wishing for some state of affairs does not, as Freud so poignantly noted, make it so. An authentic living into the future, as Binswanger pointed out, must grow out of the past and out of the given, mediated by practical action. We always run the danger of construing a possibility as impossible and controlled by the necessary, as did the boy in Chapter 5 who was convinced he could not learn to read. The reciprocal problem of construing the impossible as possible, without respect for the given was exemplified by the boy who sought to learn all his multiplication tables by next week. The latter is particularly fantastic, for it is a future that is unrelated to the past, a wish not fulfillable in terms of the limitations of the given. The former boy, who was convinced he could not read, is burdened by the past. The future's possibilities are unnecessarily closed. Unlike the fantastic future, this future lacks imagination, openness and possibility. The fantastic future attempts to transform the present without continuity and action.

C. The status-striving future

The man who saves for the future in such a way as to ignore the past and the present is also being-into-the-future in a way we might call "inauthentic." His being is not "aimed at" the future; it is limited to the future. His imagined future is also static; he will have "arrived." Possessing things will make them adhere to his person and aggrandize it objectively from outside himself. Such a future is quite different from the experience of "becoming" from within, of making future decisions whose alternatives are unseen now, of trusting one's personal growth to being something good, of relinquishing the insurance policies of acquired possessions, which, beyond a certain level of security, are notoriously ill-equipped to bring purpose and meaning into life.

3. *The Two Worlds of the Prison Inmate* *

The existential and phenomenological approaches in psychotherapy therefore call for an understanding of the world of the patient, as experienced immediately by him. Characteristics of one person's experiential world always differ from those of another, and yet there are universal features of all such worlds. These universal features supply the "structure" in terms of which comparisons can be made. Such "universals" are space, time, and identity. Every person structures space, for example, in some particular way, and such structuring is one of the crucial focal points of phenomenological inquiry. Let us look at a particular clinical group to see what phenomenology can add to our understanding of clinical problems.

Prison inmates, as a group, have certain *objective* facts of life in common; but these facts become most important to psychotherapy when one understands the *subjective* ramifications of the facts; that is, the effect of the facts on the "world" as experienced by the inmate. Let us examine one feature of this effect, one common way of construing the world by inmates, with particular reference to how it functions as a resistance to psychotherapy.

* This section was originally written with Robert Laird, (Keen & Laird, 1968).

Consider the commonly expressed sentiments of inmates in therapy: "Nothing I decide while I am here in jail makes any difference, for it is entirely different on the outside." "I don't know what I'll do then, and I can't know until I am faced with the situation out there." "I hear what everyone is saying to me, but I can't really feel it makes any difference for real life outside the walls." We see in these remarks an implicit but powerful separation between *inside* the prison and *outside* the prison in such a way that "real life" is limited to outside and the experiences inside are something other than real. Everything occurring in the limbo of prison seems irrelevant to life as experienced as real. Such a compartmentalization not only facilitates the resistance to therapy by making it unreal and irrelevant, but also carried to its logical conclusion, this restructuring successfully undercuts any and all rehabilitative programs of the penal institution.

To consider space, time, and identity separately is somewhat artificial since they are embedded in a context, the "world," but such analysis leads to a method of coping with the phenomenon as it occurs in therapy as resistance.

Time: The time spent in jail may not be experienced as a period that is meaningfully embedded in one's life-stream as, say, one's high-school years are. On the contrary, it is separated from the mainstream of life. An accurate statement of the experience of time for inmates who structure the world in this way would be, "Between the ages of 20 and 30 I didn't exist," rather than, "Between the ages of 20 and 30 I was in jail." The passing of days and months behind the wall is organized by the inmate simply in terms of his release date; it is not "between the ages of 20 and 30," but rather "between the years 1 and 10." The context in terms of which time is experienced is the sentence itself, not one's life; and further, the sentence is not part of one's life.

Identity: This construing of the passage of time is closely related to the construing of oneself. The "I" in the sentence, "Between ages 20 and 30 I was in jail" (which an inmate may indeed *say*) may be a different "I" from that in the sentence, "I went to high school in Philadelphia," "I love my wife," "I robbed a bank." The latter "I's" may all be experienced as-subject. But the prison is a place where the quality of one's self-as-subject may become quite different. We can see this difference in what "the world" becomes; indeed they are inseparable.

What may be experienced in therapy during incarceration is not really "my" experience, one that is happening to the "me" I usually am. The anger, embarrassment, longing, or any other feeling is dissociated from the personally felt "I" of "real life" in much the same way one might detach himself from a broken arm when one says, "I am not hurt; my arm, this thing, this mechanism I see is temporarily out of order."

Space: The Federal Penitentiary at Lewisburg, Pennsylvania is located 60 miles north of Harrisburg and 200 miles west of New York City. But for the inmate who has restructured his world in this way, such geographical coordinates are not only meaningless, they are nonexistent. The penitentiary is exactly "nowhere" in terms of the life-space of real life; it is outside the sphere of miles and maps; it is unreal.

Such a subjective restructuring is a defensive maneuver against the oppressions of incarceration and of course is effective only part of the time for all inmates. But when one adds the rigors of psychotherapy to the prison experience, such defenses may become all the more accentuated and important. Nothing in therapy is real; the first therapeutic task, then becomes to promote a re-integration of the experiential world so that events of therapy themselves are not successfully compartmentalized from real life. When a patient is angry, it is *his* anger, and the *him* is the same him that got angry at his wife or his father. When he says that "things will be different this time if I get out," he must realize that the "I" who is saying it is the same as the "I" who will get out.

Inmates need, of course, to perform this dissociation to help make the prison experience tolerable; but it is also important to note that many of them feel it is important to fight the process as well. Maintaining contacts with the outside world is important for many inmates in order to avoid becoming "institutionalized," which is seen as losing touch with real life. There is, in other words, a built-in servomechanism that may mitigate the danger of total compartmentalization; for the shrunken world of the prison is hardly acceptable according to what they are expected (by staff and fellow inmates alike) to feel. Looking forward to a return to real life, in other words, hope, is the saving grace of being an inmate. But by the same token, this hope paradoxically assumes the split into two worlds and is part of the resistance. It is a complex matter indeed.

The question now becomes: What are some ways of handling this particular resistance within therapy? Let us look at three approaches: frontal assault, direct interpretation, and indirect chafing.

By frontal assault, we mean an attack upon the inmate's experience itself by manipulating the world he must structure. Therapy itself is such a manipulation, but group therapy is usually a matter of about an hour a week in most prison settings. Just as the sentence itself can become an island, unrelated to the flow of real life outside, so can the therapeutic experience become an island unrelated to the prison experience, further alienating psychotherapy from real life. Perhaps a focus on identity will clarify the point further. The "I" of real life and the "I-the-prisoner" may well be radically separated. If one merely adds another identity, "I-the-therapy-patient," to the list, not much has happened. The therapeutic task is to make the "I-the-therapy-patient" experience, and all the events connected to that identity, *real*. A frontal assault on this problem would be to have therapy sessions that are longer and that thereby include a larger segment of temporal experience, and therefore a larger part of self experience. When a group meets for a "marathon" therapy session of, say, twenty hours, there is agreement among inmates that something important has happened to "me," and "me" is experienced as the "real me," the person I really am.

Other forms of frontal assault are continuously reminding the inmate of the number of miles he is from home, of his geographical coordinates, and forcing a structuring of his temporal experiences to have a continuity between what happened before he came to prison and what has happened since. This latter kind of approach is often difficult because, by and large, not much *has* happened since he came to jail—at best, a change in job or in quarters. The sequences of events in the lives of persons close to him outside thus supply a temporal grounding for this kind of frontal assault.

Second, direct interpretation includes such remarks as, "I know you would like to think that the feelings you are having now don't really count, but they are *your* feelings, no one else's. . . ."

And "I know you want to keep things that happen in therapy separate from real life, but that is merely a way to avoid taking a good look at yourself." Like any interpretation, such statements are useless unless they occur at the right time.

Third, indirect chafing is a subtle procedure and difficult to describe. It might best be described as "not playing the game" in the sense used by Eric Berne (1964). Games, in this sense, are subtle. They require complementary assumptions on the part of the participants and some degree of tacit agreement not to face certain realities. Indirect chafing is to hold noncomplementary assumptions, to violate the tacit agreement sought by the game-player and to withhold the gains that the game is supposed to yield. Concretely this technique—it could be better called an attitude—involves implicit rejection of the dissociated timetable, the nonintegrated spatial structuring, and the "inmate identity," that is, the assumption that it is legitimate to feel such and such a way because that is "the way inmates are."

Techniques like the marathon group therapy session are fine additions to the therapist's bag of tricks, but the crucial ingredient must still be the therapist. It is therefore "indirect chafing" that is finally therapeutic. What is happening here is that the therapist does not accept the patient's construing of the world as a valid one. Finally, of course, the details of indirect chafing depend on second-to-second judgments by the therapist about where he thinks the patient is and where he should be provoked to move—along the lines of the analysis of being and the interpretation of neurosis in Chapters 3 and 4.

4. The Body: Conversion Hysteria

The body occupies a unique position in this subtle but ever-present world, for it is, on the one hand, the subject of actions—it actively moves about, eating, playing, and loving. It is the physical version of me, and when it desires, I desire. When it is hurt, I am hurt. But it is also, on the other hand, the object of my experience, for I can think about it, do things to it, like it or dislike it. Hence, it is simultaneously subject and object within the life-space.

In conversion hysteria, where the body plays a central role

in symptoms, the body is also both subject and object within the life-space. The symptom, say hysterical vomiting, involves the body as an object of concern in the life-space. It plays a central role in fantasies as the "thing" I am worried about. But simultaneously, it expresses feelings as surely as if the hysteric were speaking sentences like, "I am terribly afraid to swallow things" or "I feel guilty about putting things into my mouth." We can read this body language only if we are able to see the context of the hysteric's life-space. Just as any verbal utterance becomes meaningful only if we get the verbal context, so many of the expressions of the body become meaningful only in terms of the life-space context.

For most people, the body is primarily an object. But the hysteric especially, in making his body an object, is hiding the subjectness of his body. By focusing his attention on the body-as-object, he avoids recognizing the content of the feelings he expresses. This shift is the secondary layer of the malady. However, the body is not the primary center of his fantasy, not the key reference point in his life-space. The underlying feelings expressed in body language are almost always interpersonal, and their relevant context, in conversion hysteria at least, is an interpersonal field.

The hysteric, then, first structures his life-space with pathological emphasis on certain interpersonal themes. He expresses his feelings in these relationships through his bodily symptoms. This is the body-as-subject. He then presents his situation to himself in such a way that his body is object, thus disguising the real life-space he lives in from himself and from others. The hysteric therefore lives in his body in two ways—as most of us do. In both respects, however, the feelings are disguised and hidden from view. As subject, his bodily symptoms are symbolic and idiosyncratic expressions of interpersonal feelings; as object his bodily symptoms are a ruse, further disguising his real feelings by focusing attention away from the subject-expressive aspect of what is going on in his primary life-space.*

---

* Both Janet and Binet hypothesize a "splitting" of the personality or of the ego in hysteria (cf. Reisman, 1966), and these interpretations predate Freud's key notion of repression. Splitting is also hypothesized here, but in line with the phenomenological point of view, we speak in terms of the world rather than the ego, or more accurately, we must talk about both simultaneously, for they imply one another.

It is useful to point out that we live in several structured worlds, as well as in several bodies, at once. Above we spoke of a primary and secondary layer of hysteria, which really refers to a primary and secondary life-space. In one sense this distinction corresponds to Freudian primary and secondary process, although the Freudian concepts typically describe intrapsychic events and processes rather than intentional ties between subject and object, between self and world. The emphasis upon irrational wish and the absence of logic and cognitive control, however, characterizes both Freudian primary process and what we might call the primary life-space. Similarly the emphasis on verbalized and rationalized features of the phenomena characterize both Freudian secondary process and secondary life-space. Unlike Freudian "secondary process," however, the "secondary life-space" is not imbued with the "reality principle" in contradistinction to the "pleasure principle" of primary process.

Both the primary and secondary life-space are intentional constructions of ambiguous "reality." The secondary life-space is heavily influenced by language: it will naturally have more in common with the construction of the world by others in the linguistic community, and it will conform to a kind of "social reality" to a greater extent. However, insofar as the requirements of social reality do not correspond to one's primary structuring of the world, to this extent the secondary life-space is unrealistic. For it serves to mask the real intentions that may be operative (that in neurosis *are* operative) in one's life.

Hysteria offers a good example of the "non-realism" of the secondary life-space. The neurotic with hysterical vomiting, for example, may well have a world construction such as follows: There is an interpersonal conflict, such as an erotic desire for father's attention and a fear and hatred of mother who competes with the three-year-old girl's desires. The fantasies of this Oedipal conflict are the primary life-space. They express the intentional relationship toward the parents: love for father, hate for mother. The inability to put things in one's mouth or to swallow food successfully may *express* any number of *feelings* about this situation, such as *fear* of oral actualization of father's love, or *defiance* of mother's injunction to eat. Clearly the possibilities are infinite, but for some (presumably understandable) reason, one or another of the subleties of the fantasy in this situation comes to be expressed through the symptom in body language.

The parents aid the girl in ignoring the feelings involved in the primary life-space and in diverting attention away from the expressive function of the body. Hence, the "body-as-subject" is an experience that is preempted by focusing on the body-as-object: "Something is wrong with my little girl's digestive system." The body becomes now an *object* of concern, and something is wrong with *it*. Every hysteric begins therapy with an experience of his body as a thing-gone-wrong. Indeed the logical, verbal, socially realistic world, construes the situation as one in which "I" am not my body, but something else that lives in the body much like I drive "in my car" to work every day.

The terms "primary" and "secondary" should probably be seen as relative. That is, the Oedipal life-space may not be the first in time nor the most basic context in which the expressions of the individual are to be understood. Similarly, the shift to a subsequent life-space in which the body is the central object may not be the final restructuring process. With each new "role" into which one moves in the process of growing up will come a new way of construing oneself and the world. This may be the most useful meaning of the term "role." A "role conflict" may be best understood as a life-space conflict. The "patient role" may be a way of structuring the field that adds yet another layer of resistance to the therapeutic process.

Technical Terms

The world: The context of experience of self, with certain dimensions, flavors, and characteristics. The world as subjectively experienced by an individual.

Primary life-space: That world in which the major coordinates of one's life style, self and world intentions, were formed and in terms of which "neurotic," "ego-alien," or otherwise irrational or inconsistent behavior can become meaningful.

Secondary life-space: The world of social conventions, linguistic habits, and consciously consistent meanings that may or may not be (that in neurosis, are not) isomorphic with the primary life-space.

References

Arieti, S. *The Intrapsychic Self.* New York: Basic Books, 1967.

Berne, E. *Games People Play.* New York: Grove Press, 1964.

Binswanger, L. The case of Ellen West. In R. May, et al. (Eds.) *Existence.* New York: Basic Books, 1958.

Hesse, H. *Demian.* New York: Harper & Row (Bantam), 1965.

Keen, E. & Laird, R. The two worlds of the prison inmate. *Pennsylvania Psychiatric Quarterly,* 1968, Spring.

Kelly, G. *The Psychology of Personal Constructs.* New York: Norton, 1955.

Lewin, K. *A Dynamic Theory of Personality.* New York: McGraw-Hill, 1935.

May, R. Contributions of existential psychotherapy. In R. May, et al. (Eds.) *Existence.* New York: Basic Books, 1958.

Mendel, W. Expansion of a shrunken world. *Review of Existential Psychology and Psychiatry,* 1961, I, 21–23.

Minkowski, E. Findings in a case of schizophrenic depression. In R. May, et al. (Eds.) *Existence.* New York: Basic Books, 1958.

Reisman, J. M. *The Development of Clinical Psychology.* New York: Appleton-Century-Crofts, 1966.

Skinner, B. F. *Science and Human Behavior.* New York: Macmillan, 1953.

SUMMARY OF
PART II

We have established at least provisionally, in Part I, that psychology ought to take consciousness seriously and that doing so necessitates the use of human experience as concrete data. Such data demand metaphors different from the usual scientific language of objects. A number of new metaphors were introduced which can serve psychology well and which come from existential thought. In Part II, several additional existential concepts were discussed, for they are consistent with and demanded by the concepts introduced in Part I.

We have argued that the conditions in modern life have given human experience a certain flavor that has not been mankind's usual condition. For example, the breakdown of institutional values has left the individual in a kind of hiatus; decisions must be made and there is a notable lack of clear criteria by which to make them. Only intellectuals have articulated this dilemma, but its paradox, and the threat of nonbeing in general, is present for an entire century. Most people's response to the hiatus is to fill it with some form of self-objectification. Such a procedure allows us to have criteria for deciding without activating or actualizing the experience of oneself-as-subject. This eventually produces a series of lies that in turn produce the out-of-jointness we call psychopathology.

The concrete expression of this existential situation in individual lives is the experience of anxiety. It is not pathological to experience the anxiety of having to choose without having criteria, nor other forms of nonbeing. However, when this anxiety leads to a style of being that avoids facing choice, anxiety, and nonbeing in general, existential anxiety becomes neurotic anxiety. To follow an idealized image of oneself or to look to one's image in the eyes of others (being-for-oneself and being-for-others, respectively) are ways to escape existential anxiety. But they are short-term solutions and long-term failures. The failure comes when being-in-the-world (and the accompanying experience of self-as-subject) is submerged beneath objectifications and is alienated from immediate experience.

The experience of self-as-subject, on the other hand, is the experience of making a decision in the face of ambiguity and anxiety. It penetrates rather than avoids anxiety and produces a style of being that is authentic and healthy. The experience of life in the total absence of the experience of the self-as-subject is the experience of disintegration of self and of meaninglessness, powerlessness, and loneliness.

There are two kinds of decisions, cognitive problem-solving and existential choice. Much conscious experience is of the former variety, and this model is not inconsistent with behavioristic determinism (cf. Skinner, 1953, Chapter XVI). Existential choice, in which values are created rather than followed, does not submit to such an explanation. This is the activity of being-a-subject that demands metaphors that describe phenomena in nonessentialistic terms. In psychotherapy, such moments of choice appear and have been described as "existential crises."

The concept of "intentionality" supplies a metaphor in terms of which to describe the phenomenon of existential choice and proves to be applicable also to a number of other traditional psychological phenomena such as the development of schemata, transference, and insight. This concept also supplies a point of view from which we can dissolve the apparent contradiction between two traditional lines of thought: (a) Man is responsible for everything he is and should therefore accept the consequences of his choices; (b) Man is completely the product of his environment and heredity and must not be made to feel responsible for what he is. The resolution of these two views is to realize, first, that some things are "given" and cannot be changed, but second, that even within this arena of facticity there is always the choice of interpretation of, and of our posture toward, the given. This interpretation is not unrelated to perceptual phenomena, to existential choice, to the development of a unique style of being, and to the interaction of lies and authenticity within one's being.

To focus on the intentional quality of human experience allows us to speak of "the world" as a psychological category. The world *as experienced* is always both objective (given) and subjective (chosen); neither aspect of the world is possible without the other. An exploration of the crucial dimensions and characteristics of the phenomenological world of the individual is a large part of the work of existential psychology. The experience of the body, of time, of space, and of the self-world relationship in general are all relevant data for an existential psychology.

In Part III, we want to apply some of these concepts first to a clinical case of anxiety hysteria and second to obsessional neurosis. A discussion of psychotherapy, as seen through the lens of existential psychological concepts, concludes Part III. Certain concepts from Part II have their most vivid application in the study of psychosis in Part IV, for it is the psychotic whose difference from us demands the most basic and radical awareness of human existence in order to comprehend him.

THERAPY
AND NEUROSIS III

The case of
Paula Kress 8

1. The Life-History

Paula Kress had not eaten for two weeks, since moving with her husband and three children to a new home. Paula suddenly began to suffer from uncontrollable vomiting and diarrhea. She could eat no food other than an eggnog daily, and she had lost 15 pounds. She was unable to move from her bedroom without acute attacks of anxiety. It was under these circumstances, that Paula entered psychotherapy and revealed the first aspects of a life-history presented here in as complete form as possible.

Paula's parents were Polish immigrants who lived in a lower middle class neighborhood in Chicago. There were three children born to this marriage: Victor, the oldest son; Albert, five years younger, who died of hemophilia in his first year; and Paula, born 15 months after Albert. Albert had been the family favorite, and the mother explicitly thought that Paula was to take his place. Paula was to have been "Paul," according to the mother's design, and she attempted to defeminize her unanticipated daughter. Her father, on the other hand, seems to have indulged Paula's femininity. He gave her money for permanents and jewelry while Paula's mother would have Paula's hair cut short, much to Paula's distress. Paula's mother was the dominant parent. She earned most of the family income and maintained order in the house by watchful control over everyone's actions. She was a superstitious woman who recommended drinking urine to reduce a high temperature and the application of raw bacon to cure a hernia. Paula's father was an alcoholic who, when drunk, would easily fly into a rage and violently attack anything or anyone in reach. Occasionally the parents would have a bitter fight, and Paula's father would beat up her mother. At other times they seemed to flirt with one another and talked openly about sex, about the neighbors' sex lives, and how various of their friends were deceiving their spouses. During their fights, Paula's brother, Victor, would step in to protect his mother. Paula remembers her father being knocked down by her brother, after which her father looked to her like a "poor little shrunken dwarf."

Paula always felt close to her father in spite of his erratic and sometimes cruel behavior. When he was sober, he was warm and loving toward her and seemed to favor her explicitly. His relationship to his son was openly hostile. The mother, on the other hand, rejected Paula and preferred her son, and so the children were pulled into a continuing fight and were induced to take sides.

Usually Paula's father did the housework while her mother worked. Paula's mother was not a good cook, and Paula's father would frequently complain that the food was too greasy. Her mother retaliated by berating her husband because he didn't earn the money to buy the food, and he would then stalk out in a huff. Later in the evening, or the next day, Paula's father would eat without his wife knowing it. Paula too, would then "sneak food" from the kitchen. Paula never ate much and drew attention to herself by not eating. She became ill often, but rather than responding with warmth and concern, her mother would become angry, and her father was often too drunk to respond.

Paula loved cats and kept several as pets. Her father disliked them and frequently threw them against the wall or kicked them. Finally he boarded them up in the place behind the stairs where they were kept. Paula was not free to get angry about this or many other frustrations in her young life. Every time she did get angry, she was told by her parents that red splotches were coming out on her face and that she was ugly, that these red splotches were the devil coming out in her. Perhaps her greatest frustration came when her parents would become amorous. This was mostly a matter of her mother teasing her father, but her father responded and Paula felt left out of the family while this went on. In later years, this behavior between the parents faded away.

At around two years, after Paula's tonsils were removed, she recalls having been carried home on her father's shoulders. It may have been some other operation, for she had her tonsils out again later. When she was about three or four, she recalls having crawled under the porch with a neighbor boy where they displayed their bodies to one another. They were caught by a neighbor and sent away from their hiding place. Paula felt very guilty, but did not know what she had done that was so wrong. One neighborhood boy particularly, who was three years younger than Paula, was a special friend. She and Leon would sit for hours together, digging worms or playing in the sand. They seemed to retain this rapport throughout most of Paula's early childhood.

In contrast to Leon, there was Ella, who was three years older, fatter, and always prettier than Paula. Paula and Ella quarrelled and fought for many years. Ella would tear her own dress, for example, then tell her mother that Paula had done it. Ella's mother would then chastise or try to punish Paula. Paula's only protection against such chicanery was her father, who was unreliable since he drank so heavily. Her brother would occasionally take her side in these neighborhood squabbles, and Paula came to worship him (in spite of her father's antipathy toward him), but when Paula was nine years old, Victor left for the merchant marines and did not return for six years. Paula remembers taking solace in her cats and in music.

One Christmas, in spite of the fact that there was never a Christmas tree in the house, Paula bought some Christmas tree ornaments. Her father destroyed them in a rage over the useless expenditure of money. While her grandmother was religious, neither her father nor her mother had any interest in religion. They were nominally Roman Catholic, and later Paula developed religious feelings.

In spite of the hardships at home, Paula was a pretty little girl and by the time she was eight, she was being matched up with various boys by relatives and friends who thought they were being cute. Paula was confused by and contemptuous of this whole process. While other people thought she was pretty, she did not feel pretty herself. She was always slim, a vivid contrast to the plump and shining face of her arch-enemy, Ella, and she was subject to her mother's defeminizing haircuts. When she went to Sunday school, she felt ashamed of her clothes, which her mother made, and which were never as pretty as those of other girls. She eventually quit going to Sunday school, partly to escape the prettier dresses of other girls and partly in rebellion against her mother, who thought she should go. Sunday School made her feel nauseous, a feeling that would become so familiar to her later in life. This was probably not the only time during childhood when she felt nausea, because she hated her mother's cooking and ate poorly.

There was a recurrent childhood dream that did not appear later in life. She dreamed simply that she was drowning. She would always awaken in fright just before the drowning was complete.

In school, Paula did well and was eventually advanced two years ahead of her age-mates. Although her teachers were often disapproving in ways that Paula could not understand, she enjoyed their praise of her intelligence and maintained an interest in reading through her adult life. Her early school experience, however, was a kind of island, separated from the rest of her life, and her salient memory is of being considered pretty when she felt skinny, bad, and ugly. She never really trusted any of her teachers, nor their praise, because they seemed to be interested only in whether she could do things they thought she should do.

At eleven, Paula made a concerted effort to learn how to kiss. She and a friend sought out an older girl who taught them one afternoon by kissing them and having them practice on her. Paula's attitude toward this was a combination of repulsion and fascination. This combination also applied to boys in general. A year or so later she had her first menstrual period. Her mother seemed to be disgusted and showed her how to cope physically with menstruation without offering any explanation of what was happening to her. Her mother's generally negative attitude made Paula feel very guilty for menstruating and she had vivid fears that other children, especially boys, would smell or see that she was having a period.

When Paula was thirteen, she and her friend Ann learned to smoke. Paula did not find this easy to do, and many episodes of secret smoking in the bathroom ended in nausea for her. She had the idea that it would take her about a month to smoke without getting dizzy, and so she persevered. (Later she quit smoking and promised God that she would never smoke again.) At about this time, Ann's mother had to be hospitalized for about a month. Her father had died, so for that period, Ann was without parental supervision. Paula arranged to get herself kicked out of her own house by her drunken father and stayed with Ann while Ann's mother was away. The holiday ended when the neighbors complained that many boys were going in and out of the apartment, although Paula maintained that the house was only a kind of "headquarters," that there was nothing to get excited about, that nothing bad happened. Certainly nothing sexual happened, for Paula seems to have never understood sexuality in its anatomical or interpersonal dimensions until her wedding night. Sex, feminine attractiveness, erotic pleasure, and so on, were experienced as a hazy mist in which she somehow had no part.

At fourteen, Paula developed boils on her arms, legs, and buttocks. Her mother was characteristically angry at the trouble caused her and offered no solace to Paula. Paula has a vivid memory of having one of them lanced, to which she responded with immediate vomiting and overwhelming nausea. Also during this year, she had her tonsils removed, seemingly for a second time. The boils were a socially debilitating symptom, which, combined with the fact that she was two years younger than most of her classmates, made her early adolescence a lonely one. She felt guilty about many things that were not at all clear to her. An onyx ring that had been stolen was given to her. She knew it was stolen and felt so guilty that she anonymously mailed it back to its rightful owner. But this was not a mere act of decency; it reflected a pervading guilt that surfaced whenever she felt disapproval from others for anything. For this reason she became a rigid follower of rules, all rules, no matter how often they were violated by others or how archaic they were. Even so, she could not escape the gloomy guilt that seemed always present. In about a year, her brother returned from the Merchant Marines, and she continued to admire him. However, he was only intermittently interested in his sister; she felt as though there was nothing she could do to please him.

She graduated from high school when she was sixteen. Her record had all As and Bs, but her attitude toward schoolwork by this time was one of indifference. She became involved with a series of boys in a pattern that seemed to repeat itself. She was, first at all, manifestly indifferent to them. Yet she managed to attract their attention somehow and had to systematically hide from them. Her greatest fear was that they would kiss her and try to get close to her. Hence, she seems to have seduced by playing shy and then when the chips were down to have retreated in great fear.

There were a couple of exceptions to this pattern. One boy was so nice and harmless that she allowed him to escort her to some social functions. He was, however, roundly disliked by others because he was always just being nice, even to the extent of allowing himself to be used in various ways by others. He was much older than Paula and her friends, which gave him some legitimacy as an escort, but it also made him into something of a joke. There was another boy with whom she got along quite well and seemed able to kiss him with pleasure. She did experience disturbing feelings about it all that she could not identify, but the relationship evolved to the point that they and another couple left one night for Indiana to get married. During the trip, Paula became so nauseous that the whole party had to return. This boy eventually threw her over and Paula was so upset that it was a factor in her joining the WACs at eighteen. One time he had suggested to Paula that they "play train," and she went along with the idea like a good sport. She went along with the *idea,* but when the time came for the actual game, she panicked and ran away. Occasionally another boy liked to lie on top of her, and she was vaguely aware of his erection, but somehow an actual conscious formulation of what all this meant escaped her. She avoided all such "fast" boys without ever really focusing her attention on what it meant to be "fast."

At home, she became more and more embarrassed by her father and his behavior. For a long time she had been afraid of his anger, even while being in great need of his approval. She would go out of her way to do everything in a way that would please him, but his erratic whims kept her in fear of rejection. She had feared closing her bedroom door for years because he insisted that she leave it open so he could watch her dress. Moreover, he occasionally would trap Paula or her friends in a corner and fondle their buttocks and "mammary glands." His attitude about Paula was that she was his daughter and he had a right to do whatever he liked to her. On some occasions, Paula reported, he chased her around the house for as long as an hour, until she escaped or he gave up.

After graduation from high school, Paula went to work as a file clerk. She was making "a pretty good salary," and she found the job acceptable, but somehow she drifted into a factory job that paid somewhat better. Her mother heartily disapproved of this second job, for it was unskilled and she felt her daughter ought to do higher level work. Paula therefore took another file-clerk position and eventually was promoted to be supervisor of six of her previous peers. This situation caused her so much anxiety and periodic nausea that it too was a factor in her joining the WACs.

Joining the WACs, however, was largely unpremeditated. A friend decided rather suddenly to join, and so Paula simply joined along with her. Once in the WACs she had a series of relationships with soldiers that matched her earlier romantic involvements. With one soldier, who was a "pal," for example, she felt comfortable and could have some fun, until she suddenly sighted some WAC shoes in a jeep. This image seemed to transform her "pal" into a "man" and she became so frightened she had to run away. There was also a short-lived brush with some lesbians, whom she thought awfully silly. At one point she talked it over with her CO, only to discover later from her friends that her CO was a lesbian. This episode, like everything else sexual, seems to have been lost in a cloak of bafflement. She didn't understand but didn't seem to have the self-possession to try to do so.

Various of her friends and acquaintances met with violence during this time. There was an occasional rape; one girl threw herself in front of a truck, and another girl, who had slept next to her for some months, had gone home to her husband who was mentally ill. Her husband strangled her to death and she was found with a crowbar jammed into her vagina. Paula seemed shocked at this, but was able to dismiss it as simply "crazy" without any great emotional strain.

One soldier sustained a relationship with her for about nine months. Paula became involved with him only to discover suddenly that he was married. Paula became mentally and physically upset. She had barely begun eating again a week later when she met Ed, who asked her to marry him, and she consented without much thought or feeling. She knew him slightly before this time, but she didn't like him at all. She thought his hands were too small and he seemed to her to be a spoiled brat. But as soon as she accepted his proposal, he began to be very attractive to her. All the things she didn't like about him suddenly became great assets. His "spoiled brat" behavior seemed to take on a whimsical charm. She left the WACs and married him within another week.

Her wedding night was the first time she was confronted with sexuality in such a way that she could not ignore it. She made this scene easier for herself by becoming very drunk and seems to have become acquainted with the anatomical realities of sex only gradually. She immediately disliked her in-laws, who were wealthy and seemed to have a confusing parade of unpleasant relatives: married to each other, divorced from, fathered by, cousin to, etc. Only her mother-in-law was at all nice to her; Paula resented the entire family. Within her own family there was trouble as well. She had to lie to her family that her husband was the same man she had been seeing for nine months. She soon became pregnant and at that time, particularly, her brother seemed to lose interest in her. She lived with her mother for a while, for her husband was still in service, but as soon as she became pregnant, she was shuttled off to a housing project and neglected. The marriage seems to have cost her her family.

Her involvement with her husband deepened, but he was unfortunately very casual about her. It soon became clear that she was a kind of stopping place between other women. She therefore went to great lengths to try to please him. Their sexual relationship was satisfying to her—in fact she seemed to enjoy it as the only time when he paid her much attention—but it was never enough for him. He berated her for being unable to satisfy him and she knew only to try harder to read his wishes and please him. Her slavish attitude toward him was interrupted by his progressive abandonment of her and by her pregnancy. Even so, whenever he was home, she tried to submit to every whim even as late as six years later.

Early in her marriage, Paula came to the realization that all her life she had been selfish and egotistical. It seemed to her that her meanness had been "automatic" but that it had hurt many people. She, therefore, in a crisis of conscience, tried to become "good." A couple of years later, Paula noticed that the harder she

tried to be good, the more people disliked her. This led her to conclude—and she maintained this view for years afterward—that it
doesn't really pay to try to be good; it is a dog-eat-dog world, and
nice guys finish last. This theme finds concrete expression in Paula's
behavior a few years later.

At one point she complained to her husband that he was not
satisfying her sexually because of his frequent absences. He brushed
her off with the recommendation that she masturbate, which she
dutifully tried. Her attempts, as far as we know the first self-conscious ones, were unsatisfactory to her and she gave it up.

Paula's first son, Saul, was born when she was twenty. Immediately after she returned home from the hospital, her husband
and her mother fought viciously over the details of caring for the
child. In addition, she tried to breast-feed the baby and was in
constant anxiety whether he was getting enough milk. After she
had been out of the hospital only a week, she had to return in an
emotional and physical collapse, and returned twice more before
she was able to stay home permanently with the child.

Her husband became more demanding at this time. He insisted that their sexual activity expand to fellatio and cunnilingus.
She always achieved orgasm during this time but cried immediately
afterwards for some reason she did not understand. Her husband
also did not understand and had not the patience to try, berating
her as a poor wife. She felt a sense of guilt about these sexual prac-
tices that seemed more disturbing than she had experienced before.
It was only because she was so afraid that he would leave for good
that she went along with his demands.

Also during that year, her father fell from a ladder and was
badly hurt, remaining paralyzed from the waist down for the last
eight years of his life. Immediately after the accident, Paula, with
her brother, visited him in the hospital. He appeared to her at that
time as so helpless, so much a victim of forces beyond his control,
so blameless and pathetic, and she felt so unable to help him that
the visit was the occasion of a great emotional upset followed by
vomiting and diarrhea more serious than she had experienced
before. A few months after this episode, Paula underwent an operation on her breast. She had anticipated a gruesome time, in the
hospital, but at least she would have a few days off from the pressure
of her husband, infant son, and mother. Unfortunately, the opera-

tion was minor from a medical point of view and she received only local anaesthesia. She remembers vividly the blood spurting on the doctor's glasses and she immediately became nauseous. Further, she was not even kept in the hospital overnight. She had to leave after the operation, go home, and fix supper for her husband.

While she was twenty-two, Paula gave birth to her second son, Joe. Like the first pregnancy, there was much sickness, but this time it was complicated by a brown, vaginal discharge that frightened her very much. Her doctor was very casual about it until after Joe was born, at which time it was discovered that she had a badly tipped uterus. According to Paula's description, her uterus was falling into her rectum and her vagina. The doctor put "rings" in to hold the uterus in place, but the rings kept falling out. In addition, the image of "erosions in the cervix" seemed to close this picture for her into one of bodily deterioration. She immediately began losing weight, had trouble with her gums, and developed a very bad case of acne. She was sick much of the time, and eating successfully became more difficult. Gastrointestinal problems of all kinds seemed to beset her constantly for more than a year.

Living in the housing project, where her husband rarely appeared, her family ignored her, and her two small sons demanded a great deal, she happened to rediscover her childhood playmate, Ella, with whom she had fought so bitterly. Ella had had polio and had therefore lost much of her attractiveness and her spunk, and she was able, at this crucial point in Paula's life, to be a friend. Eventually Paula's brother also became more kindly in his attitude and even gave her his car so that she could do the shopping and get around town. Her worship of him lost its adolescent flavor of adoration but became a more mature kind of dependence. She continued to worry that she was not pleasing him, just as she had worried about her father and her husband. While he was willing to be nice, even generous, he was not willing to have his sister dependent on him and so the relationship was stormy from Paula's point of view.

Paula's husband was home less and less of the time. While he was there, he would beat the children sadistically if they didn't obey him perfectly. Paula, still desperately trying to please him, would beat the children too, partly to show him that she was a good mother, partly to keep them from upsetting him, and partly because she felt occasional outbursts of violent anger at them. She felt guilty about this behavior, and she was most uncertain whether it was the right thing to do. But she seems to have felt even more guilty if they behaved badly in front of their father.

While her husband was gone, which was most of the time, the only way that Paula could get out of the house was for her mother to babysit. Paula had little confidence in her mother as a babysitter and constantly worried that she was neglecting the children. Nevertheless she greatly appreciated this form of attention her mother was willing to give. There was a more or less constant battle between Paula and her mother, and Paula's usual posture became one in which she felt obliged to please her mother's rather cranky demands. Just as always, the battles were fought in subterfuge, innuendo, and sniping. Finally the financial situation, which had never been good since Paula's marriage—largely because of her husband's indifference to the family—became critical. The mother, in characteristic fashion, began berating Paula for her inability to remain solvent and hinted strongly that Paula ought to get a job. Paula took the hint, even though it meant that her mother would do even more babysitting. The job, sorting mail at a post office, lasted only several months, and Paula gave the money to her husband anyway. Finally the burden of the babysitting became too much for Paula's mother, and the arrangement was terminated. Paula disliked her job and worried about the children, but she refused to give up before her mother did and was greatly relieved when her mother finally quit the daily babysitting. At this time Paula was also still more or less constantly ill, for she worked all day and was up all night with the children. She continued to lose weight.

Within a year or so, Paula became more social again and changed her attitude toward the neighbors, who had bickered with her about the crying children. She consciously stopped trying to please them and gave up trying to be good in this "dog-eat-dog world." She dressed up more often and began to attract the attention of men. The wives of the housing project only redoubled their petty gossiping and chicanery against her, but this bothered her less and she continued being friendly with the housing project men until she became nauseous a few times when they began to make advances.

Shortly thereafter, Paula had a bona fide affair with a young boy who was widely liked for his carefree attitude and irresponsible charm. It was a short-lived liaison; after the first sexual experience with him, Paula swore never to get involved with him again. The boy forced his way into her apartment a second time, however, and demanded sexual intercourse. After something of a fight, he got his way and Paula became sick with nausea and diarrhea. Within a month it became apparent that she was pregnant, and she felt very guilty about it. At the same time, however, she was secretly proud of being pregnant again, especially because it led her friends to be sympathetic and offer advice about abortion. With respect to the very practical matter of having another baby, Paula was not very realistic. With the coaxing and help of some friends, she made her way to a doctor and got a shot of some kind. She was not sure what it was all about. Within a day or so the baby was aborted. This was about twelve weeks after conception. Again with the advice of a friend, she froze the fetus, and took it a couple of days later, frozen, to the hospital as proof that she needed a dilation and curettage, which she received. Paula was twenty-five.

This whole matter had not come to the attention of her husband. A few months later he came back to her and moved in more or less to stay. At first, Paula thought, that Ed had finally changed into the kind of husband she wanted, and she began again all of the self-ingratiating behavior that was designed to keep him home. This introduced all the old conflicts again, about keeping the children quiet, about sexuality, about money, and about Ed's behavior when he was not in the house. He spent a good deal of time with an old army buddy who owned a gasoline station nearby and Paula cooked for him and played wife, as if her husband had a job. One afternoon she accidentally discovered a photograph of her husband with another girl, whom she recognized as one of her husband's old girlfriends, and with them in the picture was a young boy who looked very much like *her* older son. This dramatic evidence of her husband's unfaithfulness provoked a violent argument, and with her husband's urging, she decided to get a divorce. She finally did so when she was twenty-six.

The divorce alienated some of her friends, such as Ella—also a Catholic—who had no tolerance for an excommunicated friend. Her life changed rather little objectively for a while, but she began thinking of herself in a different way. The hopes for the marriage no longer made sense and she was without hope of ever having a decent life. She also became more social and flirted a bit more again, seemingly having forgotten the difficulty such behavior had led to just the year before.

One day she had to take a long taxi ride to pick up her son at a park, during which she chatted with the cab driver, whom she had seen around the neighborhood before. She eventually told him the story of the divorce and he became more or less interested in her. Many of her friends commented that this man, whose name was also Ed, was very handsome and would make a fine catch. Paula eschewed any such thoughts. On one occasion, the new Ed gave Paula twenty dollars, "just for pocket money," and she was constipated for three days, after which she suffered from diarrhea for nearly a month. However, the facts were clear to anyone who cared to look at them: he was handsome, single, financially secure, and he was interested in Paula. She did not, as usual, quite understand the situation.

The progress of this relationship was interrupted temporarily by her father's heart attack when she was twenty-seven. Her mother and her brother showed great indifference to this event in the invalid of seven years, and in fact walked out on him in the middle of the attack. Only by accident did Paula happen onto the situation, discover the seriousness of her father's condition, and call a doctor. She was furious at her mother and brother. Within a few months, her father died. Paula nearly collapsed at the funeral; her mother and brother thought she was overdoing it a bit.

By the time she was twenty-eight, Paula had decided that she would marry the new Ed, and immediately after their marriage, they moved back into her mother's house, which was large enough but which was embedded in the neighborhood of her childhood. Ed arranged to pay rent and an apartment for her mother was separated off from the rest of the house. Her brother was not in favor of this marriage, but her mother apparently was—she babysat for Paula during their courtship.

For a while, this marriage was the best time of Paula's life. Ed had a serious blood disease that he had gotten in the service, but for the most part this was no bother to them. It did mean that he had total income benefits from the government and driving a cab was not a necessity. In addition, Ed and his sisters were to split a relatively large estate soon, and so Paula enjoyed financial solvency for the first time. It was perhaps the financial aspects of the marriage that most pleased Paula's mother, who was highly conscious of money and how a woman can get it. Paula herself went overboard for a while, buying new clothes and jewelry, new gadgets for the house, and so on. Most important of all, however, Paula found that with Ed she could eat well, enjoy her food, and not suffer multiple gastrointestinal symptoms each time she ate. Ed too loved to eat and they enjoyed cooking for one another.

The paradise did not last. She was back in her mother's house and had to submit to her mother's peculiar ways all of the time. She was also haunted by her excommunication, and became victimized again, via neighborhood gossip led by Ella, so reminiscent of her childhood. The children were by now six and eight years old; they were constantly getting into trouble with other children and Paula could not avoid worrying about their behavior. She resumed harsh punishment, but felt guilty about it at the same time. She didn't even know whether to believe what her child told her or what the parent of a playmate told her after a squabble. She vacillated between punishment and trying to teach them to stand up for themselves. Both boys seemed to show signs of more or less serious emotional disturbance: Saul was excessively moody and withdrawn, Joe was always getting into fights and occasionally set fires.

There was the matter of sex with her new husband. At first his demands were moderate and tolerable by Paula. Only later did he insist on cunnilingus, which of course created anew many of the old conflicts that Paula had with the first Ed. But the final straw came when Ed refused to fight with his sisters as Paula had expected he would do. His knuckling under to his sisters, at least as seen by Paula, lost him a large part of the estate and meant that he was not really the man she thought she had married. This left her within a marriage that was different from the first one, but in other ways equally unsatisfactory. The actual development of a rift between them was avoided only by Paula's fourth pregnancy.

Her third child, Margo, was born when Paula was twenty-nine. Immediately there was another crisis—Margo had a very dangerous, infantile disease. She was near death several times, during which time Paula quit smoking, promising God that she would never smoke again if Margo was allowed to live. Margo survived. Paula herself had had heart trouble while carrying Margo, and against doctor's orders she ate foods that exacerbated this difficulty.

Against this background, Margo came into the world. They still lived with Paula's mother and things settled down somewhat with small crises and an underlying tension between Paula and her husband. Difficulties with the children continued, there were frequent alarms about her health, occasional recurrences of the vomiting, and Ed's health began to deteriorate. By the time Paula was thirty-two, she had made the first real decision, according to her description, that she had ever made in her life, namely, to take an active role in the decision to move the family from her mother's house into a Chicago suburb. Her husband procrastinated, her brother was against the move openly, her mother sniped at the idea perpetually, and Paula was uncertain for a long time. Finally she insisted and the move was initiated. It was during the actual moving process that Paula underwent the extended inability to eat and anxiety attacks that drove her into the hospital.

2. *Analysis of the Life-History*

We have just completed a narrative that describes the life events of an individual to whom we have given the name Paula Kress. Our task now is to attempt to understand that life-history and hence that person. For it is the case that Paula Kress, like every individual, *is* a history. When we see her at age 32, with symptoms of anxiety hysteria, we are not seeing a natural object that has something curious about it. We are seeing a summary of all that has come before. Her symptoms are not the beginning of something, such as a neurosis. They are the end of a long, life-history process. Paula Kress gives birth to these symptoms after a lifetime of gestation. They are her creation, or more accurately, they are how she is being at the time.

How one *is* is historical. This does not mean that we must simply understand prior "causes," gathered from the history, that explain the "effect," her neurosis. By such a definition, a car is historical; its current functioning is a product of all that has come before. But the car does not *create* a history, it does not *understand* its history, and hence cannot *transcend* its history. A car is not a being; it does not engage in the process of "aming." We understand a car by understanding *what* it is, its essential characteristics. To understand a person, we must understand *how* he is and *who* he is. A person, a being, is a process and not a thing. But even more important, it is a process of intending as well as being intended, of creating as well as being created, of deciding as well as being decided. A being, therefore, is more than a thing and more than a process in the sense of a natural processes like oxidation.

A being "temporalizes," or put another way, a person ams in a temporal way. What is the past that is remembered and the future that is anticipated, out of which the person creates a present? No being *is* (ams) outside of time. The way we *are* is always temporal and hence temporalization is always a crucial aspect of our being.

In addition to the historical dimension in this sense, to understand Paula Kress we must understand her world. Her "world" is not the objective world as seen by a neutral observer who finds causes in her mother's coldness or finds sin in her father's alcoholism. These world-creations are our own. We must try to discern Paula Kress's world creation. For it is in her world creation, and only there, that she created herself. As objective things happen to her (she is born, sees her father kill her cat, is impregnated by a husband or lover), the crucial factor is what these events mean to *her*. How does *she* weave the myriad of objective phenomena together into a coherent world in which she can place herself in some meaningful way? Her world, therefore, and her self, have a certain reciprocity. They fit into a *Gestalt*. One is not understandable without the other. To unravel how she sees herself from the multiple factors of how she sees the world and how she sees others see her is a task that cannot be taken too simply.

Finally, and very important for Paula Kress particularly, to understand a person we must understand how he is with respect to his body. How does he place it in time? At one point Paula sees time as a process of deterioration of her body. How does she place it in space? At one point we see her as hating its skinniness and its weakness to move robustly from place to place. These are specifications of the question, "How does she place her body in the world?" In what ways does she experience her body as an object? In what ways does she experience it as a subject? How does this object rattle around in her primary and secondary life-space? How does she as a body-as-subject guide and direct a path through these spaces, have impulses, and express experiences through her body?

Temporality, spatiality, and corporality are all phenomenological dimensions of her being. They describe her self-world relationship. That self-world relationship is intentional, and these are some of the dimensions of her intentionality. These are categories that apply to any person. For Paula Kress we will also find useful such dimensions as warm-cold, safe-dangerous, and aloneness. Every individual necessarily demands that we create new categories for understanding him, for every individual is unique.

For convenience, we have outlined three spheres of intentionality, three groups of intentions that can be treated more or less separately and yet must be fit together if we are to complete the *Gestalt*. She intends the world, and herein lies a basic starting point for human being. She also intends herself, reflects upon herself and judges, discerns, deceives, and recognizes herself. She also intends an image of herself as seen by other people.

The life-history that we have of Paula comes, of course, from her psychotherapy. It is an account of how she sees her past. It could be, of course, a pack of lies, or as Freud was shocked to discover of some of his early patients, pure fantasy. But that does not really matter, as indeed Freud was to conclude. It is "psychic reality" that one always works with. For us, it is not at all a disadvantage to have such a history; it is a distinct advantage over knowing simply the objective conditions of her life. We see, in this life-history, her world and her being.

There are, of course, some things that we assume were objectively true. However, the peculiar interpretation of them that congeals into Paula's unique world must also be seen as her creation. Obviously the history is a mixture of both. But separating out the objective from the subjective misses the point. Even the most objective facts must find a place in the world she created, and it is that world which is the key thing for us.

A. The beginning world

It was "given" that Paula was a girl. It's probably true that her mother wanted a boy to replace the lost son, but the important thing is that Paula always felt that her mother tried to defeminize her. It is probably also true that her father tried to feminize her, but the important thing is that the general family situation was structured by Paula in this way. Paula polarized her parents; her father was warm and her mother was cold. Regardless of how they objectively were, by so "creating" them, she probably responded to them and provoked them in such a way as to make this polarization become an objective fact. Mother became more cold, and father became more warm, as she established this order for them. It may have been, of course, that with slightly different circumstances, Paula's creation would have been different and this would have changed her behavior, thus changing her parent's behavior, thus changing the life-history. But it happened as it happened. All we can do is to testify to that fact.

Paula's world thus takes on a peculiar bifurcation, in line with her parents' probably very different personalities, within the context of her primary family. As a two-year-old child, experiencing separateness, where the best antidote to separation anxiety is the self-affirmation of the negativistic toddler, Paula already felt as though her self-affirmations had to take place within a complex political network of alliances and antipathies. What is more, she did not experience helpful guidance from her parents (even though they probably gave it some of the time), she experienced a cold rebuff from her mother and a violent unpredictableness from her father. Anger, we are told, was turned back on herself by her parents, who said that it created "red splotches" on her face and that these are the devil coming out in her.

Paula's initial feelings of self-as-subject in the stage we have called "separateness" were not very successful and not well solidified. She will need them later, and they will be absent. We see later that they are driven into bodily expressions of rebellion, such as not eating and becoming sick. These, of course, are not taken by Paula as subject-expressive but are construed as her object-body having gone wrong.

In the place of self experiences as-subject, we see an immediate reversal of focus back upon herself. The devil is coming out in her. This definition of her anger, by her parents, is an important one, for it is one of her most vivid memories (or creations). It does two things. First, it makes her responsible for, without giving her control over, the feelings—which is tailor-made to create guilt for what she *is*—which in turn tends to preempt guilt for what one *does*. Second, it establishes her parents as the authoritative definers of her self, a kind of (perhaps premature) satellization. A self as the object of these devious and contradictory gods is not a comfortable self. Whether premature or not, Paula's satellization was profound. What is more, it came to be doubly uncomfortable because she was satellized to two such contradictory gods.

The red splotches are also important in that they are bodily. Her body betrays her feelings; it is the instrument of shame. In addition, she is punished and made to feel ashamed at having revealed her body to a youthful neighbor under the porch. Should this episode have reflected some curiosity, some feeling that I-am-a-subject-who-sees-and-knows, it was hardly encouraged. We should perhaps remind ourselves that this episode is hardly unique, but what is important is that it is a salient part of Paula's past-history—salient, that is, to her. She saw it as important; it is therefore important in telling us of the role of her body, of the nature of her world, and of her being for-herself and for-others.

Furthermore, her body becomes ill, perhaps as punishment for her feelings (even while expressing them). The nourishment of her body in eating becomes a political football in her prematurely complex and bewildering world. She doesn't know why she doesn't eat, and yet this refusal is an almost perfect expression of her rebellion against her mother and her loyalty to her father, who also did not eat. Her mother does, however, make it clear that not eating is what makes her sick, and so she is held responsible for her illness. This produces more guilt for what she *is,* since not-eating does not feel to her like a choice. Shame and guilt thus pervade her being-for-others and her being-for-herself at a very early age, and her body is deeply involved in these self-experiences.

The good god, her father, whose savior-quality is expressed in the memory of his carrying her home from an operation, triumphantly, on his shoulders, is notably unreliable. Most of her early memories of him—the cats, the Christmas tree ornaments—are of his irrational violence. Finally this god is brutally dethroned by Victor, in a brawl in the kitchen, in which he suddenly becomes a weak and helpless "shrunken dwarf."

B. The wider world

The bifurcated world of the family is naturally enough super-imposed on her neighborhood friendships. We find a male, Leon, who is younger and therefore weak and pleasant, with perhaps the apparent irrationality and unpredictability of relatively younger children, and with whom Paula gets along fine. And we find Ella, older, fatter, prettier (Paula once described her mother as having been very pretty) and very dominant in a manipulative, sneaky sort of way. Leon and Ella may not have been very good replicas of father and mother, but the important thing is that Paula responded to them as if they were. One could, at this point, invoke the psychoanalytic theory of transference and say that father-feelings were transferred to Leon and mother-feelings to Ella. We are more accurate, however, not to be so specific about particular cathexes. What is happening is the creation of a world by Paula, and its total structure is what interests us rather than particular relationships.

The outside world has a more complex structure, however, with additional layers of meaning. Ella's mother, for example, seems to be an approximation of Paula's own mother: cold, hostile, scheming. And yet there is hardly a cognitive confusion between the two. It is in terms of warm-cold and safe-dangerous that they are similar. These dimensions are not something Paula could articulate, and yet they clearly are significant facts of her world-creation. So it is with so much of the phenomenological world.

Paula therefore enters the extrafamilial world still badly confused about her satellization to her parents. She could not become an apprentice for anything that she understood. It became crucial, as it always does, to understand what the gods think of oneself. But mother is very difficult to please. Insofar as she in fact wanted Paula to be a "Paul," a boy to replace the lost son, she was impossible to please. We may suppose that there was the fantasy,

"If I could only be good enough, then mother would not be so cold to me." With respect to her father, who was inconsistently warm and brutal, Paula seemed to please him sometimes by simply being a girl—exactly what displeased her mother. But at other times, she tried with great care to please him only to meet a drunken rebuff.

Similarity, the stage of later childhood, when the child begins to build a self-world relationship that goes beyond the dependency of satellization, still requires models, even if they are no longer gods. The hopeless situation with her parents leads us to wonder whether her brother Victor, seven years older, could become an important model. What we find is that he did become extremely important to Paula, but the nature of this importance was that she "worshipped" him. He was therefore not an equal for Paula, even later in life, but rather became another god around which she satellized herself. This is not surprising since the experience of similarity demands a sense of oneself-as-subject. And it is not surprising since Paula's relationships with people seem to become more and more alike. Her world is becoming rigidly structured. She is not open to new possibilities. Even her experience at school seems to be permeated with issues of acceptance and rejection of self by teachers. It never occurred to Paula that *she* had the power to accept and reject. She was barely able to hold a self together. The self-as-subject was rapidly becoming submerged in a self-as-others'-object. No wonder she dreamed of drowning.

Her school and her Sunday school experiences give us additional clues about Paula's self-world relationship. She recalls being "matched up" with boys, being called "pretty," her perceptions of a competition among girls for being pretty through having pretty dresses and her mother's sabotage of this competition for Paula by making inferior dresses. Again we see that Paula's relationship to her body is confused. There are at least three bodies here. First, there is the body that wanted to be the prettiest. This may indeed express something of her longing and her sexual impulses, in light of the relationship she had to her father, where she was acceptable primarily by being a pretty girl. Second, there was the body that she thought she had: ugly, skinny, and sick. Third, there was the body she saw other people seeing, which was pretty and match-

worthy. The first body is the body-as-subject, and her expressed feelings toward others were no more integrated into her being than her reason for getting sick eating her mother's cooking.

The second and third bodies, however, were clearly conscious and produce a very special kind of problem. She no doubt wanted to believe her father and others who called her pretty. But she could not escape the judgment of her mother that she was not. The latter is, in fact, reinforced by feelings of being sick and of being a red-splotched face. The more she received the admiration and praise of others because she was pretty, while feeling that she was in fact quite ugly, the more she felt like a fraud before other people. "If they only knew what I'm really like. . . ." Yet at the same time, we recall that she is radically satellized and she probably construed most of her relationships according to this pattern. So even while feeling like a fraud for being thought pretty, she became desperately dependent on the maintenance of the fraud. To be thought pretty is, after all, to be accepted and admired. The problem is that not too far away from the center of her attention was the felt truth that this acceptance was artificial and vulnerable. She is a long way from a more durable self-esteem in which *she* decides or achieves something that is well received by others.

C. The body

Against this background three things happened to her that fed into this confused body-self-world configuration: she learned to kiss, she began to menstruate, and she learned to smoke, all in her early adolescence. Let us consider each of these as she experienced them and try to see what they meant for her being.

The way she learned to kiss is not particularly unique insofar as most adolescents tend to occupy themselves with technique more than feelings when it comes to sexuality. The pleasure in kissing and the desire to kiss are subordinated to whether one is an adequate technician, as judged by others. One's bodily feelings are therefore subordinated to the experience of the body as an instrument to be used in playing out interpersonal and social games. We know that for Paula the primary game is one of satellization. Kissing became asexual in the sense that the body was *used* but not *lived*. Or, if we prefer to call this kind of kissing sexual, then we must say that sex became *used* and not *lived*. "Lived sexuality" demands that one's bodily feelings are expressed in bodily action. "Used sexuality" describes actions that express other, nonbodily designs, and the bodily feelings themselves get lost amidst the political gamesmanship of interpersonal relations, such as Paula's extreme satellization. If she masturbated, which at least engages the body erotically, if not interpersonally, it was totally unconscious and nonproblematic. She was probably not enough in contact with her body even to masturbate.

The first menstruation, for Paula, was traumatic in a number of respects. First of all, her mother did not take this opportunity to become a new kind of mother, an "equal," of sorts. If Paula had any fantasies that she would, in becoming a woman, escape her mother's demanding and contemptuous attitude, these hopes were dashed. Secondly, the appearance of menstruation gave Paula a vivid concern that others would know she was menstruating and therefore talk about her, ridicule her. This fear in itself is not uncommon, but the intensity with which Paula needed to please others no doubt made it more painful than usual. Finally, the first menstruation is a time when most girls are able to look to future womanhood with hope. We do not know how Paula experienced this, but we may guess that rather than signaling a hopeful future it was experienced as an invasion by an alien process, her bodily maturation, over which she had no control and which jeopardized her shaky security as the "pretty" one. This kind of experience reflects her particular temporalization of life. There is so much to lose in the future that its possible gains are not apparent. The future and its changes are threatening and gloomy rather than bright and open-ended. And the coming of the first menstruation indicates the relentless coming of change, regardless of one's wishes. One cannot turn back the biological clock. It is absolutely indifferent as it makes its way forward into the frightening unknown.

Paula's learning to smoke is perhaps the single victory over her body we see in her life-history. She successfully whips her body into shape and makes it capable of receiving nicotine without illness. But the matter does not stop there. Smoking has many layers of symbolic meaning which we can only guess about now. The victory was in the service of a project she and Ann began together. Perhaps giving up would have meant losing Ann. Smoking is also sexual in the sense that it is associated in our culture with adult activities forbidden to children, and with "sex appeal" as defined by Hollywood. We are not able to discern the extent to which these were relevant aspects of the experience. However, we might note that, as in learning to kiss, Paula was almost certainly putting her nicotine-tolerant body in the service of nonbodily needs, such as her exaggerated need for approval from others.

Paula's experience of her body is becoming complex; let us review. First, her bodily illness with mother's food expresses, in body language, a feeling toward mother. But this feeling is buried beneath the experience of her body as an object that has gone wrong, thus relieving her of the responsibility for expressing the feeling. The content, however, is preemptive: my body is sick. Second, her body became a central tool in her being-for-others, specifically in her need to be pretty. Third, there is a kind of "instrumentation" of her body as in learning to kiss. All three of these events conspire to separate any bodily feeling from her experience of herself-as-subject. Physical desires are not taken as her own and do not come to be a recognizable level of experience we have called being-in-the-world. Even the most primitive physical desire, eating, was caught up in a complex interpersonal game in which the stakes were very high. We note without great surprise, therefore, that sexuality in the adult sense has no better fate. The entire business of sexuality is cloaked in a hazy mist, never quite coming into direct focus. Her physical sexual desires met with a mammoth disclaimer. She is preoccupied with sex as a tool for satellization in the sense that she cannot forget the grounds of her being accepted (being pretty and feminine), but she is a long way from experiencing an honest sexual impulse. In good hysterical fashion, she "sexualizes everything except sex."

Instead, therefore, of a body-in-the-world, where food and stroking are the currency of exchange and bodily desire and satisfaction make a meaningful cycle, Paula experiences her body as (*a*) sinful (for being displayed), (*b*) sick (for not eating), (*c*) ugly, (*d*) a thing to impress others, (*e*) an instrument in interpersonal games, (*f*) out of control in its relentless program toward change. Even all of this would not be so impressive, compared to other adolescents, except that it is part of a process of being that has other serious anomalies that make each of these important.

It is not terribly surprising, then, that at fourteen Paula develops boils on her arms, legs, and buttocks. The boils *express*, in body language, guilt, sickness, ugliness, desire to impress others and manipulate them in interpersonal games, and lack of control over the body. The expressive nature of the boils, of course, is obscured by the experience of "my body-as-sick," all over again. Further, we learn that having one of the boils lanced produced nausea and vomiting. There is, in this experience, obvious sexual imagery in the violation of surface integrity by a long instrument. But the lancing ceremony is not just the activation of repressed wishes that must be opposed by the superego. The vomiting reaction is an outright rebellion against these wishes, in body language. The intake of mother's greasy food, of praise by those who think you're pretty, of cigarette smoke, and other things also provoked such bodily rebellion. Very likely it was chalked up, by doctor, patient, and parent alike, as some kind of chemical effect.

Even yet another aspect of Paula's relationship to her body can be reconstructed at this time. One of the crucial themes in Paula's bodily expressions is the interchange with the outside through taking-in and putting-out. Eating, smoking, getting shots with a needle, and any sexual fantasies of which we haven't heard involve taking-in; diarrhea (or elimination in general) and vomiting are putting-out. Paula seems to refuse to take-in in various ways and to insist on putting-out in various ways. An unconscious fantasy or wish could be postulated as the origin of this theme, with various personages and acts, such as fellatio with father, nursing at mother's breast, defecating on or giving birth to various people. Our approach must be less specific with respect to personages and acts and it must focus instead on how she placed her body in her world.

Paula's body was experienced by her as *vulnerable* to insidious intrusions from without. It was not really safe in the face of a threatening "putting-in" initiated from outside. Her only response to this threat was to "put-out" from within. The alien invades; it must be driven out. This way of constructing her bodily relationship to the world expresses in concrete, body-language, her being-in-the-world. Her being (her process of I-aming) rebels against interventions, influences, and interferences from other people. Most of all she did not want to *be* as her mother *was*; she did not want *her* being to be influenced by her mother's being. This "struggle with the introject" included many of mother's traits and mannerisms, but she also did not want to be as her father was. In order to prevent this, a struggle had to ensue. As we know, that struggle was blunted by her satellization and did not affirm her self-as-subject, as most intergeneration conflicts do. It remained on the bodily level where, as we have also noted, it could be interpreted as sickness instead of as existential expression. Her exaggerated being-an-object for others favored that interpretation and her struggle never (until age 32) reached an integration into her being that could result in practical action.

D. Relationships

Eventually the boils subsided and Paula entered into a series of relationships with boys. In addition to the complexities of her relationship to her body, we must remember the guilt for what she *is* (note the rigid adherence to rules), the satellization (note the reestablishing of her brother as a god when he returns), and her profound dependence on being-for-others and the general absence of her experience of herself-as-subject. We also must remember that her world, originally bifurcated by the two gods, father and mother, tends to be imposed on friends and on body experiences since then. Her body as feminine and pretty is her body through her father's eyes; her body as sick and ugly is her body through her mother's eyes. Neither is really compatible with immediate and spontaneous bodily feelings. Furthermore, we may suppose that her body as pretty suffered from the danger of attack which was a part of the world of her father (who chased her, watched her dress, fondled her) and that her body as ugly suffered from the guilt and cold demandingness that was part of the world of her mother.

We have already pointed out that to be a self in two such contradictory worlds is a very difficult task, but that she created the worlds with a self in them, and that self was a satellized self-as-others'-object. Caught between these worlds, her temporalization is without a future. "Hope," in either arena, it totally vested in the good will of the gods. She does not make decisions that are directed toward an image of the future; she can only hope to maintain her acceptability to the gods on a day-to-day basis.

This struggle fails repeatedly with boys. She can "be pretty" and attract them, at which point her object self is again affirmed and she feels a temporary security. But the boys always respond, as father did, with demands that put her squarely in the primary family again, where her only response is to get sick. The original meaning of getting sick is buried beneath later ones, such as getting her out of the situation in which she was going to Indiana to get married. And both of these are buried beneath the experience of body-as-object-gone-wrong.

Occasionally she finds a male, beginning with Leon, through to the "Pal" in the jeep, who accepts her without demanding from her. But this relationship is secure only as long as it is static. Progress and change are not promising. Her temporalization is a holding action, not a movement into the future. If she ever had adolescent dreams of a man on a white horse who would take her to a little house with a white picket fence, they were short-lived and did not influence her creation of a world of boyfriends.

Twice, before she was married, she became involved with a particular male for an extended period. In both cases, her orientation was toward whether the other person would accept her. She was object and they were subject. She never wondered if she wanted to accept them. She never became the subject.

This satellization, which has implications in her experience of her body and which informs her temporalization of life is part of the late-adolescent being of Paula Kress. Let us look at this being from yet another point of view before we see the further unfolding of her being in the third decade of her life, namely, the peculiar passivity that characterized her decision-making. A fog seems to surround her entire life when it comes to making decisions. Time after time she drifted into activities without ever quite deciding to or not to. Her dates, the trip to Indiana, her move from job to job, and finally, joining the WACs were not moves into a future she could envision, but were momentary whims that remained difficult for her to justify. The "agent" feeling of self-as-subject, which places one in control of one's life, seemed never to be a part of her experience. The existential meaning of being "other-directed," "alienated," "field dependent," and other like concepts, is two-fold: a lack of experience of self-as-subject and a predominance of the experience of self-as-object. Rape, lesbians, suicide, even violent sexual murder seemed to her to be something one feared but over

which one had no control. This renowned hysterical indifference
in the face of emotionally charged situations is not unrelated to her
entire being, as a body that is not subject, as a self that sees no connection between desire and action, as a being that is primarily for-
others.

E. Marriage

Marrying, the first time, was not a decision that was aimed toward
a future. But the experiences of this marriage did certainly confront Paula with certain things she had avoided. And her adjustment to them grew out of her self-world constructions up to that
time. Perhaps the overwhelming question that presents itself about
this marriage is why Paula put up with it for so long. Her creation
of the world of her marriage has a continuity and a difference with
Paula's previous creations.

The similarity is the radical satellization, now focused exclusively around one person. Paula's world had, as its absolute
center, her husband. She subordinated herself totally to his demands
and she never experienced herself as in opposition to him. To feel
one is in opposition, one has to feel a reciprocal subject-object relationship with the other. Paula had never constructed a world in
this way; she was out of contact with those feelings that can be
identified by saying, "I want. . . ." She had no self-as-subject. The
extent to which Ed was really the initiator of his irresponsible behavior, and the extent to which it was provoked by his wife's
behavior, we cannot tell. But we can assure ourselves that this is the
kind of world that Paula saw and thus "created."

This meant also that Paula's temporalization was still a
makeshift holding action, not pointed toward a future but aimed
at securing a tolerable present, with the haunting failures of the
past immanent in every action. At this point in her life we can see
the temporalization problem more clearly. It is not that she did not
ever think of the future. She almost certainly looked forward to his
return when he was gone and she may indeed have asked herself
whether Ed would ever be able to hold a job and to support the
family. In fact, Paula's experience of time was paced according to
her husband's periods at home. As each one ended she marked
time until the next one came. Temporalization is a more subtle and

yet more important issue than whether one *thinks* of the future. It is a question of whether one *is* of the future.

To wonder, to anticipate, even to plan is not necessarily *living into* the future. They are perhaps the cognitive component. To hope and to long for something might be the emotional component. To make arrangements by concrete action in the present may be the connative aspect. One's being is more yet than the sum of these parts. It is dependent, first of all, on the *content* of these activities. Does the thematic content reflect the past? For Paula it clearly did to an overwhelming degree. Second, we must recall that being is "I-aming." Was Paula's aming one of growth and change? It was not. The being she aimed at was static. Open-endedness and unpredictableness spelled only threat to her. In part this follows from being so severely satellized. To experience oneself as an object is to hope to have an unchanging essence, as objects do. If their essence changes, it is only a rusting or a rotting, a deterioration in time into an "old thing," weathered and worn out. *Things* do not grow nor do they transform themselves. They are mere passive recipients of the corrosive effects of time. Paula was Ed's object, and her physical deterioration would eventually make her a less desirable object. The thing-aspect of human being, the given physical processes, set the entire theme for her experiencing of herself. We note that after the breast operation and after the second pregnancy, Paula's physical being actually did deteriorate. She lost more weight, had a tipped uterus, experienced a corroding of the cervix, and developed a nasty skin disease that destroyed the "pretty" Paula forever. These bodily events are not accidental. They are part of the deterioration process of one's physical self that both expressed and further solidified her stultified and futureless being. The only future ahead, from the standpoint of this kind of being, is continued loss and finally death.

But most important of all, an authentic future-oriented temporalization is by definition under one's own "authorship." Authenticity implies self-creation through decisions. Paula Kress felt trapped; she constructed her world as a trap. There were no options open to her. She has closed off alternatives, limited her freedom, by constructing a world so enslaved to the past. One never really shakes free of the past entirely, of course. Much of it is objectively given. But to make it the predominant mode of interpreting the present and the future is to abdicate one's freedom entirely.

How often can we see options in the lives of others that they cannot see, or that they reject because of some "meaning" the options might have to them from their past? Objectively, Paula's situation was meager, of course, with an inadequate income, housing situation, and marriage. But subjectively she made it even worse by her unwillingness (inability) to oppose her husband, present herself as a subject rather than as his object, to have desires he could fulfill and thus to grow, with him, into an authentic being. Her very acquiescent choice of him as a husband in the first place was a move of her own, but it was not subjectively affirmed by her as a series of future possibilities. It was controlled by her holding action against the loss of herself as object. It was, in a word, a continuation of her satellization.

Paula Kress's future is "deteriorative" rather than "status striving" or "fantastic" (see Chapter 7), although there are elements of all three of these in her being. She has in common with the status-striver a definition of herself from the outside. But for her this outside is the single person of Ed rather than an impersonal system of prestige hierarchies. And her images of the future, like the purely fantastic future, have little connection to the given or to concrete action.

Paula's satellization and stultified temporalization grow naturally out of her prior being and become solidified in her marriage to Ed. There are also some changes in her being that the marriage provoked. Her body, for one thing, comes to play a slightly different role. As before, her physical attractiveness was a key to her security, for it made her a desirable object. But for the first time, she seems to be explicitly aware that she has sexual desires. Sexual desire can be the occasion of a new kind of being-in-the-world. It can solidify one's subjectness and feeling of agency, and it can establish a relatedness to another that makes the subject-object relationship reciprocal. One's body can become a "lived body," an intimate part of one's self-as-subject. Paula's experience of her body did not progress this way; it remained an instrument and object in her satellized world. She could not even masturbate successfully. But it was no longer possible, as it had been before, to pretend it and its impulses do not exist. Paula had to confront an aspect of "the given" that had, up until her marriage, been successfully hidden from herself.

To understand what this confrontation meant to her, we must remind ourselves why her bodily feelings had been so severely excluded from her attention. Beginning with her body-language rejection of her mother as a child, through her body-language rebellion against her "prettiness" (the boils) as an adolescent, the content of the messages within the primary life-space were perceived by her as "the devil coming out." Had Paula entered these messages into the political arena explicitly, they would have destroyed the uneasy security she felt in her satellization. And satellization for Paula was her only security. Her being-in-the-world and concommitant experience of self-as-subject were undermined, we recall, from the very beginning. To shake up her satellization was to destroy everything, and just at that time her father, to whom she had long been satellized, had a serious, nearly fatal fall from a ladder.

But in her marriage, she experienced bodily, sexual impulses. Against the background of her single source of security, this created a serious crisis. We can also say it was an important opportunity to establish an alternative and superior source of security for Paula, but everything conspired against it. The crisis was met by an even more desperate attempt to be a pleasing object.

Her husband was sexually insatiable. Had he not been so (or had she not construed him in this way), we might hope that Paula's sexuality might have led to an experience of self-as-subject from which she could operate in a more secure way. But she saw her sexual performance through her husband's eyes, and she saw him condemn it as inadequate. This occurred at the same time that she suddenly perceived "selfishness" and "meanness" in herself, and she attempted to become "good."

We may talk, at this point, about a new aspect of her being, or at least a new importance of her *being-for-herself.* As before, her damning judgment of herself came from the perceived judgment of others, but for the first time (as far as we know), it comes into the focus of her attention and it motivates a self-consciously planned self-improvement program. For the first time, we might guess, Paula experienced guilt for what she had *done,* that is, "normal guilt," instead of guilt for what she was.

One tragedy of Paula Kress's life-history was that this "normal guilt" had so little in the way of subject-initiated activity to attach itself to. Her sins were construed by her as "selfishness," but we are hard-pressed to find examples of such traits in her past behavior. What happened here in Paula's twentieth year was that a new kind of self-consciousness, being-for-herself, was being subordinated to her being-for-others. She is not enough in contact with her desires or values to make an independent judgment of herself. Therefore her husband's condemnation, occurring at a time of heightened satellization, proves decisive in determining her view of herself. Normal guilt is never really given a chance to develop.

Nevertheless, the mental act of examining oneself is established firmly at this time, and Paula proceeds with her life in a more acute self-consciousness. It is also possible for her, in this new self-consciousness, to find grounds for tolerating her bodily desires. She is still unable to feel comfortable enough with her impulses to act them out as-a-subject, but she is able to prevent a total breakdown of her being (as in psychosis) by accepting, on a superficial level, her own sexuality. The overall self-judgment is damning, but there remains a self to judge.

In the crisis, therefore, of Paula's marriage, we see some slight signs of growth from our point of view. Crises frequently produce growth. But we also see how it was poisoned by her radical satellization and how, from her point of view, it led simply to self-condemnation.

F. Mother and children

Having children is a profound psychological and existential event. Parenthood, particularly motherhood, demands a reordering of one's body in space and time, of one's identity, of all aspects of oneself. Some people are, of course, relatively more open to these changes and resolutions, others are relatively closed to them. Paula, as we might expect, was not in a position to make full use of her motherhood for her own growth. Not unlike many parents, the children were seen as extensions of herself, and the cacophony of feelings about herself got imposed upon the children. We "create" our children in more ways than just biologically. We also "create" them as we create our world; or more accurately, we place them into our created world in a particular way, having expectations of them, feelings about them, and impulses toward them.

To bear a child is to become a part of the cosmic process of life and the worldly process of human history in a more immediate and personal way. For many people whose being has ceased becoming and who have cut off their future, the future of their children serves to make life meaningful in a way otherwise closed to them. For Paula, we do not see a reordering of her temporalization. Her children are not "futures" but merely present burdens, and what is worse, remnants of the past. But most significantly of all, we see Paula punishing them so they do not disturb her husband, her neighbors, or her mother. Like her own person, she tries to make them acceptable to others. They are pawns in her complex games of being-for-others. Her overriding experience of her children, like her experience of herself, is through the eyes of others. And she sees in their gaze rejection and disapproval.

Most new mothers are able to reverse roles with their own mothers and reexperience their childhood from their mother's point of view, thus working out many problems that have never before been faced in the light of adult perspective. And motherhood is also an opportunity to reexperience oneself in the present from the point of view of the child by remembering something of one's own childhood constructions of one's own mother. Nature is indeed wonderful to have arranged it so that no one *becomes* a mother without having *had* a mother.

While Paula Kress is living with her two sons in the housing project, she uses her mother as a babysitter. Her view is that her mother is incompetent at the job. She worries that her mother will "neglect" the children. This concern is at least partly a veiled expression of anger at her mother for having "neglected" *her*. As usual, however, for Paula, who still fears "the devil coming out" in her own anger at her mother, it is one step removed from a direct being-in-the-world. It does, however, suggest that Paula also may have had some direct concern for her children.

This orientation to her mother is new. She is able to see her mother as her object, to judge and condemn her. She is no longer limited to the experience of herself as her mother's object. It is perhaps the healthiest thing we have seen in the life-history up to this time. Regrettably, if predictably, it does not last. Her mother's

judgment of her as a financial burden motivates Paula to seek out a
job; and to enable Paula to work, her mother babysits. Paula has,
in this move, regressed again to satellization around her mother. If
there was any concern about her mother's incompetence as a babysitter and any desire to protect her children from her mother, these
are subordinated to her desire to please her mother and her submission to her mother's definition of the situation. We can assure ourselves that Paula's working did not solve any real practical problem since she gave the money to Ed and since it evolved into a
contest with her mother for the saving of face. Paula refused to quit
working before her mother gave up babysitting.

This regression is followed by yet another one in which she
resumes her flirting with men. We see now the additional ration-
alization that her attempt to be nice to people only resulted in their
being less kind to her and that one must put oneself first, in this
dog-eat-dog world. In one sense, the cognition that "being nice"
didn't solve her problem was right. For to Paula, being nice meant
to be-for-the-other so pervasively that one ceases being oneself. This
does evoke from others a contemptuous using of oneself by others
and so Paula was correct. But this cognition, while *thought,* was
not really *lived.* Her world did not really become dog-eat-dog. She
did not become predatory.

What she became, in fact, was like she had been in her late
adolescence. She seduced men with her sexiness as a way of seeking
out a new god to whom to satellize herself and was, as before,
strangely indifferent and naive about the results of her behavior.
The hazy fog again moves in to obscure the facts of sexuality.
Throughout her affair, rape, pregnancy, abortion, and D and C
she remains oblivious to what was really happening. As before, the
male response to her behavior was puzzling and disconnected from
her own action, which in turn was disconnected from her bodily
feelings.

At the time of the illegitimate pregnancy, Paula experienced
both pride and shame. As we might expect, she felt very little toward the young man who had impregnated her. If ever there was
a time that Paula might have felt normal guilt, for what she had
done instead of what she *was,* this was it. We see, however, that
her experience of herself did not include a firm enough being-for-
herself to make a judgment on what she had done.

This episode is followed by yet another, and final, round with her husband, Ed, during which we see yet another, dreary repetition of her extreme satellization. However, Paula does manage finally to oppose her husband, enough to have a fight and enough to get a divorce, although the divorce was largely his idea. This rebellion, like the one a couple of years before against her mother, impresses us again as a "healthy" sign. Of course she should have worked this out and achieved a self-as-subject years ago in her childhood. But in the midst of Paula's life-history, any rebellion looks healthy. Even so, it is doubtful whether Paula experienced "jealousy" in the usual sense. Jealousy requires that the other be a possession that could be lost. Paula was not subject enough to possess; she could only be possessed. What happened was that Paula experienced the panic of a satellized child who loses his god. Paula did not lose something she chose; she lost the feeling of "being chosen." A "chosen people," who are satellized to a god, can hardly undergo a more severe trauma than to cease having such a relationship to their god.

The divorce was, therefore, the occasion of some reshuffling for Paula. Not surprisingly we note two things: that her being-for-herself underwent a period of some growth, and that the reshuffling did not profoundly change her approach to, marriage of, and relationship with the new Ed. She underwent the following sequence: her father died, she married Ed II, gave birth to Margo, made a new covenant, this time with the theological God, became disenchanted with her new husband, and finally made the move to the Chicago suburb that triggered the neurotic symptoms in full force.

G. The creation of a psychological illness

The symptoms with which Paula confronted her therapist were an inability to eat, a particularly bad episode of the old trouble with diarrhea and vomiting, and for the first time, anxiety attacks that kept her confined to her bedroom—in other words, agoraphobia. The precipitating crisis was the move from her mother's house in the city to a suburban home. To understand this picture we need to have the large perspective of her entire life-history, and we need to remind ourselves that Paula's world-creation got started in a particular way that influenced how she created her entire life-history. Her original world was severely bifurcated along the lines of how she perceived her two parents. In addition; each world was a world of satellization, which we have seen lasted over thirty years. Furthermore, we note an uncommonly severe involvement in, confusion about, and detachment from her own body, which is characterized, as all satellization is characterized, by an objectification of the self and a concommitant lack of that base of operations we have called "self-as-subject" and a similar lack of the experience of body-as-subject.

Paula spent her life recreating her two worlds from situation to situation. She was able to survive the death of her father as well as she did because of her covenant with God and because of her relationship to her second husband, which was perhaps the happiest relationship she ever had. However, she expected more than her husband could deliver in making everything all right for her, and in his progressive ill-health, he became more dependent upon *her*. However, as she weathered the various crises, we saw a halting but at times hopeful development of a self-concept, of a being-for-herself that constituted a future and a desire to actualize that future in concrete action. In trying to do this, Paula makes her "first real decision," to move. It is not a radical change into a firmly based experience of herself-as-subject, but it goes further toward the feeling of agency and initiative than anything before it.

In following this self-concept, Paula demonstrated great courage, greater courage than she had ever had. The decision was all the more difficult to make in light of her familiarity with and relative comfort in a satellized world. This was a move dramatically away from satellization and into a future where all the old sources of security would be missing. As inadequate as it is as a source of security, being-an-object-for-others is a lot safer than moving toward being-a-subject, where responsibility for decisions is unavoidable and where one must rely upon one's own criteria. Paula's move was in that direction and it is, therefore, a moment of important growth.

But she moved too quickly. Her being-for-herself (i.e., self-concept, ideal self) that guided her decision was too severely out of joint with her life-long being-for-others, particularly her satellization to mother. When the actual moving process began, and she saw her home being dismantled, her mother being left behind, and her life displaced, she had two possible contexts in terms of which to experience these sights and sounds. It could have meant she was becoming what her ideal self said she should become (her being-for-herself), and it also could have meant the loss of what she had been and the loss of the satellized world in which she was merely an object (her being-for-others). Her mother, husband, and brother were all skeptical of her decision. To stick to the decision meant to relinquish them as the definers of her life. To affirm a self-ideal yields a quite different experience of moving from that view proffered from outside.

As we see, when the chips were down, Paula's history predominated; the past, not the future, determined the meaning of moving. The stakes were so high that when she lost, she experienced a panic more severe than she had ever experienced. The future and hope collapsed under the weight of being alone without a god (the theological God proved inadequate) and she was unable even to leave her bedroom without experiencing panic.

We see in Paula's struggle a brand of heroism and of tragedy. We can only hope that she finds the courage to try again after this crisis is past. A successful attempt at growth of this magnitude may even acquaint her with her feelings of agency, of self-as-subject. We are impressed with the desire for growth in the face of what appears to be a very adverse life-history so far, and we hope she does not cease to struggle.

Being an obsessive 9

Paula Kress was, according to traditional psychopathological nosology, an anxiety hysteric. Diagnostic categories evolve, and as we continue to discover better ways of seeing psychopathology, they will continue to evolve. In this chapter we will talk about a well-established and familiar category, the obsessive-compulsive. Hysteria and obsessions are the two major "transference neuroses" in the psychoanalytic view (Freud, 1959b) and they differ from one another and from the "narcissistic neuroses" in particular psychoanalytic ways. There are certain similarities and differences among the cases reported here, and the case of Paula Kress as well. The content of these differences and similarities are, however, construed differently. As we occasionally did in the case of Paula Kress, we shall use psychoanalytic thought as a standard for comparison and a contrast for our evolving sense of the existential dimensions of psychopathology.

1. The Rat Man

For anyone who has ever attempted to understand obsessions, Freud's "Notes upon a case of obsessional neurosis" (1959a) must remain a ground-breaking treatise. There is obvious explanatory power to the metaphor of an impulse in mortal struggle with an inhibition: cathexis versus countercathexis, id versus superego, desire versus guilt, doing something compulsively and just as compulsively undoing it. Let us, however, change the metaphors to those of phenomenology to see if we can find additional leverage for understanding this perplexing and difficult symptom.

Freud reports that his patient removed a stone from the road, upon which he had stumbled, so as to avoid the outside chance that his beloved, who would soon pass by in a carriage, might wreck her carriage. After a few minutes further walk, the patient realized that such an act was ridiculous and he reprimanded himself for having gone through the excessive worry. He then felt compelled to return the stone to its original place. Freud finds an impulse and an inhibition in both acts, as well as conflicting impulses (love and hate) and conflicting inhibitions ("Don't worry so much," and "Protect her from your own hate"). And this is just the beginning of the complexity.

Let us ask different questions about this typical obsessive experience. Stubbing a toe is troublesome, but the obsessive patient must make it a major incident. Why? What was happening in his experience, in his being, during this episode? To stub a toe is to feel oneself directly in contact with the object world. Oneself is subject, here, moving in space, encountering obstacles and overcoming them. The patient may have taken revenge on the stone by kicking it angrily out of his way without leaving this predominant mode of being at the time, being-in-the-world, or he may simple have ignored it. But the patient, in typical obsessive fashion, leaves the orientation of simple moving through space, of being-in-the-world, and acts out other aspects of his being in peculiar ways. He makes a point of removing the stone to protect his beloved, and then returns, after some minutes, to replace it.

Removing the stone is a purposively moral act. It seems to imply, indeed it *requires* the question, "What will others think of me for leaving the obstacle there?" (being-for-others), or the question, "What would a really conscientious chap like me do in such a situation?" (being-for-myself). Conventional morality always involves such questions, and neither is particularly obsessive or neurotic. But the patient's morality was so compelling that he seemingly had no choice about removing the stone; he could not live with the guilt of having failed to protect his beloved. Having so failed would have yielded condemnation in his or in others' eyes. The important point here is the compelling quality of the experience so that his being an object for himself or for others completely preempts his original experience of moving as a subject in the space of the object world. The experiences of guilt and shame usurp all others.

Going back to replace the stone is of course a continuation of these modes of being: "What if someone saw my absurd act?" "How can I respect myself after yielding to such childish whims?" Either self-esteem ("I am a good person for removing the stone") or identity ("I am the sort of person who helps you") were possible experiences accompanying the moral act of removing the stone, but for the obsessive patient these experiences are far from possible. Guilt and shame are too strong.

We have now described the episode in terms of the three aspects of being. The stone's presence, and the patient's action in relation to it, have peculiar *meanings* to the patient. We can understand something of these meanings in existential terms. In Chapter 3 we pointed out that what an event *means* to a person depends on the particular quality of being at the time. In the example in that chapter, I interpreted my patient's behavior as "angry." He then ceased being angry (being-in-the-world) and ceased being indignant (being-for-himself) but perpetrated his being a good patient, or what he thought I judged a good patient to be (being-for-others). We said that his being-for-others was therefore the relevant context in terms of which he construed my remark. We also pointed out that as Paula Kress observed her furniture being moved, it could have taken its meaning from her being-for-herself or from her being-for-others. The latter predominated because of the way she *was* (was aming) at the time.

When Freud's patient stubbed his toe, the relevant context was his being-for-himself, for he was obsessed exactly with living up to unrealistic images of himself and had been for many years. Being-for-himself has thus become so prominent in his experience that periodically any vestige of being-in-the-world was completely buried and he became unable to function in a normal way. So it was, when he failed to experience himself as a subject who meets and overcomes obstacles in his path; so it was with Paula Kress; and so it is with neurosis generally, as described in Chapter 5.

But there are nonpathological ways to be-for-oneself. Why did Freud's patient suffer guilt instead of self-esteem? Why was his act one of avoiding punishment (of himself) instead of gaining praise (of himself)? Freud is no doubt correct in his assumption that we must see this symptom within the context of his entire relationship to his beloved, and that a fundamental love-hate ambivalence in this relationship underlies the symptom in an important way. He further traces the origin of the hate to the fact that the patient strongly identified with his father, who disapproved of the girl. Freud thus insists, rightly, that to understand the relationship to the girl, we must look to an even larger context of his whole life. Our view, which seeks to employ the concept of being, which is the most inclusive activity we participate in, can hardly disagree with Freud's directions here.

Identification with father has come to mean something different for us from what it meant for Freud. We have replaced the metaphor of energy dynamics with existential metaphors. Freud's accompanying analysis is complicated enough to impress us with his appreciation of the complexity of it all, but is he, finally, being complex about the right things?

Drawing on our discussion in Chapter 4, we may say that identification is a complex combination of being-for-oneself and being-for-others. It therefore becomes crucial for understanding Freud's patient to understand as much as we can of how the patient experienced his father and how he experienced himself in relation to his father. We will eventually argue that for Freud's patient and for obsessives in general, being-for-oneself looms large, indeed completely swamps one's being in general. We will argue further that such being-for-oneself is born of a particular being-for-a-particular-other with whom one has identified in a particular way.

Freud tells us that the patient's father had married a girl of position and wealth after having been in love with a girl whose poverty would have retarded his career. The patient had been currently engaged in a conflict similar to his father's (or as he construed his father's in fantasy). Freud remarks of the patient:

> And he resolved this conflict, which was in fact one between his love and the persisting influence of his father's wishes, by falling ill; or, to put it more correctly, by falling ill he avoided

the task of resolving it in real life. It is worth emphasizing that this flight into illness was made possible by his identifying himself with his father. The identification enabled his affects to regress on to the residues of his childhood (1959a, p. 336).

Freud then documents this conclusion by taking us through the network of connecting associations, of masturbation and of the rat fantasy for which the case is named, of anal eroticism and oral aggression, and many other intricately related elements.

One of the key episodes with which the symptom started was having been severely punished by his father for masturbating.

This punishment, according to my hypothesis, had, it was true, put an end to his masturbating, but on the other hand it had left behind it an ineradicable grudge against his father and had established him for all time in his role of an interferer with the patient's sexual enjoyment (Freud, 1959a, p. 342).

We have to conclude that the network of associations that are discovered in the patient's analysis are ingeniously put together by Freud, but that the cement of their connection is quite unclear. Associationism helps us to formulate associations, but it does not allow us to see the network as a whole, which is more than the sum of its parts, nor to comment upon what is happening with respect to the being of the patient. Freud is correct when he sees the symptom as an outgrowth of the patient's inability to make a decision, but the metaphors in terms of which he talks about that decision tend to direct our attention away from the psychology of making decisions—away from the anxiety of personal responsibility and the attempts to escape that anxiety by devious lies and self-objectification.

Let us recall the phenomenon of satellization, where the child experiences himself as the object of the god-parent at the cost of his experience of himself-as-subject. The experience of guilt emerges from that of shame when the criteria of judgment are internalized from the parent. When this internalization occurs within the context of prolonged and accentuated satellization, guilt is guilt for *what one is* (as-an-object) rather than for what one *does* (as-a-subject). The experience of oneself-as-an-object pervades the experiential life and crowds out one's being-as-a-subject. As in the case of Paula Kress, this shall be the direction of our account of the childhood background of the patient's symptom. Unlike Paula Kress, however, being-for-oneself is the predominant kind of self-objectification.

The patient is now, as an adult, caught in a conflict between his love for a girl and the inhibition of that love because of its violation of his identification with his father, and the consequent production of hate for the girl. The attraction toward the girl is of the nature of being-in-the-world, but it is poisoned by an invasion within the patient's being of his being-for-his-father, and eventually by his being-for-himself. His being-for-himself, stemming from the pathological identification with his father, contradicts his being-in-the-world, his love for the girl. The guilt that emerges is not from what he docs, for he is a long way from being free enough to act on his desires, but from what he is (as object), namely, a bad boy. It is exactly this experience of himself as a bad boy that interferes with his ability to live out a normal life.

The obsessive's predominant being-for-himself robs him of his immediate contact with the world and every action becomes the occasion of scrupulous self-judgment. The experience of self-as-subject, therefore, is rare indeed for the obsessive. Angrily kicking the stone out of the way is out of the question. The experiences of agency and initiative, in which one feels a pull from the environment and a push from within, and furthermore can freely move in his physiognomic life-space to obey these demands on the basis of decisions made and actions taken, these experiences are blocked by excruciating self-doubts, impossible New Year's Resolutions, and perpetual guilt and self-punishment. One's very basis for being at all (self-as-subject) is therefore smothered by the obsession itself, by a tormenting being-for-oneself.

Security is therefore replaced by anxiety. The reaction to the anxiety is further involvement in being-for-oneself. "If I can be really good at all times, I won't have to feel this way," the obsessive says. He then calculates the good (which itself can be quite time consuming) and tries to escape the anxiety by faithfully fulfilling the requirements. The demands become enormous. Any disturbance is terribly threatening, for he vaguely realizes that his anxiety is there, ready to swamp him at any time. Insignificant events, such as stubbing one's toe, then have the meaning for him that is determined by the predominance of this particular being-for-himself.

The problem is not, properly construed, one of unconscious associations. The problem is one of the patient's being. The solution is not to make conscious these unconscious associations; the solution is to make the patient aware of options he is unable to see. This is more than quibbling with words. This difference of theory has elaborate consequences for therapy, as we shall see in later chapters.

2. *The World of the Obsessive*

Having come to some conclusions about what is involved in being an obsessive, it is important to draw further on Chapters 6 and 7 and recognize that one's being, as understood here, has immediate and direct implications for how one construes the world. Let us recall the tenuous nature of the security of one whose being is dominated by his being-for-himself. His excessive demands upon himself are attempts to maintain this security. The world, then, itself becomes fearsome. Life becomes fearsome. Both are terribly unpredictable in many respects, and the renowned quest for order and more order pervades the life of the obsessive. Disorder is omnipresent and terrifying.

There are, then, two main features of the obsessive world: (*a*) It threatens to look at him, make him its object and make him ashamed, to which his response is to objectify himself even more vigilantly, and (*b*) it threatens to invade his experience with chaos and destroy the tenuous security he has achieved by his own self-objectification and by his imposition of order. Each of these deserves further phenomenological description.

The pioneering paper on the phenomenology of the obsessive's world is that of von Gebsattel (1958) whose fundamental assumption is that there is normally a certain physiognomy to the world, a map of attractions and repulsions, a light goodness and dark evil, in which objects are always "somehow animated or tuned and can, therefore, speak to us in a fundamental way. It is only that these physiognomic structures become almost completely hid-

den from us through the categorical-rational ones (1958, p. 183)."
Any of us can become aware of this physiognomy, of course, if we
open ourselves to it, and it constitutes the richness and immediacy
of meaning when one is-in-the-world. For the obsessive, however,
this sort of being and the physiognomic world that accompanies it
threaten the tenuous stability of his being-for-himself. Frightening
are

> all the features of the world which call for connection and
> union with it and thus make possible the extension of one's
> own existence, the moving into the world and being active in it,
> penetrating into it—conquest, joy, activity, spreading out. Indeed,
> it can also be plainly shown that the world of the anankastic
> [obsessive] is characterized by the omission of the harmless, the
> obvious, and the natural. What is called by Scheler the "ecstatic
> possession of world-contents" and by E. Straus "sympathetic com-
> munication" is here impeded. Threat and repulsion are all that
> remain (Von Gebsattel, 1958, pp. 184–185).

This happens to all of us some of the time, but why does it
happen to the obsessive in the pervading and uncompromising way
that it does? This alienation from the world is, in our terms, an
alienation of experience from self-as-subject and from being-in-the-
world. The world is threatening to the obsessive because his entire
being is based on a shaky experiential foundation. He construes the
world to be threatening because it is, in his terms, threatening
indeed. The meaning of the world to him stems not from the activity
of being-in-the-world, but from the desperate activities of his particular kind of being-for-himself. Everything in the world has some
potential relationship to that which is morbid and frightening. To
see only this part of the world's physiognomy is to be preoccupied
with the threat to oneself-as-object. Having no experiential sense of
oneself-as-subject makes the object world into the Great Subject
which threatens to objectify him, expose him, indeed destroy the
only self he has.

The relationship of these experiential anomalies with satellization and with the often-noted "magical" quality of obsessions
in general is easy to understand. The satellization experience, in
which one *is* the object of the god-parent, is recalled in the seeming
oppressiveness of the world to the obsessive. The threat becomes,

in the extreme case, the panic of the total loss of self-as-subject. Occasionally an obsessive patient, in a desperate attempt to have a self of any kind, must resort to paranoid delusions about the power of the environment (see Part IV). Usually a stable obsessive style of being leaves a minimum of rebellious self-as-subject which, in an effort to avoid the panic of selflessness, stubbornly affirms itself in magical and compulsive response to the physiognomic world.

3. The Obsessive Structuring of Time

Time is, the adage tells us, money; and money is, Freud tells us, feces. Be that as it may, time can become a commodity, and it is frequently horded and wasted by the obsessive just as profoundly as money, feces, and anything else. To strive for order in one's material life can be quite adaptive in our complex society, but to invade the experience of time with the same nervous overstructuring is to distort something special in human experience. For time is the great destroyer and great creator, and it passes relentlessly. The important question is whether one can accept this given quality of immediate experience or whether one must protect oneself from it.

We accept this given only on the basis of hope, and we can hope only on the basis of the kind of security that comes from the experience of oneself-as-subject. Oneself-as-object is vulnerable to deterioration with time, if not to outright destruction in the face of future events. Like things, it is static, has an essence, and does not fit with the primordial experience of life, which flows, which changes the nature of things and is unpredictable.

Oneself-as-subject, on the other hand, is not thing-like; it is a process, is alive and grows. The future is thus welcome, an infinite series of possibilities. Being-in-the-world is profoundly temporal, extending into the future. The present is embedded in a temporal flux that is familiar and comfortable, if one can be-in-the-world. It is quite different, of course, for the obsessive whose self is limited to being-an-object.

It is of course true that we are part object and that the object part of ourselves deteriorates with time. Eventually it dies. But for that to be all of one's life is a particular distortion of experience that is already a death, a death of one's being-in-the-world.

Von Gebsattel describes a patient whose obsessive world includes a foul odor, which appears to the patient as a product of his physical body.

> Behind this appearance, and making it possible, stands H. H.'s incapacity to let his energies stream into the implementation of a task-oriented self-development and thereby to purify himself from the stagnation of energy. This incapacity is the actual disturbance, perhaps related to the endogenic depressive inhibition; in any case, a choking or blocking of the life course is evidenced in it; therewith is impeded the temporalization of life—"Becoming" is blocked, and the past is fixated (Von Gebsattel, 1958, p. 176).

So we may say that, for the obsessive, the future is blocked. We can understand the "living into the future" that characterizes being-in-the-world and supplies hope for the normal person. The obsessive is denied, or rather denies himself, this luxury. But there is also something important about what the obsessive does with the past. The self-as-subject is an activity that flows out of the past smoothly, with some continuity and familiarity. For the self-as-subject, the past is inherent in the present but does not dominate it. Von Gebsattel describes the situation as follows:

> Normally, life purifies itself through its devotion to the forces of the future and the tasks that challenge us from the direction of the future. If, through the inhibition of his course toward self-realization, the person is kept back from the deep well-spring of the capacity to "Become" and to repay the debt of existence, there awakens within him a vague sense of guilt, as we find it oftentimes in inhibited melancholics; this vague sense of guilt concretizes in the latter as self-reproach which may approach delusional thoughts—thoughts that are incorrigible because they are nourished by the generalized inhibition in the capacity of becoming (1958, p. 178).

We are able, with our formulation of what is involved in an obsessive being-for-oneself, to specify something of what is involved in this guilt. For the "Rat Man," for example, all contemporaneous experience was construed in terms of the patient's particular kind of being-for himself, which solidifies the past and makes it oppressive in the present. It is not of course simply self-objectification that is oppressive; self-objectification is quite inevitable. It is the rigidity and demanding quality of the experience of self-as-object that makes it the concretion of satellization and false security.

So the future is closed and the past is oppressive to the obsessive. What is his reaction to life under these circumstances? The present becomes particularly static and all one can do is hold the line against the passage of time and against the memory of time, both of which threaten to bring chaos into his experience. Like the physiognomy of the spatial and object world, events in time are not the rich source of experiential variety but a threatening source of disruption. The obsessive attempts, in his bizarre attempt to hold the line, to make everything predictable, to protect himself from the experience of surprise and novelty and to allow nothing to chance. He dare not "let things be" for the nature of life is change and unpredictability.

It is well to recall that the obsessive experience of time and of the world are choices one makes, as indeed the solidification of oneself-as-object was a choice made at an earlier time. The choice was to avoid anxiety; the result is paradoxically to experience it more painfully in its neurotic form. Like death, pain, ambiguity, and a thousand other kinds of human finitude, anxiety can be escaped only at the costs of one's being-in-the-world, of the perversion of one's being-for-oneself, and the fear of being-for-others.

4. An Existential Obsession

I would like to report a particular obsession that is unusually instructive because of the themes it includes and the experiences it entails. The obsession is:

> There is some point in the future at which I will die. It will be, say, on the 10th of March, 1990. That means that the 10th of this month, of last month and of next month were the anniversaries of my death. They passed and I did not know the real meaning of the day as I was living it. Today may be such an anniversary, and I would not know it. How terrible it is to live through such anniversaries without being aware of what they

mean. Furthermore, it will happen at some particular time of day. I have lived all these days not knowing which minute was my death's anniversary. It is terrifying.

The patient thus lived in dread of every minute, every day, every month and year, for each might be an anniversary and his ignorance of it was profoundly disturbing. The existential themes are death and time. These two themes are not unrelated, since we can appreciate death only because we temporalize life, that is, experience it within a temporal continuity.

This individual has executed a particular movement in his being in response to the most poignant of the existential givens. The first thing to note is the *fear* of death. This fear preempts all other possible attitudes toward death that the patient could have. In spite of the fact that there is a lot of false bravado about this issue, perhaps even among existentialists, it is true that fear is not the only possible attitude toward death and it certainly need not obscure all others.

The second thing to note about the obsession is that the fear of death has become, for this patient, a fear of life. The whole future of possibilities is destroyed by the one great necessity. A sense of the possible, which is that open-ended feeling toward the future without which we could not be, is lost in the confrontation with the sense of the necessary. Both attitudes are healthy and realistic; the elimination of either is pathological, and we have seen that obsessives particularly have lost the sense of the possible.

The sense of the possible is particularly related to the experience of the self-as-subject and the sense of the necessary to the experience of the self-as-object. In this obsession, the patient seems to be saying that the most terrifying feature of his situation is that he does not know whether today is an anniversary. To know is to control; he seems to be complaining that he has lost control. This is an expression of a longing for the experience of himself-as-subject.

But he asks for too much. He asks for a kind of omnipotence that would destroy his sense of the necessary. No one knows when he will die, and to demand this as a condition of having a sense of the possible is a way of excluding the possibility of having a sense of the possible. This exclusion is consistent with the obsessive's problem: he has no future.

So this particular obsession expresses a longing for the feeling of agency involved in knowing and does so in such an extreme way as to perpetuate his not having it. The lesson from this is that one cannot have a sense of the possible that is sound without having a sense of the necessary. One cannot have a future without an ending, nor a self-as-subject without a self-as-object; in a word, one cannot be without the limits of nonbeing. This patient's experience of himself as an object (objects of course have no future and they are subject to decay with time) preempts his experience of himself as a subject because he has not faced the limits of his subjectness, his finitude and his death.

It would seem that the patient does face death, that his problem is that he cannot forget death. Perhaps if he could be conditioned to forget the topic, or persuaded that life is beautiful and should be the focus of his attention, then he would quit his morbid preoccupation. Perhaps, but I think not. The problem is more than one of his obsession; it is one of his being. What makes him sick is not that he can't forget death but that his particular manner of being does not allow him to function within the limits of the existential situation. And we have seen that to change his particular manner of being will have to involve an existential reshuffling, not merely a rearrangement of his attention. He needs a foundation for life that can only come in the experience of himself-as-subject, and those developmental conditions out of which one emerges as a self-as-subject were somehow denied him.

The obsession is also instructive in that death, the prototype of existential limitation, provokes fear. There was no religious fear of hell-after-death, no regret about unfulfilled obligations or people hurt by his death, there was just bleak, blanching terror. Under what circumstances do *limits* provoke terror? One answer is that limits are frightening when we are not certain of what they are. A child is much more afraid of his parents' punishment when he is unable to predict the limits of their patience. The child's experience of limits set by his parents is probably not unrelated to his experience with the existential limits of human life, but the relationship is a complex one. The experience, "I can play with the magazines and newspapers but not tear them to shreds" is not dissimilar to "I can become a teacher or a cab driver but not a president of the United States" and to "I have a future in which there are many possibilities but also some necessities." Also, the experience of "I don't know if I can play with *anything* without being punished" is similar to the patients' obsession.

We do not know if the patient had childhood experiences of one or the other kind. The point of mentioning these possibilities is to emphasize the continuity between childhood and adulthood *experiences*. If fear was conditioned and then "generalized" into the adult obsession, then it generalized according to experiential coordinates. The relationship between childhood and adulthood must, therefore be understood in terms of concrete experience.

One closing note about this obsession and obsessions in general. Like the content of dreams, there is a temptation to look beyond the manifest content toward an inferred "latent content" that is being disguised in various ways. This tendency directs our attention away from the being of the patient. It is not irrelevant that the world looks threatening to a dreamer or an obsessive. And certainly to seek a symbolic meaning for the various elements of the threatening dreamed or obsessive world is to miss the most important point, namely, that the patient's being is the most important thing he does. This crucial point has been made elaborately by Boss (1957) and also by Robbins (1955).

References

Boss, M. *The Analysis of Dreams*. London: Ryder, 1957.

Freud, S. Note upon a case of obsessional neurosis. In *The Collected Papers of Sigmund Freud*. Vol. 3. New York: Basic Books, 1959. (a)

Freud, S. On narcissism: An introduction. In *The Collected Papers of Sigmund Freud*. Vol. 4. New York: Basic Books, 1959. (b)

Robbins, B. S. The myth of latent emotion: A critique of the concept of repression. *Psychotherapy: Journal of the Robbins Institute*, 1955, I, 3.

Von Gebsattel, V. E. The world of the compulsive. In R. May, et al. (Eds.) *Existence*. New York: Basic Books, 1958.

Therapy and the dynamics of being 10

One's being-in-the-world, being-for-others, and being-for-oneself are quite inevitable. They all go on all the time, although at any given instant one may predominate. The other two, however, supply the context for the playing out of the one, and the relationships among the levels are complex and dynamic. Let us first explore the inevitability and interdependence among the three aspects of being.

1. Interaction among the Three Levels of Being

My activity of aming is never separate from the world; the therapeutic questions are whether that world is tolerable and whether that aming is honest. It is an ultimate question, and one that we should worry about, whether honesty makes the world more or less tolerable. It may be that the more honest we are in our relationship to the world, the less tolerable the world becomes. Perhaps the process of development is the process of learning to lie-in-the-world and that the crucial difference between normality and mental illness is merely the social acceptability of the lies.

There are, in addition, examples in history in which honest being-in-the-world has cost people their badge of normality. Socrates and Jesus were probably killed because of their honest confrontation of a world which, because of that honesty, became intolerable. Hence the question of what one is-in-the-world and the judgment of that process in one's being-for-oneself can never be totally independent of how one is perceived by others and hence of one's being-for-others.

Confronting the world honestly certainly involves, at least, a facing of existential anxiety as described in Chapter 5. The neurotic avoidance of this confrontation leads to various kinds of frustration and to neurotic anxiety. A phobia, for example, may be seen as an attempt to concretize the anxiety of being-in-the-world. That is, the world is construed in such a way as to redefine the source and nature of the anxiety. We may, therefore, schematize the neurotic process on this level as:

Existential Given	Neurotic Distortion	Symptomatic Result
existential anxiety	alienation from the experience of being-in-the-world; lying-in-the-world	frustration; neurotic anxiety

My activity of aming is also always partly for-myself. The structure of human consciousness is reflective, and I can never escape being-for-myself for very long. The therapeutic question is whether that aming is guilt-ridden and whether it is honest. Again it is probably the case that honest being-for-myself produces more guilt than certain kinds of lying-for-myself. But we must recall the distinction between guilt about what one *is* (as-object) and what one does (as-subject). The former guilt, which stems from satellization, can be characterized as neurotic, with the obsessive neurotic as an obvious example. The latter guilt is inevitable. We cannot help having hurt people; sometimes life conspires to produce a situation in which one's only choice is whom to hurt. The anxiety that comes before decisions, because we can never anticipate all the consequences of our action, is "given" in the human situation. Inevitable guilt is an *ex-post-facto* version of the same human situation. It comes reflectively and in memory rather than immediately and in anticipation. We may schematize the neurotic process on this level as:

Existential Given	*Neurotic Distortion*	*Symptomatic Result*
guilt for what one has done (as-subject); for choices made	self idealization; lying-for-oneself	guilt for what one is (as-object)

We have said that lying-in-the-world often seeks to evade rather than confront anxiety and produces frustration. The case of the obsessive fear of death, reported in the last chapter, demonstrates how a certain movement in being can transform a fear of death into a fear of life, and how certain lies therefore produce frustration. Similarly, lying-for-oneself often seeks to evade rather than face existential guilt (for what one has done), such as in the creation of an idealized self. Such a movement produces neurotic guilt (for what one is-as-object). The important point here is that these two neurotic movements often produce and support one another. If I am profoundly frustrated in-the-world, one solution is to be predominantly for-myself, to condense my activity of being into the enterprise of self idealization and to strive to live up to that ideal self-as-object. Conversely, if one is caught in such a neurotic process as this, frustration will ensue and the anxiety of being-in-the-world cannot be tolerated. Additional layers of both frustration and guilt are produced in this neurotic process.

My activity of aming is also partly for-others as well. I can never escape for very long the knowledge that others hate me, love me, judge me, and objectify me. The therapeutic question is whether that aming produces shame. Is there an inevitable and universal shame? The answer must be yes, for all the same existential reasons. Shame becomes neurotic when we cannot tolerate it and when we therefore lie-for-others, when we build a house of cards in the interpersonal world. Schematically:

Existential Given	*Neurotic Distortion*	*Symptomatic Result*
existential shame	posing, posturing for others, lying-for-others	neurotic shame

We have seen too how shame produced both guilt and frustration, as well as more shame. Therefore, we can understand the three levels in parallel, each with a similar existential given that is threat-ening in some way, a similar neurotic avoidance of that given, and a result that appears symptomatic. But we must not be too im-pressed with our own model-building. The three levels interact in a complex way within any given life. Being in general is more than the sum of its parts.

The neatness of our conceptual arrangement is therefore not matched by a neatness of what the clinician faces in the clinic. People seek psychotherapy because they have concrete problems with their feelings, their behavior and their relationships, and which they feel unable to handle without professional help. The clinician's job, simply stated, is to help the patient to handle these problems. Conversation will take place, each trying to assess the other, oneself in relation to the other, and the world in view of the relationship. The complexities of what occurs are tremendous, and we hope, in this and the next chapter, to describe in phenomenological-existen-tial terms something of the way the process should work.

The way the therapist looks at what is happening powerfully influences what is happening. This does not mean that looking at therapy this way will make one a good therapist, nor that all good therapists look at it this way. But if it is true that consciousness is the center of the human being, then it follows that we must have a way of looking that allows the therapist to look at that center, that is, we must have a psychology that takes consciousness seriously.

2. *To Let the Other Be*

It is perhaps the most difficult thing for any therapist to let the patient be, for the therapist's role tells him to influence the patient, to change him and to teach him. Ordinary and usual relationships are influential, or to use a less edifying term, manipulative. The ways in which therapy will "let be" and will "manipulate" must be different than usual relationships, and that difference must be specified.

By "letting be" we mean at least three things. We mean, first, letting the patient be-in-the-world, which in turn implies that he be allowed to construe his world as he construes it, to behave in it, feel about it, respond to it, in whatever way he does. To correct what may seem to the therapist a misperception is to run the risk of an argument, with complications in the being-for-the-other of both patient and therapist that need not occur.

Part of the patient's world is of course the therapist. This part is, strictly speaking, the only part about which the therapist is really in possession of superior knowledge. It is certainly a part of the patient's world that can very appropriately be used in the therapeutic process. If the patient does not include the therapist in his world, there can be no therapy. If the therapist presumes to correct the patient's perception of some other part of the world, he is only using his authority.

Other parts of the patient's world are of course important. There are the parts with which the patient has not been able to get along, and the therapist must understand the being of the patient in relation to them in order to understand why the patient is there. If he interferes with the unfolding of the patient's world and therefore fails to understand why the patient is there, he will be no different from the friend next door who offers kindly advice.

The patient's being-in-the-world therefore contains something of his problem and he has come to the therapist for help. Just how this "coming to the therapist" occurs must be seen on all three levels as well. With respect to his being-in-the-world, it is important to know if the therapist is construed as a healer of illness, a confessor for sins, a long-shot chance that might be of some help, a last chance to get life straight, or whether all of these and other possibilities are obscured by the patient's being-for-himself and being-for-others.

Ultimately it is the construing of the therapist that is grist for the therapeutic mill, and that mill operates by the therapist being as he is, which will violate the patient's expectations and force a change in the patient. The dynamics of therapy come from the fact that the therapist will eventually manipulate the patient's being-in-the-world by manipulating part of that world, namely, by being just as he is and nothing else.

"Letting be" means, second, letting the patient be *what* he is to himself. Any friend can tell the guilty person that he is innocent, the ugly person that he is attractive, the person who feels worthless that he is valuable. The person who tells another who feels inferior that he is not inferior fails to let the person be-for-himself. At best this substitutes shame for guilt; it substitutes fear that one will be discovered as really inferior for self-pity about one's inferiority. The person who says to such a person, on the other hand, "What are you going to do about it?" lets the patient be-for-himself and challenges the patient with his own freedom, thus opening the possibility that guilt might be replaced by self esteem, should the patient in fact choose to do something about it. (This is not always a good way to handle feelings of inferiority, for it may interact unfavorably with the patient's being-for-others, such as if he were to construe the therapist as a moralistically demanding agent of society, for example.)

The patient's being-for-himself therefore also contains something of his problem, and he has come to the therapist for help. Has he come to be persuaded by the therapist that he is really lovable, not inferior, or not guilty? The role the therapist plays in the world of the patient is not separate from the patient's being-for-himself. Or has he come to submit his ailing psyche to an expert? This construing of the therapist is a direct derivative of his construing of himself as ailing, weak, inexpert in the process of living life. Or has he come to find a person who will just listen and understand? This construing of the therapist may imply to the patient that he is so complex that no one else can understand him, or that he is so bad that no one else is willing to try.

Should the therapist fail to let the patient be-for-himself, he will fail to understand an important part of what the therapy means to the patient, and will consequently fail to see how being as he is can be therapeutic. Again the therapist's best tool is himself, and insofar as he is able to be as he is, he will not only provoke a reconstruing of the patient's world but also a reconstruing of the patient's self as an object of his (the patient's) judgment.

"Letting be" means, third, letting the patient be as he is-for-others. One important other is the therapist, and patients always begin therapy (as do therapists) with a self-presentation to the other. The therapist must attend to how the patient is being-for-the-therapist as well as how he is being-in-the-world and being-for-himself.

This level of being is the most complex because it involves at least two people, but we can say some useful things about how letting the patient be-for-others is important. The patient's being-for-the-therapist will inevitably involve something different from what the patient is-for-himself because our self revelations are always partial. Every patient will feel a difference between what he really thinks he is and what he thinks the therapist thinks of him. There may or may not be a strong tendency to bring these two levels of being into accord with one another, and if there is, it may come by adjusting what one thinks of oneself to what one thinks the other thinks, or by seeking to inform the other more accurately of what one really thinks of oneself. Each of these contingencies implies something a little different for therapy, and the therapist must be aware of what is going on.

The contradiction between the patient's being-for-himself and his being-for-the-therapist may also come from the fantasy that the therapist can see something in the patient that the patient cannot see. Again this fantasy is not independent of how the patient construes the therapist and how he construes himself.

The therapist is not the only "other" that populates the patient's world, and how the patient is-for-other-others is also of crucial importance. This is an essential part of every life and has a correlate in the therapeutic situation itself. Since the patient's being is always partly for-others, and since this may constitute a crucial point of his being out-of-joint within his being, it is particularly important to let the patient be what he is for-others until he is able to change it on his own.

Premature intervention in the patient's being-for-others occurs in behavior therapy, where patients who feel fearful of their boss are taught, for example, through conditioning techniques, to be otherwise in that relationship. This procedure runs the grave risk of increasing the out-of-jointness between the patient's being-in-the-world and his being-for-others. It is probably true that such training sometimes makes the patient more integrated, as when he really feels aggressive toward his boss and cannot express it, but it appears that conditioning therapists neglect to look at this most important issue. Furthermore, behavior therapy seems to work only when the patient has decided to let it work or make it work, in which case the patient's decision, and not the conditioning, is the important thing.

Therefore letting the patient be is the first essential task of the therapist. This is true for at least two reasons. First, the therapist must understand the patient's being and in order to do so, he must let the patient disclose himself and his world as he (the patient) sees fit. Second, the change that the therapist hopes will come must come from within the patient. To be sure, the therapist provokes, confronts, and otherwise grates up against the patient, but a change that comes because the therapist wants it to come is an inadequate change. It must come because the patient has decided it will come. The manipulation by the therapist must be geared to the expansion of the patient's range of choices, not to the therapist's idea of how the patient should live his life.

In spite of the obvious caveat against imposition of the therapist's values upon the patient, it is still true that to open up a broader range of choices to the patient is an imposition of an ideal. Indeed psychotherapy inevitably deals with moral issues. The question then becomes not whether to impose, influence, and manipulate, but in the service of what ideal to do so. It is perhaps the very first order of business for any clinical psychologist to make conscious his own values and ideals, or put another way, to become aware of how he is-in-the-world, how he is-for-himself, and how he is-for-others. The format of this self exploration will be, in part, a theory or statement of what one sees as "the good life," "psychological health," or the goal of therapy. What follows is one psychologist's view of these matters.

3. Healthy Being

A. Healthy being-in-the-world

We have said that being-in-the-world is immediate. It involves a kind of experience of self and world that is not mediated by the kinds of symbols that are ordinarily used to objectify the world. When I look at a painting, I have an experience that cannot be duplicated or produced by any nonperceptual description. The immediate experience of the painting is always more than and other than what I experience when I hear a conceptual description alone. An awareness of the world in this immediate way is the central phenomenon of being-in-the-world.

Concepts that mediate my encounter with the world are not,

of course, simply bad. The objectification of the world is the
central task of natural science, as well as of a sophisticated handling
of life. But the possibilities that objectification and abstraction
open up are not all good either. When they pervade experience to
the exclusion of immediate experience, they blind us to the very
foundation of our experience. Paintings become their description,
people become psychological theories, and life becomes an abstraction.

To open oneself to the physiognomy of the world has more
than aesthetic importance. Life becomes, to be sure, more interesting, but it also becomes more real. There are many disturbances and
interferences to this kind of immediate experience of the world, and
they are somewhat easier to talk about than the richness and real-
ness of healthy being-in-the-world. Let me, however, try to describe
something of this experience.

First, there is the experience of being "at home" in the
world. Heidegger maintains that it has been nearly impossible to
be at home in the world since Plato abstracted the reality of it and
projected it into the essences which even now govern our abstract
concepts. Few of us can deal with this issue as Heidegger does, for
few of us have his vision. But we can all experience something of
our alienation from the world and the revelatory nature of our
moments of honest being-in-the-world.

Being at home in the world implies a certain acceptance of
the world. This is not to say that one ceases to strive for improvement of the world, either through politics or science. Indeed quite
the contrary is so. When I fail to live in a way that responds to
the world (is responsible, we might say), it is not because I accept
too much. None of us accept the evil that is patently evil. It is
rather because I fear the world's reprisal, because I feel the world
is an enemy and am threatened by it. To operate firmly in the
world, even to see it clearly, I must be able to assume that I know
what is going on, that I am *of* the world as well as *in* it, and that
it and I have some kind of important but friendly business to
transact. Those who "accept" what is patently evil do not feel they
are doing so. They have really lost contact with the world; they
have become so little at home in it that they cannot even see it
clearly. Seeing it clearly presumes that one is at home enough not
to create blocks to our immediate experience of it. We must, there-

fore, accept the world in order to be-in-the-world in a way that makes sense.

We are dealing here with a very subtle but profound "orientation" or "posture" which informs everything else we do. In Chapter 12 we refer to this orientation as the "existential platform." There is at least one quality in an individual person for which our standard psychological vocabulary is inadequate. It is this fundamental orientation upon which everything else in his life is based. And one of the crucial dimensions of this posture is the degree we have opened ourselves to the world and have accepted it as the framework within which we shall be.

Things, people, and situations can be permitted to "get through" to us if we allow them to unfold as they are. Like "letting the patient be," we must "let the world be" if we are to live in it.

Second, healthy being-in-the-world involves us as-subjects in that world. The experience of oneself-as-subject has been described in Chapter 2. We omitted an important metaphor that we can now use to enrich our understanding. Being-a-subject is like a light-bulb that illuminates the objects around it. This is quite a good metaphor for consciousness, for it implies the revelatory nature, and the limitations of that revelation, of opening our experience to what the world is. Do we allow the light of our consciousness to illuminate the world, which is another way of asking, do we experience ourselves as illuminators?

I have in mind here a number of aspects of our fundamental orientation that can best be described in terms of oneself-as-object, although we may never have asked the question about ourselves as such. Do I assume (and it will be an assumption, not a conclusion) that my particular illumination of the world is genuinely unique and important? Do I assume that my light might shine from an angle that may open up visions no one else has had? Is my light really an enlightening one? Or is it really a light at all? Am I really awake? Do objects, persons and situations really "get through" to me?

We can speak of "confidence" or "security." These can be superficial words. What is at stake is not a trait, it is not a feeling about ourselves-as-object, and it is certainly not a dimension of some *thing* called personality. It is a way of being-in-the-world. I will certainly be able to change your dimensional scores and your traits, but only you can change your being-in-the-world. It is a decision of first importance because it is the first decision, upon which all the rest of one's being is based. And it is not a decision *to be a certain kind of person;* that involves one's self-as-object. It is a decision simply *to be,* which means to be awake, alive, conscious and present. A "lack of confidence" cannot be changed by changing the attributes of the object, "self," in one's own or others' eyes. It can only change within itself by "turning on" its light and meeting half way the world which, in the light of consciousness, will "shine forth."

Take as an example the following experience reported by a patient.

> When I first met you I had all kinds of preconceptions about what you would be like and what you would do. For a long time I interpreted everything you did in terms of those preconceptions. I really wasted a lot of time shadow-boxing with the image I had of you. Lately I seem to see you differently. It occurred to me when I saw you at _____ that I really didn't know you at all. And since then I have found out that I could get to know you if only I could just see and hear you . . . I mean, without preconceptions. You may not talk much, but you are definitely there, and you're not nothing. I must say I am curious about you, but in a way that is different than before. I used to wonder about how I fit into your categories, diagnosis and all that. Now I wonder more about you the way I wonder about anyone I just met. It is really amazing to me that I never could just see you before.

There are multiple things going on in this passage, but the crucial items for us now are, first, that there is an experience of the therapist that begins to get behind the initial categories; second, that this is concommitant with a notion of oneself-as-subject who can process information about the world on one's own, that one can "see" for "himself"; third, the patient is becoming more realistic, that is, he is seeing the therapist as a person and not as a role, a therapist, an objectifying subject; and fourth, that these three events are concommitant with a decrease in being-for-others that helped blind the patient, that stood between the patient and his

own immediate experience. Some patients never get to the point of
opening themselves to their immediate experience of the therapist,
even in therapy that is quite successful in terms of other kinds of
gains.

The alienation from the world becomes most vivid when we
have such an experience as seeing something anew we thought we
knew and understood. Patients have the experience of an actual
perceptual change of those important people in their lives when
they can see a parent aging, a child growing. This requires a relinquishing of the idealizations of these important persons and an
opening of one's experience to them, a letting of the world "shine
forth" as it is.

The shining forth of the world is not unconnected to feeling at home in the world. We cannot feel at home in a world to
which we have closed our eyes. Nor can we respond to it, nor be
responsible, nor act confidently, nor know what in the world is
going on.

Third, healthy being-in-the-world implies action in the world.
The question for most of us is not whether to act or not to act
(although that may be the question for some withdrawn schizophrenics), but rather it is the question of what criteria to act by.
In Chapter 4 we discussed the role of spontaneous and immediate
feelings in guiding our reactions, and we concluded that indeed
our impulses are not always best translated directly into action. But
the question here is whether they are there for us at all. Or are
they lost from view, according to lies, the origin of which involves
undue interference from being-for-myself and being-for-others?

Nonaction is, of course, not possible. Not deciding is to
decide. The fundamentality of one's immediate being-in-the-world
is seen in the observation that other human experiences, such as
rational calculation, are meaningless apart from the actual interaction between the person and the world. Man's mental capacity
would not be an advantage over animals if it did not change his
behavior. The relationship between impulse to act, a rational contemplation of that action, and the act itself is too complex to
discuss here. We must be satisfied with pointing out that a sensitivity
to the physiognomy of the world is a sensitivity to one's impulses as
well. The *experience* of the world is a product of both, and yet more

than the sum of the two. The impulse (experienced-as-subject) and an object (person or situation) combine to produce phenomena that are the basis of human experience. Analysis destroys and obscures it, and it is obscured only at the cost of considerable limitation of our lives.

Actually, of course, we rarely experience impulses in isolation from the more general feeling of subjectness, actions from the general context of being, and objects from the general context of the world. Human experience is the great organizer and clearing house of all of these, and it will be healthy to the extent that it is open to the world in which it is at home, to the enlightenment that comes from being conscious, and to the impulses as they are experienced as one's subjectness.

Fourth, healthy being-in-the-world is thoroughly temporal. Temporality is a matter of living forward into the future, but it is also a limitation, a quite intransigent one. It is only in limitation that we have possibility at all. To be able to feel at home, to let objects shine forth, and to act, one has to feel comfortable with the irreversibility of time, the openness of the future and the "closedness" of the past. We have seen in obsessive neurosis how these crucial contingencies are feared and not accepted, hidden and not faced, defended against and not built into experience itself.

Temporality suggests limitation as well as possibility; none of us is eternal. Action suggests responsibility; we are all burdened with the knowledge that we could choose differently. Enlightenment suggests openness to what is grim as well as what is pleasant. Being at home suggests meeting the world on its terms and some surrendering of unrealistic ideals on the one hand and/or idealized reality on the other hand. Being-in-the-world, as we have described it, is threatening in a number of ways. The general orientation about which we spoke, which characterizes our being-in-the-world, can be courageous and honest in the face of these threats or it can, in various degrees and various ways, be a lying-in-the-world. Courageous confrontation of the world, as we have described it here, is the only antidote to whatever oppressiveness reality imposes. Turning one's back is a decision to perpetuate our weakness, and these decisions will come, in various ways to various degrees, in accord with our accruing reservoir of courage and with the particular shape of our being-for-oneself and being-for-others.

B. Healthy being-for-oneself

To reflect upon oneself as an object of our attention is, as we have said, quite inevitable. To do so with rigor, detachment and honesty is difficult and healthy, for the truth about ourselves will have an effect anyway, and we must be prepared for that truth if we are to avoid neurotic lies which snowball into symptoms. To do so with the categories of essential traits and object-like qualities can be healthy too, in some respects, but we need to spell out the conditions and limitations that surround the healthiness of this phenomenon.

We will eventually argue that the truth about oneself must be cast in both essentialistic and existential terms. We are both object (body, finitude, and necessity) and subject (consciousness, freedom, and possibility).

The theory of intentionality seems to suggest that there is no truth about oneself apart from how one construes oneself. This leads, logically, to a kind of nihilism, subjectivism and relativism, if one takes a certain logical path. The assumption of this logical path is that we are some *thing* whose attributes we are trying to learn. However the truth about ourselves, we have argued, cannot be the same kind of truth that we have about objects, which are just things, with essences, and without a future. Oneself is not a thing and we cannot "find" or "discover" a truth about it in the usual way. The "self" we investigate is also our being. We cannot discover a truth about it apart from how we construe it because the construing of it is part of what it is, or more precisely, the construing of it is a part of *how* one *is*. For the person who says he feels inferior, we see that he construes himself that way and the very accuracy of the statement is enhanced by that self-construction, for example. Such a statement by a patient is never clear in itself. Is he saying that he *is* inferior or that he probably is not but that he *feels* inferior. What, exactly, is the problem as he sees it? If he says he *is* inferior, does he recognize that his saying it makes it so? If he says he *feels* inferior but probably is not, then he is contradicting himself. The experience of oneself-as-object, when formulated in thing-like, essentialistic terms is inherently paradoxical. The reason for this is that he could not experience anything if he were in fact a thing.

We cannot "find" or "discover" the truth about ourselves, then, in purely essentialistic terms. Our "self" is also the discoverer. To find and to discover is an act of consciousness, and consciousness is an openness; it implies possibilities as well as necessities.

On the other hand, the truth about oneself seen essentialistically is not necessarily all wrong, for we are part object. We cannot fly like a bird, for we are men, and our "manness" does not include the attribute, "ability to fly." These limitations are essential, and they may well include "causes" from our personal past that have made us "what" we are. The problem in therapy is sometimes to get patients to face this, and it is sometimes to get them to go beyond it and see that they are also possibility and open future as well. Rigorous and honest being-for-oneself is therefore always difficult and uncertain.

The process of making a decision always involves our being-for-oneself. We always make decisions in terms of what we want to be or think we are as well as in terms of the decision itself. If I decide to vote for candidate *A* instead of *B,* it is not simply because I prefer *A* to *B* in a kind of immediate spontaneity. It is also because I want to be the kind of person who prefers *A*. We cannot escape this aspect of our decision-making unless we behave in a thoroughly spontaneous and prereflective way all the time. We have seen how this aspect of the decision-making process has hypertrophied for the obsessive and become a monstrous preoccupation. It is important to describe, if we can, the ways in which this inevitable experience is healthy.

Psychology is full of labels that help us to do this with great style. Suppose one is trying to decide between two careers. He may take aptitude and interest tests that enable him to define the essence he is. There are not tests to measure the being one is, of course, because "being" is not that kind of phenomenon. Fortunately the tests will probably not appear definitive to the individual, and he must choose among several equally possible alternatives. He will ask, "What sort of person do I want to be?" Leaving aside the issues of being-for-others, which will play a more or less large role, let us ask what sort of question this is. It certainly comes up at crucial points in psychotherapy as well.

One's entire range of values will be called upon to weigh the alternatives. It is as if the individual were already in the future, looking back upon his life as an *X* and as a *Y*, and making a judgment of it. He cannot know how his values will change, or even *if* they will change. The best he can do is use the criteria that seem right to him at this point in time.

The healthy way for one's being-for-himself to be involved in decision-making is for the content of that self concept to be firmly grounded in his being-in-the-world and in his experience of himself-as-subject. It is exactly the origin of pathology to lose this primordial experience of self-in-the-world that creates a past history, present being, and chooses among infinite numbers of alternatives in making the future into history. Such a loss produces contradictions and out-of-jointness. The therapeutic task, more specifically stated, is to bring into awareness those aspects of one's being that are not being chosen honestly and that are standing in the way of integration, i.e., of one's integrity.

C. Healthy being-for-others

Since we cannot really forget that other people have consciousness and objectify us, it is impossible to escape being-for-others. The question therefore becomes: "What do we want to be for others?" "Why?" and "For whom?" Let us deal with the last of these issues first. Luijpen, speaking for Heidegger, writes:

> The subject of human actions is not always the self, and the *I* in person, but rather the *impersonal "they."* The *I* can let itself drift, it can think what "they" think and do what "they" do. The impersonal "they" can deprive man of being *himself.* It hates originality and is addicted to "as everybody knows or does" and to "being one of the crowd." Such a man makes us think of an automaton. His potentialities are less and less his own, and their execution becomes more and more a process. The impersonal "they" can account for everything, for there really is not anyone who has to render an account (Luijpen, 1960, pp. 41–42).

This kind of conformity is a familiar phenomenon. The crucial element here is that the revelant "other" has become impersonal, nobody in particular and everyone in general. The insidious aspect of such a being-for-others is that we can never know for sure what "they" really expect. We must, therefore, live in the shadow of shame, for we never know just when we will be judged badly. Healthy being-for-others must have a certain ordering of relevant "theys," and the origin of this order should come from one's being-in-the-world. It is one of the tragedies of public life, in show business or in politics, that everything rests upon a kind of popularity that must be achieved in this arena. Few people, it would seem, can survive this kind of pressure without flagrantly losing contact with their being-in-the-world. The way honesty survives in the life of a politician or actor, insofar as we understand it, is to focus one's concern, one's being-in-the-world, not explicitly on the "others" but on matters of principle or on matters of art. It is a sad but not infrequent spectacle when a public personality "loses his integrity," as we might call it. The feeling we have is that he is performing for the effect it has on the others' opinion of him, and we dislike the whole show. It is a paradox, mentioned in Chapter 3, that those who work hardest at "being loved" (as an object) tend, in the long run, to make themselves the least lovable.

For the relevant "they" to be personal and specific, then, and chosen on the basis of one's being-in-the-world, is a necessary but not sufficient condition for healthy being-for-others. The other question is, "What do we want to be for them?" Let me report a not atypical vicious circle that a patient got himself into. His greatest desire was to be loved by his family. He wanted more than anything else for them to treat him with complete respect and admiration. He therefore would buy the members of his family extravagant gifts and expect them to shower him with praise and appreciation. His family, sensitive to the manipulatory nature of the gifts, would be circumspect about the gifts, whereupon he would become furious at their lack of appreciation. This anger would create profound guilt for this patient, as well as hearty amounts of shame. In his remorse he would buy more extravagant gifts and expect forgiveness, and so on.

The crucial thing to note about this patient's being is that it is predominantly being-as-object-for-others. He badly misperceived how to get what he wanted out of life, and he wanted something that he could not, in fact, get. His misperception of how to get his family to love him can be understood by reflecting upon his immediate experience when he bought the gifts. The fact is that he really felt compelled to buy the gifts. The act of repentance was not a choice made in the light of a number of alternatives; he could not see alternatives because he could not experience himself in any way other than as their object. The *meaning* of the buying of the gifts for him did not stem from a love of his family that finds expression in this and numerous other ways, the meaning was solely in terms of their appreciation. His family sensed this; indeed we are able to "intuit," to infer or to feel what is going on in another, especially when the behavior is as blatant as this.

If the patient were to have had his way, his family would ignore what they really felt, their immediate experience of him and their concern about what they were asked to be-for-him, and they would "play the game" for him, give him the kind of love and respect that he wanted. The whole family would, under these circumstances, begin to operate on a false premise. Interactions among the family members would have become embroiled in an intricate network of lying-for-others and everybody would become increasingly uncomfortable about the feelings they really had, that is, about their being-in-the-world. To protect themselves and the family from explosion, they would have to build increasingly complex structures of lies to prevent their real feelings from showing. Conflict would have to be avoided at all costs, as would all expressions of spontaneous feeling. To grow up in such a family would almost certainly be to acquire a style of being that would serve poorly in the larger interpersonal world. We hardly need to point out that the patient came from a family not dissimilar to this.

It was, therefore, a healthy thing that this patient's family was honest enough to withhold what they knew the patient wanted. But it was practically impossible for them to do anything more for him, for they had to live with him on a day-to-day basis. The therapist enjoys a distinct advantage in this respect, and the kinds of withholding and resulting conflicts with the patient that emerge are not intolerable by a secure and consistent therapist.

What, indeed, did the patient want to be for his family? His statement of his desires at the beginning of therapy was quite reasonable as far as it went. He wanted to be loved. There is certainly nothing unique in that. He did not tell us, however, and in fact was not able to see, that this is *all* he wanted. There was some occasional spontaneous love toward members of his family, some being-in-the-world, but usually his desire to be loved pervaded his being to such an extent that he was unable to be-in-the-world. The relevant context for interpreting all the events in his life was his being-for-others. We have here a case of the god-parent being satellized by the satellites.

When his wife confronted him with her honest feelings about the situation, and told him that she did not appreciate the gifts because she saw them as selfish, the only way the patient could interpret the remark was in terms of the withholding of love by his wife. He *could not hear* her saying anything about him other than that she didn't love him. He could not interpret the remark in terms of some honest reflections about himself. At best, his being-for-himself was exhausted by an idealization of himself as the most generous father in the world. Nor could he be sensitive to how his wife's remarks made him feel in-the-world. His anger was immediate, to be sure, but it was not informed primarily by his being-in-the-world, by the love he did feel for his family, but rather it was informed by his being-for-others. And of course the anger produced guilt and shame. He could have met his wife's confrontation with more honesty if the range of alternative interpretations of her behavior were not limited only to the one great question in his life.

The question of what one wants to be for others therefore implies limits too. Other people simply are not always manipulable in their view of oneself. Honest being-for-others must recognize these limits. It must be built upon the assumption that we can afford to let the other be and upon the trust that the other's being will be minimally honest. When we cannot make such an assumption we feel trapped in the same way that the patient's wife was trapped. The patient literally did not know what he was for others. Had he known, he certainly would have chosen to be something else. The therapeutic problem, however, is that just telling him will not work. He cannot interpret such a remark in any way other than he interpreted his wife's confrontation. Certain other kinds of movements are necessary before real alternatives become open to the patient.

The presentation of oneself to others is always a complex affair. Any given instance of it will be highly unique. Honest being-for-others must live with the knowledge that one will disappoint the more outrageous expectations of others and it must be free of interferences from an idealization of oneself and from various lies-in-the-world.

Reference

Luijpen, W. A. *Existential Phenomenology*. Pittsburgh: Duquesne University Press, 1960.

The structure of psychotherapy   11

There are many difficulties in talking about psychotherapy. For our purposes, we will assume the metaphor of "structure" as a way of talking about what happens when psychotherapy is successful. The specific goal of this chapter is to describe in existential-phenomenological terms the process of movement from an experience of oneself as somehow "in need of help" to a healthy way of being. We will divide our description first into very molar movements, or a "gross structure," that apply to the process as a whole, second into less general and gross units, or an "intermediate structure," that characterize an interview or a series of interviews within the total process, and third into molecular units, or a "fine structure" of movements within a single interview.

1. Gross Structure

Psychotherapy has already been characterized generally in this book as moving from various lies to honesty, as becoming aware of alternatives and of the necessity to choose among them, as opening oneself to the immediate experience of oneself and of the world, as becoming more responsible for the shape of one's life, and as changing the meaning of events in self and world from a constricted and repetitive to a flexible and realistic repertoire of intentions. *Each of these characterizations depends upon the growth of the ability of the patient to experience himself-as-a-subject.* This growth in subject-experience is the first focus for us in describing the gross structure of psychotherapy. The second will be the growth of self-objectification, a somewhat opposite but also concomitant movement that occurs in successful psychotherapy.

A. The growth of self-as-subject

In an important sense, this movement by the patient is done in spite of the therapy as well as because of it. The therapeutic situation does not involve two equal persons participating in a common enterprise. It is structured from the start with inferior-superior, weak-strong, bad-good, and sick-healthy role implications. In our terms, this will be experienced by the patient as an object-subject structure. As long as one is in the role of "patient" in psychotherapy, one is the therapist's object and the therapist is the predominant subject. As long as the therapist assumes the therapist role at all, he is going to reinforce this inherent structure, and the movement by the patient against this structure is the movement toward health by the patient. The most difficult—and most crucial—task for the therapist is to help the patient become a nonpatient, to help him move from himself as object to himself as subject. And yet the very act of helping is permeated with the flavor of objectification. As soon as the therapist makes plans about the life of another at all, even within the interview, as soon as he interacts with the intent to change the patient, he is making a decision for the patient and therefore making the patient his object. This is quite inevitable; it does not have to be fatal to the growth of the patient's experience of himself as a subject *if* the therapist is aware of the patient's being and is able, at crucial times, to let the patient be.

Pure and total acceptance of the patient is not enough for psychotherapy, should it indeed be possible. For the interaction to be at all fruitful for either member, there must be some grating and conflict. The process of objectifying the patient, such as offering an interpretation of the patient's behavior, can be a grating that leads the patient to a fuller experience of himself as a subject, however, and we must describe now just how this can be the case.

The phenomena of transference have been described in Chapter 6 as intending the therapist in accordance with the intentions available to the patient. These intentions are necessarily constricted and repetitive and may even duplicate in great detail how the patient construes a parent or spouse. There is also, in this experience, an implicit experience of oneself for which the term "satellization" is quite appropriate.* All patients, if they are taking their psychotherapy seriously, go through a definite period of satellization around their therapist, and we can describe some of the progressions of that experience in general, even though every therapy is necessarily individual and unique.

The first stage of satellization around the therapist is to see oneself as the object of the therapist-subject. This may happen in fantasy even before therapy begins or it may occur after a number of interviews. It sometimes hits like a flash: "I see now how you see me." The patient's response to this flash may be quite varied and elaborate. At some point in therapy the patient will accept the therapist's view of him, "internalize" it, as it were, and thus will be-for-himself what he thinks he is for the therapist. This step is a deepening of the satellization and may indeed be followed by an even further identification with the therapist in which the patient comes to see the world as he thinks the therapist does. In these events lie many subtleties, some of which will be described below in the section on self-objectification. The entire process may happen several, or even many, times, depending on the course and scope of the therapy. If therapy ends during the zenith of satellization, there occurs what the psychoanalysts call a "transference cure," a change in attitude and style that will not last and will fail to generalize to other situations because it is *not* grounded on the firm foundation of experiencing oneself as a subject, nor on the making of choices from the vantage point of that experience. More movement is required for successful therapy.

At some further point in therapy, the patient will make tentative steps to transcend his satellization, and this will be the most difficult and demanding part of therapy for both patient and therapist. A first step in this process may indeed be to objectify the therapist. This will be done tentatively and defensively many

* This formulation is not dissimilar to observations on "Therapeutic symbiosis" by Searles (1965).

times during therapy: questioning the therapist's qualifications, interpreting his behavior, criticizing his manner, etc. Many therapies are broken off here, what has been called "negative transference." If it is won after many painful false starts, each blocked by the intervention of honesty, it will more likely lead to a more firmly based experience of oneself-as-subject and less likely lead to a desperate and angry affirmation of self-as-subject. In either case, objectification of the therapist and experience of oneself-as-subject go together. The task now is to discriminate between a pre-mature and a healthy objectification of the therapist.

The crucial ingredient in healthy objectification of the therapist is an accurate recognition of just who the therapist is. Ideally, the patient's transcendence of satellization will recognize not only the objectively conceived limitations of the individual therapist, but will recognize that he is a subject, even as the patient himself is a subject. The ability for patient and therapist, or for any two people for that matter, to be in one another's presence without a tacit agreement that one's judgment of the other is more important or more correct, without structuring the relationship so that subject and object are permanently assigned roles, is very difficult. Buber's intuitive description of a relationship as "I-Thou" is a good description of the end point in therapy. Both participants in the relationship are allowed to be subjects, to objectify the other without robbing the other of his subjectivity, and to freely take the role of the other in a mutual deepening of self understanding.

This description of the end point in therapy sounds so attractive that it would seem that both parties would be "naturally" attracted to it. Therapist as well as patients, indeed all of us, find this kind of relationship difficult to achieve. The greatest difficulty lies in the threat that is implied, for most of us, in the experience of oneself as a genuine subject. The patient will no doubt approach this experience of himself and of the relationship many times before he is really able to "make the move" permanently. It is indeed much safer to construe the therapist as a god-subject who has infinite wisdom and to identify with that wisdom in the fashion of satellization, even if that posture leaves one uncomfortable in some senses in the relationship. Or, it is safer to ridicule and condemn the therapist as an inferior, thus beefing up one's experience of self-as-subject with feelings of superiority, than to see the therapist and oneself as they are, as two persons, each with essential attributes and limitations and each with consciousness and freedom that is perforce unpredictable and ineffable.

This difficulty for the patient might be elucidated if we distinguish between two different kinds of identification of patient with therapist. The satellization that occurs in the middle of therapy involves an internalization of the "what" of the therapist's being. The therapist's attitudes and opinions about worldly events will be sought, inferred, and internalized *in content*. If the therapist is a Democrat, the patient will become a Democrat. If the therapist is a religious man, the patient will become a religious man. In the more mature and final identification of the patient˙ with the therapist, the *content* of what the therapist is will be seen as essentially individual, limited in validity to the being of the therapist, and finally of no more significance than the content of any other person. But the *how* of the therapist's being, his ability to make decisions as a subject and to integrate the content of these decisions with his being-for-others, his openness to himself and the world and his more varied and differentiated repertoire of intentions for interpreting events, these aspects of the therapist will still stand as a model for the patient, independent of the particular stylistic or attitudinal *content*. The patient must finally recognize, as the therapist does, that ultimate values are choices and are not subject to adjudication by an established authority; he must see the therapist's choices, in their content, as possible options but not necessarily as right for himself. But to recognize this is also to take seriously the necessity of making choices, of facing the anxiety embedded in this process, and of rising to meet that challenge. We must refer again to the "existential crisis" as described by Bugental (see Chapter 5) to capture the profundity of this final movement by the patient toward healthy being.

Ideally, therefore, the patient emerges from his satellization through a series of objectifications of the therapist, culminating in a final recognition that the therapist is a mere human subject caught in a web of objective givens just as he, the patient, is a subject, similarly caught, but similarly able to choose and enthusiastic about his own freedom. To achieve this essential ingredient in health is the key task of therapy. The neurotic symptoms and constrictions of being that had driven the patient to the therapist in the first place do not disappear automatically, but their preservation becomes vividly experienced as what it is: a choice among alternative ways of running one's life. The therapy cannot remove symptoms; it can enable the individual's being to grow and become more integrated within itself, whereupon the patient must take the final "curative" step. This is not to say that elimination of symptoms is simply an act of will. It is a decision, to be sure, but one that cannot be understood apart from the complexities of being.

B. Self-objectification

A second, almost opposite movement in therapy is from an experience of feelings that is immediate and preemptive to an objectification of them. We pointed out in Chapter 2 that the objectification of feelings sometimes can put a *distance* between oneself and the world or between oneself and one's values that essentially destroys one's being-in-the-world. It is, as we noted, a loss of the experience of love when one's primary attention becomes oneself as lover or one's feelings as physiological responses. The latter is a particularly destructive objectification not only in that the focus of one's attention is directed away from the beloved but also in that the metaphor in terms of which one intends one's feelings is the object-language of physiological mechanisms.

However, except for schizoid and some obsessive patients, every patient experiences a relationship with some part of the world whose immediacy swamps all perspective and involves him to such a degree that he cannot experience the object objectively nor himself objectively. A phobic patient, for example, may be able to reflect that his phobia is irrational, but this reflection never quite seems relevant to him in the presence of the phobic object. The only experience that has real meaning is the frightening nature of the object and the need to get away from it. The spontaneous and immediate involvement with the object is so powerful that any detachment from one's experience is out of the question. Dependent people occasionally experience their longing for the other so intensely that they are virtually unable to see their behavior from the point of view of a detached, neutral observer. Freud often pointed to the idealization of the beloved and explained it in terms of the spilling over of narcissistic libido onto the beloved object. Again, a metaphor of experience may be better than one of energy economics to describe a phenomenon Freud recognized as of crucial theoretical importance.

The objectification of one's self and one's feeling is inevitable in therapy. It is important to understand as well as we can the constructive and destructive aspects of this experience. Objectification is never the whole answer, but it is always one of the movements in successful psychotherapy. Let us distinguish three aspects of self-objectification, each having a different implication for the experience of oneself and hence each having a different place in therapy. We will label them (*a*) making oneself the object of one's attention, (*b*) detachment, and (*c*) use of an object metaphor. When I explain my feelings for my beloved in terms of physiological mechanisms, I am objectifying myself in all three ways. When I see my feeling for my beloved the way some other neutral person would see them, I am doing only the first two, making myself the object of my attention and gaining a perspective of detachment. When I focus my attention on my own joy in the presence of the beloved, I am doing only the first. When I love immediately and spontaneously, I am not objectifying at all. These are, if you like, degrees of objectification, but the quantitative relationship among these experiences should not obscure the qualitative differences among them.

It would seem that making oneself the object of one's attention is inevitable in therapy. There are two additional complexities, however. First, to do so involves some personal commitment by the patient that will likely be experienced as fairly dangerous, and second, there is a predominant tendency at the beginning of therapy not to look at oneself through one's own eyes, but through the eyes of the therapist. Hence a patient may, in satellization, experience detachment without really wholeheartedly examining oneself in one's own terms. The difficulty is, of course, that "one's own terms" implies one's choices about what is good and bad, and it is threatening to be confronted with the necessity of making these choices.

In behavior therapy, where symptoms are explained by the therapist to the patient as accidental conditioning pairings, that have a presence in one's glandular system, we have a kind of caricatured extreme of self-objectification which may or may not be accompanied by a sincere commitment to take a hard look at one-self. Here the therapist's physiological categories are offered to the patient, not for his judgment and decision, but as scientifically confirmed facts about what is going on. This may indeed enable the patient to achieve the relief of detachment and effectively reduce his anxiety about being mentally ill. But in terms of the goals of therapy formulated in existential terms, it almost certainly reduces the individual's opportunity for being healthy.

The key problem that remains in our discussion of the gross structure is to explain how an individual's experience of himself-as-subject and his self-objectification can and do proceed concomitantly. Indeed they seem to be opposite movements. They do, however, grow simultaneously in normal childhood development and in successful psychotherapy. The more one experiences one's limitations and objective qualities, the more precisely and intensely one experiences the range of options within these limits. The more one experiences one's freedom, the more one experiences the boundaries imposed by his own finitude. Interpretation and other forms of grating and conflict in therapy enhance one's experience of one-self-as-subject. The handling of any given therapy by the therapist, insofar as he is the one who "handles" it, must be geared to both aspects of the existential situation. This is, of course, never a simple matter: any individual therapy must be tailored to the patient's being as it is presented at the beginning of therapy. Therefore we turn now to some of the considerations of intermediate structure.

2. Intermediate Structure

If our reflections on the "gross structure" of psychotherapy allow us to talk about goals, the intermediate structure of psychotherapy contains the means to these ends. These means, however, stand as ends relative to the means described in the section to follow on "fine structure." We shall, in this section, focus on two kinds of phenomena, the movements that the patient makes in the first several interviews (the opening moves) and the characteristic movements that the patient makes within a single interview, as gathered from seeing a number of them (the single interview).

A. The opening moves

The first several interviews will reveal some decisive data for the therapist, whose job it is early on in the therapy to allow the individual to play it through as he sees fit. Most of us have styles of being that are layered in such a way that our interaction with another is different in the fifth hour from what it is in the first. The movements from our initial presentation of ourselves to a more intimate and trusting style later reflect crucial things about the structure of our being. Most patients are aware that there should be a paced and calculated calendar of unfolding, and they probably are aware, on some level, of just how they are calculating it. Most patients are, furthermore, torn between the feeling that they have revealed too much too soon and a kind of guilt about not having revealed themselves quickly and thoroughly enough. The crucial criterion in these doubts will be the patient's estimation of the therapist's expectations. The patient's way of handling this difficult matter of being-for-the-therapist will say something about how he characteristically is-for-important-others, and this will be a large or small part of his total problem.

Let us ask what it is like to be a patient. It is an extraordinary life event, rarely experienced although perhaps rehearsed repeatedly in fantasy, to undergo a systematic self revelation to another whose role is defined ahead of time as nonreciprocal and who will therefore not reveal himself to you, at least in the same systematic way. The therapeutic process, in its very definition, is a call for the patient to be-for-the-therapist, and whatever else is involved in the early interviews, this fact will prove decisive.

There is, in all being-for-others, a certain distance from what might be felt as the hard-core reality of oneself. Therapy in the early interviews necessarily involves some contrast between what the patient considers real and vital and what he sees himself presenting to the therapist. It is like a dramatic production, and just as there is a willing suspension of the actor's true identity as he assumes the role of the character he plays so is there a temporary willing suspension of what is felt as real in the early interviews. The two situations are different, however, in that the therapy patient cannot be satisfied with this discrepancy if he is going to get something out of the therapy, and on some level he knows it. So he must fight, in the first instance, to overcome the distance between his being-for-the-therapist on the one hand and his being-for-himself and his being-in-the-world on the other. The particular progress of this struggle, in the early interviews of therapy, discloses and releases crucial features of the patient's general style of being.

In the previous section we pointed to the increasing tendency to experience oneself-as-subject in successful therapy. We might as easily have described it as an increasing sense that the relationship with the therapist is *real*. Over the entire course of therapy, there is a movement from the "dramatic production" feeling of being in therapy to that of real participation in a real relationship with real events and vicissitudes. This overall movement is, quite understandably, closely related to the increasing experience of oneself-as-subject in life in general. But within the interview situation, this move is made repeatedly in various contexts and various ways, and the first several interviews incorporate the first version of this movement.

It is entirely possible that one may, through therapy, make substantial gains in the ability to experience oneself-as-subject in life situations before one has conquered this task in the therapeutic situation. But until it is conquered in the therapeutic situation itself, the patient is construing the therapist in a certain way that will occur also in other relationships and therefore limit his ability to deal with the most important people in his life. Until he approaches this task in the therapeutic situation, he is failing to particularize his relationship with the therapist and to see the therapist as the individual that he is. This failure in perception, or more accurately, in intending the therapist with relatively open-ended and flexible intentions, is a crucial part of the general failure that drove him into therapy.

So the question becomes, what can the therapist look for and see in this initial struggle by the patient to make the therapy situation tolerably real to him? The patient may indeed prefer to avoid this struggle, and the only real motive he has to undergo it is his motivation for therapy in the first place. Calling the patient's attention to this struggle from time to time early in the therapy will provoke either an undertaking of the struggle or a dropping of the therapy. How and with what force the therapist chooses to do this depends entirely on his own goals in the therapy; some therapists find it agreeable to seduce the patient to stay long enough to become involved in various ways, while others prefer to demand this from the patient immediately as a condition of therapy itself. The latter strategy clearly forces the patient's hand sooner and assures a quicker experience of self-as-subject at least in terms of the decision to come to therapy, but it may limit the range of patients with whom one is willing to do therapy.

The therapist can look for and see in this struggle the kinds of reasons the patient has for being in therapy and the ability of the patient to use his hard-core experience of self-as-subject as the final arbiter of important decisions. It is probably the case that the therapist will not find such a solid foundation for decision-making, for this is likely to be exactly what is lacking in the patient's experience. But he will find the various substitutes (lies and objectifications) upon which the patient relies and therefore will discover important features of the patient's being.

The most common substitutes are, of course, being-for-oneself and being-for-others. The very first task of the therapist, beyond letting the patient be, is to get this first decision, the decision to be in therapy, clear to the patient. Indeed the entire therapy may be required to complete this task, but this confrontation is a necessary place to begin what will become a series of conflicts between patient and therapist. If other life content becomes the subject of therapeutic interpretation and confrontation before this choice, important risks are taken. The entire therapy may seem to progress naturally while in fact it retains the flavor of unreality and of a dramatic production to the patient. This systematically undermines the reality of all insights gained, the cogency of all feelings felt, and the relevance of therapy to real life in general. It also will be seen, on some level at least, by the patient as exactly what it is: complicity by the therapist in avoiding difficult real life issues and preference for the safety of hypothetical and therefore nonthreatening matters.

B. The single interview

Already in the early interviews a patient may establish a customary sequence of movement through which to go in the course of the fifty or so minutes he is with the therapist. This sort of structuring of time by the patient may be on the edge of the patient's awareness or it may be totally unconscious. Or if his weekly schedule of interviews is regular, he may impose a repetitive structure upon a week-long segment of time. Other patients may repeat a series of movements in a stereotyped way from topic to topic, regardless of the clock time involved, going through detachment/involvement/anger/threat to quit therapy/repentance/detachment, for example, first in relation to talking about his work, then about his family, then about his father, etc. These cyclic phrasings by the patient may say something about his characteristic way of handling life in general. Let us talk here only about the time-structuring imposed by the patient on the single interview.

One patient hit upon and stuck with the following procedure for getting through an interview. First he reported life events that had occurred since his last interview. He then asked the therapist's advice about how to handle this or that aspect of his life. Not getting any answers, he then reflected about how frustrating it is to be in therapy and/or how frustrating life is. Then he would settle down to the business of reflecting about the problems with which he started the interview and reach a few tentative conclusions about how to handle his life. He always summarized these conclusions before concluding the interview as if to convince himself that the hour had been successful. Another patient characteristically began the interview with a report of the conclusions he had drawn about his problems since the last interview. He followed this up with a detailed plan about how to behave in this or that relationship, withholding various reasons and drawing the therapist's questions about why the plan was such and such. Yet another patient always began the interview in a state of agitation and used the hour to calm himself down, time after time. Upon reflecting on this pattern, the patient eventually concluded that his agitation was a calculated "letting go" of pent-up nervousness in the interview situation which he felt was safer than real life.

In each of the examples, the patient divides up the time with the therapist according to some set pattern. In each of these cases, the interpretation of this pattern proved to be an important turning point in therapy. The experience of having this pattern called to one's attention is at once very threatening and very reassuring, for it demonstrates how well the therapist is able to see and understand the patient, enhancing satellization, which is both threatening and reassuring. The crucial follow-up to such an interpretation must be to match the experience of oneself as the therapist's object with an equal and more salient experience of oneself-as-subject. This can be done by asking the patient why he does it and refusing to accept an impersonal, causal, responsibility-escaping explanation. Or it may be done by insisting on something like a justification, a set of reasons, not causes, embedded in the immediate experience of the patient, not in a causal matrix, and explicitly formulated as a *choice* the patient is making.

Some patients fight against this confrontation by building it directly into their hourly pattern. First comes some kind of report, then asking the therapist for advice, then the interpretation by the therapist, then a confession of guilt for making the decision, and finishing with a set of conclusions. The crucial threatening element in therapy that evokes these procedures by patients (and sometimes by therapists) is the ambiguous spectre of unstructured, uncommitted time. To sit down with another person without an agenda, without plans, without some predictability, is to submit oneself to the possibility that *anything* might happen. Just what "anything" might be will almost certainly not be clear, and the fantasies that attempt to justify the feeling of threat are quite interesting when we discover them. The point, however, is that the decision to willingly involve oneself in an open-ended future, even if it is only fifty minutes long, is a decision to let oneself be, without vigilant supervision and comparison to the criteria of oneself-as-object, either as one's own object or as the therapist's object. It is a decision to be-as-subject. For the patient to be able to begin an hour with no agenda is to have made important gains in therapy. Whether he can experience other aspects of his life this way is a different question. And in both cases, this ability to let oneself be is a necessary, but hardly sufficient, condition for or result of successful therapy.

Letting oneself be is not, of course, unrelated to the therapist having let the patient be. A decision or resolution to change before this has happened will almost certainly be a move to please the therapist, and it will very likely become another of a long list of self-curative attempts that fail, and for which the patient blames himself. Perhaps the most vivid example of a premature decision to change comes from a patient who responded to the realization of his structuring of therapeutic time with a concerted attempt to do something different each and every interview. Touching as this may be as a gesture to please the therapist, it was not a significant movement in the patient's therapy. It came before the therapist had sufficiently shown the patient that he (the therapist) was going to let him (the patient) be, and before the patient was really ready to let himself be. The commitment to change came from an atrophied sense of oneself-as-subject. As an act of self-affirmation, it was pitifully compliant. It was, however, a beginning, and when all the vicissitudes of satellization were worked out, the same resolution could be made almost playfully, now as a pleasurable exercise in letting oneself be instead of the earlier mixture of stubborn self-assertion and obsequious being-for-the-therapist.

3. Fine Structure

We have described in Chapter 3 movement in the interview, using the example of the patient who was confronted by the therapist with his own anger. We will not repeat that kind of description here, but rather continue on the more abstract level of the general role of fantasy in psychotherapy as a way of talking about some of the phenomena of fine structure.

Fantastic worlds are constructed by all of us along with the socially validated one we ordinarily live in. There are many layers of fantasy that are built into the intentions of every person's world, and the reshuffling of meanings for the patient necessarily begins with an exploration of the various layers, their relationships to one another and to his whole being. The process of free association is a systematic exploration of these relationships, as are derivative techniques of anemnesis. Reconditioning therapy is a violent reordering of meanings that may help, but it also has tremendous dangers insofar as it is done on the basis of the therapist's reconstruction of the patient's being in very simple, and usually inadequate, terms. According to the view presented here, the therapist must try to open himself to the revelations of the patient and have some firm ideas of how the patient is construing the world before making an interpretive move.

The analysis of conversion hysteria in Chapter Seven offers us an opportunity to explore how the fantastic world (or "primary life space" as it was called there) can be relevant to the interview by provoking certain movements in the patient's being. Let us recall the example of the girl (let us suppose she is an adolescent) whose primary life-space consists of love and hate relationships amid her family and whose secondary life space is the consensually validated one of logical ordering. In the context of the former life-space, her vomiting acted out, in body language, a rejection of her father's love (childishly construed according to ideas of oral impregnation), and her body is *expressive* of herself-as-subject. In the context of the latter (secondary life space), her vomiting was construed as something wrong with a body which is experienced as a part of her object-self.

The coordinates of the primary life space constitute the "unconscious fantasy" in terms of which the apparently senseless symptom becomes meaningful. The overall goal of therapy is to bring the body-expressive aspects of her self-as-subject into focus, not as an object of examination but as a felt experience of self-as-subject. Certainly the laying out of the unconscious fantasy in discursive form in an interpretation will sound bizarre to the girl and may allow her to objectify some aspects of herself heretofore not objectified. But this misses the point of therapy; she could read about the Oedipus Complex in any modern psychology book.

The "unconscious fantasy" therefore is not discursive at all. The "theory" of the Oedipus Complex, while quite appropriate in some respects, is an objectification that destroys therapy for the patient. Indeed many sophisticated patients use discursive theories as a defense against the therapeutic process. The unconscious fantasy is, on the other hand, a *world*—a fantastic and unreal one from the point of view of the therapist, but a very real and poignant one from the point of view of the girl herself. It is indeed the context in terms of which she interprets the *meaning* of life events and from which she produces the symptom.

The coordinates, that is, the meanings, channels of interpersonal attraction and repulsion, pace of temporal ordering, and so on, of the primary life-space will coexist with the secondary life-space in which she plays the role of a patient who takes her malfunctioning body to the doctor for his ministrations. The therapeutic task is to help her to experience that primary world more immediately and her bodily expression within it as herself-as-subject. Consider the following conversation.

Pt. I threw up again last night at bed time. (Patient reporting to doctor her symptoms; experience of herself-as-doctor's-object.)

Dr. You did? How did it happen? (Doctor asking patient to be his object more thoroughly.)

Pt. I was almost asleep when daddy came in and kissed me good night. I knew that I was going to throw up. (Patient reporting a self-objectification, from the point of view of the doctor whom she knew she was going to report to.)

Dr. How did you know? (Doctor asking patient to report experience of self-as-subject—i.e., knower—as well as experience of self-as-object—i.e., what she knew about herself.)

Pt. I could just tell, you know. . . . (Patient unable to describe self-as-subject.)

Dr. Surely something told you. How did you know?

Pt. I guess I could feel it in my stomach, you know, all upset and ready to upchuck. (Patient attending to body-as-object.)

Dr. You felt sick to your stomach. (Doctor bringing body feelings back into context of experience of self-as-subject.)

Pt. Yes. (Acquiescence.)

Dr. Tell me more about what that feels like.

The doctor's last comment here does two things. On the one hand it clearly aims at enriching the vividness, to the patient, of the immediate experience of self, with the ultimate aim to make the coordinates of the primary life-space clear to the patient. At the same time, the role situation, in which the patient is the subject-doctor's object, is accentuated. "Tell *me* more about what that feels like." The patient will very likely get the second point and not the first, will perform as she thinks she is expected to perform and avoid, if possible, an honest confrontation of her primary life-space. The therapist's job, in listening to the description, is to allow this way of relating to the therapist, at least early in therapy. During that time he can pick up keys to the patient's experience of self-as-subject in her way of putting things. Eventually he will want to use these keys to open up the experience of self-as-subject. Before that time the patient, if she is allowed to be, may shift gears and begin to impose some of the coordinates of the primary life-space upon the therapy itself (transference), at which time the keys may also be useful in provoking an experience of self-as-subject in choosing to be in therapy.

The world of the therapy itself is the world upon which the therapist can really operate. He does so by being honestly. Consider the following conversation:

> *Pt.* I don't know why I keep coming here. All I do is tell you the same thing over and over. I'm not getting anywhere. (Patient complaining that therapist isn't curing her; maintenance of self-as-therapist's-object.)
>
> *Dr.* I'm getting tired of hearing the same thing over and over too. (Doctor refusing to take responsibility for the progress of therapy and refusing to fulfill patient's expectations that he cure her; refusal of patient as therapist's object.)
>
> *Pt.* Maybe I'll stop coming. (Patient threatening therapist; fighting to maintain role as therapist's object.)
>
> *Dr.* It's certainly your choice. (Therapist refusing to be intimidated; forcing of patient-as-subject.)
>
> *Pt.* What do you think I should do? (Attempt to seduce the therapist into role of subject who objectifies patient-object.)
>
> *Dr.* What do you want to do? (Forcing again.)
>
> *Pt.* I want to get better. (Plea for therapist to "cure.")
>
> *Dr.* I don't blame you. (Refusing role of subject curer and supporting desire on part of patient-as-subject.)
>
> *Pt.* If you think I should stay, okay, I will. (Refusing role of subject-who-decides.)
>
> *Dr.* You want me to tell you to stay? (Confrontation with patient's evasion of the decision and calling to attention what the patient wants, or how the patient is construing the world of the therapy.)
>
> *Pt.* You know what's best; you're the doctor. (Patient's confirmation of her construing of therapy.)
>
> *Dr.* Do I act like a doctor?

This kind of interchange must occur in nearly every therapy. The doctor's moves are quite intelligible in light of his desire to help the patient experience herself-as-subject. The danger in such a procedure is that the patient will construe it as a fight, will continue to come to therapy after having lost, and thus attempt to obligate the therapist by saying, in effect, "Okay, I can't win with you. We'll do it your way. Whatever you say." The therapist must continue to contradict this construing of the world of the therapy, which will eventually lead to a more frank transference, in which the breakdown of the role relationship of doctor-patient will allow the emergence of the primary life-space in the world of the therapy.

> *Pt.* I got sick again on my way up here. (Report of self-as-therapist's-object.)
> *Dr.* You did? What happened?
> *Pt.* I threw up in the elevator.
> *Dr.* What was it like?
> *Pt.* I think I'll take the stairs from now on. (Construes body as caused by mechanical forces.)
> *Dr.* You felt like you wanted to upchuck? (Use of patient's term.)
> *Pt.* I *did* upchuck. (Sticks to objective fact.)
> *Dr.* How did you feel? (Attempt to get beyond objective fact.)
> *Pt.* Sick! (Minimum subjective report.)
> *Dr.* What was that like?
> *Pt.* I just got sick and threw up.
> *Dr.* Sick about what?
> *Pt.* The elevator; when it started to move . . . you know.

The therapist will try to get the coordinates of the world in which the patient got sick into the open. It is probably an error to call attention to the parallel between himself and the patient's father before the patient vividly experiences the coordinates of this world. Various kinds of confrontations are possible, such as "why does seeing me upset you?" may be appropriate, depending upon the patient's ability to experience herself-in-the-world.

The point of these interview fragments is to demonstrate some of the difficulties as well as the opportunities that emerge for the therapist when he focuses his attention on the world or worlds of the patient. We began this example as if we knew the content of the primary life-space of the girl in question. Much of the reporting, by the patient, which describes the shape of that life-space is omitted so that relatively simple patient-therapist interactions could be analyzed. It is well to remember that letting the patient be is essential before the therapist can move with confidence in the world of the patient.

Reference

Searles, H. F. Integration and differentiation in schizophrenia. In H. F. Searles, *Collected Papers on Schizophrenia and Related Topics*. New York: International Universities Press, 1965.

SUMMARY OF
PART III

The case of Paula Kress exemplifies such important concepts as satellization, body-as-object, and temporalization. These concepts have a presence in the chapter on obsessive neurosis as well, but their relation to the production of symptoms is different. In both cases, the future is notably blocked, and in both cases this blocking comes from an objectification of self that screens any experience of self-as-subject. In the case of Paula Kress, and in hysteria in general, the objectification of self is particularly settled in being-for-others, while in the obsessive neurotic, self-objectification is primarily settled in being-for-oneself. In both cases, the history of self-experience, particularly the nature of satellization around parents in childhood, is a crucial turning point. And in both cases, the resulting style of being is weighed on self-as-object because of an inability (unwillingness) to face the anxieties of the experience of self-as-subject.

The objectification of the body is typical of both of these types. In hysteria, objectification of the body is particularly important in that it obscures the subject-expressive functions of bodily symptoms and actions. In obsessions, this is also frequently true, but the body takes on the additional importance of being the content of many obsessions, such as in hypocondriasis. In both cases we are able, by examining the pathological experience of the body, to specify what is a healthy experience of the body, for which we used the phrase, "lived body" in contrast to "used body." To "live" one's body is to "be one's body. It is a core of self-experience, rather than extraneous to it; it expresses who and how we *are* rather than being a kind of limit that condemns us to be *what* we *are*. Traditional and natural body functions, such as sexuality, become occasions for being-a-subject as well as merely being-an-object.

In the clinical studies, we discovered that the "sense of the possible" and the "sense of the necessary" are crucial ingredients in healthy being. The necessary and the possible are not simply determined from outside, although the necessary is in fact "given," and beyond human control. The "sense of" these two aspects of human existence, however, is what is crucial, and this is as much chosen as given. The particular construing of these exigencies by the individual in his world is a particularly significant aspect of being, of one's total existential posture. This must be discovered by the therapist before he is in a position to really understand where the patient is existentially and psychologically. It is crucial, therefore, to let the patient be as he is. The patient must be permitted to reveal himself as he is without preconceived pressuring by the therapist.

The dynamic aspect of therapy, the nexus out of which comes move and countermove, is the fact that the therapist is simply as he is. This intransigence of the therapist, in the therapeutic setting, is quite enough with which to confront the patient in order for there to be conflict, struggle, and change in the patient. "What the therapist is," and "how" he is, therefore, makes all the difference in therapy. He is inescapably a person who has a certain orientation, and the content of that orientation will influence the direction therapy will take. Since therapy is always a moral enterprise, in which one person influences and changes another, it is particularly important for therapists to be clear about the content of their values and their orientation. This is important in the process of doing therapy, and in the process of writing about it. Therefore we tried to describe some of the elements of "healthy being" from this particular existential point of view.

Healthy being-in-the-world was described as being "at home" in the world, "illuminating" the world, activity, and temporality. Healthy being-for-others was described as rigorous self-scrutiny in objectified terms, but also recognition of the limits of self-objectification in exhausting our being, thus inevitably leaving an open-ended future. Healthy being-for-others was described as grounded in a conscious hierarchy of important others, whose order in turn is grounded in our being-in-the-world. It is also important to recognize that our being-for-others is never exhaustive of our being, and to be able and willing to accept the consequences of the fact that others will misunderstand us.

The primary ingredients in healthy being, must be seen in the context of therapy as well as in the abstract. Some of the aspects of therapy that lead to these ingredients were described in terms of broad movements over the entire therapy. The difficulties and opportunities of enhancing the experience of the patient's self-as-subject and of healthy self-objectification were described. On a more short-term basis, the early moves of the patient in therapy were analyzed as a sorting out of subject and object self-experiences. The decision to be in therapy at all was seen as a crucial issue early in therapy. The patterning of time within the single interview was also called to attention, with specific reference to the patient's need to structure time ahead of time. Finally, some examples of the dialogue of therapy were analyzed in terms of the therapist's attempt to work toward the goals of therapy.

In Part IV, we shall turn to psychosis, the most profound of psychological disturbances. We shall find ourselves approaching the problems of being human on a more profound level. Existential thought, as we discussed in Part II, makes a unique contribution to our understanding of psychosis, because it attempts to penetrate to the very root of human experience. That root is conceived existentially rather than biologically as in psychoanalytic theory. This extends our original conception of a psychology that takes consciousness seriously. In psychosis the existential concepts become particularly vivid, and in the existential way of thinking, psychosis becomes particularly vivid, human, and comprehensible.

PSYCHOSIS AND PSYCHOPATHY IV

The psychotic struggle 12

1. The Existential Platform

I am a person.

There are objective qualities to the person I am, such as the shape of my body and the date of my birth. These are given and final. These objective qualities are experienced by other persons whose subjective world permits me a place. Not everyone puts my objective qualities, or my behavior, in the same place, and so people disagree about what sort of person I really am.

Among those who "place" the objective person I am into a world is myself, my own subjective center of being.

I have a body that submits to my decision to move in space, but which also submits to reliable contingencies of nature, such as gravity and infection. Most of the time I feel at one with my body; it expresses what I feel; it is I. Sometimes it frustrates me with its physical limitations, those reliable contingencies of nature to which it must submit.

The other is also a person. He too has a body that submits to approximately the same limitations I do. I see his bodily expression (including speech) and read from it his mood, his thoughts and his being. He is similarly situated with respect to me.

There are, however, thoughts and feelings that I can keep from the other by inhibiting my bodily expression of them. He is similarly situated, and we know one another to the extent that we allow one another to know our subjective experience.

My body has a history and its history is my history. The sprained muscle of a year ago is still sore. I am the same person who sprained a muscle. Before that I had parents, out of whose bodies I came and in whose presence I learned my first lessons about life. My parents will die (or have died); and eventually I too will die, after which the person I am will no longer be. This will happen at some future time (I do not know when), some point ahead of where I am now as I experience myself moving toward being older.

That death will be the closing of time for me; it will complete the *Gestalt* of my life and thus give it its final form. Because I know it will have a final form, I know that what I choose to do before I die has a kind of importance, a determining importance to what that form will be. Although I will not be around to see the final form, I care about what it looks like because it is I. I care about myself. But my death is not the end of time for others, some of whom will look at that final form and judge it, be enriched or impoverished because of it, find joy or disappointment in it. I care about them too, and so I care about that form. I do not suppose that I will be here to enjoy their praise or suffer their condemnation, but they will be here to experience one or the other, and so I care about it.

Spread out in front of me is the visual space in which I move. It is regular and three dimensional. In back of me, out of my vision, there is more space essentially like that in front of me, except that life's furniture is arranged differently in different places in space.

I can shut my eyes and imagine a place where I currently am not. My imagination can, if it wants, totally ignore the data of my sense organs and my immediate memory. I can, in imagination, transport myself anywhere; in imagination I can change my identity. I can imagine what it is like to be another person, and I can look at myself from the point of view of that imagined other person.

I can do anything in fantasy, and periodically I play out elaborate plots and schemes. The fantasy world, however, is not confused with my more serious "real world." I rarely lose track of the difference; but regularly I do so in sleep, when my body is safely immobile. Sometimes I will seek verification for the reliability of my real world from others, for I know I have imagined some things that were not verified. But I trust my own perception most of the time.

These assertions are similar to what most of us would say about life. They constitute the fundamental *experiential structure* upon which our life-experience is elaborated. An experience that does not fit into that structure will be dismissed by us as illusory. We do not ordinarily challenge this basic structure, although it is amusing occasionally to contemplate infinite time and space. Rarely do such ideas take on the demand character and verisimilitude of our usual experience; and when they do, we say we have had a religious or mystical experience. This allows us to undertake conversion or to bind it up into a package we don't have to take too seriously.

We are totally dependent on such an experiential structure. Without these assumptions as a framework within which to interpret daily events, we would experience chaos and panic.

But these assertions also have a certain strangeness about them. We do not usually see them written down. We do not even think of them in sentence form as they are presented here. They are not really "propositions" at all; they are more akin to "presuppositions." They are not experienced by us in discursive form; but even more importantly, they are not *experienced* in the usual sense at all. Rather they are the ground against which the figure of our conscious experience is played out. They are the precondition for our experience in the first place. They are the "place of standing" from which we intend and interpret life. They are our *existential platform*. One cannot question such a place of standing at all except from a different place of standing. And the fact is that our individual places of standing are and have been the consensually validated ones for a long time for all of us. Our commitment toward this orientation is total. Our being is predicated upon it; indeed this orientation is our being; it is the core of how we carry on our "aming"; it is how we are.

Suppose, however, that one should find that this structure has a fundamental flaw. Suppose that one should seriously consider that some one or several planks in this platform are experientially wrong, that experience makes more sense from an alternative place of standing. Suppose that one's being is predicated upon a different structure, and that his commitment to, say, the "eternity of every moment" is just as total as ours. Such a person's behavior would appear strange to us, and our inferences about his being (a process of which we are not usually aware) would yield the conclusion that the man is insane or a mystic. (Can we really tell the difference?)

We may judge such a person to be psychotic and lock him up, out of sheer incomprehension of his being. We do, indeed, fear that which we don't understand; and we do have a tendency to insulate ourselves from those we fear, with an occasional outburst of aggression that can be witnessed in the staff of any mental hospital. And it is little wonder that we fail to understand the psychotic and his place of standing, for we usually fail to understand ourselves and our own place of standing. More accurately, we fail to understand even that we *have* a particular place of standing, an orientation that provides the framework within which our experience is meaningful. This failure is a missing of the forest for the trees by psychologists who have not taken consciousness seriously and who have therefore been unwilling to ask the right questions about human psychology.

The assertions with which we began this chapter are on a certain level of generality. There are more specific planks to the particular platform upon which I stand that will be different from yours. For example, you may operate on the assumption that if you reveal yourself honestly to another, he will reciprocate. Your commitment to such a plank is not as complete as to the assumption that you "have a body that submits to your decision to move in space. . . ." I could get you to change your mind about the former sooner than I could about the latter.

But the level of generality of these assertions is about right to describe the place of standing of sane America in the late twentieth century. The "analysis of being" in Chapter 3 is a condensation of these assertions into the bedrock fundamentals of human experience. I *am* in-the-world, and in so being I experience myself as a subject who makes decisions and has reactions to the world. I also *am* as an object of my own reflection. And I *am* as an object for the subjective scrutiny of others.

2. Panic

The natural state of man is panic. The usual achievement of man is to replace panic with security, partly by affirming himself and thus establishing a self (as subject), and partly by relying on objective qualities to supply him with the continuity of a self-as-object. The interaction of these within oneself and with other people is the crucial existential nexus out of which grows one's posture toward life. Various anomalies that lead to what we call neurosis have been discussed. The crucial existential event, the peculiar shift in orientation that underlies psychosis is a loss of something without which the panic cannot long be avoided, a loss so basic that security is out of the question, for this crucial plank in one's existential platform is the basic experience of being. It is one thing to doubt *what* one is; it is something quite different to doubt *that* one is. Psychosis is therefore a profound existential event.

Panic emerges as one's platform dissolves. The depth of that panic can be described only in the most extreme terms, for our language is not geared to such experiences:

> General misery, physical discomfort, degradation not born of intellectual concept, but a deep, bodily and inner mental state; a feeling of being lost, lost utterly with no sense of place or time, no idea as to whom voices belonged, no clear realization of my own identity, lost in mind and body and soul, lost to light and form and color; a distinct, acid nausea of self-revulsion—all these were in the feeling that swept over me. But they do not describe it any more than a list of ingredients describes any assembled whole. It was all the more complete in that I was not conscious of intellectual activity of any kind. My whole being was given over to feeling. I had not the slightest defence, either within myself or without. The sensation grew, rolled upon me like a gigantic wave. I gasped, struggled; there was a sickening, acute moment, then a welding. The emotion became *me*. I went down with it whence it had come, to some far depth beyond the bounds of any remembering (Hillyer, 1926, pp. 71–72).

> There also crept into my mind the familiar feeling of separation—separation from everything else on earth. I quite

forgot the little creature opposite me. I felt every moment as if
I were up higher and higher. I could never get down, get back;
the room opened on to . . . space, blank, void. I could never
get back, never find myself or anything. The room moved a little
as if it were gradually slipping into that all-enveloping nothingness. . . . Then the consciousness of sex again reared its head;
it made me sicker, but I could not shake it off. I did very little
thinking in the higher sense of the word. It was as if, for the
moment, I had slipped back to kinship with a primitive life
form, knowing only sex and immediate environment. The one
human element was a perfectly definite sense of revulsion, and
perhaps suffering almost to a normal level. The revulsion grew.
I did not have the energy to endure any strong emotion. For a
number of months, under such stress, I simply slipped back into
the dark, as some people faint as the result of physical injury
(Hillyer, 1926, pp. 74–75).

One cannot sustain such panic for long. The restitutive attempts to regain an orientation that will allow some measure of
security are the vicissitudes of the psychosis. Cognitive content is
imposed as a way to order the experience, and delusional and
hallucinatory phenomena result. When there is a "psychotic resolution," the search for a stable orientation reaches a plateau. Virtually
any content available to the most productive imagination may become the central organizing plank in a new platform. Lara Jefferson (1947) uses the identity of Shakespeare and the act of writing
to solidify some stability in the face of the threatening panic:

My own brain is quivering on the verge of dissolution.
Nothing can retain a definite contour when it is subjected to an
explosion such as we have this morning.

I cannot stand it! Shakespeare! For God's sake, where
are you! Sit here and help me hang on to this pencil! I tell you
I cannot stand it. I feel the roots of my hair drawing together
so I know it is standing on end and the flesh of my arms is all
goose-bumps. Feel of my hair, Mr. Shakespeare, and tell me if
it is not standing on end—no never mind, I know it is. But
no matter—you just hang on to this pencil and write something; write it fast for we cannot afford to lift our voices even
one little peep. You hang on to this pencil and put something

on paper. Anything—anything! I am not going to lift my voice in this howling. You do not like nuts, do you, Mr. Shakespeare? They are not nearly so interesting when you are one of them and have to live, see, and hear them when there are no others for variation. I cannot say I like them either, but I know I am as insane as the wildest one here. I cannot afford to let it be known by howling out loud. Sorry, Mr. Shakespeare; you should not have come to me so blithely as my delusion of grandeur. I know it was more pleasant back in your quiet English grave.

You did not know what sort of a jam you were getting yourself into. But now that you are here I cannot turn you loose to let you go back; much as I would like to go with you. I cannot stand this and I dare not dismiss you. Your education is being completed, Mr. Shakespeare. Now you can write about nuts from experience—first hand experience and you will not have to depend upon your more comfortable imagination. I know when you build characters from fancy they are more pleasant but here they are all around you charging, howling, and no one—not even you with your former skillful use of language, could construct such creatures with words—for words cannot portray them.

This is the real thing, Mr. Shakespeare. Madness. Stark, senseless, maniacal Madness. It is like a mad bull in a pasture—much safer when you can survey it through a tall fence; from a safe distance. Unless you write faster; you will be tossed on the horns of the creature; to say nothing of being gored and trampled. You are seeing Madness here, Mr. Shakespeare; at first hand—and you have nothing but the stub of a chewed up pencil to protect yourself with. You will sure as hell have to write faster. I'm going—I feel that crazy "light" feeling in the temples and my eyes are not seeing things rightly. Write, damn it. Write something. Anything, it does not matter.

There is something around my head so tight I cannot think, but you are going to sit here and keep putting something on paper. That is the law and I'm laying it down to you. You shall not run out on me. I need you now if I ever needed you. And remember, Mr. Shakespeare, one little squawk and your goose will be cooked. You are not a genius in this present inferno, only a nut in a bughouse. So it need not make the least bit of difference what you write; just so you keep at it. I cannot help you with it—for I feel my brain exploding. For God's sake keep

at it! Never mind whether it is something you would like to say—
or whether it has any beauty. You have no time to use an eraser
if you had one.

Keep writing—and write as though you were pursued by
Satan—for whether you have sense enough to know it or not—
you are! Something has caught us and is sweeping us to the devil.
You are not writing drama this time, you are living it.

Get busy, "Three Building" is worse than this. You are
not preserving the best traditions of English literature now—it is
a few glimmers and shreds of reason you hold together—if you
can. It is your sanity you are trying to rescue.

Write faster—you fool—if you do not want to disintegrate
into a jittering idiot. Your reason has left you already and the
only thing keeping you from becoming another howling maniac
is just not turning loose and being one; for you certainly have
the makings of a real one. Keep on with your writing. Do not
run out on me—I know I cannot make the grade without you.

If you can keep me from howling it will be a greater indication of genius than anything possibly conjured out of the imagination. This is not imagination—it is worse. It is a nightmare.
A nightmare while you are wide awake, so no one can come
awaken you if you yell. Wide awake in the middle of a nightmare, Mr. Shakespeare. If you were asleep you might yell and
maybe someone would hear you, come in and shake you—but
if you yell in this—all the shaking they can give you will not
awaken you. Mr. Shakespeare—My God! Do you want to yell?
Well—don't. Shut it up before it gets started, damn it.

I told you to write—write you fool! Words! Anything!
Never mind whether or not they make sense. Write! Shut up and
say it on paper! You are a bigger jack-ass than I. Genius—Bah!
Nut—brother nut! Whatever genius you may have had you lost
coming to me. You damned fool, if you give way to this hysteria
and let so much as one little peep out of you there will be no
stopping it. I know—I had that happen once, and no power on
earth can stop it. The only way to hold it is to stop it before it
gets started. The primeval chaos had nothing on this—it was as
sedate as a middleaged spinster. Poor Bill, poor Bill; what a jam
for a genius to get into.

Come next time to someone who wants to write about the
flowers, birds and bees, William, for there is nothing this side
of Hell like Madness. But hold the fort for a few minutes longer.
The rescue is coming! The rescue is coming: in the form of a

nurse, God bless her, and Mercury, dear God of speed, help her to hurry! She has a hypodermic in each hand and another nurse is bringing a cup of paraldehyde. God bless and prosper the man who discovered it! Drugs—Drugs—Unconsciousness! Quietness!

Well—that was that, William. We made it! Thank you! I have no idea what you have written the last few minutes—but I know I feel like Jacob of old who contended with the angel. I have an ankle out of joint and am so wringing wet with perspiration there is not a dry thread upon me. I am most grateful to you. The doctor can give my sick hypo to someone who did not have the good fortune to choose you for a delusion of grandeur. He can think what he likes of delusions of grandeur—but what you did for me, I could not do for myself. We made it! Whether the world ever knows it or not—the writing you have been doing for the last half hour is an indication of greater genius than all your previous works put together!

Shakespeare, we got through that crisis—though it seemed for awhile it would happen and in spite of everything I was going to go off at the deep end—with a splash. When and if that happens there is only "Three Building" left—and hopeless insanity (Jefferson, 1947, pp. 204–209).

This account is a peculiar mixture. The author recaptures the panic in her account, and in so doing she seems to be operating from the orientation of a person losing her grip. But it is written to be read and understood by sane people, as if the sane orientation were familiar and available to the author. This paradox is probably explained by the fact that considerable editing of the original documents was done by the publisher.

It is also curious, in this passage, that the author seems to vacillate between talking *to* Shakespeare, as if she had an identity of her own from which to speak, and talking *through* Shakespeare, an identity she assumed at first as a cynical put-on for the nurses in her ward, but without which she would not have been able to maintain an orientation to ward off the panic. It appears that Lara Jefferson does not, at least in this passage, ever accept the delusion as a resolution but rather uses it as a foil in the absence of any other meaningful relationship through which she could remain a person. This suggests that a relationship with another person, even a fantasy relationship, can help to supply the stability of an orientation to hold the line against the panic of psychotic dissolution.

3. The Psychotic Struggle

The psychotic struggle is against the panic of experiential chaos. Of the several excellent accounts of this struggle, we will examine closely a part of Marguerite Sechehaye's *Autobiography of a Schizophrenic Girl* (1951). Rene, unlike Lara Jefferson, had a therapist in terms of whom it was possible, for a while, to remain a person in something like the usual sense.

We begin at a point in the account when the content of experience has resolved itself into a profound guilt. This experience implies the stability of a self-orientation, but with somewhat different planks than ordinary sanity.

> For to feel oneself guilty is the worst that can happen, it is the punishment of punishments. Consequently, I could never be relieved of it as though I had been truly punished. Quite the reverse, I felt more and more guilty, immeasurably guilty. Constantly, I sought to discover what was punishing me so dreadfully, what was making me so guilty.
>
> One day I wrote a letter of entreaty to the unknown author of my suffering, to the Persecutor, asking him to tell me what evil I had done, that I might finally know. But because I did not know where to send my letter, I tore it up (p. 28).

The attempt to communicate with the Persecutor is predicated on an extreme of the experience of satellization, where one is predominantly the object of the god's subjectivity. Unlike normal satellization in childhood, however, there are no comforts in being a satellite for Rene. The content of the experience is only punishment, never protection. In the paragraph below, we see a depersonalization of the god into "the system," but the predominant theme of guilt remains, indeed is broadened. Cosmic dimensions are invoked. The temporal orientation moves from one in which a plea could be made at a point in time, after which things would be different, to a timeless, eternal quality that states the way things metaphysically are.

> Some time after, I discovered that the Persecutor was none other than the electric machine, that is, it was the "System" that was punishing me. I thought of it as some vast world-like entity encompassing all men. At the top were those who gave orders, who imposed punishment, who pronounced others guilty. But they were themselves guilty. Since every man was responsible for all other men, each of his acts had a repercussion on other beings. A formidable interdependence bound all men under the scourge of culpability. Everyone was part of the System. But only some were aware of being part (p. 28).

Within the metaphysical restructuring, there is a hierarchy of persons, some of whom are higher and others of whom are lower. In the next paragraph, Rene places herself among the chosen, in typically grandiose fashion. This shift clearly transcends the satellization and constitutes a significant change in orientation. We do not know how much time was required for this shift, but the psychotic struggle usually involves profound instability and these plateaus of restitution may follow one another rapidly.

> They were the ones who were "enlightened" . . . as I was. And it was at the same time both an honor and a misfortune to have this awareness. Those who were not part of it—though actually, of course, they were—were unaware of the System. As a result, they felt not at all guilty, and I envied them intensely (pp. 28–29).

The shift in orientation did not change the guilt. Indeed the System and its theme of culpability swallowed up an earlier, less terrifying (but equally grandiose) plateau, the Land of Enlightenment. Notice that the escape from a horrible satellization by way of a fantastic grandiosity does not supply Rene with an escape from the panic. Only a sense of subjectivity, we have argued, built on authentic relationships with the world offers security.

> At this moment, the ring closed: the Land of Enlightenment was the same as the System. That is why to enter it was to become insensible of everything except culpability, the supreme punishment, freely granted by the System. I was guilty, abominably, intolerably guilty, without cause and without motive. Any punishment, the very worst, could be imposed on me—it could never deliver me of the load. Because, as I have already said, the

most dreadful punishment was to make me feel eternally, universally culpable (p. 29).

In the next paragraph, we see how she experienced her relationship to her therapist. She seems to go through the motions of a relationship, talking and listening, but with a profound sense of unreality. For such experience to have the ordinary coherence and meaning for us, it has to be intended from a more ordinary place of standing.

> It was only when I was near "Mama," my analyst, that I felt a little better. But even for this, nearly an hour had to go by. Indeed, it was only toward the end of the hour, and sometimes not until twenty minutes after it, that I made contact with "Mama." When I arrived, I was as if frozen. I saw the room, the furniture, "Mama" herself, each thing separate, detached from the others, cold, implacable, inhuman, by dint of being without life. Then I began to relate what had happened since the last visit and relived it in the telling. But the sound of my voice and the meaning of my words seemed strange. Every now and then, an inner voice interrupted sneeringly, "Ah, Ah!" and mockingly repeated what I had said (p. 29).

Nevertheless, at the beginning of the above paragraph, there is a sense of relief with "Mama." There is an attempt, at least partly successful, to "make contact," have a relationship and use it as a thread of coherence in the chaotic shifting of orientation. However, the stability is not sufficient to prevent intrusions of memories and voices, as we see below.

> These inner voices had the aspect of the needle in the hay. They were affected, ridiculous. "Ah, ah! then the teacher said, said," and the voice dwelt stiltedly on "said, said." I struggled to repress them, to pay no attention. But they would not obey, the mocking repetitions continued. Often images were associated with the phrases. For example, if I wanted to recount that my German teacher had made some remark or that my little sister had made a row over going to school, I saw the German teacher gesticulating at his desk like a puppet, separated from everything, alone under a blinding light, waving his arms like a maniac. And I saw my little sister, rolling on the kitchen floor in a rage; but she too

was changed by some mechanism, apparently purposeless (pp. 29–30).

The only thread of coherence at this point in the narrative is the depersonalization of people who have lost their souls, i.e., their subjectivity, and who are automatons, i.e., objects, moved around by some other authority. Below even Mama becomes victimized by the System and we witness a return of the panic. The panic is accompanied by an expectable deterioration of even perceptions. This is literally a disintegration; parts become unstuck from wholes and the organization of experience dissolves.

> These people who in reality behaved in accordance with goals and well-defined incentive became void and lost their souls. Only their bodies were left them, moving like automatons, and their movements were deprived of emotion and feeling. This was awful. To get rid of these images, of these inner voices, I looked at "Mama." But I perceived a statue, a figure of ice which smiled at me. For I saw the individual features of her face, separated from each other: the teeth, then the nose, then the cheeks, then one eye and the other. Perhaps it was the independence of each part that inspired such fear and prevented my recognizing her even though I knew who she was.
>
> In the rest of the room, in the silence, everything was there, posed, congealed, stupid. And the terror, the mad anguish, mounted in me. I hid myself against Mama's shoulder, shielded by her arm, feeling her warmth and the faint fragrance of her clothes. I closed my eyes and cried, "I'm afraid, I'm afraid, the straw is there, and you don't exist. Help me, help me, the System is going to get me, the waters are rising, I am going to drown, I am cold, I am plunged in cold; oh, how afraid I am; why have you changed, why have you become a statue and let the System give you orders, oh! Why?" (pp. 30–31).

Below we see the shaping up of a conflict between two orientations, a satellization with a benevolent person and a satellization to a malevolent System. These are two alternative world-constructions. We are led to hope for the victory of the former, partly because we as readers fear the panic as much as Rene. Also, the relationship with the therapist suggests to us, in our ordinary sanity, the possibility of growth and the consolidation of security. We share the concept of a benevolent other and therefore see the therapist as more real than the System, but of course that is because of our place of standing.

> I clung desperately to her, clutching at her dress. I wanted so to take refuge in her, to hide in her heart, to escape the frightful anguish that overwhelmed me.
>
> All this time I heard the mocking sneers and the stilted unrelated phrases repeating, "And we shall see," or "Battle of Trafalgar," or "Yes, miss." (p. 31).

In the next passage we feel ourselves, as we read the narrative, cheering for the relationship and hoping for the disappearance of the System. Both are temporary resolutions, and both organize experience into a coherent world.

> Then Mama's sweet voice sounded in the midst of this madness and she was saying, "Little Rene, my little Rene needn't be afraid when there is a Mama. Rene is not alone now. Mama is here to take Rene out of the water; we will win. See how strong Mama is, she knows how to protect Rene. Rene has nothing to fear." And she passed her light hand over my head and kissed my forehead. Then, her voice, the caress on my hair, her protection, began to exert their charm.
>
> Little by little, the phrases and sneers disappeared, the unreal perception of the room no longer mattered; I closed my eyes. What did me the most amazing good was her use of the third person in speaking of herself, "Mama and Rene," not "I and you." When by chance she used the first person, abruptly I no longer knew her, and I was angry that she had, by this error, broken my contact with her. So that when she said, "You will see how together we shall fight against the System," (what were "I" and "you?") for me there was no reality. Only "Mama," "Rene," or better still, "the little personage," contained reality, life, affectivity (pp. 31–32).

It is curious that the saner of the two resolutions, the relationship with "Mama," must, for Rene, be predicated upon an impersonalization of the two characters. First person pronouns destroy the stability. This betrays how unreal the "better" of the two resolutions is. The experience of a real relationship, where both parties can be subjects and objects simultaneously, where one can objectify the other without a struggle from the other to preserve his subjectivity, and where one's self can be submitted to a situation of some unpredictability, is too threatening for Rene. It brings with it a return of the chaos and panic. Rene needs, at this point, not another person in the usual sense, but rather she needs a protective, a god-like point of reference to ward off the panic. To achieve this is still a long way from achieving a self that feels secure enough to survive a real relationship in which that self is objectified by a "you." It is also a long way from a self-world orientation that assures one that the power of one's own subjectivity cannot destroy the other by objectifying it.

These two dangers, that I will objectify and hence destroy you, or that you will me, constitute the dual threat of a real relationship. One does not have to be psychotic to feel the fear. But for most of us, whose existential platform is fairly well constructed, we can hedge our bets and move in and out of danger with some flexibility. For Rene, whose existential platform is in constant flux, such a luxury is not possible. The panic is too close, too present, too threatening. We see in the next passage that the therapist succeeds in establishing a totally nondemanding and nonthreatening ground for contact with Rene. Mama offers all the security of a relationship without any of the insecurity. She even becomes a voice instead of a person: ". . . . Mama's voice loves Rene."

> I did not know how to explain to Mama all that went on. I believed that she understood anyway. So when I complained of these distressing experiences in such words as, "I am afraid," or "the straw is spreading," or "everything is separated," or "you are disguised as ice," or "it is cold," wonderfully enough, Mama divined the horror.
>
> Sometimes when I told her "The phrases are playing tricks on me and making fun of me," Mama chased them away, saying, "Rene should listen only to Mama's voice; it is important, for Mama's voice loves Rene." Then I heard this marvelous voice which, like a talisman, could give me again a moment of reality, a contact with life. Relieved, but exhausted by the struggle and anxiety, I began to talk a little of what absorbed and interested me. But, alas, it was already time to leave (p. 32).

Mama's voice, "like a talisman, could give me again a moment of reality, a contact with life." The magical quality of the voice becomes the girder underlying a platform that enables Rene to function. The unreality of the world continues, but its panic-provoking power is blunted against an island of stability tied to Mama's voice:

> Warmed again, encouraged, softly repeating Mama's words, I went home. Once in the street, however, I saw again the pasteboard scenery of unreality. Nevertheless, I did not suffer from it as I had at the beginning of the session for I still kept a little of Mama's warmth, her words in my heart. Particularly, I no longer struggled to break the unreality but submitted to the odd perception without trying to change it. As for the way home, the people, or the objects I passed, I experienced no further pressing need to enter into contact with them as with Mama (pp. 32–33).

In the next passage, Rene offers us an extraordinary insight into therapeutic styles. The earlier, more demanding style of Mama assumed more strength in Rene's existential platform than was there, as if Rene were a neurotic.

> I was glad that Mama changed her method at the end of the first year of analysis. In the beginning, she analyzed everything I said, my fear, my guilt. These investigations seemed to me like a bill of complaints, quite as though in looking for the cause of feelings, they became more at fault and more real. As if to say, "Find out in what instances you are guilty, and why." This for me was proof that the guilt existed, that the System was really there since one could find the reasons for its actions. From these sessions I went home more unhappy, more blameworthy, more isolated than ever, without any contact, alone in my own unreal world.
>
> But after Mama sat down beside me, talked to me in the third person and especially seemed to understand without looking for causes at all, how relieved I was! She alone could break through the unreal wall that hemmed me in; she alone kept me in some contact with life (p. 33).

Presumably some time passes before Rene's existential struggle takes on a new form. In the next passage, Rene undergoes a struggle with *things,* ordinary objects whose oppressive presence constitutes another kind of threat to the shaky stability she had achieved in the relationship to Mama.

> Unreality finally reached such a point that Mama herself could no longer make contact between us. For some time I had been complaining bitterly that things were tricking me and how I suffered because of it.
>
> As a matter of fact, these "things" weren't doing anything special; they didn't speak, nor attack me directly. It was their very presence that made me complain. I saw things, smooth as metal, so cut off, so detached from each other, so illuminated and tense that they filled me with terror. When, for example, I looked at a chair or a jug, I thought not of their use or function—a chair not as something to sit in—but as having lost their names, their functions and meanings; they became "things" and began to take on life, to exist.
>
> This existence accounted for my great fear. In the unreal scene, in the murky quiet of my perception, suddenly "the thing" sprang up. The stone jar, decorated with blue flowers, was there facing me, defying me with its presence, with its existence. To conquer my fear I looked away. My eyes met a chair, then a table; they were alive, too, asserting their presence. I attempted to escape their hold by calling out their names. I said, "chair, jug, table, it is a chair." But the word echoed hollowly, deprived of all meaning; it had left the object, was divorced from it, so much so that on one hand it was a living, mocking thing, on the other, a name, robbed of sense, an envelope emptied of content. Nor was I able to bring the two together, but stood rooted there before them, filled with fear and impotence.
>
> When I protested, "Things are tricking me; I am afraid," and people asked specifically, "Do you see the jug and the chair as alive?" I answered, "Yes, they are alive." And they, the doctors, too, thought I saw these things as humans whom I heard speak. But it was not that. Their life consisted uniquely in the fact that they were there, in their existence itself.
>
> To flee from them I hid my hands or stood in a corner. I lived through a period of intense suffering. Everything was alive, defied me. Outside in the street people were struck mad, moved around without reason, encountered each other and things which had become more real than they (pp. 34–36).

Psychologists will undoubtedly read a great variety of meanings into this provocative passage. Kaplan (1964) suggests that this "surely . . . is the same phenomenon that Sartre talks about in *Nausea*" (p. 164), and one must agree. From our point of view we must say that the self-world, subject-object relationship, so basic to one's being-in-the-world, is fundamentally altered. To experience the world from our usual existential platform is to see things as objects, that is, as objectified by our own subjectivity. The object is an occasion for our being a subject, and in objectifying it we affirm our subjectivity and experience ourselves as subject. In objectifying an object, we name it, give it a meaning, and place it into the coherent picture of our world. In fact these three processes are nearly the same thing. For Rene, the names of things became detached from the things themselves, the meaning of the things was lost, and their "place" in the world ceased to make sense. In a word, Rene could not objectify the objects, and lacking this, she could not experience herself as a subject. The entire existential platform shifted in such a way that her experience of the objects followed some other rules, or perhaps it was the *absence* of rules that made objects loom up into a terrifying presence that she could not trust. Things changed their meaning, or perhaps it is more accurate to say that they became entirely meaningless. The process of controlling experience by vesting it with meaning went away.

The System now comes to have a terrible power over her again. In losing the ability to objectify and thus in losing her subjectivity, Rene also lost power relative to the ominous threat of the System. To surrender to the System is a loss of control and the occasion of panic, as we see below, but at least the System offers stability. To submit to the System is to control panic through a symbolic world-construction, even at the cost of the System running her life.

> At the same time I received orders from the System. I did not hear the orders as voices; yet they were as imperious as if uttered in a loud voice. While, for example, I was preparing to do some typing, suddenly, without any warning a force, which was not an impulse but rather resembled a command, ordered me to burn my right hand or the building in which I was. With all my strength I resisted the order. I telephoned Mama to tell her about it. Her voice, urging me to listen to her and not to the System, reassured me. If the System became too demanding I was

to run to her. This calmed me considerably, but unfortunately only for a moment.

An indescribable anguish squeezed my heart, an anguish no resolve could allay. If I refused to obey, I felt guilty and cowardly for not daring, and the anguish mounted. Then the order became more insistent. If, finally to obey, I went to the fire and stretched out my hand, an intense feeling of guilt overcame me as though I were doing something wicked, and the anxiety waxed in proportion. I should say, however, that the latter alternative provoked the greater disturbance, for I felt that if I obeyed the order, I should commit an act irreparably damaging to my personality. And yet in both cases, obedience or disobedience, was something artificial, something theatrical. Meanwhile, I was alone; no one except Mama knew of my battle.

I had, too, the conviction that my behavior was deceitful. In reality, it wasn't anything of the kind. I was deeply sincere. But if I disobeyed the System to maintain the integrity of my personality, I was deceitful since I acted as though I had no consideration for the order. If I obeyed it, I was equally deceitful, since I did not agree to burn myself. I suffered horribly from the orders and from the feeling of treachery so contrary to my character (pp. 36–37).

This is a herculean and a mortal struggle. The conflict between Mama and the System is condensed into one highly symbolic act, to burn her right hand. The conflict therefore becomes very concrete. The particular symbolic content may have come from anywhere. Certainly to follow orders to burn one's own right hand is a poignant sign of submission. The important theme, however, seems to be the feeling of a double-bind. Two injunctions are imposed; to follow either is to betray the other, with terrible consequences. Life seemed to stack up into a horrible trap. Deceit and inevitable guilt are built right into the structure of the world. Such an existential platform leaves no way out, and panic again begins to emerge. Below we see the attempt again to contain the panic in vivid symbolic images, whose bizarre and morbid content suggest primitive themes of devouring and being devoured.

While I fought with all my strength not to let myself sink in the Enlightenment, I saw things mocking me from their places, taunting me threateningly. And in my head foolish phrases floated around without letup. I closed my eyes to escape the surrounding turmoil of which I was the center. But I could find no rest, for horrible images assailed me, so vivid that I experienced actual physical sensation. I cannot say that I really saw images; they did not represent anything. Rather I felt them. It seemed that my mouth was full of birds which I crunched between my teeth, and their feathers, their blood and broken bones were choking me. Or I saw people whom I had entombed in milk bottles, putrefying, and I was consuming their rotting cadavers. Or I was devouring the head of a cat which meanwhile gnawed at my vitals. It was ghastly, intolerable (p. 37).

We shall conclude the narrative with the next passage, which concludes with Rene's hospitalization and begins with the surprising information that:

In the midst of this horror and turbulence, I nonetheless carried on my work as secretary. But with what hardship! Adding to the torment, strident noises, piercing cries began to hammer in my head. Their unexpectedness made me jump. Nonetheless, I did not hear them as I heard real cries uttered by real people. The noises, localized on the right side, drove me to stop up my ears. But I readily distinguished them from the noises of reality. I heard them without hearing them, and recognized that they arose within me.

I knew that more and more I would let myself be controlled by the System, that I would sink down in the Land of Enlightenment, or the Land of Commandment, as I also called it.

My only moments of peace were the analytic sessions, particularly toward the end of the hour when I had finally secured some contact with Mama. I implored her to save me from the clutches of the Enlightenment and the animation of Things.

But despite her good intentions, she was then powerless against the System. That she was able to resist it and that I could always run back to her when I was in danger was in itself a remarkable victory.

At last the tragedy occurred. The orders became more imperious, more demanding: I was to burn my right hand, for the right hand was the hand of the law.

In the System a formidable interdependence existed. Without knowing it, I had ordered that people be punished, and in my turn, I was to be punished. Those who had received punishment from me had the right to punish, but for each punishment they meted out, one was incurred. When I understood the mechanism of the System of Punishments which engulfed me, I fought less and less against the orders.

One day, trembling, I placed the back of my right hand on the incandescent coals and held it there as long as possible. By thinking of my duty to the System and that it might then stop issuing injunctions, I was able to stand the pain. At this moment the head of the office came in unexpectedly. Quickly withdrawing my hand, I was relieved at the thought that he had not seen me. But I was mistaken. He had no doubt grasped the situation at once, for he notified the physician of the Council for Supervision of the Mentally Ill, who happened to be my own doctor.

Realizing their intention of hospitalizing me after consultation, I spoke of the objects making fun of me and of the System surrounding me, since these had become part of me, but I kept quiet about the burn and the orders I had received, for I had never been altogether in agreement with them. However, that was enough to prompt hospitalization, lest, without it, I be officially committed to an institution (p. 38–39).

References

Hillyer, J. *Reluctantly Told.* New York: Macmillan, 1926.

Jefferson, L. *These Are My Sisters.* Tulsa: Vickers, 1948.

Kaplan, B. *The Inner World of Mental Illness.* New York: Harper & Row, 1964.

Sechehaye, M. *Autobiography of a Schizophrenic Girl.* New York: Grune & Stratton, 1951.

The psychotic resolution 13

The term, "psychotic resolution" has wide currency in the psychological literature. In no small measure this term emerges from psychoanalytic thought, which leans on the metaphor of conflict. The conflict is usually inevitable, given the state of human nature and the contingencies of a particular life history. The metaphor of conflict, however, begs the question, "Conflict of what?" The psychoanalytic answer is the entire theory of mental economics, with "energy" pushed through channels, variously blocked and deflected, culminating in phenomena of thought, feeling, and behavior. The phenomena of thought, feeling, and behavior, of course, are the concrete data. The economic model of the mind is an inferential hypothesis that has tremendous descriptive and explanatory power. We must not fail to be impressed with Freud's genius for creating a way of talking that is simultaneously personal and impersonal. A particular feeling, for example, may be private and idiosyncratic, and yet it is subject to interpretation in the most general and scientific terms of energy economics. The experiential flow that we followed in the last chapter could be described and explained in these terms if we were so inclined.

Freud (1959) offers us an example of such an analysis in the paper, "Psychoanalytic Notes Upon an Autobiographical Account of a Case of Paranoia." We shall begin this chapter with an examination of this case. Paranoia is the supreme form of psychotic resolution, but we shall change the meaning of "resolution." Especially in the matter of psychosis, "resolution" may have a meaning that does not depend on the metaphor of "conflict" between two contradictory energy vectors within the mind. "Resolution" for us means the reestablishing of an existential platform. This is not to say that people do not experience contradictory impulses simultaneously; we all surely do. But these experiences are subject to many metaphors for description. We seek to use the language of being instead of the language of energy economics.

1. Notes on Dr. Schreber

Dr. Daniel Paul Schreber, the subject of Freud's analysis, published his *Denkwürdigkeiten* in 1903 while he was still psychotic. His delusionary system had reached a stability that is manifest in his writing. The content of his delusion was that he had a special relationship to God, one in which he was destined to be transformed from a man into a woman, after which he was obliged to play out the extreme of "spiritual voluptuousness" for God. There is a definite notion of having fought God and won, side by side with the notion of submitting to God in a passive, feminine way. Freud notes that Schreber's conception of God expresses a "mixture of reverence and rebelliousness in his attitude toward him" (p. 409). Freud's reconstruction of Schreber's psychological life begins with the hypothesis of a passive and submissive attitude toward his father and brother, which looks, in sexual terms, like an unconscious homosexual wish. Further:

> . . . the exciting cause of the illness was the appearance in him of a feminine (that is, a passive homosexual) wishful phantasy, which took as its object the figure of his doctor. An intense resistance to this phantasy arose on the part of Schreber's personality, and the ensuing defensive struggle, which might perhaps just as well have assumed some other shape, took on, for reasons unknown to us, that of a delusion of persecution. The person he longed for now became his persecutor, and the content of his wishful phantasy became the content of his persecution (pp. 431–432).

Here we see the outline of a conflict. An unacceptable wish, opposed by "Schreber's personality." The latter party to the conflict was later formalized into a more specific mental institution by Freud, the ego.

But this conflict underwent a transformation:

> It was impossible for Schreber to become reconciled to playing the part of a female wanton towards his doctor; but the task of providing God himself with the voluptuous sensations that He required called up no such resistance on the part of his ego. Emasculation was now no longer a disgrace; it became "consonant with the Order of Things", it took its place in a great cosmic chain of events, and was instrumental in the re-creation of humanity after its extinction (p. 432).

Freud is now able triumphantly to point out:

> By this means an outlet was provided which would satisfy both of the contending forces. His ego found compensation in his megalomania, while his feminine wishful phantasy made its way through and became acceptable (p. 432).

This is the essence of Freud's interpretation, and one cannot read the case without being impressed with Freud's brilliant reduction of psychopathological data into the terms of the economic model. A "conflict" between two "contending forces" achieves a resolution by finding an "outlet" that would "satisfy both." Throughout the case study, detail after detail is translated into economic terms and fit into this central format. The emerging picture is coherent and sensible.

Let us now reconsider the dynamic of this not atypical case from an existential point of view. Our crucial assumption will be that the resolution comes not as a result of some new energy vector that emerges from the conflict of two contradictory ones but that "resolution" means the stabilizing of an existential platform in the face of experiential chaos. Furthermore, the explanation for *when* and *how* stability is achieved does not grow out of an image of a conflict of forces. It emerges from the dynamics of being, as we have described them, and the crucial goal of experiential resolution is an escape from panic.*

Let us begin with a statement from Freud's analysis with which we can agree. Schreber had been ill before; he recovered, and then had a series of dreams. Immediately after one of his dreams, it occurred to him "that after all it really must be very nice to be a woman submitting to the act of copulation (Freud, 1959, p. 391)." Freud concludes:

> The dreams and the phantasy are reported by Schreber in immediate succession; and if we also bring together their subject-matter, we shall be able to infer that, at the same time as his recollection of his illness, a recollection of his doctor was also aroused in his mind, and that *the feminine attitude* which he assumed in the phantasy was from the first directed towards the doctor (p. 425, italics added).

What is meant, in this passage, by "the feminine attitude"? Freud's meaning of "attitude" ultimately boils down to a wish or an impulse, conceived as a quantum of energy that had been repressed ever since he had homosexual desires for his father and brother as a child. The illness loosened the repression, as did the later dreams, and there is an *association* between the wish and other dream contents, namely, his earlier illness and his doctor. Thus the wish is "transferred" to the doctor and later "projected" to produce the delusion that the doctor wanted to emasculate him.

Let us give the term "feminine attitude" a different meaning. Rather than a quantum of energy, let us consider it a plank in Schreber's existential platform. Schreber constructed a world, into which he placed himself in a certain way. He thus intended objects in that world according to certain interpretive assumptions that were built up and systematized over the years. Instead of transference of energy (wish) from one mental image (father) to another (doctor), and later projection of the wish content to the doctor, we can suppose that the feminine attitude was a part of Schreber's orientation to life and his style in construing the meaning of certain

* This formulation bears a resemblance to a part of psychoanalytic thought, namely, that the task of the mental apparatus is to "bind" energy. However, this metaphor does not permit an elaborate experiential analysis.

people and their behavior. Schreber's "primary life space" (see Chapter 7) was structured in this way, and his construing of himself was also some part of that life-space.

The central notion of projection therefore must be reexamined. No one doubts that we see in others those things we fear or hate in ourselves. But this way of constructing a world is more than an isolated misperception based on internal psychodynamics. It involves the very basis of experience, that is, the existential platform. More specifically, to see in others what we refuse to see in ourselves is to confuse the object "me" with the object "other." This confusion is not random. It involves a lying-for-oneself and a lying-in-the-world that becomes built into one's existential platform. Suppose Schreber's immediate, prereflective attitude toward his doctor was a kind of feminine submissiveness (his first illness was largely hypochondriacal) and that this submissiveness had been characteristic of his relations with part of the world since childhood. To face and accept this (homosexual) attraction would be the first step toward choosing otherwise, should he want to. But Schreber's being-for-himself was built on the lie that such a feeling is impossible. This meant that his relationship to the doctor had to be transformed into a lie.

Now it ceased to be the case that Schreber felt he could withhold his feelings from his doctor. His ability to lie-for-others was somehow impaired. Had he constructed a life upon the "sane" existential platform we have described, where one can inhibit expression of feelings and therefore keep them from being known, he could have simply lied-for-the-doctor without resorting to further self-deception. But Schreber did not have this kind of platform. Stemming perhaps from his satellization to his father and brother, his own integrity as a self was experienced as vulnerable to the overwhelming subjectivity of the other, who could objectify him and thus destroy him. Therefore his weakness as a subject made his feminine submissive feeling toward his doctor doubly threatening, and the entire existential platform quaked under its weight. To shore up some stability in the face of this threat, it became necessary to maintain the fiction embedded in his being-for-himself (viz., that such a feeling toward the doctor was impossible) and to invoke a lie-in-the-world, namely that he was appreciative but not self-emasculating toward the doctor.

So far we have described how Schreber could have become a neurotic. But the success of this existential contortion in warding off the panic was only as great as his ability to live the lies consistently. We must infer that the entire artifice, which was elaborate and detailed, suffered from the crucial weakness with which it began, a weakness of self-as-subject. It was therefore *not* the case that Schreber merely saw in his doctor the homosexual designs in his own unconscious. "Projection" is too small a word. What should be said about his interpretation of his doctor's wishes is that his existential platform, which included the "feminine attitude," eventually proved incapable of offering security in the face of existential panic. The *what-I-am* plank (being-for-himself) was out-of-joint with his immediate relation to the world. His *what-I-can-hide* (being-for-others) plank suffered from excessive and unresolved satellization with his brother and father. And his *who I am* or *that I am* plank (self-as-subject) did not have the benefit of contact with the confrontation of certain givens, such as the desire for love, or for intimate bodily contact. These weaknesses produced a world that was profoundly insecure and which eventually came to be, in paranoid grandiosity, insane.

When we speak of this or that "plank" of the "existential platform," we are not, of course, merely referring to cognitive assumptions. Sometimes they are given cognitive expression, especially when the psychotic tries to make himself understood to us. But they really involve one's way of being, in-the-world, for-himself, and for-others. They involve that orientation toward life that is more fundamental than what one thinks, how one feels, or what one does. They involve what and how one is. Projection is not a perceptual or a cognitive phenomenon; it is an existential phenomenon.

Perhaps the most interesting conclusion we have reached about Schreber, and perhaps the one that makes him explicitly paranoid, is the inability simply to lie-for-others. Schreber seems to have felt, as most paranoids do, that he was transparent to others, particularly to his doctor. The suspicion that others know one's thoughts, invade or control them, is a common element in many delusional systems. The security of one's own privacy is essential to maintain a working existential platform we have called "sane." It is closely related to one's experience of his own subjectivity. To be a person, in the sane sense, involves an "assumption" that one can control what one reveals to others. I even suggest that a crucial part of growing up is to discover one's ability to lie, to discover one's privacy and the power to protect it, and to bring self-disclosure into the realm of things one *chooses* to do or not to do, depending on the circumstances. To operate with this kind of existential platform is to have a self, and it is a crucial ingredient in sanity and in warding off panic.

2. Megalomania

The weakness of one's sense of a subjective self, as reflected in the loss of the ability to lie, is a profound self degradation. Only total self dissolution (and total panic) are worse. But along with this self degradation we see in paranoid resolutions an exaggerated and bizarre self-aggrandizement. Terrible powerlessness and equally terrible powerfulness exist side by side. The delusion that one is about to destroy the world, or that one might accidentally do so, combines grandiosity and depravity. (Such delusions are also valid literally, if we interpret "world" phenomenologically.) Similarly, delusions of the ability to do infinite good are often combined with extreme humility in the form of a feeling of being unworthy of such power. Put another way, the active and passive modes of life are experienced only in the extremes. One is totally active and the rest of the world is subject to his power, or one is totally passive, and he is uncompromisingly subject to the power of the world. Most commonly, these two are combined in some fantastic way. The result is often a grotesque caricature of the "sane" existential platform.

Counterparts of these extreme estimates of self can readily be found in childhood. But the questions involved here are existential as well as developmental questions, that is, questions about the fundamental nature of human existence. There is, built into human existence, a realm of the possible which yields to human choice and a realm of the necessary which does not.

It would seem that life's experience offers a consistent input of information into a person's growing up. There is no reason why he should not learn to discriminate reliably the necessary from the possible. It is apparently a matter of learning. The very existence of the phenomena of psychosis, however, suggests that this "learning" is not a simple matter. The crucial addition we must make to a "learning interpretation" of paranoia is that human learning always occurs against the backdrop of an existential platform. It is not an "organism" who learns; it is a "being," which includes the organismic side of life but puts consciousness in the center of it. This implies that human learning, considered apart from the temporality, spatiality, corporality, and identity of the learner, is too superficial a framework for the understanding of psychosis.

It would also seem, from the psychoanalytic point of view, that the difference between necessity and possibility should be realistically assessed by an intact secondary process. It is the primary process that has no respect for the contingencies of reality and that persists with impossible wishes and unnecessary limitations. But to describe the crucial dynamic arena as the conflict between unrealistic wish and realistic reality already assumes that the existential platform reads this way. Indeed we may conclude that psychoanalytic thought *is* an assessment of the universal shape of man's existential platform. While this conflict between wish and reality may be universal, it may not be the central fact of human existence. Indeed the central facts of human existence are construed differently in this book.

It is in the self-aggrandizement and self-degradation of psychosis that we see an entirely different starting point for human psychology. To attribute these extreme qualities to *self* is to distort, yes, "reality," but the reality of human ontology, not the reality of material things or social norms. It is to *be a self,* embedded in a *world,* in a way that is more fundamental than secondary process conclusions about "reality."

To interpret megalomania in this way offers a vivid contrast to the Freudian interpretation of megalomania as a single phenomenon. Freud (1959) argues that the loosening of contact with and concern for reality in the psychotic is a withdrawal of libido from realistic images in the mental life of the person. Therefore:

> . . . in paranoia the liberated libido becomes fixed on to the ego, and is used for the aggrandizement of the ego. A return is thus made to the stage of narcissism (familiar to us in the development of the libido), in which a person's only sexual object is his own ego (p. 459).

It is not uncommon for a psychotic to state that he is the savior (or destroyer) of the world in affectless, almost indifferent tones. It is, for him, a statement as mundane as if I were to say that I will be the same person tomorrow that I am today. The lack of strong emotion about being the savior of the world is not due to some defensive isolation of affect; it is because such a situation seems to demand emotional response only from the point of view of *our* world-construction. In our terms, from our existential platform, such a state of affairs is indeed extraordinary. From the existential platform of a paranoid who has resolved his psychosis in this way, it is hardly extraordinary at all. It is not a startling conclusion (at least not after resolution), it is an unquestioned assumption.

It is no accident that paranoid resolutions usually appear grandiose. A resolution of the shifting and unstable orientation of the psychotic struggle into a coherent self-world relationship that does not accord with *our* existential platform will violate, in numerous details, the way we have reckoned the issues of possibility and necessity. It will violate exactly these issues because these are the central issues around which we each build an existential platform and upon which we become a self.

For Schreber, the self-as-subject becomes powerful enough to defeat God. The realm of possibility is expanded to a certain kind of extreme. In this respect, he became a kind of "total subject." At the same time, Schreber had no choice but to go along with the program. He was a "total object" as well, powerless to construct life in any other way. The realm of necessity is therefore also expanded to a certain kind of extreme. Other aspects of his life were played out against the backdrop of this orientation in ways that look more or less normal. A pen is to write with, if one wants to write. A book is to publish, if one wants to publish. For other psychotics it may be the magical qualities of writing or of publishing that organizes a new, resolved existential platform.

In addition to the usual way of being-in-the-world and being-for-himself, Schreber's being-for-others was extraordinary. The crucial other no doubt shifts, a phenomenon to which Freud assigns the term "transference." But the changing personages are not as significant as the consistent thematic content. The thematic content remains passive submission, combined with a feeble kind of rebellious struggle, with each of the personages, that condemns his self-as-subject into an extreme capitulation to his being-for-others. Had Schreber really established an orientation that was grounded firmly in a self-as-subject, he would not have had to resolve the instability in such an obsequious way. His attempts at self-affirmation, such as the indignation toward his doctor, his struggle with God, and finally his megalomanic self-estimate, have a pathetic, desperate quality about them. In loosing on all these fronts, perhaps beginning with his father and brother, Schreber turned progressively toward being an object for the other as a way to stabilize his orientation toward life. Even so, Schreber's rebellion was perhaps more spirited than many psychotics, for he did insist on publishing the book.

It cannot be doubted that being an object for the other was sexualized, perhaps every step of the way. But to call him a latent passive homosexual is to describe more than his libidinal organization. Such a description also describes, in concrete, sexual terms, his way of being. One is tempted, at this point, to suggest that the obvious success of Freud's sexual interpretations is due largely to the fact that a concrete language of bodily functions works very well as symbols and as concretizations of existential orientations. The body language of Freud may prove to be a more enduring metaphor than the more abstract language of energy dynamics, whose existential meaning is often difficult to divine.

3. Symbols and Psychotic Expression

Psychotic communication is notoriously metaphorical and obscure. The central idea that we want to add to the subject is that symbolic expression serves the purpose, for the psychotic no less than anyone else, of solidifying an existential platform.

The confusion between concrete and metaphorical thinking has often been noted about psychotics. If one should answer a question about his future by saying, "I have no crystal ball," for example, the psychotic may indeed reply that he wasn't interested in crystal and didn't want to play ball. The more abstract, metaphorical thinking, which would locate the common attribute between foretelling the future and the custom of fortune tellers, is obscured for the psychotic by the concrete and literal meanings of the terms. This is related, according to Searles (1965a) to a lack of imagination in schizophrenics. That is, all that passes through consciousness is equally real and equally concrete. The division of experience into perception of reality and playful or metaphorical elaboration in one's own thought is missing.

All this is true, but it is far from the total significance of schizophrenic communication. In addition to being a defect, this "de-differentiation" is also a source of what we may call creativity. I know of one patient who refused for many days to talk. After a few hours of playful attempts by fellow patients, attendants, and visitors to get him to talk, he maintained a stubborn, stony silence. As he left the ward where a painful version of this scene had taken place, he turned and volunteered to the group: "All the birdies go 'tweet tweet tweet.' " His contempt for the jocular helpers is perfectly expressed by metaphorically describing their behavior, and the description itself was very astute, even poignantly sensitive.

Now I do not know whether this man was unable to experience the people as people or could only see them as birds. Nor do I know if their incantations before him were any more meaningful to him than the sound of birds. But we can conlude that the comment has more force, even more veracity, than if he had said, "You stupid people disgust me!" It may indeed be that such a statement was quite impossible, since it presupposes a contact with feelings one can identify as one's own, in response to other people one can specify as not-me. But lacking such an existential platform does not decrease the necessity for expression. It forces expression into a mode not often comprehensible to others. But the expression nonetheless does something for the psychotic, namely, it organizes his experience and gives him a point of view that he may eventually be able to call his own. In our example, the patient produced a sentence that implies a definite point of view.

The general hypothesis here, then, is that psychotic expression in symbolic form is an attempt at self-cure (cf. Sechehaye, 1951). The construction of a delusionary system is an elaboration of that process into a more coherent and reliable orientation and self-definition from which to order experience.

Nearly every delusion has crucial elements of very concrete, symbolic expression, such as bodily feelings and events. In one sense, this is fortunate for us, for it is generally easier to read the existential meaning of body language than it is to unravel the associations about trees and fountain pens. Furthermore the experiences of one's body are always fundamental to one's existential platform. With the breakdown of body boundaries comes an identifiable change in the experience of one's self. In addition, Ferenczi (1950) points out that the child "learns to represent, by means of his body the whole multifariousness of the outer world (pp. 227–228)." Body language therefore is the most versatile language with which to begin a reconstruction of an existential platform. It not only demands the least in sophisticated mental processes like abstraction, but it also is capable of symbolizing the most subtle variations in orientation. Finally, of course, it need not even be verbalized.

Paranoid persons nearly always express their major fear in terms of perceived danger to their bodily well-being. Searles states that sexual fantasies of paranoids usually include such expressions. It was certainly true of Schreber. One of Searles' patients, "an intellectually brilliant and witty, but deeply paranoid, young man" produced the following parody upon Edgar Allen Poe's *Annabel Lee:*

Miss Cannibalee

It was many and many a day ago,
    In a city you all can see,
That a maiden lived whom you might know
    By the name of Cannibalee;
And this maiden she lived with no other thought
    Than a passionate fondness for me.

I was a lad and she was a lass;
    I hoped that her tastes were free.
But she loved with a love that was more than love,
    My yearning Cannibalee;
With a love that could take me roasted, or fried,
    Or raw, as the case might be.

And that is the reason that long ago,
    In a city you all can see,

I had to turn the tables and eat
    My ardent Cannibalee—
Not really because I was fond of her,
    But to check her fondness for me.

But the stars never rise but I think of the size
    Of my hot-potted Cannibalee.
And the moon never stares but it brings me nightmares
Of my spare-rib Cannibalee
    And all the night tide she is restless inside
Is my still indigestible dinner belle bride,
    In her pallid tomb, all rent free
In her carnivorous sepulchre—me.
        (Searles, 1965b, pp. 484–485).

4. The Politics of Psychosis

The fundamental nature of the psychotic resolution is a stabilizing
of an existential platform: a temporal order (often with a timeless-
eternal or a constipated-static quality), a spatial order (often following emotional closeness-distance coordinates rather than physical
ones), a self-order (often exaggerating one of the three aspects of
being into the whole of personal identity), and an existential order
that reckons the necessary and the possible. The stability of experience gained in the psychotic resolution is the opposite of (and
therefore self-cure for) the experience of panic. Searles, writing
within the psychoanalytic tradition, offers this description of paranoid experience:

> One point I wish to make at the outset is that the paranoid
> individual seems rarely, if ever—except perhaps in states of panic
> —to feel anxiety as such. I have come to believe it pathognomonic
> of him that he experiences, instead, an awareness of various sur-
> roundings—or, less often, of things within his body—as being
> charged with sinister meaning, charged with malevolence toward
> himself (Searles, 1965b, p. 465).

The anxiety of confused, fragmented and meaningless experience is overcome by creating a world that *explains* the anxiety.

If I am subjected to the panic of dissolution of my world, I combat that panic by constructing another world. But the new world must contain explanations for my previously experienced and ever-incipient panic. The process of explaining in this way is a process of controlling the anxiety and is not unrelated to the production of superstitions and rumors when unknown and unexplainable phenomena appear on the screen of experience. It is magical in flavor, just as the creation of labels dispells the puzzlement of the scientific community when it is faced with phenomena that are poorly or not at all understood. Such an enterprise is theory building, of course, and our entire culture has created a "scientific world" in the face of ultimate mysteries of life. From this point of view, religion and science are very much alike, and the polar opposite of both is the raw panic of confronting the ultimate paradoxes, puzzles, and absurdities of human existence. Our culture defines such world-constructions as sane or insane largely on the basis of majority vote, with some (usually) benevolent oligarchical behavior on the part of scientists.

The psychotic resolution is not, therefore, on one level of discourse, any different from sanity. There are however some notable differences, whose content is readily recognizable by those of us who are "sane." The ultimate question, "Which existential platform is the true one?" is a political question, both in the sense that there are always alternative models in our pluralistic culture and in the sense that each model expresses value judgments of the others. Furthermore, their champions attempt to control the course of human events in the service of these values. This book is therefore political as well as philosophical and scientific. The value position is at least, I hope, clear and not obscured by scientific disclaimers with respect to values. We have points of contention, of course, with the psychoanalysts and behaviorists. But over against the more extreme (which is defined as the less common) conclusions of those we call psychotic there is also some agreement with behaviorists and psychoanalysts. Speaking for the majority is Searles again:

> The paranoid patient is not sufficiently in tune with his fellow-men; not sufficiently able to integrate the ever-flowing nature of life with its concomitants of change and growth, ful-

fillment and loss, birth and death; not sufficiently matured in his
thought-processes to be able to distinguish the more significant
from the less significant incidents and threads in his life; and not
sufficiently loving and trusting to experience love as the ingredient which gives human existence cohesiveness and meaning;
to be able to feel the wholeness, the genuine "master plan" which
the healthy individual comes to see in his life (1965b, p. 469).

It is necessary to bring up these political considerations in
any treatment of psychosis, especially of the paranoid variety, because the problem becomes blatantly political at certain crucial
junctures (cf. Szasz, 1965). This aspect of psychosis is also inevitable
if one attempts, as we have, to cut beneath the discourse of ordinary
science and begin an investigation of human psychology at the very
roots of human existence.

So the psychotic resolution, whose most perfect form is found
in paranoia, is a solution to very human problems. We must, as
psychologists, seek to understand our common humanity with the
psychotic and to avoid being frightened into an emotional rejection
of him because of the differences. This is very difficult to do, since
the psychotic struggle is one we are quite naturally afraid of. We
must do this, that is, *if* we seek to understand him and to bring him
back into communion with us. That "if," however, is not one we
can take lightly, for our seeking to understand him may be in the
service of whipping him back into mindless conformity and it
might indeed be the polar opposite of his most central desire.

It is not clear to this psychologist at this time whether we
should assume that all psychotics want to change, or would be
"better" if they did. It may be that the psychotic desperately longs
for human contact. We sane ones would surely like to think that is
so, because we compliment ourselves as human beings with our
desirability. And there are clear signs in many psychotics that it is
so; they say it loudly and clearly. But for those who do not, notably
certain paranoids, the ethics of our intervention must be more
carefully considered than simply to assume they want to live as we
do. We must be aware of the politics of psychosis.

References

Ferenczi, S. *Sex in Psychoanalysis*. New York: Bruner, 1950.

Freud, S. Psychoanalytic notes upon an autobiographical account of a case of paranoia. In *The Collected Papers of Sigmund Freud*. New York: Basic Books, 1959.

Searles, H. F. The differentiation between concrete and metaphorical thinking in the recovering schizophrenic patient. In H. F. Searles, *Collected papers on Schizophrenia and Related Subjects*. New York: International Universities Press, 1965. (a)

Searles, H. F. The source of anxiety in paranoid schizophrenia. In H. F. Searles, *Collected Papers on Schizophrenia and Related Subjects*. New York: International Universities Press, 1965. (b)

Sechehaye, M. A. *Symbolic Realization*. New York: International Universities Press, 1951.

Szasz, T. *Psychiatric Justice*. New York: Macmillan, 1965.

The case of Ellen West
An anthropological-clinical study 14
by Ludwig Binswanger

1. Case History [1]

Heredity

Ellen West, a non-Swiss, is the only daughter of a Jewish father for whom her love and veneration know no bounds. She has a dark-haired brother four years older than she, who resembles his father, and a younger brother who is blond. Whereas the older one "has no nerves" and is very well adjusted and cheerful, the younger is a "bundle of nerves" and is a soft [1] and womanish aesthete. At seventeen he was in a psychiatric clinic for some weeks on account

From *Existence* edited by Rollo May, Ernest Angel, and Henri F. Ellenberger, Basic Books, Inc., Publishers, New York, 1958. (Translated by Werner M. Mendel and Joseph Lyons from the original, "Der Fall Ellen West." *Schweizer Archiv für Neurologie und Psychiatrie,* 1944, Vol. 53, pp. 255–277; Vol. 54, pp. 69–117, 330–360; 1945, Vol. 55, pp. 16–40.)

[The term "anthropological" is used here, as it frequently is in European psychiatry, to refer to a science of man.—Translators.]

[1] In this and the preceding chapters the procedures developed in my work, *Über Ideenflucht (On the Flight of Ideas),* are extended to the study of non-manic-depressive psychoses.

of a mental ailment with suicidal ideas, and even after his recovery he remained easily excitable. He has married.

The sixty-six-year-old father is described as an externally very self-controlled, rather stiffly formal, very reserved, willful man of action; internally, however, as very soft [2] and sensitive and suffering from nocturnal depressions and states of fear accompanied by self-reproaches, "as if a wave of fear closed over his head." He sleeps poorly and is often under the pressure of fear when he gets up in the morning.

A sister of the father became mentally ill on her wedding day (?). Of the father's five brothers, one shot himself between the ages of twenty and thirty (details are lacking), a second likewise committed suicide during a period of melancholy, and a third is severely ascetic, gets up very early, and eats nothing at noon on the ground that this makes one lazy. Two brothers fell ill with dementia arteriosclerosis and later each died of a stroke. The father's father is said to have been a very strict autocrat, the father's mother, on the other hand, to have had a gentle, always conciliatory nature, she had "quiet weeks," during which she spoke not a word and sat motionless. All this is said to have increased as she aged. The mother of this woman—that is, the patient's great-grandmother on her father's side—is said to have been severely manic-depressive. She stems from a family which produced many outstandingly capable men but also many psychotics, one of whom I have treated (an eminent scholar).

The mother of Ellen West, likewise of Jewish descent, is said to be a very soft, kindly, suggestible, nervous woman, who underwent a depression for three years during the time of her engagement. The mother's father died young. The mother's mother was especially vigorous, healthy, and gay; she died at eighty-four of dementia senilis. There were five siblings of the mother, somewhat nervous, short, physically delicate,[3] but all lived long; one died of tuberculosis of the larynx.

---

2 [The word *soft* implies in this context all the varied meanings of the German *weich*—a frequently used and important term in this paper—including physically soft as well as tender-hearted, delicate, effeminate, weak, or malleable. —Translators.]

3 [The word *zart*, translated as *physically delicate*, is a key term in the case history. It means tender, petite, fragile, subdued, and sensitive—in short, just the opposite of fleshy and heavy.—Translators.]

Life-history and course of illness

Normal birth. At nine months Ellen refused milk and was therefore fed meat-broth; nor could she ever tolerate milk in later years. On the other hand she liked to eat meat, not so well certain vegetables, some sweet desserts not at all; if these were forced upon her, a tremendous resistance set in. (As she later confessed that even as a child she had passionately loved sweets, this was clearly not a case of an "aversion" but probably of an early act of renunciation.) Unfortunately, in spite of two periods of psychoanalytic treatment in later years, we are completely in the dark about her early childhood; she no longer knows much about the first ten years of her life.

According to her own statements and those of her parents, Ellen was a very lively but headstrong and violent child. It is said that she often defied an order of her parents for hours and did not carry it out even then. Once she was shown a bird's nest, but she insisted that it was not a bird's nest and nothing would make her change her opinion. Even as a child, she said, she had had days when everything seemed empty to her and she suffered under a pressure which she herself did not understand. After attending kindergarten she went to school in her first homeland from her eighth to her tenth year. At ten she moved with her family to Europe, where, except for some trips across the ocean, she remained till her death. In her second land she went to a school for girls. She was a good student, liked going to school, and was very ambitious; she could weep for hours if she did not rank first in her favorite subjects. She did not want to stay away from school even when the doctor ordered it, fearing to fall behind the class or to miss something. Her favorite subjects were German and history; she was not as good at arithmetic. At this time too she was of a lively temperament, but still self-willed. She had already chosen the motto: *aut Caesar aut nihil!* [4] Up to her sixteenth year her games were boyish. She preferred to wear trousers. From her babyhood Ellen West had been a thumbsucker; at sixteen she suddenly gave that up, along with her boyish games, at the onset of an infatuation which lasted two years. In a poem written in her seventeenth year, however, she

[4] [Literally, "Either Caesar or nothing!"—Translators.]

still expressed the ardent desire to be a boy, for then she would be a soldier, fear no foe, and die joyously, sword in hand.

Other poems from this period already reveal a marked variability of mood: now her heart beats with exultant joy, now the sky is darkened, the winds blow weirdly, and the ship of her life sails on unguided, not knowing whither to direct its keel. In another poem from the following year, the wind is rushing about her ears, and she wants it to cool her burning brow; when she runs against it blindly, careless of custom or propriety, it is as if she were stepping out of a confining tomb, as if she were flying through the air in an uncontrollable urge to freedom, and as if she must achieve something great and mighty; then her gaze falls back into the world again and the saying comes to her mind: "Man, in small things make your world"; she cries to her soul, "Fight on." She considers herself called to achieve something special, she reads much, occupies herself intensively with social problems, feels deeply the contrast between her own social position and that of the "masses," and draws up plans for the improvement of the latter. At the same age (seventeen), following the reading of *Niels Lyhne*,[5] she changes from a deeply religious person (despite the intentionally nonreligious upbringing her father gave her) to a complete atheist. In no respect does she care about the judgment of the world.

Still other poems from her seventeenth year are available. In one, entitled "Kiss Me Dead," the sun sinks into the ocean like a ball of fire, a dripping mist drops over sea and beach, and a pain comes over her: "Is there no rescue any more?" She calls upon the cold, grim Sea-King to come to her, take her into his arms in ardent love-lust, and kiss her to death. In another poem, entitled "I Hate You," she sings of a boy, supremely beautiful, whom she now hates because of his victorious smile, just as intensely as she had formerly loved him. In a third one ("Tired"), gray, damp evening mists well up around her and stretch out their arms toward her cold, long-deceased heart, while the trees shake their heads in disconsolate gloom, singing an old, mournful song, and no bird lets its late song be

---

[5] [*Niels Lyhne* is both the title and the central character of a famous Scandinavian novel by J. P. Jacobsen (1847–1885), published in 1880. Its stark and melancholy realism, religious nihilism, and moving plot (concerning a disillusioned idealist) combined to give it a tremendous appeal to restless European youth at the turn of the century.—Translators.]

heard, no light appears in the sky; her head is empty, her heart is afraid.

In diary entries from her eighteenth year she praises the blessing of work: "What would we be without work, what would become of us? I think they would soon have to enlarge the cemeteries for those who went to death of their own accord. Work is the opiate for suffering and grief."—"When all the joints of the world threaten to fall apart, when the light of our happiness is extinguished and our pleasure in life lies wilting, only one thing saves us from madness: work. Then we throw ourselves into a sea of duties as into Lethe, and the roar of its waves is to drown out the death-knell pealing in our heart."—"When the day is done with its haste and unrest, and we sit by the window in the growing twilight, the book will fall from our hand, we stare into the distance, into the setting sun, and old pictures rise up before us. The old plans and hopes, none of which have been realized, the boundless barrenness of the world and our infinite minuteness stand before our tired soul. Then the old question crowds to our lips, 'What for—why all this? Why do we strive and live, forgotten after a short span of time, only to molder in the cold earth?' "—"At such a time spring up quickly, and well for you if there is a call for you, and work with both hands, until the shapes of the night disappear. O work, you are indeed the blessing of our life!"

She would like to gain fame—great, undying fame; after hundreds of years her name should still ring out on the lips of mankind. Then she would not have lived in vain. She cries to herself, "Oh, smother the murmuring voices with work! Fill up your life with duties. I will not think so much—my last address shall not be the madhouse! And when you have worked and toiled, what have you accomplished? What prevails around us and below us is still so much of boundless distress! There they are dancing in a brightly lighted hall, and outside the door a poor woman is starving to death. Starving! Not a crust of bread comes to her from the table of plenty. Did you observe how the fine gentleman, while speaking, slowly crushed the dainty bread in his hand? And outside in the cold a woman cried out for a dry crust! And what's the use of brooding on it? Don't I do the same? . . ."

In the same year (her eighteenth) the diary praises with the greatest enthusiasm everything new and beautiful that she experiences in Paris on a trip with her parents. New little sentimental love affairs develop. At the same time the wish now arises in her to be delicate and ethereal, as are the girl friends whom she selects. Even now her poems continue to show the contradictoriness of her mood. One sings of sunshine and the smiling spring, of radiant blue skies over a free, wide land, of pleasure and blissfulness; in another she wishes that the greening and blooming of the springtime world, the murmuring and rustling of the woods, might be her dirge; in a third the only longing left to her eyes is that for the darkness "where the glaring sun of life does not shine": "If thou still rulest behind clouds, Father, then I beseech thee, take me back to thee!"

But through clouds and darkness the light of life breaks through again and again. A journey with her parents across the ocean, occurring during her nineteenth year, lives in her recollection "as the happiest and most harmless time" of her life. In a poem of this year floods of light and "golden hands" rest upon grainfields, villages, and valleys, and only the mountains stand in darkness. And yet on this trip Ellen can never be alone—*i.e.*, away from her parents. Although she has a very good time while on a visit to friends, she begs her parents to call her back to them. Returning to Europe, she begins to ride horses and soon becomes very skilled at it, no horse being too dangerous for her; she vies with experienced riders in jumping competitions. Like everything she does, she cultivates riding "with excessive intensity," indeed, as if it were her exclusive task in life.

Her twentieth year is full of happiness, yearning, and hopes. From her poems stream radiant joy of life—indeed, wild ecstasy of life: the sun stands high, spring gales "roar through the world," then how can one lag behind, lock oneself "into the tomb of a house"? Through her veins the blood "races and roars," youthful zest bursts her breast asunder; she stretches her strong young body, for the fresh marrow of life shall not stale, the ardent yearning for a wild joy shall not dry up, "pining away bit by bit." "The earth is too stale and still, I long for a storm that is shrill." "Oh, if 'He' would come now," now when every fiber of her is quivering so that she can hardly sit still to write, now, when she is "so completely cured in body and soul," when no sacrifice would be too great for her: "He must be tall, and strong, and have a soul as pure and unblemished as the morning light! He must not play life nor dream it, but live it, in all its seriousness and all its pleasure. He must be able to be happy, to enjoy me and my children, and to take joy in sunshine and work. Then I would give him all my love and all my strength."

In the same year (her twentieth) she makes her second trip overseas, to nurse her older brother, who is very sick. She takes pleasure in eating and drinking. This is the last time she can eat unconcernedly. At this time she becomes engaged to a romantic foreigner, but at her father's wish breaks the engagement. On the return trip she stops in Sicily and does some writing on a paper, "On the Woman's Calling." Here, according to her diary, she loves life passionately, her pulse hammers out to her fingertips, and the world belongs to her, for she has sun, wind, and beauty all to herself. Her god is the god of life and of joy, of strength and hope; she is filled with a consuming thirst to learn, and she has already had a glimpse of the "secret of the universe."

The first weeks in Sicily are the last of her happiness in life. Already the diary is again reporting the shadows of doubt and of dread; Ellen feels herself small and wholly forsaken in a world which she cannot understand. To be sure, she is glad "to be far from the cramping influences of home," the pinions of her soul are growing, but this growth does not take place without pains and convulsions, indeed, in the midst of her loveliest, most exuberant moments, fear and trembling appear again. Pityingly, she looks down upon all her fine ideas and plans and closes her diary with the burning wish that they might one day transform themselves into deeds instead of merely useless words.

Along with this, however, something new emerges now, a definite dread—namely, a dread of getting fat. At the beginning of her stay in Sicily Ellen had still displayed an enormous appetite. As a result she got so fat that her girl friends began to tease her about it. At once she begins to mortify herself by fasting and immoderate hikes. This goes so far that when her companions stop at some pretty spot Ellen keeps circling about them. She no longer eats sweets or other fattening things and skips supper altogether. When she goes home in the spring, everyone is horrified at how bad she looks.

Ellen is now twenty-one years old. In the summer after her return to Italy her mood is markedly "depressive." She is con-

stantly tormented by the idea that she is getting too fat, and therefore she is forever taking long walks. She takes up her diary again,
complains that she has no home anywhere, not even with her
family, that she does not find the activity she is seeking, that she
has no peace, that she feels a veritable torment when she sits still,
that every nerve in her quivers, and that in general her body shares
in all the stirrings of her soul: "My inner self is so closely connected
with my body that the two form a unity and together constitute
my 'I,' my unlogical, nervous, individual 'I.'" She feels herself to
be absolutely worthless and useless and is in dread of everything, of
the dark and of the sun, of stillness and of noise. She feels herself
on the lowest rung of the ladder which leads to the light, degraded
to a cowardly, wretched creature: "I despise myself!" In a poem,
grim distress sits at her grave, ashy pale—sits and stares, does not
flinch nor budge; the birds grow mute and flee, the flowers wilt
before its ice-cold breath. Now death no longer appears to her as
terrible; death is not a man with the scythe but "a glorious woman,
white asters in her dark hair, large eyes, dream-deep and gray."
The only thing which still lures her is dying: "Such a delicious
stretching out and dozing off. Then it's over. No more getting up
and dreary working and planning. Back of every word I really hide
a yawn." (This and the following from a letter to her male friend
at this time.) "And every day I get a little fatter, older, and uglier."
—"If he makes me wait much longer, the great friend, death, then
I shall set out and seek him." She says she is not melancholy, merely
apathetic: "Everything is so uniform to me, so utterly indifferent,
I know no feeling of joy and none of fear."—"Death is the greatest
happiness in life, if not the only one. Without hope of the end life
would be unendurable. Only the certainty that sooner or later the
end must come consoles me a little." She wishes never to have children: what awaits them in the world?

In the fall of the same year Ellen gradually comes out of her
depression. She makes preparations for the installation of children's
reading-rooms on the American model. But along with her newly
awakening joy of life and the urge to action, her paralyzing dread
and despair continue. From her diary: "I have not kept a diary for
a long time, but today I must again take my notebook in hand; for
in me there is such a turmoil and ferment that I must open a safety
valve to avoid bursting out in wild excesses. It is really sad that I

must translate all this force and urge to action into unheard words instead of powerful deeds. It is a pity of my young life, a sin to waste my sound mind. For what purpose did nature give me health and ambition? Surely not to stifle it and hold it down and let it languish in the chains of humdrum [6] living, but to serve wretched humanity. The iron chains of commonplace life: the chains of conventionality, the chains of property and comfort, the chains of gratitude and consideration, and, strongest of all, the chains of love. Yes, it is they that hold me down, hold me back from a tempestuous revival, from the complete absorption in the world of struggle and sacrifice for which my whole soul is longing. O God, dread is driving me mad! Dread which is almost certainty! The consciousness that ultimately I shall lose everything: all courage, all rebelliousness, all drive for doing; that it—my little world—will make me flabby, flabby and fainthearted and beggarly, as they are themselves."—"Live? No, vegetate! Do you actually preach making concessions? I will make no concessions! You realize that the existing social order is rotten, rotten down to the root, dirty and mean; but you do nothing to overthrow it. But we have no right to close our ears to the cry of misery, and to walk with closed eyes past the victims of our system! I am twenty-one years old and am supposed to be silent and grin like a puppet. I am no puppet. I am human being with red blood and a woman with quivering heart. And I cannot breathe in this atmosphere of hypocrisy and cowardice, and I mean to do something great and must get a little closer to my ideal, my proud ideal. Will it cost tears? Oh, what shall I do, how shall I manage it? It boils and pounds in me, it wants to burst the outer shell! Freedom! Revolution!"—"No, no, I am not talking claptrap. I am not thinking of the liberation of the soul; I mean the real, tangible liberation of the people from the chains of their oppressors. Shall I express it still more clearly? I want a revolution, a great uprising to spread over the entire world and overthrow the whole social order. I should like to forsake home and parents like a Russian nihilist, to live among the poorest of the poor and make propaganda for the great cause. Not for the love of adventure! No,

---

[6] [The German word *Alltag* literally means any day which is not Sunday, and for this reason it is used to refer to the common and trite, the ordinary, or the humdrum and conventional workaday world.—Translators.]

no! Call it unsatisfied urge to action if you like, indomitable ambition. What has the name to do with it? To me it is as if this boiling in my blood were something better. Oh, I am choking in this petty, commonplace life. Bloated self-satisfaction or egotistical greed, joyless submissiveness or crude indifference; those are the plants which thrive in the sunshine of the commonplace. They grow and proliferate, and like weeds they smother the flower of longing which germinates among them."—"Everything in me trembles with dread, dread of the adders of my everyday, which would coil about me with their cold bodies and press the will to fight out of me. But my exuberant force offers resistance. I shake them off, I *must* shake them off. The morning must come after this siege of nightmares."

During the winter Ellen pushes with energy and success the installation of the children's reading-rooms, with the help of a benevolent association. But as early as the ensuing spring this no longer satisfies her. She longs for love and for greater deeds. In a poem entitled "The Evil Thoughts," she sees the "evil spirits" standing behind every tree: mockingly they "close her in" on all sides, fiercely they seize her, clutch at her heart, and finally they themselves speak:

> One time we were your thinking,
> Your hoping pure and proud!
> Where now are all your projects,
> The dreams that used to crowd?
>
> Now all of them lie buried,
> Scattered in wind and storm,
> And you've become a nothing,
> A timid earthy worm.
>
> So then we had to leave you,
> To dark night we must flee;
> The curse which fell upon you
> Has made us black to see.
>
> If you seek peace and quiet,
> Then we'll come creeping nigh
> And we'll take vengeance on you
> With our derisive cry.

If you seek joy and gladness,
We'll hurry to your side;
Accusing you and jeering
We'll e'er with you abide!

In the diary she continues to air her hatred of the luxury and good living which surround her, she bemoans her cowardice and weakness in not being able "to rise above the conditions," in letting herself at so early an age be made flabby "by the uglinesses and the stuffy air of the everyday. I still feel the disgrace of my imprisonment. How musty is the smell of this cellar hole. The scent of the flowers cannot drown the stench of decay. No wonder you have got such ugly yellow souls, you who have grown up in this atmosphere. Already you have ceased to notice how hard it is to breathe here. Your souls have grown dwarf lungs. Everything about you is dwarflike: thoughts, feelings, and—dreams. You look at me askance because the conditions in which you feel happy disgust me. You want to get me down . . . I want to go away, away—away from here. I am afraid of you! I pound on the walls with my hands till I sink down exhausted. Then you come out of your corners like rats, and your little eyes pursue me, like a nightmare." A month later Ellen composes a passionate riding song: she gives her horse the spur, but "the evil thoughts, the spirits of the night" follow close behind it "on bony mares, hollow-eyed and pale"; at last, however, "the pale shadows" fall behind the rousing gallop of her horse, and "life has triumphed again." But a month later she is again bewailing her "loneliness of soul"; she stands "lonely as on icy peaks," and only the winds understand her longing and her fear.

In the fall of the same year Ellen begins preparing for the *Matura*,[7] with the intention of studying political economy. She gets up at five, rides for three hours, then has private lessons and works all afternoon and evening until late at night, with the help of black coffee and cold showers.

The next spring (Ellen is now twenty-two) makes her melancholy, she cannot enjoy the awakening of spring, feels merely "how low she has sunk," not only from her previous ideal image, but from that which formerly she really was. Formerly the world lay

---

[7] [This refers to the final examination in secondary school, which in effect qualified one for entrance to any university.—Translators.]

"open before her" and she wished to "conquer" it, her feelings and sensations were "strong and vigorous," she loved and hated "with her whole soul." Now she makes concessions; she would have ridiculed anyone who had prophesied this to her; with every year she has "lost a little of her old strength."

In the fall of the same year—Ellen became twenty-three at the end of July—she breaks down. At the same time she has an unpleasant love affair with a riding teacher. Besides, she watches her body weight and reduces her food intake as soon as she threatens to gain weight. But now dread of getting fat [8] is accompanied by an intensified longing for food, especially sweets, and this is strongest when she has been made tired and nervous by being with others. In the presence of others eating affords her no satisfaction; only when alone may she enjoy it. As always since the beginning of her dread of getting fat, she has suffered from the conflict between the dread of getting fat and the wish to be able to eat unconcernedly. Even now her old governess observes that this conflict is "the cloud over her life." Especially during vacations is she in a "depressive unrest"; this does not disappear until she has regular work and a fixed daily schedule. Her plan to take the *Matura* is again given up. Instead, within a few weeks she passes the teachers' examination, in order to be able to audit courses at the university. During the summer semester of her twenty-third and the winter semester of the beginning of her twenty-fourth year she studies in the town of X. This period is one of the happiest of her life. In the summer a love relationship with a student develops. The diary breathes joy of life and sensuality. After the close of the winter semester, in a poem entitled "Spring Moods," she writes:

> I'd like to die just as the birdling does
> That splits his throat in highest jubilation;
> And not to live as the worm on earth lives on,
> Becoming old and ugly, dull and dumb!
> No, feel for once how forces in me kindle,
> And wildly be consumed in my own fire.

8 [The German is *dick,* a word which connotes thickness, stoutness, denseness, coarseness, and fleshiness. The word *dick* should be contrasted with *weich,* in Note 3, and with *zart,* in Note 4. This contrast is central to the existential analysis in Section II.—Translators.]

Ellen is enthusiastic about studying and student life. She goes with others on long excursions to the mountains, and now too she cannot be alone; her old governess is constantly with her. Nor can she free herself of her "fixed idea." She avoids fattening foods and, since she feels that she is nevertheless getting too fat, she undertakes a reducing diet, with her physician's consent, in the fall of that year.

At the same time the affair with the student turns into an engagement. Her parents demand a temporary separation. In the spring Ellen goes to a seaside resort, and here once again an especially severe "depression" sets in (she is twenty-four and one-half years old). She does everything to get just as thin as possible, takes long hikes, and daily swallows thirty-six to forty-eight thyroid tablets! Consumed by homesickness, she begs her parents to let her return. She arrives completely emaciated, with trembling limbs, and drags herself through the summer in physical torment, but feels spiritually satisfied because she is thin. She has the feeling that she has found the key to her well-being. The engagement remains in effect.

In the autumn, at the beginning of her twenty-fifth year, she takes her third trip overseas. There the physician diagnoses a "Basedow syndrome" [9] and prescribes complete rest in bed. She stays in bed six weeks and this makes her gain weight very rapidly, for which reason she weeps all the time. On her return home in the following spring she weighs 165 pounds. Shortly afterward the engagement is broken off. In May she is in a (public) sanatorium, in the summer she attends a school of gardening; she is in a depressive mood, but physically she makes a completely healthy impression. Since she soon loses interest in gardening, she leaves the school prematurely. Again she has attempted to reduce her weight by much physical activity and scanty eating. In the fall her cousin, with whom she has been friends for many years, takes a special interest in her. Until the following spring they take long hikes together, often twenty to twenty-five miles in a day. Besides this, she engages eagerly in gymnastics, is active in a children's home, though without enjoying it much, and longs for a real vocation. Although the broken engagement with the student remains an "open wound," a

[9] [This is known to the English-speaking reader as Graves' disease, a condition of exophthalmic hyperthyroid goiter.—Translators.]

love relationship with the cousin develops. The "fixed idea" has not disappeared, but it does not dominate her as it formerly did.

At this time there is a poem, evidently aimed at her former fiancé, in which she asks herself if he ever loved her at all, if her body was "not beautiful enough" to bear him sons:

> Woe's me, woe's me!
> The earth bears grain,
> But I
> Am unfruitful,
> Am discarded shell,
> Cracked, unusable,
> Worthless husk.
> Creator, Creator,
> Take me back!
> Create me a second time
> And create me better!

In her twenty-sixth year a love for music awakens in Ellen. She and her cousin plan to marry. But for two years more she vacillates between her cousin and the student, with whom she has resumed relations. Not until her twenty-eighth year, after another meeting with the student (see below), does she break off with him for good and marry her cousin. Previous to that she has taken several Mensendieck [10] courses, traveled a great deal, consulted several famous neurologists at the wish of her parents and her cousin; she has again taken thyroid periodically and gone on tremendous hikes; she has been saddened when she looked at herself in the mirror, hating her body and often beating it with her fists. Girl friends who, like her, want to be slender influence her unfavorably. She always grows depressed when she is with thin people or those who eat little.

She hopes after marrying her cousin to get rid of her "fixed idea," but this is not the case. At the wedding she weighs 160

[10] [Mrs. Mensendieck was a Swedish physician who developed a system of physical culture based on gymnastics and on certain weight-reducing devices. She opened many salons throughout Europe and even in California during the early part of this century. The popularity of her treatment program was at least in part a result of the increasing freedom for women and the new trend of fashion toward a slim figure.—Translators.]

pounds, but even on the honeymoon trip she diets, and as a result she steadily loses weight.

In the summer following the spring of her marriage her periods cease. The conflict between the "wish for harmless eating" and her dread of getting fat torments her constantly. In the fall, at the time of her twenty-ninth birthday, while on a hike with her husband in a lonely neighborhood she has a severe abdominal hemorrhage, despite which she must continue to hike for several more hours. The physician does a curettage and finds a miscarriage; he states that a good diet is a prerequisite for the possibility of a new pregnancy!

During her entire following year (her twenty-ninth) Ellen is now torn this way and that between the desire to have a child and the dread of getting fat (from adequate nourishment). "The dread retains control." Her previously regular menstruation ceases. On the whole Ellen is again in a better mood, but she is at times depressed by her repeatedly disappointed hope of a new pregnancy. She works energetically and with a great sense of duty in social welfare, goes to the theater frequently, and reads a lot. But when she happens to discover that she has gained over four pounds in one week, she bursts into tears and cannot quiet down for a long time. When another gynecologist tells her that good nourishment is not prerequisite to a pregnancy, she at once resumes the use of strong laxatives.

In her thirtieth year Ellen is even more intensely active in social welfare. She takes the warmest human interest in the people committed to her care, with whom personal relationships are kept up for years. At the same time she impoverishes her nourishment systematically and gradually becomes a vegetarian. Even after a short siege of grippe she does not spare herself. A treatment in Pyrmont,[11] prescribed by a third gynecologist, is unsuccessful, especially since she so increases the laxative dosage that she vomits every night. When she finds that she is steadily losing weight she is very pleased.

The winter of her thirty-first year brings with it a rapid decline in her strength. She continues to work just as much, but cannot get up energy for anything else. Also, for the first time she dis-

[11] [Pyrmont is a town in Germany which is well known for its health-giving waters.—Translators.]

continues the two daily hikes with her husband. She sleeps up to twelve hours, contrary to her previous custom. The laxatives are further increased, her diet is further impoverished. In spite of an occasional high fever, which she keeps secret, she goes out in the street in the hope of catching pneumonia. Her facial expression changes. Ellen looks old and haggard. However, since she thinks she has found in the laxatives a preventive against getting fat, she is not depressed.

In the spring of this year, during a hike with her husband, suddenly, with elemental force, the confession bursts from her that she is living her life only with a view to being able to remain thin, that she is subordinating every one of her actions to this end, and that this idea has gained a terrible power over her. She thinks she can numb herself by work, exchanges her volunteer work in the welfare agency for a paid position, which obligates her to seven hours of office work a day, and, after some weeks, in June she breaks down. During this entire time she has further impoverished her diet; her weight goes down to 103 pounds. At the same time she becomes intensely preoccupied with calorie charts, recipes, etc. In every free minute she writes recipes of delectable dishes, puddings, desserts, etc., in her cookbook. She demands of those around her that they eat much and well, while she denies herself everything. She develops great skill in not letting them know that she is eating almost nothing by filling her plate like everyone else and then secretly emptying the greater part of the food into her handbag. Foods which she thinks are not fattening, such as shellfish and clams, she eats with great greed and haste. Often on the way home she eats up things she has bought for her household and then upbraids herself severely for it. At every meal she sweats profusely. Ellen now goes with her husband to a sanatorium for metabolic diseases and at first follows the orders of the doctor, so that her weight increases from 99 to 110 pounds, but after her husband leaves she deceives the physician by dropping her food into her handbag and secretly carrying weights when she is weighed.

At the beginning of her thirty-second year her physical condition deteriorates still further. Her use of laxatives increases beyond measure. Every evening she takes sixty to seventy tablets of a vegetable laxative, with the result that she suffers tortured vomiting at night and violent diarrhea by day, often accompanied by a weak-

ness of the heart. Now she no longer eats fish, has thinned down to
a skeleton, and weighs only 92 pounds. Ellen becomes more and
more debilitated, goes back to bed in the afternoon, and is terribly
tortured by the feeling that "her instincts are stronger than her
reason," that "all inner development, all real life has stopped," and
that she is completely dominated by her "overpowering idea, long
since recognized as senseless." Yet her mood is rather cheerful, and
it affords her satisfaction that her friends worry about her.

At the age of thirty-two and one-half she undergoes her first
psychoanalysis, with a young and sensitive analyst who is not completely committed to Freud. She regains hope, again attends lectures, the theater, and concerts, and goes on excursions, but is extremely restless and again overdoes everything. During the times
when her husband is absent her old nursemaid must stay with her.
She soon regards the psychoanalysis as useless.

In her letters to her husband, now and again her "burning
love for life crops out," but it remains "pure mood," and the dread
of getting fatter remains unchanged in the center of her doing and
thinking: "My thoughts are exclusively concerned with my body,
my eating, my laxatives."—"And the fact that from time to time I
see emerge on the horizon the fabulous, sweet land of life, the
oasis in the desert which I have created for myself, only makes my
road the harder. For what good is it? It remains a Fata Morgana [12]
and disappears again. It was easier before, when everything was
gray-on-gray around me, when I wanted nothing but to be sick and
lie in bed. Now I'd like to be healthy—and won't pay the price for
it. Often I am completely broken by the conflict which never comes
to an end, and in despair I leave my analyst and go home with the
certainty: he can give me discernment, but not healing."

Ellen feels the opinion of the analyst, that her main goal is
"the subjugation of all other people," to be "marvelously correct
and frighteningly true." But she says she has a test, a kind of touch-
stone; she need only ask herself, "Ellen, can you eat a good serving
of beans or a pancake and afterward take no medicine?"—then, she
says, she is seized by a veritable panic, and at the mere idea dread
makes her turn hot and cold. "All good resolutions, all joy of life,
break down before this wall over which I cannot climb."—"I still

[12] [*Illusion*, from *Morgan le Fay*, once considered responsible for a particular mirage seen in Italy.—Editor.]

do not want to get fatter, or, in psychoanalytic language—I still will not give up my 'ideal.' " But now she no longer wants to die, she says, she loves life again, and longs for health, work, and her husband, but actually she "will not pay the price for it." She thinks it a matter of despair that she knows no way to "help herself out of this swamp."

During the analysis Ellen cuts down more and more on eating. Feelings of dread become more frequent, and now there appears above all the bothersome obsession of constantly having to think about food. She describes her feelings of dread as "the specters which constantly jump at my throat." Good hours seem to her like a "flood tide ," but then "low tide" swiftly sets in again.

In a letter to her husband Ellen now compares her ideal, exemplified by her former fiancé, the student, with the ideal of being thin: "At that time you [the husband] were the life which I was ready to accept and to give up my ideal [the student] for. But it was an artificially derived, forced resolve, not one ripened from within. For this reason it did not work. For this reason I again started to send him packages and to be full of opposition to you. And only much later, when I was ripe within, when I had looked my ideal in the face and realized, 'I have made a mistake, this ideal is a fiction,' then, and only then, could I say 'Yes' to you calmly and with assurance. Just so I must now be able to look at my ideal, this ideal of being thin, of being without a body, and to realize: 'It is a fiction.' Then I can say 'Yes' to life. Before I do that, everything is a fallacy, like that time in X [the University town]. But it is simpler to get into the train and ride to Y [where the rupture with the student took place] than to bring to the light of day what lies buried and hidden in me. As for the comparison of you with life, and of St. [the student] with my ideal, of course it is a lame one; there is only a superficial analogy. My saying 'Yes' [to the husband after her visit with the student in Y] was also not yet the right thing. I chose you—but then I still did not really become your wife. The thought of my secret ideal, by which I do not mean St. [the student]—for that was something external—I mean my life's ideal, to be thin, continued to occupy me more than all else. I shall really become a wife only when I have finally given up my life's ideal. And that is so difficult that today I am again just as desperate as weeks ago. Poor ——, always I have to keep disappointing you!

As for externals, I have not yet taken medicine again. But that makes me constantly touch my abdomen and eat with dread [13] and uneasiness."

At another time Ellen writes her husband, "The only real improvement, which must come from within, is not yet here; Nirvana in a figurative sense, 'the extinction of greed, hate, and delusion' has not yet been reached. Do you know what I mean by this? The greed to realize my ideal; my hatred of the surrounding world which wants to make this impossible; the delusion which lies in my seeing this ideal as something worth while." To which is annexed the very characteristic outcry: "The thought of pancakes is still for me the most horrible thought there is." Moreover, meat and fat, she says, are so repugnant that the mere thought of them nauseates her. For the rest, she now has (during the analysis) the will to become fatter, but not the wish. She describes it as a fight between duty and desire in the Kantian sense. However, as long as it remains that, she is not "redeemed"; for this categorical imperative, this "thou shalt," comes from the outside, as it were, and therefore can do nothing against the tenacity of the morbid urge which rules her. At the same time she feels her present state, just because she is making an effort to take no laxatives, to be "more torturing than all that I have gone through hitherto. I feel myself getting fatter, I tremble with dread of this, I am living in a state of panic." —"As soon as I feel a pressure at my waist—I mean a pressure of my waistband—my spirit sinks, and I get a depression as severe as though it were a question of goodness knows what tragic affairs." On the other hand, if she has a "good bowel movement" there is "a kind of calm" in her and she feels at ease. In spite of this she feels "the entire time, every minute," how terribly her life is dominated by her "morbid idea."

Now that Ellen knows her husband has told her parents what is the matter with her, she feels a great longing for her parents, especially for her mother; she would like to lay her head on her breast and have a good cry. But this, she says, is a passing mood. Basically she feels no desire at all to be at home, indeed, she feels dread of "the grave and serious nature" of her father.

In August, soon after Ellen's thirty-third birthday, the analy-

[13] [The German word is *Angst*, which may mean either dread or anxiety. —Translators.]

sis begun in February comes to an end for external reasons. Upon his return, her husband finds her in a state of severe dread and agitation. Her food intake becomes quite irregular; Ellen leaves out entire meals, to throw herself indiscriminately with all the greater greed upon any foods which may happen to be at hand. Each day she consumes several pounds of tomatoes and twenty oranges.

A three-week visit with her parents at first goes better than expected. Ellen is happy to be out of the hotel atmosphere, to be able to spend the evenings with her family, and to talk things out with her mother. From the second week on, however, the picture changes again. For days Ellen cannot get over weeping, dread, and agitation, walks in tears through the streets of her home town, and suffers more than ever from her hunger, especially since at home she has to sit at the table with others who eat normally. She now despairs completely of her illness being curable and can hardly be calmed down any more. The physician does a blood count and finds "irregularities in the composition of the blood." He advises a consultation with the internist at the University Clinic in X, where she had audited lectures, and where she returns at the beginning of October with her husband and her old nursemaid. The internist advises a clinical treatment. Ellen cannot make up her mind to it. Instead, she undergoes psychoanalytic treatment for the second time. The second analyst with whom she enters treatment is more orthodox than the first.

Ellen is now at the beginning of her thirty-third year. On the 6th of October her husband leaves her, at the request of the analyst but against his own wishes. After having previously expressed suicidal ideas, on the 8th of October she makes an attempt at suicide by taking fifty-six tablets of Somnacetin, most of which, however, she vomits up during the night. The analyst ascribes no importance to this attempt and continues with the analysis. For the rest, Ellen is left to her own devices and walks aimlessly and tearfully through the streets. These and the following weeks until the middle of November are, according to her own account, "the most horrible of her life." In her dreams, too, she is incessantly concerned with eating. Her husband is with her from the 16th to the 24th of October and again continuously after the 6th of November.

On the 7th of November she makes her second suicidal attempt by taking twenty tablets of a barbiturate compound. On the

following day she is in a condition which the analyst describes as a
"hysterical twilight state." She cries and whimpers the entire day,
refuses all food, and declares that in some unguarded moment she
will take her life after all. On the 9th of November she again takes
food greedily. On the 10th, she attempts several times on the street
to throw herself in front of a car, on the 11th she tries to throw
herself out of a window in her analyst's office; on the 12th she moves
with her husband into the clinic of the above-mentioned internist.[14]

From her diary, resumed upon the advice of the analyst, the
following October entries are of special interest.

> October 19.   I don't think that the dread of becoming fat
> is the real obsessive neurosis, but *the constant desire for food*
> [E. W.'s emphasis]. The pleasure of eating must have been the
> primary thing. Dread of becoming fat served as a brake. Now
> that I see the pleasure of eating as the real obsessive idea, it has
> pounced upon me like a wild beast. I am defenselessly at its
> mercy. It pursues me constantly and is driving me to despair.
>
> October 21.   The day begins like all others. I see it lying
> before me filled with the uninterrupted desire for eating and the
> dread of eating. I get up and go away. My heart is full of de-
> spondency. Shall I ever in my life be able to rejoice again? The
> sun shines, but there is emptiness within me. The dreams of the
> night are confused. I have slept without joy.
>
> What is the meaning of this terrible feeling of emptiness
> —the horrible feeling of dissatisfaction which takes hold after each
> meal? My heart sinks, I feel it bodily, it is an indescribably
> miserable feeling.
>
> On the days when I am not tortured by hunger, the dread
> of becoming fat again moves to the center. Two things, then,
> torture me: First, hunger. Second, the dread of getting fatter. I
> find no way out of this noose. . . . Horrible feeling of emptiness.
> Horrible fear of this feeling. I have nothing that can dull this
> feeling.
>
> Anyway, the picture has shifted. Only a year ago I looked
> forward to hunger and then ate with appetite. The laxatives I
> took daily saw to it that I did not put on fat. Of course I also

14 [It was not at all uncommon in European institutions at this time for
the family of a wealthy patient, and even a corps of servants, to live in the institution with the patient.—Translators.]

chose my foods accordingly, avoided everything fattening, but still ate with pleasure and enjoyment the allowable things. Now, in spite of my hunger, every meal is a torment, constantly accompanied by feelings of dread. The feelings of dread do not leave me at all any more. I feel them like something physical, an ache in my heart.

When I awake in the morning I feel dread of the hunger that I know will soon appear. Hunger drives me out of bed. I eat breakfast—and after an hour get hungry again. Hunger, or the dread of hunger, pursues me all morning. The dread of hunger is something terrible. It drives all other thoughts out of my head. Even when I am full, I am afraid of the coming hour in which hunger will start again. When I am hungry I can no longer see anything clearly, cannot analyze.

I will briefly describe a morning. I sit at my desk and work. I have a great deal to do; much that I have been looking forward to. But a tormenting restlessness keeps me from finding quiet. I jump up, walk to and fro, stop again and again in front of the cupboard where my bread is. I eat some of it; ten minutes later I jump up again and eat some more. I firmly resolve not to eat any more now. Of course I can summon up such will power that I actually eat nothing. But I cannot suppress the desire for it. All day long I cannot get the thought of bread out of my mind! It so fills up my brain that I have no more room for other thoughts; I can concentrate neither on working nor on reading. Usually the end is that I run out into the street. *I run away from the bread in my cupboard* [E. W.'s emphasis] and wander aimlessly about. Or I take a laxative. How can that be analyzed? From where does this unconquerable unrest come? Why do I think I can dull it only with food? And why then does eating make me so unhappy? One might say, "Eat up the bread, then you will have peace." But no, when I have eaten it, I am unhappier than ever. Then I sit and constantly see before me the bread I have eaten. I feel of my stomach and have to keep thinking and thinking, "Now you will get that much fatter!" When I try to analyze all this, nothing comes of it except a theory. Something thought up. All I can feel is the disquiet and the dread. [Here follows an attempt at analysis.] But all this is only fantastic pictures; I must exert my brain to think them up. It would be easy to analyze someone else like this. I myself, however, continue to wander about in my deathly dread and must go through thousands of frightful hours. Every day seems to me to have a thousand hours, and often I am so tired from this spasmodic [15] thinking that I no longer wish for anything but death. After dinner my mood is always at its worst. I would rather not eat at all, so as not to have the horrible feeling after dinner. All day I am afraid of that feeling. How shall I describe it? It is a dull, empty feeling at the heart, a feeling of dread and helplessness. Sometimes then my heart pounds so strongly that it makes me quite dizzy. We've explained it in the analysis in this way: I attempt to satisfy two things while eating— hunger and love. Hunger gets satisfied—love does not! There remains the great, unfilled hole.

In the morning when I awake I begin to be afraid of the "dread after dinner," and this dread goes with me all day long. I even dread to go into a grocery store. The sight of the groceries awakens longings in me which they [the groceries] can never still. As though a person tried to quench his thirst with ink.

Perhaps I would find liberation if I could solve this puzzle: The connection between eating and longing. The anal-erotic connection is purely theoretical. It is completely incomprehensible to me. I don't understand myself at all. It is terrible not to understand yourself. *I confront myself as a strange person* [L. B.'s italics]. I am afraid of myself, I am afraid of the feelings to which I am defenselessly delivered over every minute.

This is the horrible part of my life: It is filled with dread. Dread of eating, dread of hunger, dread of the dread. Only death can save me from this dread. Every day is like walking on a dizzying ridge, an eternal balancing on cliffs. It is useless to have analysis tell me that I want precisely this dread, this tension. It sounds brilliant, but it does not help my aching heart. Who wants this tension, who, what? I see nothing any more, everything is blurred, all the threads are tangled.

The only work I do is mental. In my innermost being nothing changes, the torment remains the same. It is easy to say: everything is transparent. I long to be violated—*and indeed I do violence to myself every hour* [L. B.'s italics]. Thus I have reached my goal.

But where, where indeed is the miscalculation? For I am boundlessly wretched, and it sounds silly to me to say: "That is just what I want: to be wretched." Those are words, words, words, . . . and in the meantime I suffer as one would not let an animal suffer.

---

[15] [This word is used to approximate the German *kramphaft,* which refers to cramp-like, convulsive effort.—Translators.]

In the clinic to which, as already mentioned, Ellen went with her husband on the 12th of November, a spiritual relaxation sets in, and a complete revolution in her nourishment. From the first day on she eats everything which is put before her, including things she has not touched for years, such as soup, potatoes, meat, sweet dishes, chocolate. Her weight, which was 102 pounds on admission, nevertheless does not increase to more than 114 pounds in two months. From the clinic Ellen attends lectures at the University in the morning and afternoon: in between, from three to four o'clock, undergoes analysis; and in the evening often goes for a walk or to the theater. In class she takes notes with great concentration. It seems to her husband as if real improvement were now beginning. Her notes and poems show new hope and new courage. She wants once again "to be human among humans"; "softly on sun-billows comes a new time"; "and thus I was reborn and the world has me again"; "deep gratitude quivers through my heart that I have lived through this night." But still she does not quite trust this peace:

> I see the golden stars and how they dance;
> It's night as yet, and chaos utterly.
> Will with the early morn's clear countenance
> Peace come to me at last, and harmony?

All these poems (reproduced here merely in small extracts) were written in the night of November 18–19. She writes, "As soon as I close my eyes, there come poems, poems, poems. If I wanted to write them all down I should have to fill pages and pages—hospital poems . . . weak and full of inner restraint. They only beat their wings softly; but at least something is *stirring*. God grant that it may grow!"

From the same night we have the following entries: "I have been awake for two hours. But it is beautiful to be awake. Once before it happened, in the summer. But then everything fell apart again. This time, I believe, it will not fall apart. I feel something sweet in my breast, something which wants to grow and become. My heart throbs. Is love coming back into my life? More serious, more quiet than previously, but also more holy and more purified. Dear life, I will ripen toward you, I spread out my arms and breathe deeply, timid and glad.

"I am reading *Faust* again. Now for the first time I am beginning to understand it. I am beginning; much will have to come, and many more heavy things in my life, before I may say, 'I understand it. Yes, now I understand it.' But I am not afraid of what is coming. It is sweet to fear and to suffer, to grow and to become."

But on the very next morning (November 19) "the beautiful mood of the night is as if blown away. I am tired and sad." She does continue to go to lectures, to write, and to read, but the thought of eating never leaves her. For the attraction of this thought she finds a very characteristic comparison: "The murderer must feel somewhat as I do who constantly sees in his mind's eye the picture of the victim. He can work, even slave, from early until late, can go out, can talk, can attempt to divert himself: all in vain. Always and always again he will see the picture of the victim before him. He feels an overpowering pull toward the place of the murder. He knows that this makes him suspect. Even worse—he has a horror of that place, but still he must go there. Something that is stronger than his reason and his will controls him and makes of his life a frightful scene of devastation. The murderer can find redemption. He goes to the police and accuses himself. In the punishment he atones for his crime. I can find no redemption—except in death."

Ellen is painfully aware that "by this fearful illness I am withdrawing more and more from people." "I feel myself excluded from all real life. I am quite isolated. I sit in a glass ball. I see people through a glass wall, their voices come to me muffled. I have an unutterable longing to get to them. I scream, but they do not hear me. I stretch out my arms toward them; but my hands merely beat against the walls of my glass ball."

At this time she begins to write the "History of a Neurosis." We quote from it:

> Since I acted only from the point of view of whether things made me thin or fat, all things soon lost their intrinsic meaning. My work too. I sought it for the purpose of diverting myself: away from my hunger or my fondness for sweets. (During the time I was working from nine to one and from two to six, I was not tempted to eat things that would make me fat.) For a time work served its purpose. It also gave me joy. When everything

collapsed in me, that too broke to bits: Work neither diverted me nor gave me joy. However, that did not come till later.

In the fall of 19—— (at the beginning of my thirty-second year) I felt dread for the first time. Only a very indefinite and faint dread; really rather an inkling of the fact that I had become enslaved to an uncanny power which threatened to destroy my life. I felt that all inner development was ceasing, that all becoming and growing were being choked, because a single idea was filling my entire soul: and this idea something unspeakably ridiculous. My reason rebelled against it, and I attempted by will power to drive this idea out. In vain. Too late—I could no longer free myself and longed now for liberation, for redemption which was to come to me through some method of healing. Thus I came to psychoanalysis.

I wanted to get to know the unknown urges which were stronger than my reason and which forced me to shape my entire life in accordance with a guiding point of view. And the goal of this guiding point of view was to be thin. The analysis was a disappointment. I analyzed with my mind, and everything remained theory. The wish to be thin remained unchanged in the center of my thinking.

The months which followed were the most terrible I have ever experienced, and I have not yet gotten over them. Now it was no longer the fixed idea alone which embittered my life, but something far worse was added: the compulsion of always having to think about eating. This compulsion has become the curse of my life, it pursues me waking and sleeping, it stands beside everything I do like an evil spirit, and never and nowhere can I escape it. It pursues me as the Furies pursue a murderer, it makes the world a caricature and my life a hell. It seems to me that I could stand any other pain more easily; if my existence were darkened by a really heavy sorrow, I would have the strength to bear it. But the torture of having each day to tilt anew against the windmill with a mass of absurd, base, contemptible thoughts, this torment spoils my life.

When I open my eyes in the morning, my great misery stands before me. Even before I am entirely awake I think of— eating. Every meal is associated with dread and agitation, every hour between meals filled with the thoughts, "When shall I get hungry again? Would I perhaps even like to eat something now? And what?" . . . and so on and so on; a thousand different forms, but always the same content. No wonder I can no longer be glad. I know only dread and sorrow, lack of pleasure and lack of courage.

Since the curve again takes a serious drop after the end of November, at the beginning of December Kraepelin is consulted and diagnoses *melancholia*. The analyst considers this diagnosis incorrect and continues the analysis. In the first half of December her course is again uphill: Ellen again attends lectures, reads *Faust,* Part II, but is torn to and fro by the differing views of the doctors regarding her illness and her treatment. The internist, who judges the illness most correctly, considers continued hospital treatment necessary, the analyst advises leaving the clinic and "returning to life." This advice completely shakes her faith in the analyst. In her diary she noted on December 19, among other things, "I continue living only because of a sense of duty to my relatives. Life has no further lure for me. There is nothing, no matter where I look, which holds me. Everything is gray and without joy. Since I have buried myself in myself and can no longer love, existence is only torture. Every hour is torture. What formerly gave me joy is now a task, an intrinsically senseless something contrived to help me pass the hours. What formerly seemed to me a goal in life, all the learning, all the striving, all the accomplishment, is now a dark, heavy nightmare of which I am afraid." For her condition she again finds pertinent analogies:

Karl (her husband) says, she tells us, that she does have joy in some things; but he should "ask a prisoner of war sometime whether he would rather stay in the prison camp or return to his homeland. In the prison camp he studies foreign languages and concerns himself with this or that; of course, only to help himself get over the long, hard days. Does he really enjoy the work? Would he for its sake remain in the prison camp even a minute longer than necessary? Certainly not, and nobody will even dream up such a grotesque idea. But of me it is required. Life has become a prison camp for me, and I long as ardently for death as the poor soldier in Siberia longs for his homeland.

"The comparison with imprisonment is no play on words. I am in prison, caught in a net from which I cannot free myself. I am a prisoner within myself; I get more and more entangled, and every day is a new, useless struggle; the meshes tighten more and

more. I am in Siberia; my heart is icebound, all around me is soli-
tude and cold. My best days are a sadly comic attempt to deceive
myself as to my true condition. It is undignified to live on like this.
Karl, if you love me, grant me death."

Another analogy: "I am surrounded by enemies. Wherever
I turn, a man stands there with drawn sword. As on the stage: The
unhappy one rushes toward the exit; stop! an armed man confronts
him. He rushes to a second, to a third exit. All in vain. He is surrounded, he can no longer get out. He collapses in despair.

"So it is with me: I am in prison and cannot get out. It does
no good for the analyst to tell me that I myself place the armed
men there, that they are theatrical figments and not real. *To me
they are very real* [E.W.'s emphasis]."

Ellen complains that for months she has "had not one hour
of complete freedom." At the same time, she says the daily picture
keeps changing. In one week the morning hours are the worst, in
another the evening hours, in a third the midday or the late afternoon hours, but in no week is she "completely free." What is constantly denied her is unconcern. She "knows" about herself un-
ceasingly, does everything "with awareness," can never be simply
here and live. If once in a while she "grasps at the faith" that her
life does still make sense, that she can still be useful to others and
help them, then fear comes and "stifles this weak spark of life
again." It becomes clearer and clearer to her that she cannot live
on if she does not succeed in "breaking the ban" and getting out
of this preoccupation with self. Her "spiritual confusion" during
and after meals is terrible. She swallows every bite with awareness
and an inexplicable feeling of sadness. *"The entire world-picture
is disarranged* [L.B.'s italics]. As if I were bewitched. An evil spirit
accompanies me and embitters my joy in everything. He distorts
everything beautiful, everything natural, everything simple, and
makes a caricature out of it. He makes a caricature out of all life."—
"Something in me rebels against becoming fat. Rebels against becoming healthy, getting plump red cheeks, becoming a simple,
robust woman, as corresponds to my true nature. . . . It drives me
to despair that with all my big words I cannot get myself further.
I am fighting against uncanny powers which are stronger than I.
I cannot seize and grasp them. . . ."

At the beginning of the new year, on the 3rd of January, the internist intervenes decisively, prohibits the continuation of the analysis, to which the patient agrees, and advises her transfer to the Bellevue Sanatorium in Kreuzlingen. On January 7th she writes her younger brother to pardon her for writing him so frankly, but she will no longer lie to him; she wants to tell him that she is full of dread, even though she does not know of what: "Life burdens me like a cloud." During the preparations for the trip, increased depression and agitation sets in. The trip, which takes place on January 13th and 14th, is undergone amid states of fear, feelings of hunger, and depression.

2. *The Stay at Kreuzlingen Sanatorium from January 14 to March 30, 19——*

The referral note of the internist states that menstruation has been absent for years and that the salivary glands are slightly enlarged. Certainly, therefore, there are endocrine disturbances too. The neurosis has expressed itself for many years in obsessive ideas, especially in the fear of becoming too heavy and then again in a compulsive urge to eat copiously and indiscriminately. Between these opposing feelings the exceptionally intelligent patient, many-sided in her interests, vacillates back and forth. To this was added in July of the previous year a very severe cyclothymic depression with exacerbations approximately once a month, strong feelings of dread, and periodic suicidal ideas. During periods of increased depression the obsessive thoughts have been more in the background. In the clinic her condition improved decidedly during the constant presence of her husband, who has a very favorable effect upon her. Her body weight increased markedly on an initial diet of 70 calories/kilo and at the present time is steady at about 52 kilos (114 lb.) on a diet of 50 calories/kilo. Because of her last depression, she was to undergo the prolonged rest urgently recommended by Kraepelin in our institution. Admission to the locked ward seems unnecessary.

The second analyst states in his detailed report that the patient is suffering from a severe obsessive neurosis combined with manic-depressive oscillations. He is convinced that the patient is on the way to a cure! Evidence of this is also a far-reaching physiognomic alteration; for whereas during the summer she was repulsively ugly, since then she has grown more and more feminine and almost pretty. The report confirms in general the above anamnesis, but also contains some important additions and opinions of the psychoanalyst. He considers the depression as "strongly and purposefully aggravated." The patient stated at one time, he says, that her father did not understand her obsessive ideas, but that he did have full understanding of the depression. She had feared that by becoming fat she would displease her previous fiancé (the student), and anyway, for her, being thin was equated with a higher intellectual type, and being fat with a bourgeois Jewish type. After the termination of her engagement her first action was, with a sigh of relief, to raid her own larder! "But when she learned from a statement of the gynecologist that she would have no success along the womanly—motherly—line, despite her renunciation of higher intellectuality (in her marriage she concerned herself ostentatiously with the household and the copying of recipes, especially when in the presence of her younger brother's wife, who is a slim blonde, artistically oriented, has children, etc.), she now resolved 'to live for her idea' without any inhibitions, and began to take large daily doses of laxatives." Since she saw the blond, higher type in the person of her analyst, he succeeded in quieting her during the first consultation (a fact which her husband also confirms). She has also shown pronounced hysterical traits, visibly calculated to impress her husband. Anal-eroticism was the focus of the treatment for a long time. She recognized the relationship between chocolate and anal-eroticism, as well as the equation: "Eating = being fertilized = pregnant = getting fat." The transference then became so clear that on one occasion she sat down quite suddenly on the analyst's lap and gave him a kiss, which, in spite of their previous friendly relations, was very unusual. On another occasion she came to him with the wish that she might lay her head on his shoulder and he should call her "Ellen-child." Since the beginning of December the analysis had flagged more and more, and this as a sequel to their discussion of the father-complex, which however could only be treated peripherally. She had made it clear to herself that "her obsessional idea" meant turning away from the paternal (Jewish) type. For the incest-wish, no material could be obtained, not even from her dreams. The infantile amnesia, unfortunately, was not illuminated by either analysis.

During the intake interview at the sanatorium on January

14th, after a few words the patient bursts out into loud wailing and cannot be calmed down for a long time, but reports abruptly and intermittently disconnected fragments of her case history. She readily follows her husband to her room and is glad that she will have an opportunity at once to report details of her illness. She then tells circumstantially the main features in the development of her suffering, from its inception thirteen years before to the latest events in the University town. Kraepelin had rejected the analyst's assumption of an obsessive neurosis, had assumed a genuine melancholia, and had declared to her that the obsessional thoughts would surely disappear with the melancholia; what would happen to her fixed idea after that would soon be seen. Even now she differentiates between the obsessional idea of always having to think about eating and the "fixed idea," the "one goal" of not becoming fat. She reports that during the last weeks she has felt a slight improvement, but has never really been happy and glad. She has come here with a thousand good resolutions, but even on the way over she has become terribly hopeless. Every trifle now seems to her like an insurmountable obstacle. She has the feeling that if one of her symptoms is better, another is so much the worse. "I need the carefree feeling again while eating; to me every meal is an inner conflict. Constantly I have the feeling that if somebody really loved me he would not let me live on." In the clinic, she says, she finally became afraid of everyone because she must always expect they would tell her she looked well. "Everything agitates me, and I experience every agitation as a sensation of hunger, even if I have just eaten." Now she has the feeling that all inner life has ceased, that everything is unreal, everything senseless. She also reports readily on her suicidal attempts. Even now she wishes for nothing so much as to be allowed to go to sleep and not wake up again, for she does not dream that she can ever become healthy again. After the second attempt she had constantly thought only this: if only her husband would come back soon, otherwise she would throw herself under some car, she had constantly longed for him when he was away. She turns against psychoanalysis with particular vigor. In contrast with this, her husband states that she let herself be analyzed quite willingly and that she was by no means detached from the second analyst.

Further extracts from the case record:

January 16. After a discussion of the daily schedule as to

rest, walks, etc., and the question of eating, the first night went well, with the help of a mild sedative. The patient is allowed to eat in her room, but comes readily with her husband to afternoon coffee, whereas previously she had stoutly resisted this on the ground that she did not really eat but devoured like a wild animal —which she demonstrated with utmost realism.

Her physical examination showed nothing striking. She is a woman of medium height, adequately nourished, tending toward pyknic habitus, whose body build is characterized in the case record as boyish. However, signs of pronounced male stigmatization are missing. The skull is described in the case record as relatively large and massive, but otherwise no signs of acromegaly are present. Facial form oval and evenly modeled. Salivary glands are markedly enlarged on both sides. Thyroid gland not palpable. An earlier gynecological examination is said to have revealed "infantile genitalia." On clavicle, callus formation from an old fracture while riding. Internal organs, no comment. Pulse full, soft, but the rate is unstable. Periods absent for several years. The neurological examination shows, except for a very weak (Jendrassik enforced) patellar reflex (with a moderately active Achilles' reflex), absolutely nothing remarkable, nor any tremor of hands.

January 21. The facial expression is very changeable, corresponding to frequent fluctuations from one affective state to another; on the whole, however, somewhat stiff and empty, her look now empty, now strongly "saturated with feeling." Also, her posture is somewhat stiff. Her gait is erect and very quick. Her behavior is very amiable; she seeks contacts but without notable eroticism. Basic mood hopelessly despairing. Even at this time I noted: "One has less the impression that she suffers under a genuine depressive affect than that she feels herself physically empty and dead, completely hollow, and suffers precisely from the fact that she cannot achieve any affect. Strong feeling of illness in the sense of a flagging of her mental energy. Seriously longs for death. In the foreground, vexation and torment because of the obsession of always having to think of eating. Feels herself degraded by this. Striking is the objectivity with which she reports things from which properly the release of a strong affect must be expected. Train of thought shows neither flight of ideas nor dispersion; but she has difficulty concentrating since her thoughts keep revolving about her "complex."

Hence will not yet let her husband read to her. Power of appre-
hension, attention, and memory intact, however. The Rorschach
test was unfortunately not available at that time; the result would
have been of the greatest interest in presenting experimentally a
picture of the patient's entire world-view.

January 22.   Nights tolerable with mild sedatives. Only during her second night so agitated that her husband had to call the
head nurse. Mood fluctuates from day to day and often several times
during the same day. On the whole, quieter; slight attacks of
dread beginning with a "fluttering" in the cardiac region, "as if
there were bats there." Eats nearly everything that is set before
her, only makes occasional difficulties about desserts. Has lost one
pound in the last week, since then has eaten better. During walks
lets herself be diverted from her despair with relative ease. Though
as a child she was wholly independent of the opinion of the others,
she is now completely dependent on what others think about her
appearance and her being fat.

Since everything now depended on our arriving at a definitive diagnosis, I asked the patient and her husband to work out an
exact anamnesis, a labor which visibly calms the patient.

February 8.   She suffers greatly from obsessional impulses to
throw herself upon food and gulp it down like an animal (confirmed by observation). One night devoured seven oranges in suc-
cession. By contrast, during the meals there appear ascetic impulses, forcing her to deny herself this and that, especially the des-
sert. She is least restrained during walks but is also quite orderly
with the other patients; however, she can never get away from herself and constantly has the feeling "of being like a corpse among
people."

February 15.   The findings already noted in the report of
the internist are again shown here clearly: feelings of hunger,
ravenous desire, and "compulsive thoughts" about eating superseded
by a severely depressive dejection, indeed, despair. Suicidal impulses, self-reproaches for beginning to lie once more—it had come
to that today. Had recently taken six tablets of laxative daily but in
response to a direct question had lied to the physician, saying she
was taking nothing.

February 26.   Agitation, quickly subsided again. Has attached herself to an elegant, very thin female patient. "Homoerotic component strikingly evident." Dreams very vividly and always about food or death; sees the finest things before her, feels terrible hunger, but at the same time the compulsion not to be allowed to eat. The death dreams are:

> *Dream 1:* "I dreamt something wonderful: War had broken out, I was to go into the field. I say good-by to everyone with a joyous expectation that I shall soon die. I am glad that before the end I can eat everything, have eaten a large piece of mocha cake."
>
> *Dream 2:* In a semisomnolent state she dreams she is "the wife of a painter who cannot sell his paintings. She herself has to work at sewing or the like, cannot do it because she feels sick, both have to go hungry. She asks him to get a revolver and shoot them both. 'You're just too cowardly to shoot us; the other two painters shot themselves too.' "
>
> *Dream 3:* Dreams that on her trip overseas she jumped into the water through a porthole. Her first lover (the student) and her husband both attempted artificial respiration. She ate many chocolate creams and packed her trunks.
>
> *Dream 4:* She orders goulash, says she is very hungry, but only wants a small portion. Complains to her old nursemaid that people are tormenting her very much. Wants to set herself on fire in the forest.

For psychotherapeutic reasons, an analysis of her dreams was not made.

During a morning agitation in a semisomnolent state she speaks of the deceased, who have eternal rest while she is still tormented; speaks of her burial. Will eat no oranges because her husband will tell the doctors. Offers a farmer fifty thousand francs if he will shoot her quickly. Speaks of her younger brother, who has left the New World because he has been tormented day and night by the buzzing of a fly; she herself, though in the same tormented state, is not allowed "to leave from overseas," but must continue to live. If she knows no other way of dying, she will set fire to herself or ram her head through a pane of glass. She says we are all sadists and take pleasure in tormenting her, the doctor included.

It is very easy for her husband to achieve rapport [16] with
her, not only when she is half asleep but when she is fully asleep.

March 9.   After fourteen relatively good days, there are five
days of agitation, which reached their climax yesterday. In the
foreground a "colossal gluttony," to which, however, she did not
yield. She says she cannot wait until her "melancholia" is cured.
It is terrible that her husband has such a "bad" influence on her,
since his presence makes it impossible for her to take her life. Wants
to look at the locked wards, possibly to transfer there.

"I feel myself, quite passively, the stage on which two hostile
forces are mangling each other." She has the feeling that she can
do nothing at all about it and must look on in complete helplessness.

March 11.   Her visit to the locked wards has had a rather
unfavorable effect. "I would want to smash in the solid panes immediately." Feels gluttony again "as when a wild animal throws
itself on its food." Full of self-reproaches for having eaten too much.
Wants permission from the doctor to take her life. Attempts ob-
stinately to convince her husband and doctor of the correctness of
this trend of thought, rejects every counterargument.

Even as a young girl she could not sit quietly at home, but
always had to be on the go, which even then struck those around
her. At the age of eighteen she wrote to a girl friend, "Melancholy
lies over my life like a black bird, which hovers somewhere in the
background until the time has come to pounce upon me and kill
me." Now, too, she has the feeling that in everything she does a
ghost stalks her in order to kill her, or she is only waiting until
"insanity comes and, shaking its black locks, seizes me and hurls
me into the yawning abyss." Periods absent for four and one-half
years, sexual intercourse discontinued for three years; previously
normal.

March 21.   Suicidal threats become more serious. Wants only
to wait for the consultation scheduled for March 24. "If there were
a substance which contained nourishment in the most concentrated

16 [This word is not used here in its customary sense of a close and har-
monious relationship but in the special sense of communication between a
hypnotist and his subject. In hypnotic rapport the subject responds without
awakening to the questions and commands of the hypnotist. The use of the term
at this point may be taken to indicate the extent of the husband's influence over
Ellen.—Translators.]

form and on which I would remain thin, then I would still be so glad to continue living."—"I want to get thinner and thinner, but I do not want to have to watch myself constantly, and I do not want to forego anything; it is this friction between wanting to be thin and yet not wanting to miss any food which is destroying me."—"On all points I am clear and sensible, but on this one point I am insane; I am perishing in the struggle against my nature. Fate wanted to have me fat and strong, but I want to be thin and delicate." The capacity to enjoy spring increases more and more, but also the torment while eating.

Second postscript to the anamnesis: She says she already had depressive dejections even before the appearance of the fixed idea in her twenty-first year. In her diary, some months before the appearance of this idea, she expresses wonderment that a damper suddenly tones down her cheerful mood, so that she feels like crying. She wonders whether she is too sensitive for the great battle of life. "How often I begin a morning cheerily, my heart full of sunshine and hope, and before I am able to understand why I am so happy, something comes and strikes my mood down. Something quite insignificant, perhaps a cold tone in the voice of a person whom I love, or some other usually insignificant thing to disappoint me in someone. I see how the world darkens before my blurred vision."

In response to my request her husband gathers together the following material on the theme of suicide: The wish to die runs through her entire life. Even as a child she thinks it "interesting" to have a fatal accident—for example, to break through the ice while skating. During her riding period (at nineteen, twenty, and twenty-one) she performs foolhardy tricks, has a fall and breaks her clavicle, and thinks it too bad that she does not have a fatal accident; on the next day she mounts her horse again and continues to carry on in the same manner. When sick as a young girl, she is disappointed each time the fever subsides and the sickness leaves her. When she studies for the *Matura* (at twenty-two), she wants her tutor to repeat this sentence over and over again: Those whom the gods love die young. The teacher is annoyed by this and finally refuses to do this again and again. When she hears of the death of girl friends, she envies them and her eyes shine at the death announcement. While working in the Foundling Home, despite the warnings of the supervisor she visits children who have scarlet fever and kisses them in the hope that she, too, will catch it. Attempted also to get sick by standing naked on the balcony after a hot bath, putting her feet into ice cold water, or standing in the front of the streetcar when there is an east wind and she has a fever of 102°. The first analyst at the first consultation in late December 19—calls her behavior a "slow attempt at suicide."

March 22. Was very cheerful yesterday during her walk; sat down to her meal at noon quite calmly, but then, as always, was suddenly as if inwardly transformed. Wonders then immediately whether she can make herself leave something on her plate. Becomes more agitated, the more the meal progresses. "Everything in me trembles, the desire to eat up everything fights within me a furious battle against the resolve not to eat everything, until finally I jump up and have all that I have left taken away, in order not to get into the danger of eating it up after all." Then feels as if beaten up, completely exhausted, her whole body covered with perspiration; all her limbs ache as if she had been whipped; would like to shoot herself at once. Only after some time (one to two hours) does this condition fade away.

March 24. Consultation with Professor E. Bleuler and a foreign psychiatrist.

The preliminaries of this consultation are as follows: In view of the increasing risk of suicide, continued residence of the patient on the open ward could not be justified. I had to put before her husband the alternative of giving permission to transfer his wife to the closed ward or leaving the institution with her. The very sensible husband saw this perfectly, but said he could give his permission only if a cure or at least a far-reaching improvement of his wife could be promised him. Since on the basis of the anamnesis and my own observations I had to diagnose a progressive schizophrenic psychosis (schizophrenia simplex), I could offer the husband very little hope. (If shock therapy had existed then, it would have offered a temporary way out of the dilemma and a certain postponement, but it would certainly have changed nothing in the final result.) Since it was clear that a release from the institution meant certain suicide, I had to advise the husband in the light of his responsibility not to rely upon my opinion alone—certain as I was of my case—but to arrange for a consultation with Professor Bleuler on the one hand, and on the other hand, with a foreign psychiatrist whose views were not too close to the Kraepelin-Bleuler theory of schizophrenia. The complete anamnesis (excerpts from which are given in the following section), as well as our case record, was handed to the consultants in advance.

Result of the consultation: Both gentlemen agree completely with my prognosis and doubt any therapeutic usefulness of commitment even more emphatically than I. For Bleuler the presence of schizophrenia is indubitable. The second psychiatrist declares that schizophrenia can be diagnosed only if an intellectual defect exists. In our case he would label it a psychopathic constitution progressively unfolding. The "idea" of wanting to get thin he correctly designates not as a delusional idea (since logical motivation is absent), but with less justification as an overvalent idea (we shall come back to this). All three of us agree that it is not a case of obsessional neurosis and not one of manic-depressive psychosis, and that no definitely reliable therapy is possible. We therefore resolved to give in to the patient's demand for discharge.

March 30. The patient was visibly relieved by the result of the consultation, declared that she would now take her life in her own hands, but was much shaken when she saw that despite her best intentions she could not master her dilemma with regard to eating. Externally she controls herself powerfully and is quiet and orderly, but inwardly she is very tense and agitated. She ponders this way and that what she is to do now, and finally resolves to go home with her husband this very day. She continues precisely her whole way of life until the last, since every change "confuses her and throws her completely off the track." She is tormented in the extreme by her "idea" up to the last moment. Weight upon leaving approximately the same as upon arriving, namely 104 pounds.

3. Her Death

On her trip Ellen is very courageous. The reason for taking it gives her strength. The glimpse into life which the trip gives her hurts her. Even more than in the institution she feels incapable of dealing with life. The following days are more harrowing than all the previous weeks. She feels no release of tension; on the contrary, all her symptoms appear more strongly. The irregularity of her way of life upsets her completely; the reunion with her relatives only brings her illness more clearly into view. On the third day of being home she is as if transformed. At breakfast she eats butter and sugar, at noon she eats so much that—for the first time in thirteen years!—she is satisfied by her food and gets really full. At afternoon coffee she eats chocolate creams and Easter eggs. She takes a walk with her husband, reads poems by Rilke, Storm, Goethe, and Tennyson, is amused by the first chapter of Mark Twain's "Christian Science," is in a positively festive mood, and all heaviness seems to have fallen away from her. She writes letters, the last one a letter to the fellow patient here to whom she had become so attached. In the evening she takes a lethal dose of poison, and on the following morning she is dead. "She looked as she had never looked in life—calm and happy and peaceful."

Binswanger's analysis of Ellen West 15

Ellen West is important for us because Binswanger's analysis is one of the most complete and insightful in the psychiatric literature. Binswanger, one of the leading European existential psychologists, also uses this opportunity to demonstrate the "philosophical anthropological" approach to existential psychology. That approach, and this case study in particular, has not been widely appreciated or even understood in this country, and so we shall attempt here an account and description of Binswanger's analysis, as well as an analysis from the point of view of the present book.

Binswanger's *Daseinsanalyse* (cf. Binswanger, 1963) is based, as all existential psychology is based, on an ontological framework that sees man's existence as necessarily embedded in and inseparable from a unique world. We do not examine a person, or a life-history, except that we examine the world in which that person is (ams). Since that examination itself is inseparable from the examiner's being and his world, our task is to place the data of the case into a framework that is "basic," that encompasses the fundamental aspect of human being, namely, the self-world relationship as it is embedded in a past-future flow. What is more, however, as scientists attempting this anthropological task, we must recognize that our framework too is a creation of a temporal flow, both in the sense that we as individuals are histories and in the sense that we belong to a scientific community that is a history. In both senses, the past and the future, as experienced by us, are relevant to our creation of a framework for analyzing Ellen West. For example, the framework of the present author includes, in an important and relevant way, an intellectual confrontation of Freud and of Binswanger, both of whom contribute to my understanding of Ellen West. The reader, in turn, is a history; he does not read this book from some neutral standpoint outside of his individual and cultural history.

To realize this is to submit to devilish intellectual problems. Binswanger insists that we need not be condemned to a solipsism or relativism that destroys all meaning. Men transcend this intellectual impass through "love" and the imagination originating from it. This is not fuzzy sentimentalism. It is a recognition that man does transcend himself, that we do escape our solipsism—by becoming involved in and related to other persons, and by imagination, which can and regularly does violate the static present and the single perspective. To be anthropologists in Binswanger's sense, then, we needn't be more than human; we need only become systematic and disciplined in our humanity. Unlike objective science, where knowledge is reduced to mechanics and all else is condemned as "mere subjectivity," we seek to use our transcendence in the service of our science. We can do this insofar as our categories are ontologically basic, and only insofar as they are. Therefore, we must temporalize our thought and in so doing we must be able to see the patient's self-world relationship as a history. The patient's being transcends the single perspective and goes out into the world, and it transcends the static present and lives the past and the future in a particular way.

1. The World

In his search for metaphors that describe the ontological structure, the basic categories of human being, Binswanger resorts to two sets of categories that differ in minor ways from the major categories of this book. The "world," for Binswanger, is divided into three "regions": the *Umwelt* is the region of natural, environmental things to which one is related in experience; the *Mitwelt* is the region of other people in which one is embedded; the *Eigenwelt* is the region of self that is experientially differentiated from objects and from other people. In some ways these categories correspond to being-in-the-world, being-for-others, and being-for-oneself (respectively), and in some ways they cut across them. To follow Binswanger's analysis, we shall use his language and refer to our own when it is appropriate. In addition to the "regions" of the self-world relationship, Binswanger describes three "basic forms" of human existence, which are decisive for understanding Ellen West and central to his entire approach. These are also elaborated in Binswanger's major work (1953). First, there is the world of the air, in which one "flies" in the freedom of imagination and idealism. Wishes and ideals, which are not actual but may be possible, populate this world; and one's movement therein has a characteristic temporalization and spatialization recognizable in certain experiences. Ellen West's ecstatic moments are of this form and are not unrelated to what we have called the open-endedness of the future and of possibility.

Second, there is the world in and under the earth, in which one "crawls" like a worm, crushed by the burdensome necessities of natural limitations. Desires, which are "given" and intransigent, along with the entire structure of objective qualities not subject to human whim, populate this world. The temporalization of this world is ultimately that of mere decay, or at best, ponderous and relentless movement into a foreordained and essentially closed future. Third, there is the world of the earth, in which one has one's feet planted on the ground but in which one moves by "striding," through practical action, into a future that envisions possibilities but recognizes necessities. To move in this world is to combine the ideal, the hoped-for, and the possible with the given, the recognized and the necessary, in concrete expression of human being.

These categories seek to describe the basic forms of being and they do so by describing worlds in which one's being is. The view of Ellen West that emerges from these categories obviates the limited perspective of a particular theory or theorist because these are the ontological forms of all human being. No human *is* except in these terms. No theory of human nature that falls short of the ontology of human being describes the most basic, and hence the most important, aspect of that being. Let us now follow Binswanger's analysis of Ellen West.

Binswanger notes that the refusal to take milk is an immediate demarcation of the *Eigenwelt* over against the natural surroundings of the *Umwelt*. In addition, the first verbal assertion of which we know, that "This bird's nest is no bird's nest" is a similar refusal of intercourse with the *Mitwelt,* that is, with the communal consensus that this is a bird's nest. The *Umwelt* and *Mitwelt,* therefore, were experienced very early in an oppositional way, that is, in opposition to a rigid assertion of self. This exaggerated affirmation of the *Eigenwelt,* which continues to play a role in Ellen West's being throughout her life, may appear to be an expression of self-confidence and fullness of life. However, Ellen West's demarcation of a rebellious and obstinant self impoverished the *Eigenwelt,* for the exchange with and enrichment from the *Um-* and *Mitwelt* failed to occur. The region of the self, in its defiance, was locked into a self-definition that closes, rather than opens, being and that constricts, rather than expands, possibilities.

Such a structuring of experience puts one in complete control of oneself, in the sense of warding off any influences from the outside, but that self becomes a peculiarly empty self. It is totally defined in terms of resistance to what it is not. The autonomy of such a self is therefore a by-product of the struggle with the outside; this autonomy is merely negative. By excluding intercourse with the world, Ellen West deprived herself of something to affirm in her self-affirmation. Possibilities deteriorated. Submission to other people, or even mere agreement with them, and invasion by objects, or even mere swallowing of milk, were no longer possibilities.

In addition to misconstruing possibilities in this way, Ellen West misconstrued necessities. Binswanger points to her rejection of womanhood until age 17. Here it is not only a rigid demarcation of the *Eigenwelt* over against the *Um-* and *Mitwelt,* but an alienation of the *Eigenwelt* from the "world of fate," or what we have called the "given." A self-sufficient and an uncompromising flavor of Ellen West's being, which is consistent with this alienation, is seen in her thumbsucking until the sixteenth year and her ambitious, self-defining principle, *"aut Caesar aut nihil!"*

The religious faith which she seems to have enjoyed until her seventeenth year is the great exception to Ellen West's radically individualistic existence. Perhaps the nursemaid was also a point of community for her. But in connection with her first love affair, her religious faith and her rebellion against her femininity both crumble. Her world therefore shifts; any modesty that might characterize a religious person disappears. Binswanger points out, in addition, that her reading of *Niels Lyhne* had a great impact on the creation of a new *Gestalt*. This book is an example of the "rigorous esthetic individualism and religious nihilism, so characteristic of the late nineteenth and early twentieth century." Niels experiences disillusionment: "It was a lie, any belief in the melting of one soul into another. Not the mother who took us on her lap, not a friend, not the wife who rested in our heart . . ." (Binswanger, 1958, p. 272). Ellen West's response was to reaffirm herself by raising her own self-concept to superlative heights.

This newly emerging existential platform has differences from and continuities with her earlier structuring of experience. Her *Eigenwelt* continued to be the major region of her being, but it became more grandiose and more addicted to its own passions and dreams. Her relationship to the *Mitwelt,* which had previously been one of defiance and independence, acquired not only a lover but also a burning interest in social change. However, rather than supplanting her original willfulness, her new social involvement retained unbridled ambition. Her sights were set on revolution and on herself as a heroine whose name will be remembered by posterity. She condemned her own family for their wealth. Her love was poisoned by the exclusiveness of her *Eigenwelt*.

Both her love affair and her social conscience, however, were manifested in images of "practical action" which solidifies one's relationship to the world and prevents withdrawal into fantastic self-absorption. According to Binswanger, it is only through practical action that we become truly certain of our own existence. She attempted to stand with both feet firmly on the ground and to know where she stood. Ellen West's existential posture was not devoid of at least a longing for authentic communion with others. In fact, without this human longing, for love, for a "homeland," for community, Ellen West would have been incapable of psychosis. This longing, which is at once universal and yet not totally realizable, makes possible the incurable emptiness that eventually makes her life a living hell. It is a longing rooted in man's existential condition rather than in his psychodynamics. Ellen West was not oblivious to existential limitations; indeed she suffered acutely from them. But because her ideals were so grandiose, the paradoxes of human limitation were intensely frustrating. Ellen West could have loved; to one who cannot love, existence can become a burden but not a hell.

Ellen West's "practical action" was, alas, spotty and inconsistent. She did not succeed in her attempt to stand "with both feet firmly on the ground." Neither her independence nor her possibilities could take root in practical action. She could move on the earth only with effort, for her movement on earth was constantly opposed by a flying in the air, on the one hand; and by a being-confined in and under the earth, on the other. These two worlds, in the air and under the earth, as Binswanger characterizes them, have vivid representation in Ellen West's poems, diary notes, letters, and utterances. The flying through an airy world with volatile spirits ran into contradictions. Her lofty idealism was not reconcilable with the "given," and so she experienced the realities of life as "the darkening of the sky," "the sinking of the sun's fireball into the ocean," "the eeriness of the whistling winds," "the pilotless drifting of the ship of life on the water," "the rising of gray, damp evening mists," "the hopeless dreary shivering of the treetops," "the gradual waning of the birdsong," and eventually as an "icy coldness." Ellen West therefore added to her rigid demarcation of the *Eigenwelt* a radical split in the way her being is-in-the-world. At times it soars; at other times it is gloomy. Her being was thus, alternately, in two different worlds: the airy, light world (the Artemis ideal) and the dark, sullen one. These two worlds, these two modes of being, constitute a contradiction that lies at the core of all human existence but that is especially visible and determinative of the life-history of Ellen West.

Her practical action, therefore, took on a desperate quality. It was to be the resolution of the contradiction. Possibility and necessity must be resolved, and practical action must mediate their mutual influence and express her being, as indeed it must for all of us. But the given, existential contradiction was augmented by the older, more idiosyncratic, contradiction within her own being: the violent exclusiveness of her *Eigenwelt*. If practical action were to help her, it must be for its own sake, not as a means of gaining undying fame, nor as an opiate for sorrow and grief in order to make her forget. Practical action built upon so desperate a contradiction became a mere ploy to rescue her from insanity and the madhouse.

Failure, therefore, becomes devastating. Her death will negate everything unless she achieves an "undying name." Her being was not experienced as a temporal flow within the historical age, but as a thing, as merely extant, as something which eventually will no longer be extant but will molder and be buried in oblivion. Ellen West's inability to have an exchange with the world yielded an isolation from communal and historical events. This isolation severely restricted what life could mean to her, and led to a reification and a stultification of life.

Binswanger has taken us, up to this point, through the experiential coordinates that characterized Ellen West's being. Her most salient "symptom," and the one that eventually led to her death, appears against the background we have described and is meaningful only within that context.

In her eighteenth year, Ellen West discovered that she would herself like to be petite and ethereal as her girl friends were. This wish of the ethereal world permeated not only the *Umwelt* and *Mitwelt,* but also the *Eigenwelt.* Yet it is a region of the *Eigenwelt* which offers the most powerful contradiction to the wish by its very gravity, solidity, and compact filling of space. The body is and must inevitably be massive and opaque.

Ellen West extravagantly dramatized life into two opposite worlds, the "ethereal" world where she can soar through idealism and possibilities, and the world of confined dullness and dark necessities of the tomb. At eighteen these two worlds took up concrete representation in her body. The idiosyncratic existential contradiction later came to be experienced concretely as contradictory directions for her body to change: toward objective stodginess and intransigence, substance and fat, or toward ethereal lightness and spiritual freedom.

At this point, Ellen West began to shift to yet another existential platform, yet another order for her experience. God the Father was implored to save her from her dilemma. The ethereal world as such cannot supply a firm footing and becomes vulnerable to the threat of the moldy world beneath the earth, the world of the grave. Ellen West needed a stable anchor of salvation, and so she turned to a bond with the father and an erotic-mystical longing

for return to and union with him. She says in so many words, however, that this union is possible only in death.

Death was thus transformed, for her, from the end of the
thing she feels herself to be, to a wedding with salvation. This movement broke the earlier reification of herself but still failed to combine possibility and necessity in practical action. The more she
indulged in these fantasies of salvation, the more salvation on earth,
the "standing with both feet firmly on the ground," or practical action, receded. The more radiant and animated the ethereal world
became, without cognizance of the given, the more the world in
and beneath the earth became consolidated.

To begin with, she exalted the ethereal world even further
and flew with exuberance from daring horsemanship to infinite joy
in the freedom of open spaces. Next, an attempt was made to
harmonize the ethereal world and the earthly world on the home
ground of sexual love. Even though there were threats from the
restrictiveness of the house-tomb and the "damp fog and dark
clouds," she became engaged to the "romantic foreigner." It was
not a successful solution, for when she broke the engagement, she
did not experience the failure of a frustrated lover. Her spirits continued to soar; she became more expansive. She was filled with a
desire to learn and wrote an article about woman's calling. She
later saw this last serious attempt at fusing the ethereal world with
the world of work as her last period of happiness. Eventually she
looked upon her effort with contempt. Practical action was not a
consistent form of being that does what it must. She despaired.

> Tossed back and forth from one world to the other, feel-
> ing wholly at home in neither, repeatedly failing in her attempts
> to bring the ethereal world into harmony with the earthly world,
> more and more "pulled down" into the subterranean world of the
> tomb, and no longer hoping for rescue by either an earthly-
> practical or a super-mundane love, she is even in her most ex-
> uberant moments beset by "pains and spasms." Nowhere does her
> existence find a loving shelter, nor can it anywhere lay hold of
> its ground (Binswanger, 1958, pp. 279–280).

Our interpretation of this shaky existential platform emphasizes the role of the impending panic of total dissolution into
Nothingness, in other words, dread (*Angst*). To use the language of

Chapter 13, a new "resolution" emerged, a new world-construction that can at once express and explain to oneself one's being-in-the-world, a new orientation toward self and world that can hold the line against the panic of experiential chaos. This new resolution, of course, was her radical preoccupation with her own body.

The fear of becoming fat and the wish to be thin were the final expression of the cosmological contradiction between the airy world of possibility and the tomb-like world of necessity. This contrast invaded the *Eigenwelt* in a way that is condemned to failure, for one's body cannot become ethereal if one is to remain a living, breathing human being. The intransigent world of natural objects, when not integrated into one's style of being, invaded like an insidious and relentless cloud of doom. Unable to wed necessity with possibility in practical action, and yet so caught up in the richness of her own imaginative idealism and passions, Ellen West built a fantastic future of salvation which tried to eroticize death and reduce the necessary to an airy world design. But the given exigencies, in death, in the need for action to be practical, in bodily existence, and in the grim realities of social injustice, cannot be so reduced. Nonbeing was ignored, and it inevitably invaded. Binswanger therefore concludes:

> The dread of becoming fat, which appears in her twentieth year in Sicily, and with which the true illness in the psychiatric sense manifests itself, has thus to be seen anthropologically not as a beginning but as an end. It is the "end" of the encirclement process of the entire existence, so that it is no longer open for its existential possibilities (1958, p. 281).

Ellen was now trapped in her own resolution. The body imagery was the final and "definitive psychophysical garb" of her confinement to a steadily diminishing circle of narrowly defined possibilities. Her being became again, and finally, stultified. The openness to the future was now replaced by an objective enslavement to her own body, and she was condemned to fruitless attempts at escaping from this circle. Binswanger notes finally that if in place of this picture we want to set down its existential expression, it must read—hell.

The relationship to the *Mitwelt* underwent a corresponding change; she constructed her world of others according to the emerging existential platform, which was both different from and continuous with her past. Toward others, her resistance took the form of hostility, hate, and contempt. The *Mitwelt* and the workaday life demand compromise, but compromise was impossible for her. Thus the *Mitwelt* was experienced not as mere limitation but as a positive burden, from which she tried to free herself in rebellious and wild insurrection. Convention, possession, comfort, gratitude, and even love became intolerable.

This movement with respect to the *Mitwelt* reenacted the violent obstinancy of the *Eigenwelt,* which defined itself in terms of what it is not and thus sought to preserve its inner purity at the expense of closing off the normal intercourse of social relationships. The desperate attempt at self-affirmation in this respect was just as self-defeating as her attempt to obviate the necessary solidity of her body. In both cases, something was given, was seen as a threat, and attempts were made to ignore it. And in both cases the existential limitations invaded that idealistic inner purity of the *Eigenwelt* with relentless inevitability. For Ellen West the stakes were high. Her perpetual state of anxiety about her body and about others was an awareness of impending doom, not merely with respect to her body and her relationships but indeed with respect to her very platform of being. She was certain that her "little world" was "softening" her and making her into a "puppet," that finally it would condemn her to "mere vegetating." These metaphors are poignant existential expressions of her alienation from herself, the more so the more she tries to preserve herself.

Eventually, Ellen West's self-world relationship became one in which she herself was "a nothing, a timid earthworm smitten by the curse surrounded by black night." The uncanny grew insidiously, poisonously, threatening. Life became various guises of evil. "How moldy smells this cellar-hole," she writes. "The scent of flowers cannot drown out the odor of rottenness." We hear now of "ugly, yellowed souls, of dwarf lungs and dwarf thoughts." The world of beneath-the-earth closed in, and its various nauseous images of vegetating life and decaying death became amalgamated with sin, guilt, and evil.

Ellen's body came to take a more and more central role in what Binswanger calls the dramatic "game of the existence with itself." The "body," of course, is meant existentially and not anatomically or physiologically. It is the thing, the necessary given that I am as an object, and it is the medium of expression of myself-as-subject. For Ellen West, of course, the former body-experience predominated, and the body's forward-looking, desiring, and intending role was reduced to the desire for sweets, which in turn was relegated to the weighty and substantive, dark and morbid side of life. This is a true "existential standstill." Being with others threatened her and made her tired. She could not recover from this burden of fatigue and oppression by means of poetry, work, or athletics, but only through eating.

More vicissitudes followed, with another attempt to exalt death as salvation. She became engaged to the blond student, which is the last and most desperate attempt to harmonize her two worlds through sexual love. Various tricks were tried to avoid eating and getting fat. The ethereal world became more and more a longed-for memory, an ideal unencumbered by substance of body, others, reality. She progressively lost the light and the air of possibilities while experiencing the necessities as only mud and rot. Suicide attempts followed.

Her psychoanalysis helped her consolidate her position temporarily by construing the problem as an obsessional neurosis whose chief content is gluttony. But "gluttony" as a label for her malady does not dissolve the progressive encirclement and entrapment that her entire being conspired to create. If we are dealing here with something new from a psychiatric point of view, such as the appearance of a new symptom, we can see that there is nothing new anthropologically. It is an extension of the same existential posture.

It is only an apparent contradiction that a full stomach made her feel most empty, for the physical being-full and being-round represents the dull world of decay and the tomb, of glutted vegetating and rotting, finally of evil and of guilt. When seen from the ethereal world, eating and being full is the quintessence of spiritual emptiness. She became more eloquent in finding similes for expressing her encirclement: prison camps, the compulsion to return to the scene of the murder, being encased in a glass wall. "If you love me, grant me death."

Before her death, there was a period in which she seemed to somehow escape the tightening net of her own existential posture. For passing moments she seemed capable of, or at least saw the possibility of, authentic love. She realized that becoming round is natural and good. But something in her rebelled against this insight; it was, of course, the ethereal or Artemis ideal.

2. *The Death*

In considering the death of Ellen West, we must again consider the matter of our own perspective. Our task, simply stated, is to understand the meaning of the event within the context of the *Gestalt* of Ellen West. To understand is not to judge, condemn, idolize, romanticize, nor to psychologize, but to grasp the event in ontological terms. All other approaches fall short of the anthropological task. They provide partial and special perspectives but they do not require of us our fullest transcendence, nor do they offer to us a total understanding. To look for a "motive" for the suicide is a partial perspective, for it does not answer the question of how some motive we may see in the case *can* be a motive in the first place. What indeed do motives construed from a theoretical perspective enable us to understand about the unique being of Ellen West? To ask whether the suicide was a choice that could have been made differently or a necessity fated by something beyond her control is to apply a partial perspective, for "arbitrary act" and "necessary event" already assume that we understand the meaning of the death. The truth is simply *that* it happened as it happened, and in so happening the death closed the *Gestalt* of Ellen West. It was necessary *and* voluntary, depending on one's perspective. We seek to understand it from the more basic perspective of ontology, which illuminates the fundamental ground of human being instead of collapsing human being into a voluntaristic or fateful framework.

We are confronted with the following problem. On the one hand, the idea of death "overshadowed her entire life" and provoked profound dread, and yet on the other hand, as she approached her actual suicide, "death shows itself as brightness." We cannot allow ourselves the luxury of a motivational explanation, for motives are still problematic. Our analysis seeks to get behind motives to the ground of human being out of which they can somehow become meaningful.

As a kind of general statement, one can point out the Heraclitian insight that life and death are not opposites, that death too must be lived, and that life is totally surrounded by death. Hence, life is a continued process of dying and neither can be separated from the other in our attempt to understand them. There is no life that will not end in death, and the life that attempts to avoid this fact is not living fully. But more in line with an explicitly existential analysis, one can inquire into the temporal *Gestalt* that was completed by her suicide. That is, Ellen West's death, like all deaths, is the completion of the totality of the life-history we are examining. As in most cases, it was not introduced from without, as an irrelevant interruption. It emerged in its own way, that is, in the way the particular human being has determined it. The progressive supremacy of the past that we observed during her life closed a circle and cut off the future. This is the way her life-history was. That is just how it was. Binswanger states:

> As a young woman Ellen West had already become old. The life-meaning of the *Dasein* * had already been fulfilled "in early years," in accordance with the stormy life-tempo and the circular life-movement of this existence, in which the *Dasein* had soon "run idle." Existential aging had hurried ahead of biological aging, just as the existential death, the "being-a-corpse-among-people," had hurried ahead of the biological end of life. The suicide is the necessary-voluntary consequence of this existential state of things (1958, p. 295).

The festive celebration of her own death cannot be dismissed as irrelevant. It forces us to ask what death as such meant to Ellen West. Her nihilistic *Weltanschauung* precluded hope of an afterlife. The psychoanalytic notion of death-eroticism is contradicted by her last letter, in which she clearly foregoes eroticism, and certainly abandons the mystical eroticism connected to her earlier suicide attempts. We cannot grasp the meaning of Ellen West's celebration apart from understanding the meaning of her existence. Unlike a celebration of life, which emerges from the robust striding upon the earth, Ellen West's celebration was possible only as death ap-

* The term *Dasein,* central to Heidegger's philosophy and to much existential-psychological thought, can be understood here as "being" in the sense of "aming."

proached. Nonbeing, by its extraordinary presence in her life, ceases
to be a negation and becomes instead the precondition of her being
at all.

> In her death we perceive with special impressiveness the existen-
> tial meaning, or more accurately, contrameaning, of her life. This
> meaning was not that of being herself, but rather that of being
> *not* herself. If we wish to speak of a foundering of this existence,
> then this is what it foundered upon (Binswanger, 1958, p. 297).

The desires to be oneself and to be not-oneself make a contradiction that is more obvious in the case of Ellen West than
most life-histories. The contradiction, in this case, because of the
particular being she was, led to the resolution of suicide. In the
voluntary-necessary resolve for death, Ellen West was no longer
desperate but rather has become authentic. One *is* authentically
when one decisively resolves the situation by action, when one takes
account of the possibilities and the necessities and then takes a stand
in relation to them. Ellen West's suicide was such an act. Her being
had evolved into a closed circle; nonbeing invaded at every point;
all previous practical action had failed to unite the extremes of
her being and she was left face to face with nonbeing in a most
poignant form, her dread of bodily survival. The final act, unlike
the emotion-ridden and escapist suicide attempt earlier, was con-
templative and affirmative. It was an act that affirmed nonbeing and
thus affirmed her being, for her being was, as Binswanger has said,
peculiarly not itself. But when being can be affirmed only in the
sacrifice of life itself, as was the case for Ellen West, then that being
is tragic.

3. Time

In consideration of time we approach the phenomenon of Ellen
West with one of the ontological categories that conditions everything else. We understand something central about her life and
her death when we understand how she temporalized. She was different from most of us, but she was not merely "psychotic," if by
calling her psychotic we allow ourselves to avoid making sense of
her being. No more nor less than any of us, Ellen West had her

being within the universal limits and contingencies of human existence. She did not run away from the ground of her existence but ran squarely into it. Her manifest concerns, such as the refusal to become old, dull, and ugly, in a word, fat, were a kind of temporalization, just as all of us temporalize life. In her peculiar being, however, she wanted to stop time. By rebelliously demarcating her *Eigenwelt,* she struggled with the "given" and created a self which was not a temporal self but a "timeless" and ethereal wish-self. This struggle forced her up against the limits of human being in a way that is fundamental; she wrestled with time itself. Indeed her struggle was not different in one sense from the rest of us, but it was more direct and her commitment to it was greater—in fact was total. What emerged was a slow sinking, the uncanny creeping of time, and finally its congealing.

Temporality is a fundamental "horizon" or frame of human being, and Ellen West's struggle is tragic. Eventually she forced her self into the position that her only victory was to affirm death. For her, this was an affirmation in that it enabled her, for the first time, to authentically choose her being, to bring together her own being with the given. This is not the only affirmation available to most of us, but it was the only one available to her.

All human beings "temporalize." The *experience* of time is not quite what is meant by temporalization. When we experience time, we objectify it and separate it off from our selves and trivialize it. Temporalization is not experienced time, then, but "lived time." Minkowski (1967) and Von Gebsattel (1968) have described temporalization as a part of the platform from which one looks and lives, not as something we look *at.* It is not a "process" to be examined from some point of view outside of time; it is a fundamental way of examining, or more broadly, of being. Ellen West herself made few actual statements about time. Our attempt to understand her temporalization goes beyond her utterances to her being, from which platform such utterances could be made at all.

Ellen West was forced (forced herself) into the choice between suicide and "hell" in her peculiar bifurcation of life into "ethereal" being which stood opposed to the given. The given therefore appeared as the tomb-world. She was never able to synthesize the ethereal world with the world of practical action, where the present includes a "having been," a past, and a series of definite possibilities for the future. Her future never was "realistic" in the sense that it continually floated in the ethereal limitlessness of pure fantasy.

The evolution toward her entrapped conclusion began with the rigid demarcation of her *Eigenwelt* from the other regions of being. This demarcation cut Ellen West's being off from the "ground" of being, that is, from temporal continuity in which time is a process of getting older, of becoming, of living "out of" a past and "into" a future. The loss of this kind of temporalization is the loss of the world of practical action and the stubborn affirmation of the world of the air. Oneself in the world of the air and its particular temporalization is a "fantasy self," unrelated to the past and future, eternal, and hence static. If we can speak of a future at all for this ethereal world, it is one of unlimited, unimpeded and unrestrained optimism. Everything becomes possible and hence the realm of the possible becomes particularly empty.

The pervasiveness of this world was a predominance of fantasy in her life. But the fantasy did not undermine her being simply because it was "unrealistic" in any scientific sense. Rather it destroys one's footing on the ground, and it alienates one's self from the given and the necessary. Once alienated, Ellen West's being had to struggle perpetually with the given and with nonbeing, a struggle that culminated in her body-language dread of corporality. The atemporal and unauthentic future came to be constantly in the shadow of the boundary, even while and because it seeks to overcome that boundary of human limitation. One may change one's temporalization through self-willed ambition, perhaps, but one cannot eliminate its relevance. The passage of time is simply given.

Binswanger states:

> In unauthentic futurization, in self-designing for the sake of a wish-self, the meaningfulness of the world is falsified and "artificially" leveled. . . . To be sure, everyone may "swing himself up" into such a world temporarily, but with the full knowledge of its fantasy-nature—i.e., of the fact that there is no staying in it. But when this contour-less world replaces the present world of practical action, in which "things collide harshly in space" (Schiller), ground makes itself evident once more, but now no longer as a call back to the having-been, as a knowing about the "having-

to-return to earth," but as an unknowing, blind, uncanny being-threatened by the shadow—that is, as dread! And the farther the existence climbs away into the ethereal world,. the more threatening, more compact, more impenetrable the garb of this shadow becomes (1958, p. 304).

The incipient tomb-world that constantly threatened Ellen West is also "unauthentic" in that its temporal aspect is the "ever-present past" without future. Her images of rotting life and foggy stench express this temporalization perfectly. It is "hell," understood not theologically but existentially, as a kind of being that is condemned to an eternal bogging down in one's past, from which there is no escape.

As the ethereal world progressively lacked, for Ellen West, relevance to "practical action" and a temporalization in which past is synthesized with a future, so also did the impending tomb of the dark world become divorced from a future in terms of which practical action can make sense. The world as practical action therefore lost its "referential character," its function as a point of reference in terms of which being can understand itself. The tomb-world, as it took over, was an extremely rigid, amorphous world, where being can no longer understand itself from anything "new." Only the decaying of the accustomed and the familiar supplied a context in which there is meaning.

Late in her life another form of temporalization emerged for Ellen West, namely, the temporalization of greed. This temporalization was not the expecting of the future, but was solely a living in the present, neither born of the past nor aimed at the future. The "animal seriousness" of this present is impressive; everything revolved around eating and devouring, which was the only context in which her being could understand itself.

But of course greedy eating, for Ellen West, led to being fat. Being fat was the quintessence of the given she denied, and hence it was her guilt—a guilt for what one is. The greed, like the ethereal world, did not escape dread. Nowhere could Ellen West find an existential platform that could protect her from dread. The contradiction between the two worlds was not one between nondread on the one hand, and dread on the other. It was between two different forms of dread, the dread of old age and dying and the dread born of unauthentic living. This reminds us of the "existential obsession" analyzed in Chapter 8, where the fear of death led the individual into, finally, a fear of life.

Temporalization thus supplies us with the fundamental dimension in terms of which to understand a human being. For Ellen West, we see contradictory worlds with contradictory time orders. Binswanger repeatedly points out, however, how she sought to bring her being into harmony with the "given," to seek out a way to become authentic. In practical action, for example, she attempted continually to bring order into her scattered being, but her other worlds were too diverse for a synthesis. Therefore, instead of an authentic temporalization of "ripening," Ellen West was condemned to a pedantic "taking care of time." It was a "makeshift." Like her need for food, her temporalization became a greed, and finally it dropped deadly into the vacuum of futureless experience.

The case of Ellen West is more than the study of a being. It is the study of an exceptional being. Her claim to our attention is not so much her "psychosis," which is, after all, a very small concept. Nor is it because her story is a tragic one, although indeed it is. Ellen West demands our attention because she pressed human being to its limits, struggled with these limits, and in so doing reveals to us in her "psychosis" something of the ultimate shape of the ground of being—that, by virtue of which, there is human being at all.

Let us go beyond Binswanger's published notes on the issue of the death of Ellen West and consider again what it means. We cannot say that her uniqueness lies in having bright and dark moods, for we all have such moods. Nor can we say that her uniqueness lies in the failure of her practical action to unite these two moods, to integrate the possible and the necessary, to effectively articulate her idealism within the framework of the given realities of life. Indeed, few of us in this century can have a visible effect upon the atrocities modern life has "given" to us. Nor can we locate her uniqueness in her struggle with this impotence. To be sure, her existential situation came to be expressed in bizarre images of body and world, and the encirclement process was highly idiosyncratic in many ways. But to see the suicide within the context of these movements alone is to divorce the entire event from that which is universally human, or put another way, from that which is ontological.

We all experience moods—ups and downs—and it is easy to dismiss them as physiological phenomena. The existential viewpoint, of course, directs our attention to the fact that different moods entail different worlds, that a mood is not a chemical state of affairs but a way of being, and that the worlds in which we *are* during our moods make *the* difference. Ups and downs, therefore, are experiences that have ontological significance.

The ontological significance of universal moods, and the ontological underpinnings of Ellen West's life—and death—are the same. Ellen West is, more than is immediately apparent, very much like all of us. Her "psychosis" lays bare for all of us that which we would rather keep hidden. And now we must confront the most challenging issue of all: how could it be that Ellen West's ontological situation produced the paradox that the only way to affirm her being was to take her life? Is this paradox also universal, or can we point to a "perversion" in her particular case? Perhaps the major difference between her and us is merely that she was more consistent, more honest, more in need of or committed to self-affirmation. Perhaps and perhaps not. Ellen West's life and death therefore leave us with some positive insights, no doubt, but her primary legacy to us is a question. Our reluctance to ask that question—to experience that question—perhaps accounts for the misunderstanding that has so often accompanied the reading of the case.

References

Binswanger, L. *Grundformen und Erkenntnis Menschlichen Daseins.* Zurich: Max Niehaus, 1953.

Binswanger, L. The case of Ellen West. In R. May, et al. (Eds.) *Existence.* New York: Basic Books, 1958.

Binswanger, L. *Being-in-the-World* (translated and with an introduction by Jacob Needleman). New York: Basic Books, 1963.

Minkowski, E. Spontaneity. In N. Lawrence and D. O'Connor (Eds.) *Readings in Existential Phenomenology.* Englewood Cliffs: Prentice-Hall, 1967.

Von Gebsattel, V. E. The world of the compulsive. In R. May, et al. (Eds.) *Existence.* New York: Basic Books, 1958.

Being a 16
psychopath

When we speak of "the psychopath," we are referring to an "ideal type." No one fits the classical description perfectly and all of us are more or less this way; most of us are less. The psychopath, like all diagnostic groups, is defined by a number of characteristics that tend, in clinical experience, to go together, but one or several traits can appear in any diagnostic category, including "normal." Getting to know "psychopaths" personally, however, is a powerful experience for any clinician. This experience is bound to make this chapter more than an exercise in diagnosis.

The practice of creating types treats persons as objects, of course. It follows the scientific routine of classification. This is legitimate as long as we are able to transcend our objectified thinking, to take human consciousness seriously, and to orient to individuals as subjects as well as objects.

The traits that characterize the "psychopathic type" are summarized by McCord and McCord:

> The psychopath is asocial. His conduct often brings him into conflict with society. The psychopath is driven by primitive desires and an exaggerated craving for excitement. In his self-centered search for pleasure, he ignores restrictions of his culture.

The psychopath is highly impulsive. He is a man for whom the moment is a segment of time detached from all others. His actions are unplanned and guided by his whims. The psychopath is aggressive. He has learned few socialized ways of coping with frustration. The psychopath feels little, if any, guilt. He can commit the most appalling acts, yet view them without remorse. The psychopath has a warped capacity for love. His emotional relationships, when they exist, are meager, fleeting, and designed to satisfy his own desires. These last two traits, guiltlessness and lovelessness, conspicuously mark the psychopath as different from other men (1964, pp. 16–17).

Let us try, in this chapter, to understand what the being of a psychopath is like, beyond a list of his objective qualities. We will seek, therefore, to understand how he is-in-the-world (and the shape of that world), how he is-for-himself, and how he is-for-others. We will also attempt to understand something of the developmental processes that culminate in this kind of being. Not everyone who gets called "psychopathic" fits our description, for it is indeed a "wastebasket" diagnostic category. But clinicians encounter persons more or less like our description, and we must try to understand them.

1. The World of the Psychopath

Like everyone else, the psychopath lives in a world of his own construction. It is experienced as "out-there" and in some kind of contradistinction to "self" "in-here." Frankenstein adds:

The relationship between the ego and the non-ego . . . is disturbed also in neurotic or psychotic diseases [as well as in psychopathy]. . . . But in all these pathologies, the feeling of otherness is not only eliminated but, on the contrary, is accentuated and the specific forms in which it is accentuated constitute the essential characteristics of the various clinical units. The perception of the non-ego may be distorted by projection (in neurosis), or the non-ego may engulf the ego (in psychosis); the non-ego may be the area of chance occurrences (in waywardness) or the absolute enemy (in primary behavior disorders) (1959, p. 6).

One of the "traits" that characterizes the psychopath is a tendency to express conflicts directly in behavior rather than to produce neurotic symptoms. Traditionally, this has been described as a lack of the usual conflicts that keep most of us in check. This, in turn, indicates the lack or weakness of an inhibiting mechanism in the personality, i.e., of the superego. This description of the psychopath defines "the normal" as well. It is normal to carry around, from situation to situation, inhibitions that characterize the norms of the culture. The psychopath is different primarily in the *absence* of these inhibitions. He therefore produces little internal conflict, and little in the way of neurotic symptoms. The arena of his conflict is between himself and society.

To describe psychopathy as the absence of something may miss the point. The tendency to act out conflicts in behavior rather than in neurotic symptoms also expresses a different way of being. Most concisely, the psychopath tends to be alloplastic instead of autoplastic. "Adjustment to" reality is not as common as "adjustment of" reality. In terms of social reality, persons and norms, psychopathic being is a mixture of ignoring these realities and of attacking them when they interfere with one's desires.

A. Other persons

The world of the psychopath is unique in its peculiar omission of other *persons*. Of course the psychopath knows the difference between people and things, but the "normal" tendency to treat persons as essentially like oneself, as having feelings that are as real to them as experience is to oneself—to identify with others, have empathy, feel their suffering, to put oneself in the role of the other—these processes seem strangely absent. Instead, therefore, of living in a world with multiple points of view and multiple subjectivities, the psychopath walks through a world with one center of subjectivity—himself. His relationships are not two-way streets. Allies are seen as objects to be manipulated; they are not persons with whom there is some communion. The "other person," for the psychopath, loses both his "otherness"—his legitimacy of being as another—and his "personness"—his subjectivity and point of orientation. The interpersonal process is "devoid of polarization" in Frankenstein's terms. Frankenstein continues:

In other words, normally the incorporated [other] continues to exist as a separate reality in its own right. . . . In
psychopathy, on the other hand, the lack of polarization manifests
itself in a more or less radical disappearance from consciousness
of the objective counterpart of what is being incorporated. It
exists, as it were, in the consciousness of the psychopath, as his
property only, to be used and disposed of at will, but it has lost
its individual independence (or its independent individuality)
(1959, p. 7).

Put yet another way, Frankenstein suggests:

It is needless to add that intentionality in the psychopath
is not the same as in a "normal" individual. The latter directs
himself intentionally toward a specific object with which (or
whom) he establishes, through the very act and process of his
"intending," a specific, and constantly reversible, subject-object
relationship; the former knows of the non-ego as an object only
(1959, p. 92).

I recall asking a very psychopathic young man about what
he thought I thought of him. The very hearing of the question
was an occasion of puzzlement and confusion for this otherwise very
bright and articulate person. In one sense, he understood the question; of course I must think something of him. In fact he went to
great pains to manipulate my view of him. But the possibility of
talking about this, of treating the relationship as an exchange of
information in the service of mutual understanding, this possibility
was totally foreign to his *modus operandi*. I was an object to
manipulate. The question suggested that I wanted to share with
him our perceptions and our subjectivities. He could not respond.
Halleck (1967) defines psychopathy as the repeated efforts of an
individual to search for a painless freedom from personal relationships, and Redl and Wineman (1965, Chapter 4) discuss at length
this aspect of psychopathy.

This definition suggests that the psychopath also has a
peculiar kind of being-for-others. The psychopathic "con man" is
a master at deception. He recognizes my subjectivity in one sense—
as a factor to be handled by him. But he does not recognize it in
another sense—as something to be respected, as a point of orienta-

tion with which to be in dialogue. His talking to me and listening to me are enterprises that go on in the service of a being-for-others that does not really transcend his egocentricity. Being-for-others for the psychopath is never simply seeing oneself from another's point of view; it is having to control the whole process in the service of goals more or less (often less) well established in his own mind.

Of the traits that McCord and McCord list as being typically psychopathic, we have perhaps explained the last two: the lack of guilt and the shallowness of interpersonal relationships. Guilt is heartily augmented by (if not created by) an identification with and vicarious experience of the suffering one causes others. This absence in the psychopath is also relevant to McCord and McCord's first trait, that the psychopath is often in conflict with society. Surely, part of the reason people don't usually steal and rape is because they identify with and feel sorry for their would-be victims.

B. Time

Unlike the compulsive for whom time has bogged down, and unlike those psychotics for whom it has opened up wildly, the psychopath seems to experience a continuing present that is unattached to the past and the future. This kind of world also accounts partly for the frequency with which psychopaths are involved in crime. They do not "plan" in the usual way. The future may include getting arrested or drowning in the bathtub, but it is not meaningfully related to behavior now. Most of us in American middle-class culture are oppressed by the future. Anticipation of the consequences of our actions are never absent from our experience of performing them. We have, indeed, been taught this lesson all too well by the agents of popular morality. But for the psychopath, performing an action is always just present tense. Behavior, therefore, looks "impulsive" and "uncontrolled," and these are indeed good descriptions if one thinks in terms of the psychoanalytic metaphor: impulses seething under a lid of more or less well-organized ego controls. But the temporal anomaly must also be seen as central to this behavior.

With respect to the past, psychopaths rarely draw on their body of past experience in order to inform their present behavior. They are, in spite of sometimes impressive intelligence, notoriously unable to learn from past experience. Repetitive behavior patterns click off from one situation to another, and the connections are not made. Or if they are made, they are not really taken seriously. No matter how many times one points out such repetitions, say in therapy, the awareness of the past is never built directly into the experience of the present. This, too, stands in vivid contrast to, say, the more common neurotic of our culture whose experience of the past is so preeminent in the present that he "projects" and "transfers," that is, he reads the situation as if it were a replay of something already experienced.

The temporal nature of so-called normal experience is so pervasive that it is difficult to imagine extreme atemporality. Anxiety is an experience that is often felt as an impending future. Something terrible (unspecified) seems to be going to happen. When the psychopath experiences anxiety, he does not experience it in this way at all. The experience of a vaguely threatening future presupposes the experience of the future. It is difficult, therefore, to say that the psychopath experiences "anxiety" in the usual sense at all. He may panic, and seem to fall apart, but it is not projected out into anticipatory fantasies as it is for most of us.

C. The object world

The psychopath experiences people much as most of us experience objects, i.e., as instruments of our purpose. The psychopath experiences objects, then, in yet a different way than we do. They may indeed be instruments of his purpose, but to a surprising degree they seem to loom up as impediments to his purpose. I recall a number of movies in which the escaping bad guy, upon running out of ammunition, throws his gun at his pursuers in anger upon discovering that it no longer produces missiles. This always seemed a waste; the gun may be useful in some other way. However, this seems to be the attitude of the psychopath toward his implements. At the first frustration, they become objects of rage. He is ready to lash out at whatever seems available in moments of pressure. Again the psychoanalytic model comes to mind: angry impulses that get "transferred" or "displaced" when frustration produces a strain on ego controls.

Let us consider the possibility, however, that the psychopathic way of experiencing objects is different from ours in a more fundamental way. There seems to be no "respect" for things. We do not mean here the kind of respect that is paid to persons; it is more like the respect the carpenter has for his tools. Tools have a kind of otherness, a kind of presence, a kind of integrity that is independent of one's wishes. A screwdriver does not make a good hammer; but in addition to the functional failure of a screwdriver to drive nails, it is not supposed to be used for that purpose. Someone, somewhere, made the screwdriver for driving screws. That person had a purpose that cuts across, at this minute, my need of a hammer. In refusing to use the screwdriver for a hammer, we do not pay homage to that mysterious artisan and his plan (it was probably mass-produced anyway)—we are respecting the screwdriver as an independent thing, which has its limitations and uses, its own existence, independent of our needs of the moment. For the psychopath, every thing is reduced to its usefulness to him and his purpose. There is no world that stands there, to be confronted in its own terms. The entire world of things is subordinated to the one giant subjectivity, his atemporal self.

Related to this peculiar way of constructing a world is Frankenstein's observation on "the psychopath's lack of concern for objective facts."

> Why, indeed, should he be concerned with the independent, objective significance of what has no *raison d'être* outside his "ownership." And why concern himself with facts which have not, or have not yet, aroused his egocentric needs? Objective facts are meaningful only for those who are able to recognize their independent existence, their right and power to limit the ego. They are meaningless for the psychopath unless they are connected with an immediate act of "incorporation" (1959, pp. 7–8).

2. The Psychopathic Self

What sort of self-experience goes along with this kind of world-construction? The two are necessarily related in an intimate way. Let us again make some contrasts with other ways of experiencing oneself. I am definitely limited by the existential situation, and one of the challenges of human existence is to face up to these limitations. The psychotic misconstrues the realms of the necessary and the possible in wildly erratic and fantastic world-constructions that serve, however inadequately from the sane point of view, to stabilize his existential platform. The psychopath is not crazy in this sense. The self-world relationship that emerges is not the desperate self-affirmation of grandiosity, which is the outcome of a futile struggle with the "otherness" of the world. The psychopath has never really had this struggle, for he has never really taken the objective world quite seriously. Should his (at times) wild schemes fail, he is temporarily confused or enraged, but he never experiences reality's right to impinge upon him or to be intransigently what it is. In a kind of blind subjectivity, he trudges on through life without giving credit to the world for existing.

His self is therefore grandiose in quite a different way from the psychotic. Frankenstein (1959) gives this tendency of the psychopath the label "ego-inflation." Following a psychoanalytic metaphor, Frankenstein characterizes the psychopath's experience as "incorporating" wildly and indiscriminantly. If we see experience as fundamentally rooted in a self-world relationship, it follows that the degradation of the world and the "inflation of the ego" are two sides of the same coin. They reflect each other.

In our discussion of the development of being (Chapter 4), we distinguished four stages in the evolution of the self-world relationship: fusion, separateness, satellization, and similarity. In the second stage, separateness, the child learns of the intransigence of reality. This frustration is compensated in part by the child's growing feeling of self-as-agent, and the two-year-old, who loudly affirms his independence, seems to protest too much. A crucial step in moving from the arrogant egoist of two years to a more social person is satellization. It is probably through becoming the object of others (in one's own experience) that one really acquires a sensitivity to the subjectivity of others.

When we consider the usual deprivations and/or brutalities that characterized the parental care of psychopaths when they were children, we begin to see how the peculiar self-world relationship we have described might develop. The experience of satellization may well be missing entirely. Or more likely, rather than traverse this stage into the experience of similarity, a different route was followed. It is, in a way, a kind of regression to separateness. In the face of extreme parental cruelty, for example, the self may seek to preserve itself not by becoming an equal but by becoming absolute. Such a desperate grabbing hold of self-feelings would not be noteworthy except for the fact that, by age seven or so, the world is different from that of a two-year-old. Other children are moving from satellization into similarity, and there is a raft of attitudes toward reality that one should be acquiring at this time. The child is in school and ordinarily comes, however reluctantly, to realize that he must respect "intransigent reality." The reversion to the egoism of separateness, on the other hand, does not allow such developmental processes to take place. What is missing most of all is the openness to reality that characterizes polarization, a give and take attitude with people and with things.

It is perhaps no wonder, under circumstances of painful satellization, that the child's attempt to save himself must be executed at the cost of reality. There may not be damage to the cognitive processing of reality, but there is an absence of the usual affective overtones to his relationship to reality. Most important of all, this peculiarity includes an unwillingness to be a satellite, which in turn closes off the normal fantasies and experiences of communion that comprise the process of identification and the most effective way of learning how to be like other people.

Satellization is an attitude of smallness in the face of a more powerful god-parent. In order for this experience to be tolerable, there must also be some acceptance of the otherness of the other, some admission that he exists. This requires that the relationship not be totally exhausted by fear and hate. Ordinarily satellization includes an attitude of admiration, which is a confession that the other is something—or more precisely, someone. If the satellized child experiences only fear of and anger at the god-parent, the fantasies that he may become like him are unlikely to develop and the vicarious experience of the other's subjectivity cannot occur. The parent becomes merely a part of an environment that spells danger. For a child struggling to experience himself as someone consistent, he must rely on the fantasies of separateness in order to survive. Reality thus becomes, as it is for the two-year-old, devoid of any meaning except the most immediate one for oneself right now. Things are not enriched by their meaning to other people, for there are no other people in his experience. The complex network of attitudes that ordinarily leads to a respect for reality is undercut by the overwhelming need to be a self-as-subject. The self-as-subject that emerges under such duress is not acquainted with a reality of objects to which it stands in some kind of dialectic; it is merely affirmed in a vacuum.

These rather speculative reconstructions do not cover the idiosyncrasies of any individual psychopath. There may be concrete manifestations of the earlier relationship with a parent in contemporaneous behavior. One psychopath may have a particular vendetta against women; another a particular indifference to the suffering of children. In any individual, however, these behavioral peculiarities do not exist in a vacuum but are part of a coherent self-world relationship. Underlying the differences we are tempted to describe a similarity which, once recognized, demands a coherent developmental hypothesis.

3. Confronting the Psychopath

The psychopath tends to evoke from other people some measure of fear and moral repugnance. The psychopath, more than even the psychotic, reveals to us the intricacies of our own sensibilities and feelings of propriety. He does this because he does not share them and seems to violate them without the discomfort that his behavior causes us. For example, it may never have occurred to us that we place a value on the integrity of natural objects until a psychopathic companion repeatedly violates that integrity by carving into tree trunks, kicking apart rock formations, and destroying birds' nests. The experience of our own repugnance reveals to us a layer of sensitivity and sensibility that may have no counterpart in our verbalized world-view. But in the presence of a psychopath who does not share this existential platform, we discover not only that this sensibility is there, but also that it is a powerful part of our being.

This kind of experience is similar to the "culture shock" that emerges from contact with a foreign culture. Without knowing it, we have acquired all sorts of ways of being that are typical for our culture. It is only in the experience of their negation by others that we see them as they are. The psychopath does not confront us with another culture, but he offends us in ways that make us aware of the "personal culture" of our own existential platform. Truth is discovered in the experience of being wrong; beauty is discovered as a contrast to the experience of ugliness; certain planks in our existential platform are discovered only in their violation. The psychopath is uniquely suited for acquainting us with our own sensibilities.

We have heard of the sadistic child who captures insects and carefully and gleefully dismembers them. In an adult, we say simply that such behavior is "perverse." What offends us gives him pleasure. It is different with the psychopath. He is not "perverse" in the sense of *reversing* the aesthetic and ethical value of morbid activity. Such a reversal seems still to operate within our frame of reference, but with all the signs changed. The psychopath does not reverse values that are comfortable for us; he simply finds them to be irrelevant. He may dismember insects, books, or humans, but *not* because he defines his pleasure by our pain, as the sadist tends to do, nor because he is involved in a dialectic with social norms, such as the Nazis were (cf. Rubenstein, 1966). Rather his pleasure in such activity has no reference to anyone else; it is purely a fleeting whim and is not oriented toward offending us; it emerges from an existential platform that is not the *opposite* but rather is simply *different,* radically different, from ours. Therefore, the psychopath seems unpredictable to us. We can predict the pervert's behavior often as a negation of our values. The psychopath is totally individual. Such a person is frightening.

Moral repugnance, fear, and noncomprehension are not the only responses we have to the psychopath. He also has, as has been frequently noted (e.g., Halleck, 1967), a kind of charm and fascination to "normal" persons. Alexander (1930) says of the "neurotic character," who is also noted for his conflict with social norms:

> The external struggle between man and society is exemplified not in elusive intrapsychic processes, but in the visible drama of their own lives. That is why they are born heroes who are predestined to a tragic fate. Their defeat is the victory of society and the spectator who has had some conflict within his breast (and who is without it) is able to live out both the rebellious and the social tendencies of this personality by sympathetically feeling themselves into the lives of the vanquished.

We can interpret this appeal of the psychopath as an expression of our repressed impulses and conflicts, but we can also be more existial in our interpretation. If we are right that the psychopath construes the realms of the possible and the necessary very differently from us, we may suggest that the psychopathic style expresses a desire for more possibility and less necessity. That desire may be in all of us. It is, finally, the confrontation of the necessary that provides the tragedy and drama of life. To fly off into life without being troubled by this struggle may be a universal human fantasy. The psychopath, with great aplomb and abandon, sometimes with grace and style, bypasses this conflict. And in the end he succumbs to the final authority of existential necessity, death. His lack of concern for the necessary in life is an escape and a denial, but we are likely to see it as courageous.

Who should be given the moral approval of the term "courageous," the psychopath who whimsically ignores life's limits or the "normal" who accepts life within boundaries that are given from without? How much, indeed, should one "accept"? Is a direct confrontation of one's own death, of the intransigence of reality, of the rights of the subjectivity of others, of the inexorable passage of and ubiquitous presence of time, of the otherness of the world—is constructing one's world with all of these givens built-in worth it? Have we a choice about these issues? The psychopath, in his very style of being, seems to suggest to us that we do have such a choice, and herein lies his profound effect on us.

References

Alexander, F. The neurotic character. *International Journal of Psychoanalysis*, 1930, II, 292–311.

Frankenstein, C. *Psychopathy*. New York: Grune & Stratton, 1959.

Halleck, S. *Psychiatry and the Dilemma of Crime*. New York: Harper & Row, 1967.

McCord, W., & McCord, I. *The Psychopath*. Princeton: Van Nostrand, 1964.

Redl, F., & Wineman, D. *Children Who Hate*. New York: Free Press, 1965.

Rubenstein, R. Religion and the origins of the death camps, a psychoanalytic interpretation. In R. Rubenstein, *After Auschwitz*. Indianapolis: Bobbs-Merrill, 1966.

SUMMARY OF
PART IV

When we think about psychosis, the most profound versions of psychopathology, we find ourselves dealing with the most profound aspects of human experience in general. In Part II we discussed existential anxiety; in Part III we discussed the "orientation" of being "at home" in-the-world. But it is only when we see the psychotic experience vividly that these basic aspects of human being come into focus. For the psychotic is exactly the person whose differences from ourselves are on this most fundamental level of human existence. To deal with these differences, we found that the metaphor of a "platform," particularly of an "existential platform," is helpful. The "existential platform" is not a series of cognitions, nor a content that can be submitted to some kind of judgment. The existential platform is our "place of standing," our vantage point and our orientation. It too is chosen with respect to its content, but whether to have one is not chosen; it is inescapable as long as we hold life together at all.

The crisis of psychosis is the deterioration of the existential platform and the inability to hold life together. The only experience that is left, when the existential platform is dissolved, is sheer, stark-raving terror; for here one is forced to confront life's most serious challenge without the benefit of any stable footing, the challenge of nonbeing. To experience panic, and to survive it, is something we have all done to some small extent. Psychotic episodes are not common, but dreams and nightmares are, anxiety attacks are, and the fear of death is. Fortunately, these are transient experiences. They are unpleasant, they do not usually demand anything from us but a firming up of the familiar platform upon which we have built our lives. But to experience this panic chronically or as always incipient, to feel the desperate need perpetually to solidify some platform—any platform—that is the psychotic experience.

If we see nonbeing as the perpetual context of being, and if nonbeing has its concrete presence in our lives in the form of anxiety, as we argued in Chapter 5, then we must conclude that life is a perpetual struggle with anxiety. We assume these statements to be a better description of the situation than the traditional notion of derangement and psychosis, which makes them something nearly inhuman and totally foreign. We find that we must accept psychosis as very human, along with our rejection of the so-called medical model and along with our desire to take human consciousness seriously.

The experience of security, which is the opposite of the experience of anxiety, depends upon establishing an existential platform that has some stability. This may best be achieved, we have said, through the affirmation of the experience of self-as-subject, but the experience of self-as-object is also a source of stability and continuity for us. The superiority of the experience of the self-as-subject is a result of the fact that as-subject I must face existential anxiety in experiencing my own freedom. To face the anxiety yields, if we survive it, a better mode of dealing with life than to turn away from it in an objectification of ourselves that relieves us of our freedom and thus protects us from the ambiguities and anxiety of non-being. The resolution of the human situation will be a platform that is more or less, depending on the style of one's being, inoculated against the threat of nonbeing by having taken nonbeing into itself as a given limitation of human existence.

In the grandiosity of psychosis, we see a reshuffling of exactly these issues. The ordering of a "sense of the necessary" and of a "sense of the possible" takes fantastic turns, with both extremes often being simultaneously affirmed. This suggests to us that the building of a psychology capable of dealing with psychosis and capable of taking consciousness seriously would better follow existential metaphors than the biological or electrical ones of Freud. The sexual and bodily language of Freud has profound existential meaning; the language of energy dynamics does not. The body-language of psychotics, therefore, both verbal and acted out, solidifies an existential platform for him and communicates to us, if we are able to see what he means. And the first step in discovering what he means is to recognize that his reckoning of his body is a fundamental plank in his existential platform.

We must also, it was noted, be aware of the political aspects of dealing with psychosis. The fundamental political situation is that the hostile and suspicious paranoid and the sane doctors who treat him have alternative existential platforms, both of which are responses to the same existential situation. They each provide judgments of the other and attempt to make the other like oneself. The participation in this political battle should not be undertaken by treatment agents who would use the club of majority opinion without coming to terms with the nature of their own existential platforms.

The examination of the case of Ellen West gave us further opportunity to demonstrate the point of existential psychology. We see in Binswanger's "anthropological" approach a combination of total detachment with total involvement. The philosophical anthropologist is detached in the sense of being nonjudgmental and phenomenological in the philosophical sense. He is involved in what Binswanger calls "love," without which we cannot transcend our solipsism. We see again in this case the graphic way in which body-language expresses the existential posture of the individual, and how for Ellen West the reckoning of the possible and the necessary is a crucial and fundamental issue of her being and her psychology. For Ellen West, the sense of the possible becomes so oppressed by the necessary that only suicide can affirm a possibility in a positive way. Even more intriguing, however, is Binswanger's suggestion that in love we can transcend the categories of the possible and the necessary. This particularly Binswangerian point remains one of the frontiers of existential thought.

In the final chapter of Part IV, we moved from psychosis to psychopathy and from individual case analysis to a description of a diagnostic type. Insofar as we are able to describe the existential platform that underlies a diagnostic type, we characterized the psychopath as having a self-world relationship in which the self is exalted at the specific cost of respect for reality. The reality that is not respected includes both persons and things. This is a particular way to construe the world, and we discover important features of our own existential platforms by confronting the psychopath.

In Part V, we will deal with two remaining issues and attempt to summarize the progress of the evolution toward an existential clinical psychology. The issues that await us are the relationship between values and psychology—particularly as these orientations have a presence in psychotherapy—and the problem of methodology.

TOWARD
AN EXISTENTIAL V
CLINICAL PSYCHOLOGY

Psychotherapy
and values 17

1. The Politics of Psychotherapy

To say that psychotherapy involves both therapist and patient in moral questions is, by now, to say the obvious. Adjustment to society as a goal of therapy has been sufficiently debunked (cf. Fromm, 1955) to place the therapist in the position of having to make some personal decisions himself. The coordinates of these decisions are in many respects "given" by the social and historical context in which the therapist operates. His obligation is, therefore, not simply to have the courage to decide but to recognize, through intelligent penetration of his own situation, what he is deciding about.

There are social, philosophical, historical, and legal as well as psychological coordinates of the therapist's decisions in therapy. Being unaware of these can hardly be compensated by moral courage, just as a lack of moral courage can hardly be compensated by great intelligence. Put yet another way, responsible decisions are not made in an intellectual vacuum, and intelligence in a moral vacuum is hardly wise. Everything said about the therapist and his decisions, of course, can and must be said about theorists and writers of books.

We have spent a good deal of time contrasting an existential-phenomenological approach with orthodox psychoanalytic theory. If this is to be more than a scholastic game (and if therapy is to be more than a superficial playing with life), we must make clear the moral implications of the contrast. Very briefly, the moral addition of the current theory is to make explicit what is only implicit and rarely appreciated in psychoanalytic thought: the centrality of individual choice. It would be a great tragedy if we were to ignore, as some Neo-Freudians have done (cf. Marcuse, 1955), the fundamental challenges of Freudian thought. In *Civilization and Its Discontents,* Freud revealed a basic contradiction between the biological heritage of man and the requirements of (at least our kind of) civilization. To reject Freud's instinct theory because it is "unproven" is to apply entirely the wrong criteria. To reject it because it is not cross-culturally sophisticated is to avoid its applicability for us in this culture. We are really talking here about the fundamental conflict between the individual and society, and this conflict hardly needs to be validated since the very existence of clinical-psychological work depends on social norms and their violation by the individual.

Freud's theory is a defense of the integrity of the individual against society, even as it is a theory of how that integrity is systematically compromised by society (cf. Rieff, 1959). This becomes then, an intensely political matter. Is it possible for the individual to be socialized? Is it *possible* for persons who are socialized to be individuals? To say that the individual is merely an abstraction from society, or that society is merely an abstraction from individuals, is an attempt to make the problem go away by intellectual sophistry and is to deny a simple experiential fact. This denial is just as much a lie-for-oneself, a lie-in-the-world, and a lie-for-others as any childhood defense mechanism.

The practitioner in therapy cannot, therefore, avoid the question asked by Szasz (1965): whose agent is he? Is he the agent of society, whose job it is to get the patient to conform to social norms? Is he the agent of the individual, whose job it is to help the individual manipulate society to get what he really wants more efficiently? This is one of the crucial dimensions along which every clinician, perhaps every psychologist, must decide, and this dimension is "given" by our peculiar cultural-historical situation.

Is our society's treatment of certain minority groups (or

nations) acceptable or unacceptable? Is the decision to resist such socially sanctioned treatment pathological? If it is illegal? If it is violent? If it is in bad taste? It is certainly in bad taste, and consensually pathological, to be schizophrenic. But does that mean we should prevent it? Change it? "Treat" it? Some would say a hearty "No" (Laing, 1967); others would point out the danger of denying to individuals civil liberties on the basis of psychiatric good intentions (Szasz, 1963). Whatever one thinks of these issues, one must recognize (a) that we choose our position, (b) that this choice can be intelligent only in terms of a recognition of the political and moral context in which it occurs, (c) that the particular shape of our theoretical psychology will influence how we see the options, and (d) that that theory ought not contradict the content of our political position.

2. Being a Bureaucrat

The existentialists have not refrained from various sorts of social and sociological criticism (e.g., Heinemann, 1958), and indeed streamlined bureaucratic America offers a fine target for those who want to push for the integrity of the individual. The present chapter takes some of the issues raised in these criticisms and attempts to see their relationship to clinical psychological practice.

Bureaucracies function in ways that produce a certain kind of self-world relationship and self-world experience. The essential ingredient, not only in modern bureaucracies, but in social organization of many kinds, is the impersonality of experience. Parsons' (1951) distinction between "particularistic" and "universalistic" roles describes this phenomenon. When the written constitution of an organization defines "recording secretary," for example, it defines requirements that an individual must fulfill to occupy the role and prescribes his functions in certain ways. Anyone who fulfills the prerequisites may occupy the role; the concrete personality of the occupant is supposedly irrelevant for his performance of the function. This is therefore a *universalistic* role. Similarly, production-line workers are replaceable, as are executives and organizational functionaries in general.

In contrast, one's role as the "father" of a particular family is heavily influenced by and dependent upon the personality of the occupant. The concrete relationship of a particular father to his family is a *particularistic* role. There is a culturally defined "father role," to be sure, but the father who brings to this role all the universalistic requirements and not his individuality is a poor father indeed. Conversely, the social functionary, such as the recording secretary of an organization, may seek to particularize his role and to structure his power in terms of personal relationships to him rather than in terms of the definition of the role within the entire system of roles. He does so, however, only at the risk of violating the universalistic prescriptions of the role.

The distinction is always a relative one, and most roles are in some degree both universalistic and particularistic. However, the experience of oneself in-the-world is radically different in the two cases. Consider the difference between one's experience of oneself as father and as production-line worker. The family does not see its father as replaceable by a new functionary; its members are personally involved in the personality of the father. The production-line foreman, on the other hand, *must* see his workers as replaceable if he is to be a good foreman. These radically different contexts of self-world experience cannot be ignored in a phenomenological psychology.

The legal system, it should be noted, makes a virtue of its universality. All persons, regardless of *who* they are, are subject to the law. This prevents favoritism and assures equality; it is the purpose of having a government of laws instead of a government of men. While such universalization occasionally appears anachronistic, there is a certain efficiency gained by treating individuals as members of a category instead of as individuals. For example, a mail order house may automatically send catalogs to customers who have made *two* purchases in a given year. Under this policy, a man who bought two pair of socks, each in a separate order, will get a catalog while a man who bought an entire wardrobe (in one order) will not. This is unfortunate for the company, who wants to send catalogs to its best customers. But for the decision to be made impersonally, according to a simple and universalistic criterion of *two* purchases, is a lot more efficient than to judge each case individually and qualitatively.

Bureaucracies are notoriously universalistic. Whatever else

is true of our current society, it is more bureaucratic than it has ever been. The Industrial Revolution produced the phenomenon of selling one's time. The world's work thus became "labor" and ceased being "work" in the sense of investing oneself in a task to which one is personally committed. One's daily toil thus became separated from the core experience of oneself; labor became "alienated." A job is performed for the paycheck and not for its intrinsic value. A portion of one's day is sold, like a thing, to the highest bidder. One's "self," insofar as one's daily toil is concerned, is reduced to performing functions defined ahead of time and by a system not of one's own creation. One therefore becomes alienated from a part of himself.

As we move from a production-line society into a bureaucratic society, the problem of alienation becomes *more,* not less, acute. The bureaucrat, like the production-line worker, is essentially replaceable, but the demands made upon him by his job include more than the physical functions he performs. These demands include his attitudes, his style of relating to people, his values and his very being. His concrete personality becomes important, but not in its individuality. The person he *is* now becomes subject to universalistic judgment. As long as one works on the production line, who and how one *is* is irrelevant. One's job is secure as long as he is able to perform the function. But as production lines themselves become bureaucratized and more and more of the work force become bureaucrats, the alienation cuts even deeper into the experience of oneself, and the relationship of oneself to the world is even more profoundly invaded by impersonality.

The effects of large historical and sociological trends are not without significance for the kinds of problems of being that are experienced, that is, for psychopathology. To understand this, we must describe in general terms the experiences of self and world that characterize the bureaucratic way of life. Our description may be somewhat of a caricature, but we hope it is a caricature with a point.

The bureaucrat is faced with a number of special conditions. First, his job is likely to be relatively secure if his behavior conforms to the expectations of his immediate superior. This means that the personal idiosyncrasies of one's immediate superior become crucial environmental contingencies that one dare not violate.

Ideally, the universality of the bureaucracy should rule out the personal dislike a boss might have for an underling, but it rarely works this way. Grievance committees in unionized shops and impersonal job descriptions are designed to combat this kind of arbitrariness, but the bureaucrat often does not have such power. It is always possible to go over the boss's head, but to do so is often risky and generally assumed to be precipitous. This riskiness is augmented by the interests of the boss's boss, whose job contingencies are probably heavily influenced by the consideration of keeping "trouble" at a minimum, and who finds it less "trouble" to take the boss's side than that of the bureaucrat in question.

The contingencies of the boss's life are also important. His major agenda may also be to prevent "trouble" and herein lies the fragment of power available to the bureaucrat. The boss needs to look good to *his* boss, and any underling can spoil this for him. We have, therefore, a social and political arrangement in which fights between individuals must be carried out in entirely different terms from the biological model of the survival of the fittest or the capitalistic model of economic competition. Anger, should it be felt, or ambition, or even devotion to the purpose of the bureaucracy, must be filtered through a series of rituals ("regular channels," they are called) that are remarkably elaborate.

These filters are, in a bureaucratic setting, predominantly and pervadingly of the quality of being-for-others. This kind of awareness of oneself, that is, a vigilant guard over how one appears to others, can be neglected by the bureaucrat only at his occupational peril. But even more important is the long term effect of this context for self-experience upon the being of the individual. The bureaucrat is in real danger of lying-for-others for so long and in such detail that he comes in time to lie-for-himself and to lie-in-the-world.

Suppose, for example, that a salesman is encouraged by his company to be aggressive. His supervisor is aggressive and thus supplies a model for the salesman. Because of the power structure, satellization around the supervisor occurs and the individual internalizes the value, "aggression = good" as a criterion against which to measure himself. He comes, then, to see himself as aggressive (whatever that might mean to him) and to feel that he is not being the "real him" when he is not. Idealization of one's self around this concept and guilt for not living up to the idealized image grow together in the vicious circle of lying-for-oneself. The guiltier one feels, the more adamant is the affirmation of the standard, and vice versa. Soon the salesman has identified with the role to such an extent that his immediate perception of the world is changed. Neutral persons become potential sales targets; relationships are subordinated to the goal of sales.

This example is actually from a rapidly disappearing era. Objective criteria, like the number of sales, are disappearing from the bureaucratic scene and replacing them is the *appearance* of being a certain kind of person. Aggressiveness (or some other trait) ceases being a means to the end of selling and becomes an end in itself. The behavioral trait is no longer replaceable by some other style as long as sales are made. What one is (for-others) becomes the sole criterion. The ticket to job security becomes less and less what one *does* and more and more how one appears. Being-for-others takes on exaggerated significance, and any lies therefore become more vital necessities.

3. Therapy and the Bureaucrat

To call the bureaucratic style "lying" is to imply that the therapist's job is to help him to be "honest," which may indeed be a maladaptive stance to take given the social and political contingencies of bureaucratic life. The question is not, however, whether a behavior is adaptive within a social system but whether it violates the ontological structure of being. It is taken as "given" that certain relationships among the levels of being are "healthy," and such a normative position underlies every psychology. The crucial ingredient of the existential view, however, is that this "given" is peculiarly empty of content and open to decision by the individual. To lie is a choice that must be considered legitimate and necessary, though costly in certain respects.

The attempt to force overt honesty in a patient may subject the patient to the wrath of his bureaucratic context and do him a great disservice. The goal must be, therefore, to open up for the individual the *option* of honesty. If he decides to run the risk of honesty in a system built on lies, he does so presumably in the service of other than bureaucratic values. To become aware of his own experience of self-as-subject may enlighten latent values. This may put him into agonizing conflict between his personal values and his bureaucratic values, and the therapist must be willing to accept responsibility for his role in bringing that conflict to a head. Often, however, the conflict was there all along and may well have been central in driving the bureaucrat into therapy. And concrete political circumstances in the bureaucracy itself usually are the precipitating conditions for conflict, rather than what the therapist does. Finally, it must be said that it is hardly the therapist's fault if a patient has internally conflicting values, nor is it his fault if bureaucratic values themselves put a particular strain on being as it is given ontologically.

Let us make our original distinction between personal and impersonal, gross as this may be, into a distinction between "worlds" within which we operate. Each world has its own values objectively, in the sense that these values are there independent of any particular subject. The bureaucracy has its values; one's family and primary group may have different values. As soon as the person *is* in these two worlds, he appropriates these values as his own even as he influences them by his participation in the worlds. A conflict between these values can become a conflict between two ways of being-in-the-world. If a man says, for example, "From the point of view of what I stand for in my family, X is good; but from the point of view of what I stand for in the bureaucracy, X is bad," then he stands for contradictory values and experiences a conflict within being-in-the-world.

However, the more usual statement reads something like this: "From the point of view of my primary group, X is good; but from the point of view of the bureaucracy, X is bad. I don't know where I, as an individual, stand." Here the individual does not experience himself as in either world. Indeed the conflict may best be construed as one between significant "others" for which he must "be" (i.e., being-for-others). Or the statement may read, "From the point of view of what I stand for in my family, X is good; but from the point of view of what the bureaucracy stands for, X is bad," in which case it is a conflict between being-in-the-world and being-for-others. One can imagine a conflict between being-for-oneself and being-for-others. None of these "statements" are quotations, of course. They are merely ways we may use here to represent critical experiential conflicts.

Such conflicts as these are not "merely" role conflicts, although we may indeed construe them as such. More to the point, we must see them as ontological conflicts that can produce or represent a profound rift within one's being. There is often more at stake than the question, "Which role shall I play?" At stake rather is, "Which role is more important?"—a decision that demands a commitment by the individual, or more pointedly, "Which role is the real me?"—which is another way of asking, "Who am I?" The growing importance of bureaucratic arrangements in the social context of all of us makes this question a particularly modern one (cf. Wheelis, 1958; Riesman, 1951). The crisis that sometimes occurs because the bureaucracy has a ready-made identity did not occur as frequently when, in the production-line situation, one could say that he was not personally but only bodily present on the job, or when, in the preindustrial situation, one never asked such questions at all.

The particular experience of the conflict that any given patient may undergo will no doubt evolve during the course of therapy, with one's being-for-the-therapist playing some role in this evolution. As the experience of the conflict by the patient evolves, it will, if our initial categories are correct, move toward a sharper focus between two or all three of the aspects of being we have described. The important task of therapy, here as always, is to make the individual aware of his options within his situation, which is to confront him with a choice, which in turn is to enable him to experience himself as a subject. He may indeed choose the values of the bureaucracy, even while the therapist may have made some other choice. The essential ingredient is that he choose rather than evade that choice through misrepresentation of his situation to himself and subsequent perversion of his being to support such misrepresentation.

Virtually every psychotherapy case today has some version of this problem inherent in it. The more bureaucratic society becomes, the more appropriate are the terms used here. But even for nonbureaucrats, the problem is not dissimilar, and Freud's *Civilization and Its Discontents,* published in 1930, recognizes a not dissimilar problem. The underlying issue in all these cases is how to survive as an individual in a society that can maintain itself only by denying or controlling or in the worst case, ignoring, that individuality.

References

Fromm, E. *The Sane Society.* New York: Rinehart, 1955.

Heinemann, F. H. *Existentialism and the Modern Predicament.* New York: Harper, 1958.

Laing, R. D. *The Politics of Experience.* New York: Pantheon, 1967.

Marcuse, H. Critique of neo-Freudian revisionism. In H. Marcuse, *Eros and Civilization.* New York: Vintage, 1955.

Parsons, T. *The Social System.* Glencoe, Ill.: Free Press, 1951.

Rieff, P. *Freud: The Mind of the Moralist.* New York: Viking, 1959.

Riesman, D. *The Lonely Crowd.* New Haven: Yale University Press, 1953.

Szasz, T. *Psychiatric Justice.* New York: Macmillan, 1965.

Szasz, T. *The Ethics of Psychoanalysis.* New York: Basic Books, 1965.

Wheelis, A. *The Quest for Identity.* New York: Norton, 1958.

Methodological puzzles 18

In this chapter, we will attempt to state some of the methodological issues in psychology as seen from the phenomenological-existential point of view. In the end, we should strive for an objective (this term is discussed below) theory of subjectivity.

1. Measurement in Psychology Is Not Objective

Whether measurement yields objectivity is an issue that revolves around how we define "objective," and there is an alternative to defining it the way traditional, objective psychology does. Let us assume that there is just one objective world and that I, and a number of other human beings, somehow "know" what it is—that is, there are statements I can make about it that make up this activity of "knowing" and the product of this activity is "knowledge." The crucial question becomes: What is this activity and how does it work?

Modern science, including most traditional psychology, has followed Descartes. The theory of knowing runs something like this: My body is covered with sense organs that are in a mechanical relationship with the mechanical world (light rays affect my retina in such and such a mathematically describable fashion).

Somewhere in me is a soul that observes these events and by the God-given faculty of reason puts together knowledge of the world. Conscious experience, then, is a quality of my soul.

Beginning in this way, the soul is one of three possibilities for conceptually dealing with conscious experience. The second alternative is to follow Locke (and eventually Wundt and Titchener) and to extend the Newtonian image of mechanical atomism to the "mind" itself, in which case the mind is the "container" of images, sensations, affections, etc., and conscious experience is somehow not only made up of, but also exhausted by, the workings of the laws of association. The third alternative is to deny that conscious experience is important at all, and hence concentrate, as behaviorism does, elsewhere.

There may be other alternatives, but these are the historical outcomes of starting the theory of knowledge from the mechanical relationship between sense organs and the world. To start here is to start with the Cartesian split between body and soul, the former being completely mechanical and the latter being the exclusive locus of consciousness. In line with other advances in secularism and science, the soul (and experience) was progressively discarded until behaviorism excluded it altogether. These trends have been very fruitful in the history of man and the physical sciences, but they have put psychologists into the extraordinary position of neglecting conscious experience.

The definition of "objectivity" thus became consistently mechanical. While on the one hand ignoring consciousness and subjectivity as the object of investigation, psychology at the same time took great pains to rule out subjective factors in the knowledge-producing process. The logic runs as follows: Individual observers may impose preconceived ideas and biases upon the observations, and in order to make sure this is not happening, many different observers must be able to repeat the operations and emerge with the same product and the same knowledge. The surest way to facilitate this procedure is to quantify. Little subjective bias can sneak into the process of counting and meter-reading. Or, put another way, the product, knowledge, comes from either the subject or the object. To assure ourselves that it is not from the biases of the subject and that it *is* from the object, i.e., is objective, many different subjects have to be able to agree. And one simply cannot quarrel with numbers that are consistently and logically used. Thus contemporary psychology is, in this respect, a clear outgrowth of the Cartesian starting point in the theory of knowledge, but yet without the soul and hence, without an explanation of the experience of the observer.

Phenomenology and existentialism do not begin with the Cartesian split between the nonexperiencing, mechanistic senses and the nonmechanistic, experiencing soul. The activity of "knowing" is not my consciousness (homunculus) passively observing what my sense organs mechanically give me about the world, but rather conscious experience and "the object" are inextricably bound together in an *intentional act*. I intend an object, and from this act emerges knowledge. I cannot be conscious without an object to intend, nor can I know an object without intending it.

Knowledge emerges out of the meeting of subject and object in this kind of activity, and thus what we know is limited to what we intend. It is interesting that in the late days of prebehaviorist associationism, "directedness" of thinking was offered as a refutation of the passivity and homunculosity of the associationistic process, but its later psychological statement in Gestalt psychology made little impression on a continent swept by behaviorism.

This way of reckoning knowledge solves the problem of the soul, or homunculus, who watches the sense organs from the inside, by including *experience* at the very basis of knowing. That is, experience (a process or activity, and not a thinking thing or ghostly spirit) is intentional, active, and focused. No longer are we faced with the choice of saying (*a*) there is a nonmechanical (free) soul who watches the sense organs, or (*b*) experience itself is as mechanical as the rest of the universe. The primary phenomenological datum —intentionality—is built into the theory of knowledge in the first place.

Having established, at least provisionally, that intentionality is a better model for understanding our own knowledge-creating processes than the Cartesian split between subject and object, in what sense may we say that measurement is not really "objective"? The crucial point is that we see what we intend, and that we cannot see without intending. The question of objectivity is: Where does the knowledge come from, the subject or the object? Since we cannot see the object without being an intending subject, the greater amount of information will come from the object when the intentions of the subject are more varied, more open-ended and less constricted.

One thing is clear about measurement: Of all the possible features of the object that may be incorporated in the knowledge, the measuring intention is extremely selective. It admits only the quantitative aspects of the object. It intends the object with eyes closed to all but a narrow range of the possible features that may be observed.

Now it is still the case that by narrowing the focus to quantitative dimensions, there is a substantial reduction in the variation among observers. There is more agreement, and agreement, the argument runs, rules out subjective bias. But agreement is not objectivity. It does not mean that the information contained in the knowledge comes from the object and not from the subject. Agreement, rather, simply signals intersubjectivity, that is, it indicates that the intentions of the various subjects are the same, that they are attending to (and ignoring) the same attributes of the object.

The compelling conclusion to all this is that measurement assures us of less, not more, objectivity in psychology. But does this mean that we will be more objective as psychologists if we stop measuring and begin arguing again about who has fewer biases? Are we to return to the terminological confusions and vain abstract controversies of preoperational psychology? This can hardly be recommended, and yet there is a sense in which the kind of psychology dealing with humans may be better off without measurement. For measurement, by concentrating upon the quantitative dimensions of a person, gaits out and excludes one very important attribute of our subject matter, namely, consciousness. Human beings, while having thing-like qualities, are not merely things. They are not only objects of our study; they are also subjects, persons who intend us even as we intend them. To have somehow missed this feature of our subject matter can be seen only as highly non-objective, highly influenced by the intersubjective biases of ourselves as psychologists.

This rather massive fact about our subject matter cannot be ignored if we are to have a psychology that is in any sense complete, or, for that matter, objective. Just what are we missing in traditionally defined, objective psychology? What features of the person are we not appreciating? It is, of course, the fact that he has a point of view. Let us call this the "actor's" point of view in contrast to the "observer's" point of view.

2. The Point of View of the Actor

It is said that all the data we have in our effort to understand another person is his overt behavior: his speech, his gestures, his way of life. These may well be the only data available to the psychologist, but in themselves they are *meaningless* bits of observation. They derive their meaning from the categories and conceptual field glasses of the observer—what we have called above the "intentions."

A. The problem of agreement

Suppose that we are psychologists who are asked to "explain" the behavior of a man who drinks too much. Is it not predictable that the Skinnerian will look for (and find) the schedule of reinforcement that is responsible for shaping this behavior? And that the Freudian will look for (and find) the oral eroticism and frustrated passive needs that lie behind it? And that the social psychologist the interpersonal message that is being transmitted, and perhaps the socioeconomic origins of this behavior? Our interpretations can be as varied as the conceptual schemes we can impose on the data, and in fact, without some such conceptual scheme, the data will be meaningless. And each conceptual scheme is, theoretically at least, capable of being verified; thus each interpretation is in a very important sense "true" (pending verification); and thus we have arrived at the sophisticated view, in the social sciences, of multiple causation.

But there is yet another kind of meaning that the data can acquire, another kind of explanatory program for interpreting the data; another complex of associations and categories that gives the data a context in which they can be comprehensible to the observer. All of the above examples ask: "What do these data mean to me, the psychologist?" Let us ask, "What do these data mean to the man himself, who drinks too much?" Does he think it is too much?

Does he feel that he is sinning? That he is exercising his male prerogative? That he likes the taste of it?

Can we, as outside observers of his behavior, leave this behavior undefined until we can discover what the behavior means to him? Can we hear about his behavior without interpreting it? Ultimately, no, unless we refuse to listen (for we hear what we intend to hear), and yet there are varying degrees to which our interpretation, the very meaning of the data, stems from *our* conceptual scheme as opposed to *his*. The extreme in one direction is to reduce all data to one's own categories immediately upon discovering the data; that is characteristic of measurement psychology. The extreme in the other direction is the impossible task of seeing it only through his eyes, i.e., by being him. Somewhere in the middle is the standard clinical attitude of swinging with the patient for a while, then interpreting what we think is going on in his life according to our theory and to the accumulating quantitative findings that support it.

B. The problem of generality

Our interpretation of the data must ultimately be comparative: this behavior is like X behavior and unlike Y behavior, and thus the uniqueness of that datum is lost to the extent that all Xs are seen as essentially the same, and to the extent that our intentions limit us to a very narrow range of attributes. To say that our man drinks because it is reinforcing to drink, and it is reinforcing because A, B, and C reinforcement schedules existed for him in the past, is to make the phenomenon comparable to (and meaningful in terms of) laboratory data collected on pigeons, rats, and humans, and will have little to do with his specific situation.

On the other end of the continuum lies a repetition of his own statement: because it relaxes him, and he needs to relax because his job makes him tense, which in turn is a result of his boss who is a tyrant, he cannot relax around tyrants because they remind him of his father. Here all the uniqueness of his life history comes to the fore, and the data of the man's behavior means something quite different if we withhold our conceptual forging long enough to hear his point of view. Naturally, and inevitably, we must bring to bear our own categories in order even to hear what he is saying, and the extreme of appreciating the data in their full uniqueness, independent of any comparative and interpretive work on our part, this extreme is impossible. For I am, after all, another person; I am not him.

The crucial question, then, can be stated in a number of ways: How broad a range of attributes of the person are allowed to enter the knowledge? How broad are the intentions of the observing psychologist-subject? How much of the person's own interpretation is interpreted by our interpretation? How much do we, as observers, intend his interpretations? To what extent are our intentions open to his point of view? The more so, the more objective we are—in each of these questions. The more his subjectivity is included in our interpretations, the more objective we are. The more our point of view as observers is capable of dealing with his point of view as actor, the better is our psychology.

Insofar as we are interested only in psychotherapy, the methodological problem is hardly problematic. For it is not a generalizing kind of knowledge that makes a difference in psychotherapy but rather the kind of knowledge that one lives, in a highly personal and often intellectually noncommunicable fashion. We may call this "existential knowledge." It is obviously something that we "know" rather than "don't know," for we live out our lives on the basis of it (such as questions of identity and values), and yet unlike scientific knowledge, it is not demonstrable.

However, we cannot be satisfied with personal, noncommunicable and existential knowledge in the field of psychology. We must generalize; we must build theory, we must be essentialistic as well as existential.

3. Husserl and Method *

From the discussion of objectivity emerges the problem of agreement, and from the discussion of the actor's point of view emerges the problem of generality. If we stick to our definition of objectivity, it appears that the more objective we are (i.e., the more the information in our knowledge comes from the object and not from the

* For a more detailed study of Husserl, cf. Kockelman (1967). For a more elaborate program for research, cf. Van Kaam (1967).

subject, or put another way, the less constricted our intentions as observers are) the *less* generality we will have in our knowledge. Because we must take the definition of objectivity very seriously, let us try to point to the broad outlines of how these problems can be solved. Psychology runs the great risk of being irrelevant without this kind of definition of objectivity and without some resolution of these problems.

Operationalism in the broad sense will have to serve us. That is, we must be able to state unequivocally what operations the observing subject shall undergo to arrive at the knowledge first-hand. This is not to endorse operationalism in the sense that every concept has a measurement technique. We have already seen that measurement sacrifices too much of the data merely to agreement. *Can we have agreement on the meaning of terms without the kind of operational definition that constricts our intentions so severely and is so costly in terms of objectivity?* Nor is it to endorse operationalism in the sense of telling the observer what operations to perform on the object in order to get the desired response. "The object" is really a subject and it is *his* performance of operations on the world that we seek to understand. We have already seen that leaving the intentionality of man out of our theory has led us to be highly non-objective about him. *Can we have generalizable concepts through which to intend him that take into account his subjectivity?* The first question is the agreement problem; the second is the generality problem.

Husserl felt it was possible to solve these problems by going back to the roots of our knowledge. Husserl's view was that knowledge, as we generally understand it, is the end product of a series of mental operations which had their beginning in experience. But the experience that underlies all knowledge is raw, primitive, and untransformed by subsequent operations. If we can understand the operations, we can undo them and achieve again the raw, primitive experience which underlies all knowledge. Then to progress again from this primordial experience toward the finished product—knowledge—carefully and scrupulously, this is the program that could yield knowledge as certain as is possible for the human being.

Let us outline Husserl's program and then comment upon it giving examples of how it would work for psychology. The end point of this discussion is rather ambitious: it is to rebuild psychological theory. The new psychological theory must be cast in a language of experience, for the key to human psychology is human experience. This is the (by now familiar) point about objectivity. In the process, we hope also to solve the problems of agreement and generality.

Husserl's program contains the following steps: (*a*) attend to phenomena as they appear; (*b*) discern what aspects of the phenomena are essential to their particular presentation as they appear; and (*c*) explore the workings of consciousness that are responsible for the constituting of these essences.

(*a*) Attend to the phenomena as they appear. The starting and ending within the range of conscious experience is phenomenology's attempt to avoid the perhaps rational but nevertheless (at this stage) irrelevant "hypothetical constructs" that grow up out of the need to force the data to fit a theory. For example, if we already assume that early childhood affects later behavior in a casual fashion, we must have mediators like "personality" and "character structure" to carry the force of the early cause to the later effect. Such terms as these may eventually emerge in the theory, but at this stage we want to undercut these categories as much as possible and stick to the data.

(*b*) Discern what aspects of the phenomena are essential to their particular presentation as they appear. This is simply sorting out those aspects to which we are in fact attending in order that we experience the phenomena as we do. For example, if I look at a patient and see him as "depressed," I must ask what aspects of the total phenomenon of the patient I am attending to in order to experience him that way. If it is his manner of speaking, I need to specify exactly *what* about it, etc.

It is clear that the variety of concrete experiences of persons that comes about under the term "depressed" is immense. Depression is a mood, but a mood of many nuances. This term must be broken down, of course, and the crucial point here is that the subcategories of the term must be clearly explicated with adequate criteria for inclusion and exclusion. Hence a new language of moods must be developed. The only way to be clear about the language is to insist upon full and scrupulous description, with examples and counterexamples.

This appears to be a tremendous task. However it is already

going on in phenomenology. Adjectives such as "depressed" must refer to adequately defined experiences (in this case the experience of depression). Such experiences that are already defined include "sympathy" (Scheler, 1954), "anxiety" (May, 1950), "loneliness" (Moustakas, 1961), "shame" (Lynd, 1961; Sartre, 1956, Part III) to name only a few. We have added some to this list in Chapter 3.

(c) Explore the workings of consciousness that are responsible for the constituting of these essences. That is, the "essential" aspects mentioned above are here called "essences." This step in the program is a kind of critique of what went on in step two above, so that the explanation of terms must include an account of the movement from the raw data to the descriptive content. This step remains to be done for those concepts introduced in Chapter 3.

The primary problem of objectivity, namely, to develop concepts that cover the person's experience as well as how he is experienced by the psychologist, is solved by using only terms that refer to concrete experience in the first place. Subsidiary problems of objectivity, such as assuring ourselves that the terms we use do in fact describe a person (rather than missing the mark) depend upon an adequate carrying out of step *a*. The problem of agreement must ultimately depend upon an adequate carrying out of step *b*. Most disagreement is a matter of misunderstanding of terms, and if terms are clear, then this problem will hopefully be solved. Disagreement that is not a matter of misunderstanding of terms will have to be resolved by step *a*. The problem of generality has been solved in the phenomenological literature by step *c*. For to move from the concrete data to a concept, such as "shame," is a matter of abstraction of the crucial elements of the situation, and it requires an understanding of this process.

Assuming that this is clear, we have a psychology of adjectives. We have stuck to adjectives because they are the most obvious kinds of words that need redefinition. But the truth of the matter is, of course, that theory is not all adjectives, but nouns and especially verbs. We want to describe states and processes as well as qualities. Beyond that, our psychology must ultimately do more than describe: it must ultimately explain. There is still a long way to go.

The movement to verbs is quite easy here, for when a person is "depressed," he is doing something in the world, interpreting it in a particular way. His manner of experiencing himself and his world, or to be even more inclusive, his manner of *being,* is the "thing" that is depressed. Hence Binswanger (1964) has written a short but fine paper entitled "On the manic mode of being-in-the-world" which describes not just the experience of mania but the experience of the world in mania. This is a crucial step.

Nouns traditionally refer to things, and while the human being is part thing his experiences are not things. Hence nouns really have little role in a phenomenology of man. The grammatical place of nouns will no doubt most likely be filled with participle forms of verbs, such as "being" and "intending." Finally, to move from a descriptive to an explanatory model will simply have to follow when we are ready for it. The continuity in human existence can be accounted for in a way that is better than the model of causality found in natural science. May (personal communication, 1962) has used the metaphor of birth to refer to the emergence of symptoms, dreams, and other phenomena of human existence. This metaphor has the advantage of connecting an event with prior events without the rigid formula of cause and effect. It also focuses our attention upon the creative nature of personal products such as dreams and symptoms, and accounts for the apparent taking of disparate elements and weaving them into an original combination that grows out of the individual life-history. This metaphor deserves serious thought.

Technical Terms

Problem of objectivity: Whether the content of our knowledge is determined by the biases built into the "subject" or by the actual characteristics of the object.

Problem of agreement: Whether terms used in formulating knowledge carry the same information from one observer to another.

Problem of generality: Whether one can have terms that describe the uniqueness of what is studied (such as a person's being) and still be general enough to allow communication and comparison.

References

Binswanger, L. On the manic mode of being-in-the-world. In E. Straus (Ed.) *Phenomenology Pure and Applied.* Pittsburgh: Duquesne University Press, 1964.

Kockelman, J. J. *Edmund Husserl's Phenomenological Psychology.* Pittsburgh: Duquesne University Press, 1967.

Lynd, H. M. *On Shame and the Search for Identity.* New York: Science Editing, 1961.

May, R. *The Meaning of Anxiety.* New York: Ronald Press, 1950.

Moustakas, C. *Loneliness.* New York: Prentice-Hall, 1961.

Sartre, J.-P. *Being and Nothingness.* New York: Philosophical Library, 1956.

Scheler, M. *The Nature of Sympathy.* New Haven: Yale University Press, 1954.

Van Kaam, A. *Existential Foundations of Psychology.* Pittsburgh: Duquesne University Press, 1966.

Conclusion 19

Every psychological theory has its assumptions about the nature of man, a series of "givens" that are not so much put to empirical test as they are used to organize empirical data. *Behaviorist learning theory,* for example, assumes a basic set of given drives taken over from biology. Behavioral data are then *organized* into theory about how the organism satisfies (given) basic survival needs. Hunger, sex, and thirst served for decades as the "basic needs" or "givens" in terms of which data were organized into "secondary reinforcement" hypotheses and so on. *Psychoanalysis* also proposes a set of givens, but being particularly aimed at human neurosis, hunger and thirst seemed less important than striving for erotic gratification and the societal blocks to this striving. Thus the givens in psychoanalytic theory form the core around which Freud's clinical data were organized, leading to elaborate theory about the development of characterological anomalies that emerge from the conflict of givens to create neurosis.

It is at the point of the givens that existential-phenomenological theory differs from behaviorism and psychoanalysis. It is important to note that the givens are derived not from biological theory nor from the observations of neurotics; they stem from existential philosophy, which is an attempt to come to terms with the inexorable givens of immediate human experience. Death, for example, is not seen as a biological event but rather is interpreted in terms of the profound experiences that it provokes in the lives of men. An end to the life of an organism is one thing; the end of my life is something quite different in terms of the experiences it provokes in myself. Similarly, pain is not simply a biological danger signal nor an instinctual frustration. Pain becomes profound for humans when the total arbitrariness of life's distribution of pleasure and pain becomes apparent to us. We thus graduate from a biological, or even simply psychological (in the sense of traditional psychological theory), interpretation of human experience into a frame of reference that is existential, that is, a frame of reference designed to deal with the exigencies of human experience.

We began this book by comparing the units of analysis used by behaviorism, psychoanalysis, and an existential psychology. It should be clear at this point that the units of analysis are not all that is at stake. Indeed, behavioristic psychology has gone beyond the single habit as the analytic unit, and indeed the individual character structure is not the only unit of analysis in later, more interpersonal versions of psychoanalytic theory. What is really in question, after the advent of existential psychology, is the overall approach of the psychologist. Both psychoanalysis and behaviorism, even in their modern versions, are very much in the natural scientific tradition. This tradition formulates the knowledge-getting situation as one in which there is a world of objects, and an observer-subject who tries to match the object world's essential attributes with a theoretical structure inside his own awareness.

This posture is not the only way to have a psychology. The existential alternative involves, however, more than a different theory of psychology. It involves an entirely different approach to the knowledge-getting process, to being a psychologist, indeed to being. One's total relationship to the "object of knowledge" is different, once we take intentionality seriously. Sartre's short essay (1947), translated by J. P. Fell and quoted below, vividly describes this difference.

>   "He devoured her with his eyes." This expression and
> many other signs point to the illusion common to both realism
> and idealism: to know is to eat. After a hundred years of
> academicism, French philosophy remains at that point. We have
> all read Brunschvicg, Lalande, and Meyerson, we have all be-
> lieved that the spidery mind trapped things in its web, covered

them with a white spit and slowly swallowed them, reducing them to its own substance. What is a table, a rock, a house? A certain assemblage of "contents of consciousness," a class of such contents. O digestive philosophy! Yet nothing seems more obvious: is not the table the actual content of my perception? Is not my perception the present state of my consciousness? Nutrition, assimilation! Assimilation, Lalande said, of things to ideas, of ideas by ideas, of minds by minds. The corpulent skeletons of the world were picked clean by these diligent diastases: assimilation, unification, identification. The simplest and plainest of us looked for something solid, something not just mental, but in vain; everywhere they would encounter only a soft and very genteel mist: themselves.

Against the digestive philosophy of empirico-criticism, of neo-Kantianism, against all "psychologism," Husserl persistently affirmed that one cannot dissolve things in consciousness. You see this tree, to be sure. But you see it just where it is: at the side of the road, in the midst of the dust, alone and writhing in the heat, eight miles from the Mediterranean coast. It could not enter into your consciousness, for it is not of the same nature as consciousness. One is perhaps reminded of Bergson and the first chapter of *Matter and Memory*. But Husserl is not a realist: this tree on its bit of parched earth is not an absolute which would subsequently enter into communication with us. Consciousness and the world are given at one stroke: essentially external to consciousness, the world is nevertheless essentially relative to consciousness. Husserl sees consciousness as an irreducible fact which no physical image can account for. Except perhaps the quick, obscure image of a burst. To know is to "burst toward," to tear oneself out of the moist gastric intimacy, veering out there beyond oneself, out there near the tree and yet beyond it, for the tree escapes me and repulses me, and I can no more lose myself in the tree than it can dissolve itself in me. I'm beyond it; it's beyond me.

Do you recognize in this description your own circumstances and your own impressions? You certainly know that the tree was not you, that you could not make it enter your dark stomach and that knowledge could not, without dishonesty, be compared to possession. All at once consciousness is purified, it is clear as a strong wind. There is nothing in it but a movement of fleeing itself, a sliding beyond itself. If, impossible though it be, you could enter "into" a consciousness you would be seized by a whirlwind and thrown back outside, in the thick of the dust, near the tree, for consciousness has no "inside." It is just this being beyond itself, this absolute flight, this refusal to be a substance which makes it a consciousness.

Imagine for a moment a connected series of bursts which tear us out of ourselves, which do not even allow to an "ourselves" the leisure of composing ourselves behind them, but which instead throw us beyond them into the dry dust of the world, onto the plain earth, amidst things. Imagine us thus rejected and abandoned by our own nature in an indifferent, hostile, and restive world—you will then grasp the profound meaning of the discovery which Husserl expresses in his famous phrase, "All consciousness is consciousness *of* something." No more is it necessary to finish off the effeminate philosophy of immanence, where everything happens by compromise, by protoplasmic transformations, by a tepid cellular chemistry. The philosophy of transcendence throws us onto the highway, in the midst of dangers, under a blinding light.

Being, says Heidegger, is being-in-the-world. One must understand this "being-in" as movement. To be is to fly out into the world, to spring from the nothingness of the world and of consciousness in order suddenly to burst out as consciousness-in-the-world. When consciousness tries to recoup itself, to coincide with itself once and for all, closeted off all warm and cozy, it destroys itself. This necessity for consciousness to exist as consciousness of something other than itself Husserl calls "intentionality."

I have spoken primarily of knowledge to make myself better understood: the French philosophy which has molded us understands little besides epistemology. But for Husserl and the phenomenologists our consciousness of things is not limited to knowledge of them. Knowledge, or pure "representation," is only one of the possible forms of my consciousness "of" this tree; I can also love it, fear it, hate it, and this surpassing of consciousness by itself that is called "intentionality" finds itself again in fear, hatred, and love. Hating another is just a way of bursting forth toward him; it is finding oneself suddenly confronted by a stranger in whom one lives, in whom one suffers from the very first, the objective quality "hateful."

So it is that all at once hatred, love, fear, sympathy—all these famous "subjective" reactions which were floating in the malodorous brine of the mind—are pulled out. They are merely ways of discovering the world. It is things which suddenly unveil themselves to us as hateful, sympathetic, horrible, lovable. Being dreadful is a *property* of this Japanese mask, an inexhaustible and irreducible property which constitutes its very nature—and not the sum of our subjective reactions to a piece of sculptured wood.

Husserl has restored to things their horror and their charm. He has restored to us the world of artists and prophets: frightening, hostile, dangerous, with its havens of mercy and love. He has cleared the way for a new treatise on the passions which would be inspired by this simple truth, so utterly ignored by the refined among us: if we love a woman, it is because she is lovable. We are delivered from Proust. We are likewise delivered from the "internal life": in vain would we seek the caresses and fondlings of our intimate selves, like Amiel or like a child who kisses his own shoulder, since everything is finally outside, everything, even ourselves. Outside, in the world, among others. It is not in some hiding-place that we will discover ourselves; it is on the road, in the town, in the midst of the crowd, a thing among things, a man among men.

Returning to psychology, the point is that as psychologists we must construe the situation in such a way that we are not trapped in a tradition that leads us to consume reality with theoretical ideas, that sets the world up as an opponent of human experience, and that reduces experience to a two-stage process that condemns those features of the world not measurable as "merely subjective" and hence irrelevant. Such an approach is natural science.

This posture puts two restrictions upon the scientist. First, it forces him into a language of essential attributes of the object world, which is perforce a language of things, and second it puts his relationship to his subject matter in an ideal, or theoretical plane and divorces him from his own immediate contact with his subject matter. These two limitations are, I fear, fatal for psychology.

The first one, that of essentialistic metaphors, requires little elaboration by now. The fatal aspect lies in the fact that when the subject matter is human beings, one is dealing with an existing subject (being) as well as with an essence-laden object. The additional ramification of essentialistic language, that the relationship between perceiver and perceived becomes merely ideal, deserves comment here.

I have a friend who reports the following revelatory experience. He was confronted with the task of shortening the legs on a coffee table. In good, rational fashion he calculated that if he took exactly four inches off every leg of the table, he would lower the height of the table four inches and maintain the good balance among the four legs. Ideally, and in terms of geometric theory, this theory is impeccable. It turns out, however, that for this particular table, with its unique angle of legs, the desired effect was achieved by taking 4, $4\frac{1}{4}$, $4\frac{1}{4}$, and $4\frac{1}{2}$ inches off of various legs. In addition to rejoicing with him that he still has a table at all, instead of a table top with shredded stumps, we should rejoice with him in the insight that the table he was working with was not the ideal table, from the celestial collection, with perfect geometric properties, but rather it was a stodgy and concrete, particular table.

The practical import of this experience is obvious. What is not obvious, because we are so deeply enmeshed in our ideal way of thinking, is that the "model" or "theoretical" table has become, for the natural scientific observer, more real and more meaningful than the concrete object. In psychology we run the grave risk of our models and theories becoming not only more real and more meaningful than individual persons we confront in the consulting room, but also these models become *the only* means through which our experience of the individual person can be meaningful *at all*.

I hope that this book has not produced another "model" of behavior, although I am afraid we have come dangerously close to that. If so, there is some comfort in the knowledge that multiple models are probably better than a single model. Certainly it is true that the distinction among levels of being looks like a model in the usual sense. But its greatest virtue is not, finally, its representational function. Its greatest value is, in its author's view, its attention-directing function and in its metaphorical flexibility. The crucial thing in clinical psychology is not the theory in terms of which we interpret phenomena—although it is very important not to have a bad theory—but rather it is the choice of what phenomena to interpret, that is, to attend to and to worry about. This in turn depends, to be sure, on something like a theory of what is "essential" in man—a philosophical-anthropological model, if you will—but these "assumptions" are more than "assumptions" in the sense of premises for logical constructions. These assumptions are fundamentals of one's own total orientation to life as well as one's orientation to psychology. They must be understood in terms of the being of the psychologist rather than merely in terms of his thinking.

And it is, finally, the being of the psychologist that is decisive in therapy—especially if we gauge therapy according to the being of the patient. To say this gives psychotherapy an almost mystical tinge, and that is an unfortunate piece of public relations in a society dedicated to combat mysticism. But it does not make it less true. And if it looks mystical to us, we must be willing to entertain the hypothesis that we really make difficult psychological problems more difficult by dismissing them as mystical and insisting that a bad theory must be good enough.

The problem of *knowing* is only a small part of all of man's problems, and insofar as science has ceased to be just a way of knowing and has become a more generalized way of living (or can we say, way of being?) of modern man, it has gone beyond its role as a solver of problems and has become a culturally relative style of life embedded in a historical process. Why should this concern psychologists? It should because psychology's subject matter is man, his relation to the world and to one another, and man challenges psychology with problems beyond how he knows things. The saying that "facts cannot be translated automatically into values" demonstrates the point. Human problems today, which psychology in its broadest tradition should attack, are also problems of feeling, of behaving and relating to the world, in a word, problems of being.

To attack the problem of knowing in a certain way already makes assumptions about our total relationship to the world. For example, natural science strives for objective knowledge of the object that is supposed to be in no way related to the individual or collective subject who reckons it. But data never really speak for themselves. Numbers are abstract and contentless. Interpretation of the numbers will be common among subjects (and hence considered objective) only insofar as all the subjects agree on various conceptual conveniences. And it is also true that the data are gathered within an existing frame of reference so that what is measured is subject to whatever theoretical biases the investigator has.

These so-called biases are part of what else we are besides knowers. We are also, and in a prior way, believers. While it would be ridiculous to challenge the notion that there is, say, a law of gravity, and that we know this law absolutely, it is not ridiculous to suggest that knowing the law is only a small part of our relationship to it, and that we also have attitudes toward it, feelings about it, and that in fact, our total stance toward gravity is prior to knowing it.

These two points, that (a) the problems of man that challenge psychology are not limited to his knowing processes and cannot be solved simply by making him more scientific, and that (b) the scientist himself has solved the problem of knowing only with regards to the collection, but not the interpretation, of data, these two points lead to a third more general one about the relativity of science to historical processes: being is prior to knowing.

It is at this point that the relationship between existential and traditional psychology becomes clear. In no way is existential psychology antiscientific. It is not, of course, opposed to "knowing" things as objectively as we can. But while existential psychology is as concerned as any branch of psychology with knowing as certainly as we can about the subject matter, it is also concerned with how this knowing relates to the larger question of man's being.

Science is a tool of man's intercourse with the world. Like any tool, it is a means that can be put to whatever ends man chooses, just as atomic energy can be used for destruction or construction. It has become more and more fashionable to blame science for inventing the bomb, for trivializing life into gadgetry, and so on. This is an easy kind of scapegoating, for the failure (if one sees a failure) is not the failure of science. Science has been eminently successful. The failure is man's failure. Existential psychology, insofar as it is concerned with something more than knowing our subject matter, namely, our total relationship to it, including how we use the knowledge, is not therefore being antiscientific; it is being pro-mankind. Concern about values, then, is not antiscientific; it is metascientific. It is, however, still part of the enterprise of psychology. The view that psychology is mere knowing, and all else is "politics and poetry" not only ignores important parts of the field that are directly concerned with values (e.g., SPSSI, psychotherapy, educational psychology), but also is based on a view of man's relation to the world that is philosophically uninformed.

I have great respect for human intelligence, but not through a natural science that omits being. We must not lose certain aspects of the scientific tradition, such as its rigorous self-scrutiny and premium on systematic work. But we must, as psychologists, not be bound by a crystalization of this rigor and system into a bad theory and a constricted notion of what qualifies as "understanding."

References

Sartre, J.-P. Une idée fondamentale de la phénoménologie de Husserl: L'intentionnalité. In Jean-Paul Sartre, *Situations I*. Paris: © Editions Gallimard 1947. Translated by J. P. Fell.

Epilogue

While reading the proofs for this book, I have had a very sudden and powerful realization that once you take existentialism seriously, once you accept face-on the idea that human beings are being, living proactively and intentionally into the future, the whole business of reading books and of writing them becomes transformed. One is no longer comfortable with writing or thinking about the state of things, of life, or meaning, but one is thrown, bodily hurtled into the task of saying how he should, can, ought to become. I cannot really "report" the way it is in any simple sense, I am obliged to have a vision, a projection, a direction. Readers too can no longer just learn how things are; they must take up the questions personally and live them. I see, as I read what I have written, that I realized this before, but I fear that the urgency and the demand of this realization is not clear enough.

Since writing the book I have also been studying Heidegger more carefully and more thoroughly. In this marvelous expanse and thoroughness of perspective, he takes it upon himself to write about how it is, against the backdrop of how one wants or hopes it to be. Or rather he fills in the backdrop of how it is so that one's visions and hopes can be ontologically grounded. The situation is, I now think, more complex and simpler than I had thought. It is a simple matter, in one sense, to take existentialism seriously. But it is frightfully complex in its implications as soon as one begins to do so. The work of R. D. Laing, especially the newer books, vividly expresses that simplicity—complexity—urgency.

In practical terms of society's shape, of war and its self-creation and self-destruction, and of psychology as a discipline and profession amidst all this, Heidegger's perspective and Laing's urgency seem to me to open a possibility for a future, that is, a future in which we and our children can continue as human beings. It is this perspective and this urgency that can become existential—and all clinical—psychology. It is these that I would communicate.

Name Index

Adler, A., 13–14, 22
Alexander, F., 316, 317
Arieti, S., 7, 12, 93, 108

Bateson, G., 74, 79
Berne, E., 104, 108
Binet, A., 105 n
Binswanger, L., 50, 57, 98, 108, 248–86, 287–305, 345, 346
Boring, E. G., 24, 38
Boss, M., 165
Brentano, F., 81, 91
Buber, M., 45, 57, 189
Bugental, J. F. T., 24, 38, 66, 72, 76, 77, 79

Combs, A., 82, 91
Cooley, C., 45, 57

Descartes, R., 335

Erikson, E., 75, 79
Eysenck, H. J., 72, 79

Federn, P., 4, 12
Fell, J. P., 50, 57, 348, 355
Ferenczi, S., 243, 247
Flavell, J., 19, 22
Frankenstein, C., 70, 79, 307, 308–09, 312, 313, 317
Frankl, V., 21, 22
Freud, S., 7, 10, 35, 40, 46, 50, 52, 72, 79, 87, 99, 106, 131, 152–58, 160, 165, 191, 232–38, 239, 240, 247, 326, 333, 334, 339
Fromm, E., 74, 79, 325, 334

Goldstein, K., 10, 12
Greene, N., 72, 79

Halleck, S., 309, 316, 317
Heidegger, M., 81, 91, 174, 181
Heinemann, F. H., 327, 334
Hesse, H., 29, 32, 38, 93–94, 108
Hillyer, J., 215, 216, 231
Hoffman, L. W., 53, 57
Hoffman, M. L., 53, 57
Horney, K., 10, 12, 13, 22, 35, 38, 46, 57
Husserl, E., 16, 81, 90, 341–45

Jacobson, E., 40 n, 57
James, W., 13, 22, 40
Janet, P., 105 n
Jaspers, K., 21, 45, 57
Jefferson, L., 216–19, 231

Kant, E., 16
Kaplan, B., 15, 22, 228, 231
Keen, E., 100 n, 108
Kelly, G., 93, 108
Kockelmans, J. J., 341 n, 346
Kohler, W., 14, 23
Kostenbaum, P., 20, 23

Laing, R. D., 7, 12, 17, 19, 21, 23, 70–71, 74, 78, 79, 80, 327, 334
Laird, R., 100 n, 108
Lecky, P., 82, 91
Lewin, K., 82, 91, 94, 108
Locke, J., 336
London, P., 9, 12
Luijpen, W. A., 181, 184
Lynd, H. M., 344, 346

Marcel, G., 45, 57
Marcuse, H., 326, 334
Maslow, A., 10, 12
May, R., 21, 23, 70, 72, 80, 93, 108, 344, 345, 346
McCord, I., 306–07, 310, 317
McCord, W., 306–07, 310, 317
McCurdy, H. G., 82, 91
Mead, G. H., 45, 57
Mendel, W., 95, 96, 108
Minkowski, E., 96, 108, 301, 305
Moustakas, C., 344, 346
Mullahay, P., 35, 38

Parsons, T., 327, 334
Perls, F., 14, 23
Piaget, J., 18, 40, 41, 85
Poe, E. A., 243

Rachman, S., 72, 79
Redl, F., 309, 317
Reisman, J., 105 n, 108
Rieff, P., 84 n, 91, 326, 334
Riesman, D., 21, 23, 333, 334
Robbins, B. S., 165
Rogers, C., 10, 12, 13, 23, 82, 91
Rubenstein, R., 316, 317
Russell, B., 7

Sartre, J. P., 15, 17, 23, 27, 34, 35, 38, 45, 46, 50, 57, 64 n, 65, 72, 80, 228, 344, 346, 348–51, 355
Scheler, M., 159, 344, 346
Schreber, D. P., 233–38
Searles, H. F., 188, 204, 242, 243, 244, 245–46, 247
Sechehaye, M., 220–30, 242, 247
Shakespeare, W., 216–19
Skinner, B. F., 108, 110, 339
Snygg, D., 82, 91
Spitz, R., 45, 57
Straus, E., 158
Sullivan, H. S., 35, 40 n, 45, 57
Szasz, T., 246, 247, 326, 327, 334

Tarde, G., 52
Tillich, P., 11, 12, 16, 23, 66, 72, 80
Timasheff, N. S., 52, 57
Titchener, E. B., 9, 13, 24, 38, 336
Tymieniecka, A. T., 21, 23

van Kaam, 341 n, 346
von Gebsattel, V. E., 158, 165, 301, 305

Wheelis, A., 333, 334
Wild, J., 81 n, 91
Wineman, D., 309, 317
Wundt, W., 9, 336
Wylie, R., 14, 23

Subject Index

Action, practical, 99, 140, 289
 and Ellen West, 291, 292, 294, 303
 necessity for, 67, 177
Actor's point of view, 339, 341
Agency, sense of, 15, 18, 22, 41, 44, 65,
  141, 144, 150, 157
 loss of, 69
Agreement, problem of, 339–40, 342,
  344, 345
Alienation
 of labor, 329
 and obsessions, 159
 from self, 69, 71, 74, 141, 296, 329
 from the world, 159, 177, 227–28
Ambiguity, 63
Anthropology. See also Binswanger, L.
 basic forms, 288–89
 philosophical, 287, 353
Anxiety. See also Dread
 and action, 67
 avoidance of, 66, 68, 73, 76
 and choice, 65–66
 and death, 66
 and Ellen West, 302–03
 existential, 66–69, 71–72
 existential and neurotic, 72, 78, 167
 and isolation, 68
 and meaninglessness, 67
 and paranoia, 244
 and psychopathy, 311
 and psychotherapy, 75
 and self-as-subject, 69
 separation, 41
Authenticity. See also Being, healthy
 and choice, 65–66, 73
 and Ellen West, 291, 300, 303
 and the future, 98–100, 143–44, 303

Bad faith, 15, 46, 64 n. See also Lying
Basic forms of being, 288–89

Behaviorism, 15, 44. See also Conditioning; Habit
 and anxiety, 72
 assumptions, 347
 as existential platform, 245
 as therapy, 164–65, 172, 192–93, 199
 as a tradition in psychology, 3, 336
Being
 aspects of, 27, 37
 basic forms of, 288–89
 defined as aming, 24, 37
 development of, 39–57
 healthy, 173–185. See also Authenticity
Being-at-home-in-the-world, 174–75,
  178
Being-in-the-world. See also Self-as-
  subject
 alienation from, 73, 157
 as aspect of being, 27, 37
 and development, 42
 and Dr. Schreber, 237
 and healthy, 173–78
 and identification, 53
 and letting be in therapy, 169–70
 and obsessive neurosis, 157, 160
 and Paula Kress, 147
Being-for-myself. See also Self-as-Object
 as aspect of being, 27, 37
 and Dr. Schreber, 237
 and evasion of anxiety, 73, 76
 healthy, 179–81
 and identification, 53
 and intentionality, 86
 and letting be in therapy, 170–71
 and lying, 47
 of obsessive, 47, 157
 and Paula Kress, 145, 150
Being-for-others. See also Self-as-Object

361

Being-for-others (*cont.*)
  as aspect of being, 27, 37
and the bureaucrat, 330, 331
  and depression, 28
  and development, 42, 44
  and Dr. Schreber, 237, 240–41
  and evasion of anxiety, 73, 76
  healthy, 181–84
  and identification, 53
  and intentionality, 86
  and letting be in therapy, 171–72
  and lying, 44
  and obsessive neurosis, 158
  and Paula Kress, 140, 147
  of psychopath, 309–10
Body
  and choice, 50
  and Ellen West, 293, 295, 296–97
  language, 105, 145, 241, 243
  and Paula Kress, 135–36, 136–40
  and separateness, 40–41
  as-subject and as-object, 104, 133,
    200, 296–97
  used versus lived, 136–37, 144
Bureaucrat, 453
  and alienation, 329
  conflicting worlds for, 332–33
  lying of, 330–31
  and satellization, 330
  therapy of, 331–34
  world of, 328–31

Care. *See also* Love
  as primordial experience, 36
  and self-as-subject, 75
Causality, 40. *See also* Given
  and experience of self, 71, 198
  as frame of reference, 83, 345
Choice, 39, 78. *See also* Decision
  and anxiety, 63
  and the body, 50
  as it confronts psychologists, 325–27
  development of, 41, 42, 43
  inevitability of, 67
  and intentionality, 83
  and psychotherapy, 75, 196, 198
  and punishment, 53
  and self-as-subject, 65
  and self-deception, 46
  two kinds of, 64–65
Commitment, 21

Conditioning, 4, 8, 25, 39, 79, 164, 165,
    172, 199. *See also* Behaviorism;
    Habit
Conflict. *See also* Psychoanalysis
  and the bureaucrat, 332–33
  in contrast to existential framework,
    234–35
  individual with society, 326
  and the psychopath, 308
  as theoretical framework, 4, 152–53,
    232–35, 326
Consciousness. *See also* Experience; In-
    tentionality
  and behavior, 9
  and dualism, 335–37
  and intentionality, 337
  as subject-matter, 4, 25
  and the nature of man, 4, 5
Conversion hysteria. *See* Hysteria, con-
    version
Courage, 72, 77, 83
Creativity, 84, 87, 131, 133, 134, 242,
    345
Culture. *See also* Individual and So-
    ciety
  breakdown of, 63
  distractions of, 66

Death, 66, 483. *See also* Finitude
  as anthropological event, 298–300
  for Ellen West, 293, 294, 298–300
  and obsessions, 162–63
Decision. *See also* Choice
  and being-for-oneself, 180
  and cognition, 11
  and intentionality, 83
  and Paula Kress, 150
  to be in therapy, 195–96
Depression, 28, 78, 343, 479
Determinism. *See* Causality
Diagnosis
  as clinical procedure, 36–37, 75, 152
  and the psychopath, 306–07
Dread, 302–04. *See also* Anxiety
Dualism, 8–9, 335–37

Ego, 4
  and self, 13
  splitting, 105 n
  transcendental, 16

Eigenwelt, 93, 288
  for Ellen West, 290, 292, 296, 301
Existential Crisis, 77, 190
Existential Platform. *See also* Orientation, life
  defined, 211–14, 237
  of Ellen West, 291, 293, 294, 303–04
  and megalomania, 238, 41
  of psychopath, 315
  stability in a relationship, 219–20, 224–26
  and temporalization, 301
Existentialism, versus essentialism, 10–11, 16, 22, 345
Experience. *See also* Consciousness
  as starting point for psychology, 4–5
  as subject matter of psychology, 6–7
Explanation, 4, 339–40, 345. *See also* Science

Facticity, 72
Families, 183
Fantasy, and therapy, 199–204. *See also* World
Finitude, 67, 162. *See also* Death; Limits
Free Association, 199. *See also* Psychoanalysis
Freedom, and determinedness, 76, 83, 89–90. *See also* Given
Frustration
  and loss of openness, 51
  and neurosis, 74, 76, 167
  as primordial experience, 36
Fusion, as developmental stage, 40, 56
Future. *See also* Temporalization; Time
  children as, 147
  and death, 66
  deteriorative, 99, 144
  and Ellen West, 302
  fantastic, 99, 144
  and healthy being, 177–78
  and objectification, 99
  and obsessive neurosis, 160–62
  and Paula Kress, 137, 140, 141–44
  for the psychopath, 310
  status-striving, 100, 144

Generality, problem of, 340–41, 342, 344, 345

Gestalt Psychology, 14, 17, 337
Given, 10, 39, 41, 289, 301. *See also* Causality; Limits
  and the body, 50
  and existential anxiety, 66–69
  theoretical assumptions about, 347
Guilt
  and choice, 67
  and lying, 45, 46
  and neurosis, 167
  and neurotic anxiety, 74, 76
  and obsessive neurosis, 153
  as primordial experience, 36, 76
  and the psychopath, 310
  psychotic, 220–21
  for what one does, 55, 56, 133, 145–46, 167
  for what one is, 55, 57, 133, 167, 303

Habit, 3, 25, 348. *See also* Behaviorism; Conditioning
Health. *See* Being, healthy; Courage
History
  as an approach to psychology, 97–98, 129–30
  personal, 84
  and psychotherapy, 325, 333
  and theory, 287–88
Horizon, 301
Hysteria
  anxiety hysteria and Paula Kress, 115–151
  conversion hysteria, 104–107

I. *See also* Self-as-subject.
  as agency, 15, 18, 22
  loss of, 70
  and me, 14–15
  and schizophrenia, 15
I-thou, 189
Idealization
  and the bureaucrat, 330–31
  and lying, 46
  relinquishing of, 177
  of self, 35, 55, 73, 184. *See also* Being-for-myself
Identification
  In development, 51
  patient with therapist, 188, 190
  for psychopath, 308, 314

Identity, 15, 29
  as primordial experience, 36
  of prison inmate, 101–02
Ideology, 21
Illumination of the world, 175
Imitation, 52
Individual and Society, 317, 325–27.
    See also Culture
Inferiority, 15, 179
Insight, as therapy, 9–10
Intentionality, 18, 51. *See also* Con-
    sciousness
  and aspects of being, 86
  as frame of reference in theory, 83
  and knowledge, 337
  and measurement, 338
  and personal history, 84
  and phenomenologists, 81
  of psychopath, 309
  and transference, 87
Intervening variable, 5–6
Interview. *See also* Psychotherapy
  early sessions, 194–96
  fine structure of, 199–204
  movement in, 30
  structure of, 196–99
Isolation, 68, 70

Language
  body, 241, 243
  of experience, 343–45
  Freud's, 7, 241
  of self-knowledge, 179, 180
  of theory, 7, 343–45, 351
Learning
  of existential platform, 238–39
  in the psychopath, 310–11
Legal system, 328
Letting be
  and healthy being, 175
  and obsessions, 162
  as patient behavior, 198
  as therapeutic strategy, 169–73
Life-space. *See also* World
  compared with primary and second-
    ary process, 106
  and Dr. Schreber, 236
  primary and secondary, 105, 106,
    145, 200
Limits, 41, 164, 177–78, 304. *See also*
    Finitude; Given

Love. *See also* Care
  and being-for-others, 182–84
  and Ellen West, 292, 294, 297, 298
  and philosophical anthropology, 288
  and self-degradation, 28
  and self-objectification, 20, 191, 192
  withdrawal of, 45
Lying. *See also* Bad Faith
  and the bureaucrat, 330–31
  and families, 183
  and Dr. Schreber's existential plat-
    form, 236
  inability to, 237–38
  -for-myself, 45, 56, 168
  and necessities/possibilities, 47
  and neurosis, 75
  and obsessions, 47
  -for-others, 44–45, 56, 168
  psychology of, 43
  and trauma, 89
  -in-the-world, 48, 56, 167

Meaning, 26, 33, 183, 200
  of data, 339
  and the existential platform, 213–14
  and intentionality, 82
  and love, 288
  for obsessive, 154
  for Paula Kress, 151
  for the psychopath, 314
  of stimulus, 6, 26, 33
  of world in context of self, 17
Meaninglessness, 67, 69, 70, 228
Measurement, 335–39
Megalomania, 238–41
  and activity-passivity, 238
  and possibility-necessity, 240
  and power, 238
Mental Illness, 5. *See also* Neurosis;
    Psychosis; Schizophrenia
Mitwelt, 93, 288
  for Ellen West, 290–96
Model
  in identification, 53
  in science, 352
  therapist as, 190
Moods, 304–05, 343
Morality. *See* Values
Mother, 41, 146–47
Motivation, 31, 82, 298
Movement, 30, 37

Necessities and Possibilities, 47
Neurosis. *See also* Hysteria; Obsessions; Phobia
  and anxiety, 72
  and lies, 73–74
  and Paula Kress, 129, 149
Nonbeing, 68, 164, 295, 300
Nothingness, 17, 216, 294

Objectification of therapist, 189–89
Objectivity
  and measurement, 335–39
  problem of, 337–38, 344, 345
  in psychology, 335–39
Obsessions, 152–65
Oedipus Complex, 106–07, 200
Ontological Insecurity, 21, 70. *See also* Laing, R. D.
Ontology, 28, 239, 287–89, 298, 304, 305, 331–32
Openness, 39
  development of, 44
  and healthy being, 174–77
  loss of, 50, 89
  and the psychopath, 314
Orientation
  and existential platform, 175, 213–14, 220, 235, 237
  life, 67, 82, 83, 175
  loss of, 69
  point of, 17–18, 22, 308, 309
Otherness, 307, 308, 309, 312
Out-of-jointness, 31, 36, 49, 73, 78

Panic, 214–20
  and Ellen West, 294
Paradoxes, existential, 71, 292
Paranoia, 232–47
Phenomenology
  and Adler, 13–14
  as approach to psychology, 4–5
  and Husserl, 341–45
Phobia, 167, 191
Physiognomy, 158–59, 174, 177
Physiology, 50–51, 95, 192, 305
Politics. *See also* Values
  and existential platform, 245–46
  of psychosis, 244–46
  of psychotherapy, 325–27

Possibility
  closing of, 290
  and Ellen West, 289
  and the future, 99
  and healthy being, 177–78
  and intentionality, 84–85
  and learning, 238–39
  and megalomania, 240
  and necessity, 11, 47, 68, 289
  and obsessive neurosis, 163–65
  and philosophical anthropology, 289, 290
  and psychoanalysis, 239
  and the psychopath, 312–13, 317
Primordial Experiences, 36, 37
  and psychotherapy, 75
Projection, 235, 236, 237
Psychoanalysis, 15, 44, 76, 87, 134, 188, 232–38, 239. *See also* Freud, S.
  assumptions of, 347
  and Ellen West, 297
  as existential platform, 239, 245
  and megalomania, 239
  as psychological tradition, 3–4
  and the psychopath, 310, 311, 313
Psychopath, 70, 306–20
  ambivalence toward, 315–17
  anxiety and, 311
  being-for-others of, 309–10
  characteristics of, 306–07
  conflict in, 308
  existential platform of, 313, 315
  intentionality of, 309
  otherness for, 307, 308, 309, 312
  possibility and, 312–13, 317
  self of, 312–15
  time for, 310–311
  world of, 307–12
Psychosis, 15. *See also* Megalomania; Paranoia; Schizophrenia
  behaviorism and, 3
  cultural norms and, 4–5
  speech of, 241–43
Psychotic Resolution, 232–48
  defined, 233–34
  and Ellen West, 294–95
  and megalomania, 238–41
Psychotic Struggle, 220–31
Psychotherapy. *See also* Interview
  and being-for-myself, 167
  and being-for-others, 168
  and being-in-the-world, 166

Psychotherapy (*cont.*)
    and the bureaucrat, 331–34
    and existential crisis, 77
    and fantasy, 199–204
    goal of, 32, 37, 39, 75, 76, 84, 181,
        186–87, 190–91, 325–27, 333
    and history, 325, 333
    and intentionality, 87–90
    motives for, 195–96
    and primordial experiences, 75
    and prison inmates, 102
    and self-as-subject, 187–91
    and self-objectification, 191–93

Relationships as stability, 219–20,
        224–26
Religion, 63, 245
Repetition, 89–90
Resistance, 76, 100
Responsibility
    and causality, 83
    escape from, 15, 65
    and healthy being, 174
    and Paula Kress, 150
    psychotic, 221
Role, 26, 34–35
    flight into, 75
    and life-space, 107
    particularistic, 327–28
    of therapist, 169, 187, 189
    universalistic, 327–28
    and world, 333–34
Rules, 43

Satellization
    of the bureaucrat, 330
    as developmental stage, 41, 56
    in Dr. Schreber, 236
    and obsessive neurosis, 156, 158
    in Paula Kress, 133, 141, 142, 145
    and the psychopath, 313–14
    and punishment, 54, 221, 222
    in therapy, stages of, 188–89
Schizophrenia, 211, 306
Science. *See also* Causality; Explana-
        tion
    as approach, 82, 351–55
    as existential platform, 245, 353
    and measurement, 335–39
    and objectivity, 335–39

Security, 70, 141, 145, 158, 175, 215,
        216
Self, 22
    known versus lived, 20
    and lying, 44
    of psychopath, 312–15
    and punishment, 54–55
    as-subject and as-object, 14
Self-actualization, 10–11
Self-as-object. *See also* Being-for-my-
        self; Being-for-others; Self-objec-
        tification
    and avoidance of anxiety, 68, 73
    defined, 14, 22
    and development (satellization)
        41–42, 45
    flight into, 76
    and healthy being, 179, 191–93
    and lying, 45
    and obsessions, 157, 160
    and security, 215
Self-as-subject. *See also* Being-in-the-
        world; I
    and anxiety, 68
    and choice, 65
    defined, 14, 17, 22
    and development, 40–41
    and Dr. Schreber, 237, 238, 241
    growth of in therapy, 187–91, 200–04
    and healthy being, 175
    loss of, 20, 75, 88, 228
    and obsessions, 156–60
    and Paula Kress, 132, 141
    and the psychopath, 312–15
    and schizophrenia, 15, 228
    and temporalization, 141
Self-deception, 46. *See also* Bad Faith;
        Lying
Self-esteem. *See also* Being-for-myself
    in development, 43
    and Paula Kress, 136
    as primordial experience, 36
Self-fulfilling prophesy, 86
Self-objectification. *See also* Self-as-ob-
        ject
    aspects of, 192
    and commitment, 21
    as experiential datum, 20
    and the future, 99
    and healthy being, 179–81
    and loss of self-as-subject, 20
    in obsessions, 157, 162

Self-objectification *(cont.)*
  and satellization, 45, 150
  in therapy, 191–93
Separateness
  as developmental stage, 40–41, 56
  and Paula Kress, 132
  in psychopathy, 313
Sexuality
  and body, 136–37, 144
  and Ellen West, 294, 297
  and hysteria, 138
Shame, 44, 45
  existential and neurotic, 168
  and neurosis, 74, 76
  and obsessive neurosis, 154
  and Paula Kress, 134
  as primordial experience, 36, 76
Similarity
  a developmental stage 43, 56
  and Paula Kress, 135
Social reality, 106
Space. *See also* World
  life, 105
  phenomenological, 95, 130–31
  physical space as theoretical metaphor, 7, 96
  of the prison inmate, 102
  various kinds, 95–96

Taking the role of the other, 45, 189, 308
Temporalization. *See also* Future; Time
  as co-ordinate of being, 98, 129–30, 300–05
  in Ellen West, 293, 300–05
  and healthy being, 178
  and obsessive neurosis, 160–62
  and Paula Kress, 130, 141, 142–44
  and philosophical anthropology, 300–05
Theory
  as existential platform, 245
  in psychology, 343–45, 352, 354
They, 181–82
Time. *See also* Future; Temporalization

Time *(cont.)*
  as aspect of world, 96
  of prison inmate, 101
  of psychopath, 310–11
  unstructured, 198
Tragedy, 67
  and Ellen West, 300, 301
Transcendence, 97, 130
  and philosophical anthropology, 288
Transference
  -cure, 188
  and Dr. Schreber, 235, 240
  and intentionality, 87, 90, 134
  and satellization in therapy, 188
Trauma
  and intentionality, 88–90

Umwelt, 93, 288
  for Ellen West, 290, 293
Unconscious, 3, 8, 36, 71, 197, 200
Units of analysis, 348. *See also* Language, of theory

Values. *See also* Politics
  and the bureaucrat, 332–34
  and choice, 64–65
  cultural, breakdown of, 63–64, 70
  and facts, 353
  and psychology, 10–11, 44, 84 n, 317, 325–27
  and psychosis, 245
  and psychotherapy, 173

World, 51. *See also* Space
  and Dr. Schreber, 235
  of Ellen West, 288–98
  fantasy as, 199–204
  and moods, 305
  as object of psychological study, 82–83, 84–85, 92
  in obsessive neurosis, 158
  in Paula Kress, 130
  of prison inmates, 100
  in psychopathy, 307–12
  and self, 93–95, 131, 313
  of therapy, 202–04